Secondary Instruction

Secondary Instruction
A MANUAL FOR CLASSROOM TEACHING

JOEL M. LEVINE

Mount St. Mary's College, Los Angeles

Foreword by Ralph Tyler

Allyn and Bacon
Boston London Sydney Toronto

Series Editor: Sean W. Wakely
Production Administrator: Annette Joseph
Production Coordinator: Susan Freese
Editorial-Production Service: Sally Stickney
Text Designer: Denise Hoffman, Glenview Studios
Cover Administrator: Linda K. Dickinson

Library of Congress Cataloging-in-Publication Data

Levine, Joel M., 1950–
    Secondary instruction : a manual for classroom teaching / Joel M. Levine;
    foreword by Ralph Tyler.
       p. cm.
    Includes bibliographies and index.
    ISBN 0-205-11790-2
    1. High school teaching.   I. Title.
LB1737.A3L48   1988   88-27416
373.11'07'12—dc19   CIP

Printed in the United States of America

10 9 8 7 6 5 4 3 2 1   93 92 91 90 89 88

Credits

    Excerpts on pages 156–158, 168–169 (Table 4.6), 312, 320, 329, and 333 from *Better Teaching in Secondary Schools* (3rd ed.) by Marvin D. Alcorn, James S. Kinder, and Jim R. Schunert, copyright© 1970 Holt, Rinehart and Winston, Inc., reprinted by permission of the publisher.

    Material on pages 153, 155, and 159 from *AV Instruction: Technology, Media and Methods* (4th ed.) by J. W. Brown, R. B. Lewis, and F. F. Harcleroad, 1973, New York: McGraw-Hill. Used with permission of the publisher.

(continued on page 396)

To my father, the late David Levine
of Windsor, Ontario

and

To Master Ramanand Maharaj
of the Himalayas

Brief Contents

Contents

Foreword

Ralph W. Tyler
*Director Emeritus, Center for Advanced Study
in the Behavioral Sciences*

A manual that is helpful to classroom teachers and to those preparing to teach must surmount several serious obstacles. Most teachers think of their role as presenting material in the textbooks that students are to memorize and assigning exercises on which students can practice and perfect their skills. This conception of teaching may be appropriate for an authoritarian society in which students are expected to learn to be obedient followers of authority but not for a democratic society in which students are expected to learn to identify problems they encounter and work out practicable ways of attacking them in order to be responsible citizens. Few manuals are based on the conception of a teacher as a stimulator and guide of student problem solvers.

Many teachers want a manual to present rules that they should follow in order to be effective. But the great variety in the background experiences and interests of students and in the homes and communities in which they live makes it impossible to formulate a set of rules that will cover this variety of situations. Teachers must learn to identify the problems they encounter and to use appropriate principles of learning to guide them in designing ways of attacking these problems. Few manuals furnish assistance to the teacher in identifying his or her problems and in designing an appropriate attack.

The principles of learning that teachers find helpful are generalizations from experience, and to be meaningful they must be relevant to the experience of the teachers using them. But meaningful interpretations of experiences do not automatically come from the experiences but are gained from reflection upon them. From experience alone one learns to like "it" or dislike it, to seek more of it or avoid it. In reflecting upon experience, one seeks answers to such questions as how did it come about, what were its consequences, how could it have been better, and the like. Few manuals are designed to stimulate reflection and to raise questions to help guide the teacher's reflections.

The overall conception of teaching that has been formulated from many years of experience and experiment is that of stimulating and guiding the learning of students. If students are not learning, the teacher is inadequate. Few manuals for teachers focus on students' learning as the primary concern of the teacher. But Levine's manual makes clear from the first that teaching and learning are necessarily closely related. In the second chapter he discusses learning and basic theories of learning and presents a practical model of a continuous learning sequence. To enhance the discussion he presents three case studies of learning as an active process, and then the teacher is asked to make a study of the readiness for learning of the students in his or her classroom. This focus on the teacher's experience and the interpretation he or she is asked to make is maintained in every chapter of the book. Also in every chapter, a carefully selected list of annotated readings furnishes additional opportunities for the teacher to reflect upon the activities he or she is asked to carry out and to compare his or her interpretations of these experiences with the ideas outlined in the readings.

This manual presents no simple rules to follow, but it asks the teacher to make his or her inquiry into the classroom, into the characteristics and values of the various available instructional resources, and into an effort to understand students' assets and limitations in their efforts to learn what the schools are expected to teach. From these studies the teacher formulates generalizations that guide his or her teaching. It is a hands-on manual, not to provide answers to questions the teacher has not asked but to stimulate and guide the teacher in seeking to identify serious problems students are having in learning and to test out ideas that offer ways to attack these problems. I believe that those preparing to be secondary school teachers as well as those already in the classroom will find this manual very helpful in their efforts to gain greater competence in their profession.

Preface

Teaching involves three inseparable aspects: the teacher, the students, and what is taught. In terms of effective secondary school teaching these three aspects correspond to knowledge of teaching methods, the adolescent, and subject matter, respectively. Mastery and understanding in one or even two of these three areas alone is not sufficient for success in the classroom. Because the true test of knowledge is found in its application, this manual aims to assist the reader in developing not only the requisite knowledge and related skills but also the sense of responsibility, dedicated effort, and creativity essential for effective teaching. To accomplish this goal each chapter is divided into the following five sections.

1. *Basic Theories.* Theories and ideas covering topics relevant to each chapter are presented. The experiences and insights of previous generations of leading educators, scholars, and thinkers are joined with the most recent research and practices as a guide to effective secondary school teaching. Numerous tables and figures are included in this section to clarify and summarize the discussion of essential points as well as to serve as self-assessment guides for practice.

2. *Practical Models.* A practical model is presented in each chapter to illustrate an exemplary classroom application of ideas examined in the Basic Theories section. The models have been selected from materials that have been used successfully in the classroom by junior and senior high school teachers.

3. *Case Studies.* Each chapter has three case studies derived from actual observations and accounts of student teachers and teachers in-service who are working in a variety of classroom settings. (Although the case studies are based on actual observations, all people in them are fictional creations.) Each case study relates to a major topic within the chapter and is introduced by several orienting questions that focus on the main points being highlighted. The Brief at the end of each case study serves as an excellent basis for group discussion and for sharing perceptions, ideas, and experiences.

4. *Chapter Projects.* Each chapter culminates in a major project. (One, two, or three phases of the project can be completed as deemed necessary or useful.) Successful completion of the project requires the synthesis and application of several of the main ideas presented in the chapter. The work completed for all the projects is designed to form a unified body of ideas, plans, and resource materials for effectively organizing and carrying out a secondary school classroom program. In addition, developing original case studies or practical models can serve as worthwhile supplementary or alternative exercises.

5. *References and Annotated Readings.* At the end of each chapter is a list of the references cited followed by an annotated list of supplemental readings featuring accounts of recent and relevant literature for further exploration of the topics examined.

The manual consists of eight chapters covering all the areas essential to secondary school teaching. Chapter 1 examines the roles and responsibilities of the teacher in the classroom and the school community as well as the nature of teaching both as an art and a science. Chapter 2 focuses on understanding the nature of the learner and the dynamics of the learning process as the basis for planning effective classroom learning experiences. Chapter 3 emphasizes the teacher's creative role in developing a complete course curriculum to serve as the basis for planning and carrying out daily classroom lessons. Chapter 4 focuses on understanding the nature and uses of various instructional resource materials and discusses how these materials may be procured or developed. Chapter 5 examines how to reach students and meaningfully touch their lives through developing an understanding of their natures, backgrounds, and needs. Chapter 6 presents numerous ideas and recommendations for developing and carrying out daily lessons using a variety of teaching methods. Chapter 7 examines ways of creating and maintaining a classroom environment conducive to effective student learning and cooperation. Chapter 8 presents ideas and recommendations for measuring and interpreting the effects of classroom instruction on student growth as a guide to developing and modifying instructional plans, methods, and activities.

To best use this manual I recommend that whatever time is spent reading the material, double that much time should be spent thinking about it (e.g., how it can be applied, adapted, or combined with other ideas), and double that much time again should be spent applying it in the classroom so that it may be fully comprehended and assimilated.

◆ Acknowledgments

I would like to express my gratitude to Professors Ralph Tyler and John McNeil, Dr. Naomi Aschner, Carmela Weiss, and my family of friends whose guidance and support made this book possible. I would also like to thank the distinguished reviewers who showed great confidence in my views.

CHAPTER 1
◆ ◆ ◆ ◆ ◆ ◆ ◆

Teaching

INTRODUCTION

BASIC THEORIES
- ◆ Teaching: Art and Science
- ◆ Roles and Responsibilities of the Teacher
- ◆ Teaching Behaviors
- ◆ Broad View of Teaching

SUMMARY

PRACTICAL MODEL 1.1   Home Reading Record

PRACTICAL MODEL 1.2   Professional Growth Plan

CASE STUDIES
- ◆ 1.1   Teacher as Leader
- ◆ 1.2   Teacher as Instructor
- ◆ 1.3   Teacher as Counselor/Guide

CHAPTER PROJECT   Analyze the Classroom Behavior of an Exemplary
                  Teacher

REFERENCES

ANNOTATED READINGS

INTRODUCTION

The two main attributes of the teacher as a professional, in the highest sense of the term *professional*, are dedication to service and the ability to adapt to situations and needs whenever and wherever they arise. The teacher must have a passion to serve young people by continually seeking to better their lives, thereby directly affecting the quality of life in society. He or she must also have a passion to learn, remaining always a student at heart, striving to learn more about his or her subject, students, and teaching. In

1

short, "a good teacher must not only know something about what he is teaching but care about it and the pupils he is teaching it to" (Passmore, 1980, p. 162).

Although meeting these two conditions does not ensure effective teaching, it does put a prospective teacher in the best possible position to obtain the learning and experience necessary to be an effective teacher. Those who lack these qualities are unlikely to touch a vital part of students' lives no matter how much knowledge they have acquired or how many models of teaching they have mastered.

"The mediocre teacher tells. The good teacher explains. The superior teacher demonstrates. The great teacher inspires" (in Alcorn, Kinder, & Schunert, 1970, p. 7). These words convey the idea that a teacher is a leader. But we could ask the question, Leading who, where? In the immediate sense the teacher is leading his or her students to an appreciation for and an understanding of a particular body of knowledge. However, the teacher's role as a leader extends much further.

> The [teacher] more than the member of any profession is concerned to have a long look ahead. The physician may feel his job done when he has restored a patient to health. He has undoubtedly the obligation of advising him how to live so as to avoid similar troubles in the future. But, after all, the conduct of his life is his own affair, not the physician's; and what is more important for the present point is that as far as the physician does occupy himself with instruction and advice as to the future of his patient he takes upon himself the function of an educator. The lawyer is occupied with winning a suit for his client or getting the latter out of some complication into which he has got himself. If it goes beyond the case presented to him he too becomes an educator. The educator by the very nature of his work is obliged to see his present work in terms of what it accomplishes, or fails to accomplish, for a future whose objects are linked with those of the present. (Dewey, 1938, pp. 90–91)

In a philosophical sense the teacher comes to realize that all of life is educative, as every situation and experience modifies the individual and produces new adjustments. Viewed in this way, education is an evolutionary process with the teacher serving in a pivotal position to lead students on a path of continuing growth and development.

The teacher is a leader on two levels: the instructional level, dealing with students' intellectual growth, and the personal level, dealing with students' emotional, social, and spiritual growth. These two levels of leadership are inextricably bound together so that at any given time the teacher's efforts on one level will have concomitant effects on the other level.

Another question arises: What are the basic requirements for assuming this leadership role? Two areas of requirements need to be considered. One area, related to leadership on the instructional level, concerns the knowledge and skills needed to effectively plan, implement, and evaluate a classroom instructional program. Theories, ideas, materials, and recommendations relating to this area are presented in Chapters 3, 4, 6, 7, and 8. The other area, related to leadership on the personal level, concerns the personal growth and insight needed to reach every student in a meaningful way. Theories, ideas, materials, and recommendations related to this area are presented in Chapters 2 and 5 (Table 1.1). Because these two areas are closely interrelated, how one area (instructional level) relates to the other (personal level) is frequently discussed throughout the book.

BASIC THEORIES

◆ Teaching: Art and Science

Whitehead (in Hendley, 1986) describes teaching as an art that, like any other art, attempts to turn the abstract into the concrete and the concrete into the abstract. The ability to do so is what Dewey called the "science" that is naturally embedded in teaching.

The art of teaching involves the immediate and creative as well as practical competence to put together various skills in new forms at the spur of the moment as new situations arise. The science of teaching involves the ability to gain understanding through carefully observing teaching practices and examining the ever-growing knowledge in the field. Put simply, art deals with practice and science deals with the study of practice. Over-emphasizing either area results in uninformed practice on the one hand and baseless theorizing on the other—and thus ineffective teaching. The teacher needs to be both artist and scientist (Table 1.2).

For the most effective teachers, practice (what is referred to here as the art aspect of teaching) is always guided by reflection (what is referred to here as the science aspect of teaching). Practice unguided by reflection is bound to be blind to many signals and occurrences in the environment. Likewise, reflection without practice, in time, becomes divorced from reality.

TABLE 1.1 *Teacher as Leader*

LEVELS	AREAS OF GROWTH	REQUIREMENTS	CHAPTERS
Instructional	Intellectual	Knowledge and skills to plan, implement, and evaluate classroom instructional program	3, 4, 6, 7, 8
Personal	Emotional Social Spiritual	Personal growth and insight to meaningfully reach every student	2, 5

TABLE 1.2 *Art and Science of Teaching*

AREA	DEFINITION	CONCISE DEFINITION	EXAMPLE
Art	Immediate practical competence	Practice	Putting together various skills in new forms at the spur of the moment as new situations arise
Science	Ability to ascertain knowledge through systematic observation	Study of practice	*Micro:* Momentary reflection on effects of a particular classroom activity
			Macro: Examination of teaching practices over a period of time

On a micro level, for example, the teacher reflects momentarily on the effect a particular classroom activity is having on one or more students. From this momentary reflection comes a spontaneous modification of the teaching practice to suit the needs of the situation. On a macro level, for example, the teacher critically examines the effects of his or her classroom practices on the students over a period of time. This examination becomes the basis for planning changes in the overall instructional program.

Dewey, asking if there is a science of education, realized:

> The important thing is to discover those traits in virtue of which various fields are called scientific. When we raise the question in this way, we are led to put emphasis upon methods of dealing with subject-matter rather than to look for uniform objective traits in subject-matter. (1929, p. 8)

The science of teaching cannot be reduced to a set of principles to be applied regardless of who is teaching what to whom and under what circumstances. Because of the complexity and uniqueness of each teaching situation, systematic methods of inquiry are essential to understanding classroom problems and intelligently finding solutions to those problems.

Sri Aurobindo Ghose (1966, p. 21) defined "the 'true art of teaching' as the ability to lead the student on step-by-step, interesting and absorbing him in each [step] as it comes, until he has mastered his subject." To successfully lead the student to subject mastery as well as personal growth, however, requires the continual observation and reflection characteristic of the science aspect of teaching. In reality, therefore, the art and science aspects of teaching are inseparable.

Einstein (1950, p. 198) determined that for schools to be successful in educating students and guiding them to important fields for society the teacher must be a kind of artist in his or her province. He asks, "What can be done that this spirit be gained in the school?" He had no simple answer for this, but he did point out that at least two necessary conditions can be met. "First, teachers should grow up in such schools." In other words, students need to see teachers functioning as artists so they have that as their model. "Second, the teacher should be given extensive liberty in the selection of the material to be taught and the methods of teaching employed." Einstein considers teachers as artists because to a large extent they shape their own work and, further, through their work they shape the lives of their students. In a sense this is the classic view of what an artist is. Because the teacher needs to be directed by an inner impulse, he or she can be likened to "the artist, the philosopher, or the person of letters" (Russell in Hendley, 1986, p. 71). Thus to follow his or her creative impulses, the teacher needs more opportunities for self-determination and more independence to decide what is to be taught and how it is to be taught. Einstein and Russell recommend that in situations where teachers do not have artistic freedom, the data obtained by studying their classroom practices cannot be considered a valid source for formulating modes of inquiry to examine the usefulness of those practices. To the extent that there are external controls on the practices of the teacher, in that proportion is the teacher's artistic prerogative to apply scientific principles to modify practice based on reflection diminished.

The use of scientific principles to enhance and guide instruction is at a rudimentary stage when basic teaching skills of instructional planning and classroom management are not yet well developed. At a beginning stage, the teacher can be called neither an artist nor a scientist. Rather, he or she is at an apprentice or intern stage of development where the focus needs to be on observing and practicing various teaching skills and then reflecting on the effects that result. By doing this the artistic and scientific aspects can grow side by side. Thus "the final reality of educational science is not found in books, nor in experimental laboratories, nor in classrooms where it is taught, but in the minds of those engaged in directing educational activities" (Dewey, 1929, p. 32).

◆ Roles and Responsibilities of the Teacher

The various roles and responsibilities of the teacher fall into two main categories: interpersonal and pedagogical. The roles of counselor/guide and member of the school community are interpersonal, and the roles of curriculum developer, instructor, and researcher are pedagogical (Table 1.3). The role of leader, discussed above, applies to the roles in both categories.

Interpersonal Roles
These roles pertain to the emotional, social, and spiritual growth of students.

Teacher as Counselor/Guide. The teacher gets to know each student as an individual who has a distinct nature characterized by certain needs,

TABLE 1.3 *Roles and Responsibilities of the Teacher*

CATEGORY	ROLES	AREAS OF STUDENT GROWTH	BASIS FOR PERFORMING ROLES
Interpersonal	Counselor/Guide	Emotional Social Spiritual	Knowledge of students' interests, strengths, weaknesses, and way of communicating
	Member of school community	Cooperative, supportive work	Development of keen sympathetic awareness of environment
Pedagogical	Curriculum developer	Intellectual	Mastery of subject area and structure
	Instructor	Intellectual	Knowledge of teaching methods
	Researcher	Intellectual	Knowledge of formal and informal assessment techniques

interests, strengths, weaknesses, and ways of communicating. Central to being able to perform this role successfully is the teacher's maturity, patience, and deep interest in each student's welfare. Thus, a key indication of how well the role of counselor/guide is being performed is the extent to which the teacher is familiar with the characteristics and needs of each student. It is in this regard that Heck and Williams (1984) consider the teacher's role of understander of student behavior as one that distinguishes the teacher as a professional from the teacher as a mere technician.

Teacher as Member of the School Community. The teacher communicates and works with fellow teachers, staff, administrators, and parents both formally and informally, giving and receiving continuing social and professional support. The importance of this role must be recognized for two principal reasons. First, "a cooperative and supportive work environment will help teachers deal with the varied expectations placed on them and the stress they cause" (Heck & Williams, 1984, p. 15). Second, a keen awareness of the environment in which students live and learn helps teachers stay in tune with students' needs above and beyond what can be observed in a single classroom setting.

Pedagogical Roles

In these roles the teacher functions as both artist and scientist. Each role in this area corresponds to one of the three major phases of a classroom instructional program (i.e., development, implementation, and evaluation).

Teacher as Curriculum Developer. The teacher's first task is to determine the goals to be attained. These objectives then become the criteria by which materials are selected, content is outlined, instructional procedures are developed, and tests and examinations are prepared (development phase). From one perspective the teacher is involved in the development of general curriculum goals and policies; from another perspective the teacher is involved in the curriculum decisions that need to be made daily (Heck & Williams, 1984, p. 115).

Teacher as Instructor. The teacher serves as the director of learning, planning interesting and meaningful learning experiences for students using a variety of instructional materials and procedures; providing for individual differences; and monitoring, recording, and reporting student growth and achievement (implementation phase). "The ideal learning environment is one in which students work with rather than depend upon the teacher" (Hunter in Heck & Williams, 1984, p. 60). As instructor the teacher is, in effect, a navigator for learning by serving as guide, consultant, and resource person to students.

Teacher as Researcher. The teacher searches for theories, ideas, and practices that will help create an effective teaching-learning environment for all students. The role as researcher has two intimately related aspects. One aspect, *field research,* concerns the teacher's present and developing subject-area expertise and is based on expert, continuous, disciplined inquiry into a subject area and into the teaching of a subject. To effectively carry out field research it is important for the teacher to become informed about the best ideas, past and present, in the particular area being investigated, such as organizing classroom routines or handling behavior problems. The other aspect, *classroom research,* also requires continuous, disciplined inquiry but focuses instead on all the daily happenings in the classroom. Effective classroom research is based on careful observation of all instructional practices and the effects these practices have on students, both individually and collectively.

Preoccupation with subject matter itself rather than with how it can be effectively related to the students, however, places the teacher in a poor position to effectively carry out classroom research. "Simple scholarship is not enough. In fact, there are certain features of scholarship or mastered subject matter—taken by itself—which get in the way of effective teaching unless the instructor's habitual attitude is one of concern with its interplay in the pupil's own experience" (Dewey, 1928, p. 215).

In their comprehensive work on classroom research methods, Waples and Tyler (1930) consider that problem recognition consisting of three elements is essential to meaningful classroom research: (1) a definite conception of desirable attainments by the students, (2) an estimate of the actual attainments of the students, and (3) a comparison of the actual with the desired attainments. The shortcomings discovered are thus recognized as specific problems.

The relationship between classroom research and field research is cyclical in that the diagnosis of classroom problems leads the teacher to search for ideas and exemplary practices (field research) to adapt and use to meet students' needs and abilities. Barr (1961, p. 7), in recounting nearly forty years of study on the topic of teacher effectiveness, points out that "what is frequently lost sight of is that theory by its very nature tends to emphasize the generalizable and to neglect the specifics. [Teachers] are seldom allowed to forget specifics." Thus, the teacher who can carry out and link the more general, theoretical research with the more specific, classroom research is better able to intelligently select, combine, and adapt ideas and methods for classroom use.

Teacher as Leader. The teacher must help students attain their fullest creative potentials by encouraging imaginative endeavor rather than conformity to any particular patterns. "The teacher has a double function. It is for him to elicit the enthusiasm for self-discipline and continuous progress from the students by resonance from his own personality, and to create the environment of a larger knowledge and a finer purpose" (Whitehead, 1929, p. 62). Further, the teacher "must never substitute his own intelligence for that of the [student], but rather make the [student] himself think, and induce him to exercise his own activity" (Montessori, 1917, p. 44).

To focus the discussion on the roles and responsibilities of the teacher, teaching is seen on a continuum of occupations (Figure 1.1). The element common to each occupation on the continuum is the need for mastery of a particular body of knowledge and related skills. This is also an element

FIGURE 1.1 *Continuum of Occupations*

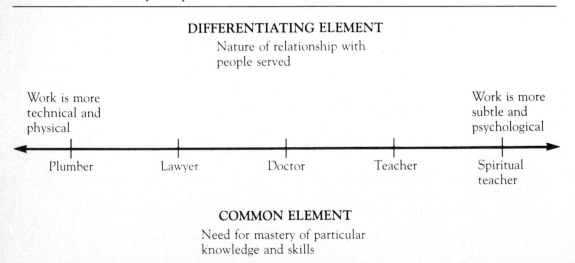

DIFFERENTIATING ELEMENT
Nature of relationship with
people served

Work is more
technical and
physical

Work is more
subtle and
psychological

Plumber   Lawyer   Doctor   Teacher   Spiritual
                                                                    teacher

COMMON ELEMENT
Need for mastery of particular
knowledge and skills

common to what are termed *professions*. Although this element of mastery is important in the profession of teaching (see "Pedagogical Roles" above), a more subtle element concerning emotional, social, and spiritual growth (see "Interpersonal Roles" above) is involved. The main difference, therefore, between occupations toward either end of the continuum is not only in the type of work done but in the nature and closeness of the relationship that exists with the people they serve. It is for this reason that the teacher is closer on the continuum to the spiritual teacher than to those in more technical occupations.

It is hardly a compliment to call a spiritual teacher a highly skilled professional, because spiritual teachers (e.g., priests, ministers, rabbis, gurus) understand that their work goes well beyond any particular technical expertise. They realize the intimate relationship and bond that is developed in guiding the very lives of the people with whom they work. Similarly, a major aspect of the teacher's work is to develop a close and caring relationship with students and to serve as a model and guide for their personal growth.

From this perspective, two personal traits are essential to successfully fulfilling the responsibilities of a teacher: a caring attitude and an interest in developing close relationships with students. Without these traits all efforts in the classroom can only have limited success at best.

Caring Attitude

After years of firsthand experience and tireless effort educating children, Bertrand Russell (1926) and Mahatma Gandhi (in Patel, 1953) both came to the conclusion that a caring attitude toward students is the foundation of the teacher's work. As they saw it, the caring teacher naturally evolves a philosophy and way of functioning in the classroom based on a knowledge of teaching and learning acquired not through books or courses but by participating actively in the lives of students, their work and activities, their joys and sorrows. A caring attitude helps the teacher cut through many of the fruitless and often confusing prescriptions and much of the verbiage that surround teaching and go to the heart of classroom problems.

Developing Close Relationships

Teachers' personal and professional goals are important factors in determining the nature of their relationships with their students.

> Teachers who see their primary role as the transmission of knowledge (information) will react quite differently from teachers who feel their primary responsibility is to establish a close relationship with students and to help them experience success in the pursuit of knowledge. The latter are more likely to develop strong affective responses to students and to be concerned with their development as total persons rather than only with the more narrow range of cognitive development. (Heck & Williams, 1984, pp. 5–6)

It is extremely difficult for secondary school teachers to develop a close relationship with each student in their several classes. Even if they attempt to do so, a close relationship, by definition, must be a two-way street, and some students are just not ready for such a relationship with their teacher or perhaps with anyone else. Despite this, it is still important for teachers to make the effort to know each student as an individual and to let each student feel that they are personally interested in him or her. This effort, at the least, demonstrates to each student that the conditions for a close relationship exist and that the lines of communication are open. Further, a sincere effort by the teacher in this way, even though it may not immediately reach some students, eventually has its positive effects. Little by little, trust and respect for the teacher develop and barriers initially put up as a defense come down as students are given the opportunity to realize and experience the value of sharing their feelings and thoughts with another person.

◆ Teaching Behaviors

Teaching behaviors are the types and patterns of behavior common to all teachers as they carry out their various roles. A classification system developed by Wallen and Travers traces the origin of six patterns of teacher behaviors:

1. Patterns derived from teaching traditions (for example, a teacher teaches as he was taught).
2. Patterns derived from social learnings in the teacher's background (for example, a teacher reinforces the behaviors of pupils so as to develop middle-class values).
3. Patterns derived from philosophical traditions (for example, a teacher teaches in accordance with the Froebel or Rousseau tradition).
4. Patterns generated by the teacher's own needs (for example, a teacher adopts a lecture method because he needs to be self-assertive).
5. Patterns generated by conditions existing in the school and community (for example, a teacher conducts his class in such a way as to produce formal and highly disciplined behavior because this represents the pattern required by the principal).
6. Patterns derived from scientific research on learning. (In Alcorn et al., 1970, p. 15)

The teaching behaviors discussed in this section relate directly to the interpersonal and pedagogical teaching roles and responsibilities described in the previous section. Each general area of teaching behavior is related to teachers' interpersonal and pedagogical roles and responsibilities respectively and is briefly described according to its specific constituent behaviors (Table 1.4).

Each constituent behavior listed below is thoroughly examined in a later chapter, as indicated in parentheses. The purpose of this section is to provide a useful guide to teaching behaviors essential for effective teaching.

TABLE 1.4 *Outline of Essential Teaching Behaviors*

INTERPERSONAL BEHAVIORS	PEDAGOGICAL BEHAVIORS
Counselor/Guide	**Curriculum Developer**
Getting to know students	Delineating course of instruction
Demonstrating exemplary values and character	Identifying and using basic sources
	Determining course objectives
Member of School Community	**Instructor**
Working with colleagues and parents	Carrying out classroom instruction
Participating in school and community events	Tailoring instruction to reach the students
	Managing classroom environment
	Researcher
	Examining theories, ideas, and practices
	Observing and assessing effects of classroom instruction

Interpersonal Behaviors

This category of roles and responsibilities is comprised of two general areas of teaching behavior: teacher as counselor/guide and teacher as member of the school community.

Teacher as Counselor/Guide. The constituent behaviors of the teacher as counselor/guide are getting to know students and demonstrating exemplary values and good personal character.

1. Getting to know students (see Chapter 5)
   ◆ Carefully observing students
   ◆ Establishing rapport and communicating with students
   ◆ Understanding students' needs and interests (intellectual, emotional, social)
2. Demonstrating exemplary values and good personal character (see Chapter 5)
   ◆ Handling situations with fairness, honesty, and patience
   ◆ Caring for students' welfare and feelings
   ◆ Fostering respect, confidence, and conviction

The behaviors of the teacher as counselor/guide are closely related to the nonstatic aspects of personality (e.g., psychological and emotional characteristics). Discrepancies between potential and observed effectiveness of teachers can often be attributed to behaviors in this area.

For many reasons many individuals do not live up to expectancy. These dis-crepancies may arise from many reasons: lack of physical energy, determina-tion and drive; lack of adaptability, flexibility, or the ability to adjust to different needs, persons, and situations; personality conflicts, rigid value sys-tems, and attitudes unacceptable to majority groups; teachers, parents, pu-pils, administrators, supervisors and all others with whom the teacher may come in contact. These deal chiefly with the feeling components of behav-ior and are part of the teacher's potential other than measures of potential that deal chiefly with the cognitive aspects of behavior. Since, for various reasons, people do not live up to expectations, those who would predict ef-ficiency [of teachers] must include in their machinery of prediction some of the non-static aspects of behavior. (Barr, 1961, p. 7)

Teacher as Member of the School Community. The constituent be-haviors of the teacher as a member of the school community are working with colleagues, staff, and parents and participating in school and com-munity events.

1. Working with colleagues, staff, and parents (see Chapters 5 and 8)
   ◆ Giving and receiving support
   ◆ Planning and carrying out interprogram and interdepartmental activities
   ◆ Communicating formally and informally
2. Participating in school and community events (see Chapter 5)
   ◆ Coordinating and assisting with fund-raisers, cultural events, and other projects
   ◆ Holding and attending seminars, workshops, conferences, and dis-cussion groups

An environment in which trust has been established among colleagues promotes and facilitates staff interaction. "Through interactions with col-leagues, teachers can benefit from what others know, prefer, and value. One teacher can help another to become aware of various views and prac-tices" (Heck & Williams, 1984, p. 14).

Likewise, supportive relationships between the home and school play an important role. Students have many learning experiences from the time they wake up in the morning until going to bed at night. Motivating them to work hard and succeed in learning requires a joint effort between the school and home to create a supportive environment for learning. Where this is accomplished, "parents shift from being clients, or silent partners, to becoming full partners in the education of their children" (Gordon, 1971, p. 28).

Pedagogical Behaviors

This category is comprised of three general teacher behaviors: teacher as curriculum developer, teacher as instructor, and teacher as researcher.

Teacher as Curriculum Developer. The constituent behaviors of the teacher as curriculum developer are delineating the course of instruction, identifying and using basic sources (i.e., ideas and materials for the instructional program from relevant sources), and determining course objectives.

1. Delineating the course of instruction (see Chapter 3)
   ♦ Determining major areas to cover
   ♦ Determining topics to cover
   ♦ Determining scope and sequence of units, topics, and lessons
2. Identifying and using basic sources (see Chapter 3)
   ♦ Enriching understanding of subject area
   ♦ Enriching the instructional program
3. Determining course objectives (see Chapter 3)
   ♦ Setting objectives concerning content of subject
   ♦ Setting objectives concerning students' growth
   ♦ Setting objectives involving different levels of understanding

Covering particular topics and trying to develop specific skills in isolation without relating them to other topics and skills within the structure of a subject puts students at a disadvantage in terms of both being able to understand and develop interest. "The curriculum of a subject should be determined by the most fundamental understanding that can be achieved of the underlying principles that give structure to that subject" (Bruner, 1960, p. 31). Any understanding of facts and principles students gain is likely to be lost if there is no unifying structure to tie those facts and principles together. "The best way to create interest in a subject is to render it worth knowing, which means to make the knowledge gained usable in one's thinking beyond the situation in which the learning has occurred" (Bruner, 1960, p. 32).

Thus, when topics and skills are taught with the basic structure of the subject in view, students are more likely to grasp the general principles inherent in the subject and thereby develop not only a greater interest but a greater capacity for learning in the subject area as well. Developing a curriculum in a way that recognizes the basic structure of a subject and that makes that structure clear to students, however, requires a deep interest and understanding of that subject.

Teacher as Instructor. The constituent behaviors of the teacher as instructor are carrying out classroom instruction, reaching the students, and managing the classroom environment.

1. Carrying out classroom instruction (see Chapter 6)
   ♦ Sequencing the presentation of topics
   ♦ Using various types of instructional methods and activities
   ♦ Integrating various resources into lessons

2. Reaching students (see Chapter 5)
   ♦ Adapting instruction to students' intellectual, emotional, social, and spiritual needs
   ♦ Relating instruction to students' home and daily lives
   ♦ Relating instruction to other school subjects
3. Managing the classroom environment (see Chapter 7)
   ♦ Coordinating and pacing instructional activities
   ♦ Organizing the physical environment
   ♦ Establishing daily routines
   ♦ Maintaining disciplined, cooperative behavior

In the role of instructor, the teacher strives to create a classroom environment and organize instructional activities in a way that brings about learning experiences most beneficial to students. To accomplish this the teacher must understand students' interests and backgrounds so that he or she "can make some prediction as to the likelihood that a given situation will bring about a reaction from the student; and, furthermore, will bring about the kind of reaction which is essential to the learning desired" (Tyler, 1950, p. 41). Further, the teacher must first master, as thoroughly as he or she wants students to, any learning he or she hopes to impart to students. This requires not only an abiding interest in the students and the subject but also an effort to learn with students and thus place "himself in a position not only to gain a complete grasp of the subject with which he wishes to become acquainted, but also to observe the children themselves and all their reactions when learning" (Pestalozzi in Heafford, 1967, p. 46). In this way the teacher can monitor students' reactions, determine their needs, and guide them step by step to the desired learning goals.

Teacher as Researcher. The constituent behaviors of the teacher as researcher are searching for theories, ideas, and exemplary practices and observing and assessing classroom instruction.

1. Searching for theories, ideas, and exemplary practices (see Chapters 3 and 6)
   ♦ Visiting libraries and curriculum centers
   ♦ Pursuing advanced study, degrees
   ♦ Attending workshops and seminars
   ♦ Communicating with colleagues (local, state, national)
2. Observing and assessing classroom instruction (see Chapter 8)
   ♦ Monitoring instructional plans
   ♦ Monitoring effects of instruction on students
   ♦ Assessing students' progress and achievement

There is a clear distinction between the nature of the research the teacher carries out in the classroom and the more general research carried out in the field.

Educational research [i.e., classroom research], properly conceived, undertakes to test existing theories and to formulate new ones. Research [i.e., field-oriented] accordingly belongs to the specialist who has time to carry on a search for abstract truth, no matter where it leads and no matter what practical difficulties arise where findings are applied to the improvement of existing conditions. (Waples & Tyler, 1930, p. 7)

An example of such practical difficulties is seen in the disastrous results obtained when classroom innovations that are theoretically and statistically sound are applied blindly, without respect for the specific conditions and needs of particular school and classroom settings. On the other hand, classroom research

tries to determine the effects of various specific conditions upon the processes of teaching and learning. . . . Teachers have important problems to solve, and the solutions will be wise or unwise in proportion to the evidence at hand. This evidence can only be secured by investigation. Hence some investigating must be done by someone. Since the research worker has his own theoretical problems to solve, the investigation of service problems (i.e., classroom teaching problems) must usually be undertaken by the teacher if it is undertaken at all. How much investigation is necessary depends upon the complexity of the problem and upon the desired results. The investigation may consist simply in preparing a test upon the words used in a given textbook in order to determine whether the text is too difficult for the class; perhaps to identify the vocabulary that needs to be taught before the class can read the book intelligently. Or the investigation may be far more extensive, as when the teacher of general science undertakes to construct a new course of study on the basis of topics or problems that have special importance in the local community for the particular pupils concerned. (Waples & Tyler, 1930, pp. 7–8)

Section Summary

As a summary to this section, the teaching behaviors that shape the total classroom environment are examined (Figure 1.2).

FIGURE 1.2 *Three Determining Elements of the Total Learning Environment*

---

1. Modes of functioning
   - Teaching methods used
   - Nature of students' work and activities
2. Organization of classroom and of instructional program
   - Breadth and sequence of instruction
   - Design and use of classroom facilities and resources
3. Personal example of the teacher
   - Personal character and maturity
   - Care for others

A serious misconception is to regard student achievement of objectives in a particular subject (e.g., knowledge of facts, concepts, operations) as the primary goal of teaching. Those who view achievement in this way will perforce focus their energy on taking students toward this goal. It is important to place academic achievement in perspective to form a wider view of classroom teaching and learning that takes into account three major elements constantly influencing the growth of students: (1) the teacher's and students' modes of functioning, (2) the organization of the classroom and of the instructional program, and (3) the personal example of the teacher. Together these three elements create the total learning environment—the environment in which the students work and grow every day.

To measure student and teacher success by attainment of curriculum objectives alone fails to take into account that much more than information is being learned in the classroom. It also leads to very unproductive classroom situations similar to what Popkewitz et al. (1982) refer to as "illusory schooling," where students are seen to be busy at work, curriculum objectives seem to be attained, and achievement is apparently taking place but where in reality instruction is merely mechanical and efforts to reach the students are negligible. What on paper and through superficial observation looks successful (e.g., materials organized and being used, students being "on task" and quiet) is actually bankrupt in terms of the growth of students' inner and creative faculties. Table 1.5 outlines the requirements for establishing a positive classroom learning environment according to the three major elements that shape the total classroom environment (outlined in Figure 1.2). The aim of fulfilling these requirements is not only to increase students' capacity to learn a subject (though that is an important part of it) but to increase their capacity to learn from and deal with life situations as well.

In the previous section the various roles of the teacher were examined, and in this section teaching behaviors corresponding to those roles were discussed. The next section offers a broad view of teaching by looking at the context in which the various roles and behaviors are carried out.

♦ Broad View of Teaching

In this section the complexity and cyclical nature of the teaching process are examined, followed by a discussion illustrating three fundamentally different approaches to teaching based on the work of Popkewitz, Tabachnick, and Wehlage (1982).

Complexity Model

The three diagrams in Figure 1.3 represent a basic teaching model that illustrates how complex the task of teaching can be. In (a), point A is the starting point (i.e., the beginning of the school year) from which the teacher seeks to put a classroom instructional program into operation. Point G is the teacher's goal (i.e., the intellectual, emotional, social, and spiritual

TABLE 1.5 *Requirements for Establishing a Positive Classroom Environment*

DETERMINING ELEMENTS	REQUIREMENTS
1. Modes of functioning	
◆ Teaching methods used	Must be well planned and varied
◆ Students' work and activities	Must encourage interest and disciplined, thoughtful effort
2. Organization of classroom and instructional program	
◆ Breadth and sequence of instruction	Must be thorough, imaginative, and tailored to students' needs
◆ Design and use of classroom facilities and resources	Must facilitate learning and provide sense of security
3. Personal example of the teacher	
◆ Personal character and maturity	Must embody honesty, discipline, respect, and cooperation
◆ Care for others	Must demonstrate dedication, selfless service, objectivity, and tolerance

growth of all students). Diagram (b) shows that once movement from point A is made, it should be done with careful and skillful planning. For example, lines AD and AB depict movement that, for whatever reason (e.g., poor planning, incompetence), is away from the goal. Lines CD and CB also move away from the goal, revealing that the initial problems and mistakes have been compounded. These lines indicate how much time and effort

FIGURE 1.3 *Basic Model of Teaching (Complexity)*

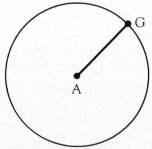

(a) Shortest path to the goal

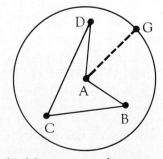

(b) Movement in directions away from goal

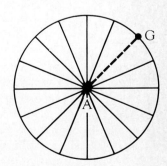

(c) Sixteen major factors to bring into line

can be wasted if a teacher's plans and classroom activities are not sound. The teacher who has moved in the direction of any of the four paths (AB, CB, CD, DA) will first have to get back to at least the starting point (point A) before progress can be made. Thus the distance to the goal will have been greatly increased compared to the most direct path to reaching it (line AG). For example, if at the beginning of the school year (point A) the teacher spends the first two weeks using a text that is too difficult for students to read, then considerable time and effort may be required just to regain students' interest and attention, to clear up misunderstandings, and to get instruction restarted appropriately. In essence, this teacher is back at the beginning (point A). This assumes that the teacher recognized the problem after two weeks and took appropriate steps to remedy it. If the teacher did not recognize the problem and in fact added another problem to it—for example, not establishing with the class that only those who raise their hand or who are called upon (as opposed to calling out) will be allowed to answer questions—then the teacher will have moved even further on a path away from the goal. Not only will the teacher have lost students' interest, attention, and understanding but also an important way of assessing each student's understanding from day to day. Again, before progress can be made toward the goal (point G) the two problems will have to be solved.

Considering how many factors need to be thought of and managed (see Table 1.6 for a list of sixteen important factors), if the teacher at point A is to move on a straight path to the goal, it becomes clear just how complex the teacher's task is. Four basic steps for guiding the teacher through this complexity are:

1. Become aware of the sixteen important factors at work in the classroom. [In Figure 1.3(c) the lines representing the sixteen factors that need to be brought into line to reach the goal indicate how difficult it is to make significant progress.]
2. Determine how much attention each factor needs to be given at the start of the school year and as the school year proceeds.
3. Maintain a log to help keep track of how well each factor is being addressed.
4. Develop a plan to strengthen areas where problems are noted.

Table 1.7 depicts these four basic steps on a matrix so that their relationship with the sixteen important factors can be made clear as a guide to channeling the teacher's efforts toward the goal.

Cyclical Nature of the Teaching Process

Dewey (1929) referred to education as an endless circle or spiral because, as he said, "In its very process it sets more problems to be further studied . . . in everlasting sequence" (p. 77). Similarly, teaching is a process of ever-recurrent cycles from diagnosis, to preparation, to guiding instruction,

TABLE 1.6 *Sixteen Important Factors to Consider for Effective Teaching*

DEVELOPMENT	IMPLEMENTATION	EVALUATION
1. Delineating course of instruction (units, topics, lessons)	8. Getting to know students (their needs, interests, backgrounds)	14. Assessing students' readiness for learning
2. Identifying and using basic sources (to enrich understanding and course)	9. Establishing rules and standards of conduct	15. Designing and using various assessment techniques
3. Determining course, unit, and lesson objectives	10. Managing routines and resources (rollbook, seating, materials)	16. Assessing and grading students' progress and achievement (daily, weekly, monthly)
4. Procuring and using instructional resources	11. Motivating students	
5. Getting to know other teachers, administrators, and staff	12. Determining teaching strategies and pace of instruction	
6. Becoming familiar with school policies and expectations	13. Utilizing various instructional methods and activities	
7. Maintaining emotional stability and physical health		

to evaluation (diagnosis), and back to preparation, as the pattern repeats. Table 1.8 presents the main characteristics and purpose of each phase in this cyclical process.

Three Approaches to Teaching

The names of the three approaches to teaching identified in Table 1.9—technical, constructive, and illusory—are based on their dominant styles of classwork and on their conditions of knowledge.

From the lists of characteristics under each approach presented in Table 1.9 it would appear that the constructive approach is logically the one to follow. However, this is not always true. It is clear that all aspects of the illusory approach should be avoided, but some aspects of the technical approach are relevant and necessary at times. For example, in most courses the principles and concepts taught have to be based upon a definite body of knowledge that needs to be both accepted and absorbed by the students as a prerequisite to understanding more abstract processes and conceptual analyses. It would be meaningless for students to attempt to derive principles about British colonialism, for instance, without knowing some basic facts about the peoples and lands the British colonized as well as the key events surrounding colonization. In fact, a combination of the constructive and the technical approaches will prove most effective in the classroom. When

TABLE 1.7 *Guide for Classroom Teaching*

SIXTEEN IMPORTANT FACTORS	BECOME AWARE OF THE SIXTEEN FACTORS	DETERMINE AMOUNT OF ATTENTION TO BE GIVEN	MAINTAIN DAILY LOG OF EFFORTS	DEVELOP A PLAN TO STRENGTHEN PROBLEM AREAS
1. Delineating course of instruction (units, topics, lessons)				
2. Identifying and using basic sources (to enrich understanding and course)				
3. Determining course, unit, and lesson objectives				
4. Procuring and using instructional resources				
5. Getting to know other teachers, administrators, and staff				
6. Becoming familiar with school policies and expectations				
7. Maintaining emotional stability and physical health				
8. Getting to know students (their needs, interests, backgrounds)				
9. Establishing rules and standards of conduct				
10. Managing routines and resources (rollbook, seating, materials)				
11. Motivating students				
12. Determining teaching strategies and pace of instruction				
13. Utilizing various instructional methods and activities				
14. Assessing students' readiness for learning				
15. Designing and using various assessment techniques				
16. Assessing and grading students' progress and achievement (daily, weekly, monthly)				

TABLE 1.8 *Teaching as a Cyclical Process*

PHASE	CHARACTERISTICS	PURPOSE
Diagnosis	Determine present state of students' knowledge and needs Determine present state of students' readiness to learn	To determine what should be done (focus planning and efforts)
Preparation	Plan course of instruction Locate resources and carry out research Organize and develop curriculum	To master subject material and be ready for instruction
Guiding instruction	Select activities and methods appropriate for students, subject, and objectives Motivate students Foster good work habits and character	To carry out instructional program
Evaluation (continuous and summative)	Keep to plans; assess plans as instruction proceeds Determine success of teaching and learning Modify plans (note: recycle to preparation phase)	To assess effectiveness of instruction

and to what extent the various aspects of one approach or the other should be emphasized can only be determined by the needs of a particular teacher in a particular teaching assignment.

SUMMARY

In this chapter several points about teaching were presented:

1. The basis for effective teaching is a passion to serve and a passion to learn.
2. Above all, the teacher is a leader, guiding students toward intellectual and personal growth.
3. Teaching is an art with science embedded in it because effective practice (art) is always guided by careful observation and reflection (science).
4. The primary roles, responsibilities, and behaviors of the teacher are interpersonal and pedagogical in nature.
5. Teaching is an enormously complex task with as many as sixteen major factors that must be successfully managed in the classroom for progress to be made.
6. Teaching is a process of ever-recurrent cycles from diagnosis, to preparation, to guiding instruction, to evaluation, back to preparation that can be thought of as a repeating endless and growing spiral.
7. A caring attitude and interest in developing close relationships with students are essential to successful teaching.

TABLE 1.9 *Three Approaches to Teaching*

AREAS	TECHNICAL TEACHING	CONSTRUCTIVE TEACHING	ILLUSORY TEACHING
Curriculum	Curriculum development emphasizes certainty and standardization.	Curriculum development emphasizes interdisciplinary and higher-order skills.	Curriculum outlined in teachers' manuals or texts is followed exactly (no curriculum development).
Learning	Creativity and nonstandardized learning are assigned peripheral status.	Aesthetic knowledge is incorporated into classwork encouraging expression and insights.	Conventional mental learning of skills and knowledge is thought to be unattainable for most students.
Students	Students are presented with information they are expected to accept and absorb.	Student initiative and responsibility for learning are encouraged.	Students are presented with information they are not expected to know.
Discipline	Discipline refers to students being able to independently carry out predetermined tasks.	Discipline refers to inner control, attitudes toward schoolwork, responsibility, and initiative.	Discipline refers to obedience.
Classroom tasks	Classroom tasks emphasize ideas and skills that are measurable and expressed in a discrete, sequenced form.	Classroom tasks emphasize relational ideas and exploration of principles and concepts using facts and skills as guides.	Classroom tasks are independent of what is known about students' levels of understanding and ability and are used to maintain control.
Instruction	Instructional activities require students to work in isolation and are characterized by learning packets and commercial materials.	Instructional activities require students to work together or cooperate in some fashion and are characterized by problem solving and discovery learning.	Instructional activities do not require students to work together; interaction between students is considered to be a discipline problem; and activities are intended to make students look busy.

8. Most teaching can be characterized by one or some combination of three basic approaches: technical, constructive, or illusory.

Teaching is among the most important fields of work one can take part in to help better the condition of humanity. This is as true now as it was when the celebrated German philosopher and educator, Immanuel Kant, said,

All culture begins with the individual, and radiates from him as a center. It is only through the efforts of people of broader views, who take an interest in the general good, and who are capable of entertaining the idea of a better condition of things in the future, that the gradual progress of human nature towards its goal is possible. (In Painter, 1905, p. 330)

♦ ♦ ♦ ♦ ♦ ♦ ♦
PRACTICAL MODEL 1.1   Home Reading Record

Introduction   This practical model represents a means of allowing students and their parents to take responsibility for what is certainly a key component of education—a regular, self-monitored home reading program.

Submitted by   Paul Kerwin, junior high school English teacher, West Los Angeles, California

Purpose   To provide students and parents with a structure for organizing a regular program of reading at home

Setting   Junior high school in a large urban school district

♦ Rationale

Teachers are often frustrated by the fact that their students are "aliterate" in the sense that they seldom read books of their own choosing outside the classroom. The traditional book report assignment is hardly a cure. In my experience, students who have not developed the habit of reading regularly at home usually fabricate a report at the last minute. While these fabrications are often easy to detect, catching the fabricator clearly does not solve the problem of the aliterate.

I have found the home reading record to be effective for several reasons. It gently provides a structure in which students can develop a regular reading routine. It also provides a structure for parents to take part in both creating an environment conducive to reading and monitoring their children's progress in developing reading skills.

When using the reading record, students can be guided to gradually develop key self-monitoring techniques, thus letting them feel a sense of responsibility for their own growth. Besides maintaining a record of their daily readings, students are required to summarize key events, use context and the dictionary to understand new vocabulary words, and, perhaps most important, provide interpretive comments to express their understanding of and feelings about what was read.

Below are brief descriptions of the roles played by the parent, student, and teacher in using the home reading record.

◆ Parent

By reading and regularly initialing the reading record sheet (Figure 1.4), the parent assumes responsibility for seeing that reading takes place in the home and specifically affirms that the student has done a minimum of thirty minutes of reading each night. Through the use of parent-student activities and assignments, parents are also encouraged to go beyond mere clock watching and take an active interest in what their children are reading and how it is being understood.

◆ Student

In order to get a grade of "A" on the reading record, students must make sure they read regularly, maintain their reading records appropriately, and keep their parents informed of their progress. This provides them with the unique opportunity to achieve success in the eyes of both teachers and parents—the most important and influential adults in their lives.

◆ Teacher

Without adding hours to an already daunting workload, the home reading record provides the teacher with an insight into each student's progress in developing good reading habits and essential reading skills. For example, the required chapter summaries provide the teacher with material to serve as the basis for short, meaningful, and timely discussions with the students about the books they have read. If chapter summaries are incoherent, this may signal that the students need help in their approach to reading as well as in understanding what they are reading. Most important, the home reading record allows students to receive crucial support from the teacher and parents in developing habits and practicing skills essential to the mature reader.

◆ ◆ ◆ ◆ ◆ ◆ ◆

PRACTICAL MODEL 1.2   Professional Growth Plan

Introduction   Lifelong learning needs to be a goal for each professional teacher. One way to help a teacher reach this goal in a practical and realistic way is through this suggested model for professional growth. Teachers can use this model as a guide, making adaptations in the model as seems appropriate to their particular situations and needs.

FIGURE 1.4 *Home Reading Record*

READING RECORD

Name _____ Week of _____

Dear Parents:

Students become accomplished readers by reading on a regular basis. This home reading record is meant to provide you with a structure for helping your child organize a regular program of reading at home. After your child has read from a book of his or her choice for a minimum of thirty minutes, please initial and date the calendar. Also, actively taking an interest in what your child is reading and how it is being understood will be a great source of encouragement and help foster the development of good reading habits.

Book Title _____ **Author** _____

Calendar

Monday _____

Tuesday _____

Wednesday _____

Thursday _____

Friday _____

Saturday _____

Sunday _____

Vocabulary Words

1. _____ (on page ____)

Context definition _____

Dictionary definition _____

2. _____ (on page ____)

Context definition _____

Dictionary definition _____

3. _____ (on page ____)

Context definition _____

Dictionary definition _____

Chapter Summary

1. _____

2. _____

3. _____

4. _____

(continued)

FIGURE 1.4 *(Continued)*

5. _____

6. _____

7. _____

Overall summary sentence _____

_____

_____

Interpretive Comments

Express your feelings about some of the ideas or situations presented in the book.

What do you think the author was trying to say? Has the author successfully gotten his or her message across to you?

_____

Submitted by   Jane Rudolph, high school English teacher, Los Angeles, California

Purpose   To provide teachers with a list of areas to consider for designing a comprehensive plan for continued professional growth

◆ Areas to Consider for Professional Growth

1. *Monthly readings of professional journals and periodicals.* These readings provide a teacher with information about current trends in education, new research, and a variety of ideas for classroom application. Special monthly features present additional information on specific topics, such as how to use computers creatively to enrich instruction in a variety of curricular areas.

    Some of the many journals and periodicals available include the following:
    - *Educational Leadership*
    - *Journal of Teacher Education*
    - *Phi Delta Kappan*
    - *Curriculum Review*
    - *Media and Methods*
    - *Instructor and Teacher*

2. *Biweekly readings of* The Master Teacher *issued by The Master Teacher, Robert L. DeBruyn (author and publisher).* Many of the issues of this pamphlet offer teachers practical suggestions for classroom use. *The Master Teacher* provides a yearly index of all the issues so that

teachers can locate relevant material when a particular concern or interest arises.

A few of the titles to be found in *The Master Teacher* are the following:

♦ The big question: How do good teachers teach? *17*(32).
♦ Never stop letting students seek, search, and blunder. *17*(33)
♦ Student motivators that we control. *18*(11)

3. ***Attendance at workshops, conferences, and lectures.*** No matter how long one has been a teacher it is always possible to learn much more. Attending a workshop, conference, or lecture at least once a year can be beneficial and invigorating by providing opportunities for teachers to become aware of and share practical suggestions and new ideas for teaching in their particular subject areas.

4. ***Enrollment in education courses or degree programs.*** Lifelong interest in learning is essential for successful teaching. Many universities and colleges offer an excellent variety of interesting courses and advanced degree programs in such areas as curriculum and instruction, counseling, special education, administration, and research. These educational opportunities help teachers increase their skills and widen their perspectives of the field in general. In addition, a teacher should occasionally sign up for a course or lecture series in a field in which he or she has not had much experience. For example, The Origin and Evolution of the Universe, Rethinking Arms Control, Contemporary Films and Filmmakers, and Poetry and the Human Experience, courses offered by the University of California, Los Angeles, have proven to be stimulating and enriching learning experiences for teachers.

5. ***Regular readings from a variety of books in the field of education.*** Many excellent books are available in the field of education. High schools should be encouraged to maintain a curriculum library for the faculty to encourage personal and professional growth. University and county educational libraries are the best sources of books written by authors from all over the world and spanning many time periods that cover a wide array of topics on education.

A few recommended books are the following:

♦ Dell, H. D. (1972). *Individualizing instruction.* Chicago: Science Research Associates.
♦ Goodlad, J. (1984). *A place called school: Prospects for the future.* New York: McGraw-Hill.
♦ Johnson, D. W., et al. (1984). *Circles of learning: Cooperation in the classroom.* Alexandria, VA: Association of Supervision and Curriculum Development.

6. ***Use of videotapes.*** Faculty members should have access to videotapes on effective teaching, learning styles, and writing, to name only a few topics, that are produced by the Association of Supervision and Curriculum Development (ASCD), college and university teacher education programs, and a variety of professional development centers.

Videotapes represent an effective use of technology for professional growth. In addition, joint projects by teachers to videotape each other's classroom teaching, followed by constructive analyses of the tapes, can provide all involved with rare and useful insights into understanding problems and building on strengths.

7. ***Subscription to the Learning Styles Network.*** This network is located at the School of Education and Human Services, St. John's University, Grand Central and Utopia Parkways, Jamaica, NY 11439. The network aims to help teachers keep abreast of important and exciting research that is continually becoming available in the area of student learning styles.

8. ***Visits to university, college, and school district curriculum libraries and professional resource centers.*** These resource centers contain a display of textbooks that have been adopted state- and district-wide, collections of films and videotapes that can be used in the classroom, and numerous books, journals, and periodicals in the field of education. Most important, these resource centers usually make available a variety of teacher-made materials that represent ideas and activities that have proven effective in the classroom. Teachers would do well to spend several days a year reading and doing research at such centers to develop ideas that can be incorporated into their classroom instructional programs.

9. ***Regular sharing of experiences and ideas by faculty members both informally and formally.*** Faculty members should be encouraged to share their experiences, knowledge, and skills with each other. This can be done informally over lunch, at break time, after school, and during conference periods, or formally at monthly faculty meetings and a variety of staff development activities such as team planning workshops, seminars, and interclassroom visitations. In addition, faculty members can be encouraged to hold inservice activities to share some of the ideas, knowledge, and skills they have gained from other professional growth experiences.

10. ***Observations and conferences with school administrators and supervisors.*** School administrators and supervisors are responsible for supervising teachers to determine areas of need and to help increase their effectiveness. An open and constructive approach on the part of both teachers and administrators to the supervisory process, including pre- and postobservation conferences in combination with an ongoing dialog can contribute much to each teacher's professional growth.

11. ***Visits to other schools to observe other teachers.*** There is always room for teachers to develop their skills and learn about new ideas and methods. As part of a school inservice renewal program, a day or two can be set aside during the year to allow each teacher to visit a different school to observe other teachers. A great deal can be learned from

these visits, because teachers often gain many insights into recognizing and handling their own problems by observing other teachers in action.

12. *Quarterly self-evaluation of teaching effectiveness.* Each teacher should take time to evaluate his or her effectiveness in the classroom. One suggestion is to reflect on the appropriateness of the teaching methods used to carry out classroom activities in terms of students' needs and the subject being taught. As part of this evaluation, teachers can also review the effectiveness of the various types of classroom and homework assignments given to students. The self-evaluations prove to be even more useful when teachers share some of the results among themselves at department meetings or in other more informal ways.

13. *Regular reading of daily and weekly newspapers and periodicals.* Teachers should be well informed so they can help students develop an interest in and an awareness of the world around them. Discussing local, national, and world news and issues and applying the issues raised to particular lessons or activities is an excellent opportunity to foster student interest in reading and watching the news as a daily routine.

14. *Getting sufficient rest, relaxation, and exercise.* Teaching demands alertness and stamina. Personal well-being, in terms of emotional and physical health, is essential to effective teaching. To avoid emotional and physical stress and to have both mind and body functioning optimally, it is important to develop regular, healthy habits of eating, sleeping, and exercising. In addition, teachers need a balanced approach to life; they should find recreational outlets so that all their time is not spent concentrating on their work.

◆ ◆ ◆ ◆ ◆ ◆ ◆

CASE STUDY 1.1   Teacher as Leader

Orienting
Questions   As you read this case study ask yourself these questions:

Specific
◆ How effectively is this teacher functioning as an instructional leader?
◆ Does this teacher appear to be providing for students' personal growth?

General
◆ What points in this lesson stand out as indicators of this teacher's strengths and/or weaknesses?
◆ What recommendations would you make for addressing the problems this teacher seems to have?

Setting   School – High school in lower-middle-class neighborhood
Subject – Algebra 1A (fifty-five minutes)

Teacher – Ms. Fowler, first-year teacher

Students – Thirty tenth- and eleventh-grade students who are below average in math

Topic – Absolute Value

Lesson

Note: Under Time Frame the numbers represent the minutes that elapse as the period progresses. Under Dialog the names of the students and the teacher appear as they speak. The symbol ► represents a brief description of a particularly noteworthy action or observation.

Time Frame	Dialog	
	►	The bell for second period has just rung and over the next five minutes (i.e., until the late bell) the students in Ms. Fowler's Algebra 1A class enter the room and take their seats.
1 to 10	►	As the students enter the room Ms. Fowler is quickly putting five new absolute value problems on the board as most students quietly converse.
	Jose:	Ms. Fowler, what do you want us to do in number 1?
	Ms. F.:	Wait until I finish writing these problems on the board; look at the sheet I gave you yesterday.
	►	Jose's notebook is a mess and he makes a brief but futile search for yesterday's sheet. He then goes on to see if he can do any of the other problems.
10 to 25	**Ms. F.:**	Okay, you know these problems are just like the ones we did yesterday in class, and for homework last night. Who wants to tell me the answer to number 1?
	Lily:	$9x + 5$.
	Ms. F.:	Right! Do we all see that?
	►	Three or four students say "yes" with an "of course" tone of voice while most remain silent, and some of the more reserved students say "no," more or less to themselves.
	Ms. F.:	Bill, come up to the board and do number 2.
	►	There is no answer at first, and then several students call out "Bill is absent, Ms. Fowler." Ms. Fowler quickly takes attendance using her seating chart.
	Ms. F.:	Rosa, come up and do number 2.
	Rosa:	I don't know how to do it.
	Ms. F.:	Follow me, Rosa, and anyone else who doesn't know this one.
	►	Ms. Fowler proceeds to do the problem at the board (with her back to the class), asking "Do you understand?" after completing each step of the problem.

Time Frame	Dialog	
	Luis:	Ms. Fowler, didn't you want to cancel out the "3x" when you did step 2?
	Ms. F.:	Where?
	Luis:	On the left side of the equation in step 2 "3x" looks like it should have been cancelled. I think that's how you showed us yesterday.
	Ms. F.:	Wait a second, let me look at this. (She quickly retraces her steps and realizes she missed cancelling "3x.") You're right, Luis. Class, let me explain this problem again from step 1.
25 to 35	►	Ms. Fowler goes through problems 3 and 4, pausing briefly at a few points to ask, "Do we all see that?"
35 to 42	**Ms. F.:**	Take out your homework. I want to go over it now. Okay, here are the answers. (She proceeds to read the answers to each problem as several students take the opportunity to write down the answers for the first time.)
42 to 50	**Ms. F.:**	Okay, open to a new clean page. I'm going to show you how to do domain problems. Here are the steps to follow; watch closely. (She goes through four steps.) Does anyone have a question?
	John:	Yes, Ms. Fowler. How did you get a negative 2 after doing step 2?
	Ms. F.:	Before I show you I want to pass out this sheet that explains how to go through domain problems. Look at this if we don't have time to finish now. Okay, follow me, John, and everyone else. (She then does steps 1 and 2 exactly the same way as before but more slowly.) Now do you see that?
	John:	Yeah (rather hesitatingly).
50 to 55	**Ms. F.:**	Here is your homework. Do problems 1–7 and 9, 11, and 14 on this sheet (homework sheet is being passed out) for tomorrow. Leave the other problems; we'll do those for homework after we discuss how to do them in class tomorrow.
Brief		*Key Facts* – List three key facts verbatim (e.g., "John: Yeah") that characterize the main positive and/or negative aspects of the lesson.
		Strengths/Weaknesses – Briefly explain how the key facts selected indicate strengths and/or weaknesses in the teacher's performance.
		Recommendations – Briefly describe what the teacher could have done to alleviate or avoid the problems that were seen.

♦ ♦ ♦ ♦ ♦ ♦ ♦

CASE STUDY 1.2   Teacher as Instructor

Orienting
Questions   As you read this case study ask yourself these questions:

Specific
- ♦ What can be said about this teacher's style of conducting daily lesson activities?
- ♦ Has this teacher designed a meaningful learning experience for the class?

General
- ♦ What points in this lesson stand out as indicators of this teacher's strengths and/or weaknesses?
- ♦ What recommendations would you make for addressing the problems this teacher seems to have?

Setting   *School* – Junior high school in upper-middle-class neighborhood

Subject – Physical science (lab class) (fifty minutes)

Teacher – Ms. Daman, veteran teacher

Students – Thirty-two eighth-grade students; the majority were in a low-track class last year. (This year there is no longer a low-track science class.)

Topic – Metric System Measurements

Lesson   *Note:* The teacher confided that she feels particularly tense with this class and she tries to exert a higher level of control over them. She stated that four of the students (i.e., three boys and one girl) are particular behavior problems. She has seated them in strategic places in the room. The lab is intended for twenty-eight students. Some stations are crowded.

Time Frame	Dialog	
1 to 5	►	The tardy bell rings. Students are in their seats but talking.
	Ms. D.:	The bell has rung. Let's please be quiet. Please do not touch the equipment on the tables.
	►	Ms. Daman takes roll. The students are nearly quiet.
5 to 22	**Ms. D.:**	Please quiet down and listen to directions for this lab.
	►	The class was prepared for the lab the previous day.
	Ms. D.:	Today's lab deals with measurements in the metric system. If you look around the lab you will see twenty-five stations set up with equipment and questions. For example, one station asks you to measure the mass of a

Time Frame	Dialog	

		rock; another asks the volume of water in a flask, and so on. I have an answer sheet for you to use.
	►	Ms. Daman passes out a ditto of the answer sheet. Several students start talking.
	Ms. D.:	Put your name, today's date, and period 4 on top. Fold your paper lengthwise. You need to be quiet. You don't have to go in order. For example, you could start at station 5, but be sure to put your answer on 5 on the answer sheet. Work by yourself and keep your paper folded so no one copies. When you are finished return to your seat and work on the assignment due Friday. Just a reminder: Today, I will be watching to see how well you can behave in lab. Is there anyone here who feels they will not be able to handle the lab? (A few murmurs of "no" are heard.) Anyone who cannot behave and be safe will not be allowed to participate in the Bunsen burner lab. Are there any questions?
	Dave:	Do we have to be exact on this?
	Ms. D.:	No. You can be plus or minus .1 gram or 1 milliliter. If 83 is correct I would accept 82, 83, or 84. Any other questions? Okay, you can go to the stations and begin.
22 to 45	►	The class begins to work at the stations. Ms. Daman walks around, observes, and answers individual questions.
	►	Three boys start talking loudly.
	Ms. D.:	You are talking too loud. I want it quiet.
	►	Five minutes later the same three boys are talking loudly and not working at a station.
	Ms. D.:	This is the second time I have had to ask you to quiet down and do your work. If it happens again you will be out of the class.
	►	Ten minutes later the same three boys are again loud and are now asking other students for their answers.
	Ms. D.:	That's it! Take your books and go to the counseling office. You will come here after school today to finish this lab, and you had better show up!
45 to 48	►	Most students are done with the lab and are either at their desks or walking around.
	Ms. D.:	I should see people at their desks working quietly.
48 to 50	**Ms. D.:**	It's time to clean up. Please check inside your desk and on the floor around you for trash. We will line up as soon as I see that everyone is quiet.
	►	The students shush each other.

Time Frame	Dialog
	Ms. D.: All right. You may line up.
	▶ The dismissal bell rings and students leave the classroom.
Brief	*Key Facts* – List three key facts verbatim that characterize the main positive and/or negative aspects of the lesson.
	Strengths/Weaknesses – Briefly explain how the key facts selected indicate strengths and/or weaknesses in the teacher's performance.
	Recommendations – Briefly describe what the teacher could have done to alleviate or avoid the problems that were seen.

♦ ♦ ♦ ♦ ♦ ♦ ♦

CASE STUDY 1.3   Teacher as Counselor/Guide

Orienting Questions   As you read this case study ask yourself these questions:

Specific
♦ How well does this teacher relate to the students?
♦ How effective is this teacher in guiding the students to an understanding of the topic being discussed?

General
♦ What points in this lesson stand out as indicators of this teacher's strengths and/or weaknesses?
♦ What recommendations would you make for addressing the problems this teacher seems to have?

Setting   *School* – Private high school drawing from all income levels

Subject – Social studies (fifty minutes)

Teacher – Mr. Golub, history teacher and part-time counselor

Students – Thirty-five freshmen and sophomores

Topic – Objective versus Subjective Knowledge

Lesson

Time Frame	Dialog
0 to 5	▶ The bell for third period rings and students begin pouring into the classroom. On the board are the words, in bold print, OBJECTIVE and SUBJECTIVE. Next to each

Time Frame	Dialog	

		word is a dictionary definition. The instructions say to copy all the information and reflect on an example that illustrates the difference between the two terms.
	Peter:	Do we need to put this in our notes?
	Mr. G.:	That might be a good idea.
	Paul:	Can I go to the bathroom?
	Mr. G.:	No.
	►	By the second bell each student is seated and roll has been taken using a seating chart as the students entered.
5 to 10	**Mr. G.:**	Good morning. Today we will begin our discussion of the difference between how we know people objectively and how we know them subjectively. This will lead us to our discussion tomorrow of how we come to know and appreciate people from other cultural backgrounds. By the end of today's class, you should have a fairly good idea of the distinction between the two terms on the board.
	►	A pause.
	Mr. G.:	Has everyone got these?
	►	No response.
	Mr. G.:	Good. At this point I would like to ask you to include the example from reflection in your notes. Has everyone finished?
	►	No response.
10 to 15	**Mr. G.:**	Would anyone like to share with the class their example?
	►	No response.
	Mr. G.	Tina, turn your notes over please, and tell us the definition of objective knowledge.
	Tina:	I'm not sure I can.
	Mr. G.:	There is always the temptation to give up too soon, Tina. I want you to concentrate a bit more in class. You shouldn't be such a drifter. Jim, would you help us out?
	►	Jim repeats the definitions verbatim from the board but hesitates to provide an example.
15 to 30	**Mr. G.:**	I can see we need to spend a bit more time on this idea than I had planned. Let me see if I can help distinguish the difference between the two terms. Let's say your family hires a maid to do household chores. If she comes only once a week, you might only learn a few things about her, things such as her name, where she lives, and if she has a family or not. Your association with her is

limited to basic facts and thus your knowledge of her as a person is objective. Do you see that?

► Minimal response.

Mr. G.:   Now let's say the maid lives with your family full-time. After a while, you would get to know much more about her than the basic facts. With more contact, she becomes part of the family and you begin to share experiences. Perhaps your conversations with her reach a more personal level and you feel comfortable enough to talk to her as if she were your own sister. In this way, your knowledge of her would be subjective. Okay, I've been in the limelight enough. Now is your chance to share your examples with each other. You have five minutes to discuss in your small groups.

► Mr. Golub moves to his desk.

Mr. G.:   Before you begin, please pass in your homework from last night, which defines the major aspects of cultural heritage.

30 to 49   ► Students pass in homework assignments and then quickly break into their preset small groups. Mr. Golub collects the work and proceeds to put a check on each of the papers. After recording the checks in his grade book, Mr. Golub returns each paper personally and reminds the four freshmen in the back of the room that they have two assignments missing.

49 to 50   **Mr. G.:**   Okay, there is only a minute left. Please return to your original seats and copy the following assignment.

► Mr. Golub writes the day's homework assignment on the board. The bell rings just as he finishes writing "Explain in a paragraph your objective knowledge of someone from another culture."

Brief   *Key Facts* – List three key facts verbatim that characterize the main positive and/or negative aspects of the lesson.

Strengths/Weaknesses – Briefly explain how the key facts selected indicate strengths and/or weaknesses in the teacher's performance.

Recommendations – Briefly describe what the teacher could have done to alleviate or avoid the problems that were seen.

♦ ♦ ♦ ♦ ♦ ♦ ♦

CHAPTER PROJECT   Analyze the Classroom Behavior of an Exemplary Teacher

Goals
1. To become familiar with how an exemplary teacher carries out daily lessons.
2. To develop an effective method of observing a teacher so that useful ideas and insights can be gained.
3. To write a brief report of the observations to have as a resource for future reference.

Phases
One, two, or three phases (i.e., planning, partial implementation, full implementation) of the chapter project can be completed as is deemed appropriate to student needs and the design of the course.

Planning
1. Make arrangements for three classroom observations of an exemplary teacher in your subject area.
2. Design a general framework to focus the observations. For example, a framework to use as a guide could focus on how the teacher carries out the major parts of the lesson (i.e., beginning the lesson, review of work from the previous lesson, introduction of objectives for the lesson, presentation of new material, assignment of homework, and summary of the day's work), or his or her pedagogical and interpersonal roles.

Partial Implementation
1. Carry out the classroom observations.
2. Make a log of the observations using the observation guide developed. Allow for flexibility and spontaneity by using the guide mainly as a starting point and an instrument to help focus attention.

Full Implementation
1. Review the observation log that was kept.
2. Write a two- to three-page report that includes the following:
   a. A description of the setting (i.e., classroom environment, number and characteristics of students, subject area of course).
   b. A description of the lesson presentations (i.e., outline of the topics covered, description of the teaching strategies and materials used and of the teacher's personal interactions with the students, discussion of the strengths and/or weaknesses noted, and insights gained concerning the use of methods and materials of instruction).
   c. An analysis of the teacher's performance focusing on how the main parts of the lesson and pedagogical and interpersonal roles were carried out.
   d. A summary of the observations discussing the strengths and weaknesses noted and insights gained concerning the use of methods and materials and personal interaction with the students.

◆ ◆ ◆ ◆ ◆ ◆ ◆

REFERENCES

Alcorn, M. D., Kinder, J. S., & Schunert, J. R. (1970). *Better teaching in secondary schools* (3rd ed.). New York: Holt, Rinehart and Winston.

Barr, A. S. (1961). *Wisconsin studies of the measurement and prediction of teacher effectiveness.* Madison: Dembar Publications.

Bruner, J. S. (1960). *The process of education.* Cambridge, MA: Harvard University Press.

Dewey, J. (1928). *Democracy and education: An introduction to the philosophy of education.* New York: Macmillan.

Dewey, J. (1929). *The sources of a science of education.* New York: Horace Liveright.

Dewey, J. (1938). *Experience and education.* New York: Macmillan.

Einstein, A. (1950). *Out of my later years.* New York: Philosophical Library.

Ghose, A. (1966). *Sri Aurobindo and the mother on education.* Pondicherry: Sri Aurobindo Ashram.

Gordon, I. J. (1971). Parent involvement in early childhood education. *National Elementary Principal, 51,* 26–35.

Heafford, M. (1967). *Pestalozzi: His thought and its relevance today.* London: Methuen.

Heck, S. F., & Williams, C. R. (1984). *The complex roles of the teacher: An ecological perspective.* New York: Teachers College Press.

Hendley, B. P. (1986). *Dewey, Russell, Whitehead: Philosophers as educators.* Carbondale, IL: Southern Illinois University Press.

Montessori, M. (1917). *Spontaneous activity in education.* New York: Schocken Books.

Painter, F. V. N. (Ed.). (1905). *Great pedagogical essays.* New York: Great American Book Company.

Passmore, J. (1980). *The philosophy of teaching.* Cambridge, MA: Harvard University Press.

Patel, M. S. (1953). *The educational philosophy of Mahatma Gandhi.* Ahmedabad: Navajivan Publishing House.

Popkewitz, T. S., Tabachnick, B. R., & Wehlage, G. (1982). *The myth of educational reform: A study of school responses to a program of change.* Madison: The University of Wisconsin Press.

Russell, B. (1926). *On education.* London: George Allen & Unwin.

Tyler, R. (1950). *Basic principles of curriculum and instruction.* Chicago: University of Chicago Press.

Waples, D., & Tyler, R. W. (1930). *Research methods and teachers' problems: A manual for systematic studies of classroom procedure.* New York: Macmillan.

Whitehead, A. N. (1929). *The aims of education and other essays.* New York: Macmillan.

◆ ◆ ◆ ◆ ◆ ◆ ◆

ANNOTATED READINGS

Anderson, C. J., Barr, A. S., & Bush, M. G. (1925). *Visiting the teacher at work: Case studies of directed teaching.* New York: D. Appleton.
  A complete and detailed treatment of the reasons for failure in teaching due to causes other than poor teaching technique. See Chapter 5 for a series of case studies of teaching.

Barzun, J. (1945). *Teacher in America.* Boston: Little, Brown.
> *A personal and philosophical examination of the teacher in American society by one of the nation's most prominent writers and thinkers. See Chapter 1 for a unique look at the profession of teaching.*

Bolton, F. E. (1911). *Principles of education.* New York: Charles Scribner's Sons.
> *A comprehensive study of all facets of education from psychological and biological viewpoints. See Chapter 1 for an insightful interpretation of education and teaching.*

Callahan, J. F., & Clark, L. H. (1982). *Teaching in the middle and secondary schools* (2nd ed.). New York: Macmillan.
> *A basic self-instructional text on teaching methods. See Chapter 16 for a method of analyzing one's teaching.*

Fenstermacher, G. D., & Soltis, J. F. (1985). *Approaches to teaching.* New York: Teachers College Press.
> *A book designed to stimulate thought about ways to conceive of the role of the teacher. Three distinct yet related approaches to teaching are examined, including the executive approach, the therapist approach, and the liberationist approach.*

Henson, K. T. (1981). *Secondary teaching methods.* Lexington, MA: D. C. Heath.
> *A basic text in secondary school teaching emphasizing practical applications of the principles of teaching. See Chapter 1 on the foundations of learning and teaching.*

Hunter, M. (1982). *Mastery teaching.* El Segundo, CA: TIP Publications.
> *A book designed to help the beginning teacher develop effective classroom techniques. See Chapter 1 for a practical guide to classroom decision making for the teacher.*

Lortie, D. C. (1977). *Schoolteacher: A sociological study.* Chicago: University of Chicago Press.
> *An examination of a variety of issues concerning the organization and nature of the teacher's work, including a discussion of how teachers view their daily classroom tasks. See Chapter 5 on the personal purposes of teachers for a discussion of the teacher's role beyond the curriculum.*

Montessori, M. (1912). *The Montessori method.* New York: Schocken Books.
> *A complete and detailed examination of Montessori's methods for "structural freedom." See Chapter 4 on pedagogical methods.*

Mursell, J. L. (1934). *Principles of education.* New York: W. W. Norton.
> *A book full of ideas and examples concerning issues and topics considered to be most relevant to teachers and teacher educators. See Chapters 2 and 3 for a thorough discussion of the foundations of education.*

Orlich, D. C., Harder, R. J., Callahan, R. C., Kravas, C. H., Kauchak, D. P., Pendergrass, R. A., & Keogh, A. J. (1985). *Teaching strategies: A guide to better instruction* (2nd ed.). Lexington, MA.: D. C. Heath.
> *A book presenting a broad spectrum of instructional methodologies, techniques, and approaches tailored to the secondary school classroom. See Chapter 1 for a discussion of the teacher as decision maker.*

Plato. (1956). *Protagoras and Meno.* Baltimore: Penguin Books.
> *See "The Meno" for a dialog illustrating the Socratic method of teaching.*

Schulman, L. S. (1986). Paradigms and research programs in the study of teaching. In M. Wittrock (Ed.), *Handbook of research on teaching* (3rd ed.). New York: Macmillan.

An examination of teaching behaviors according to three fundamental cognitive processes—judgment and policy determination, problem solving, and decision making.

Strike, K., & Soltis, J. F. (1985). *The ethics of teaching.* New York: Teachers College Press.

A thought-provoking book focusing on the nature of ethical inquiry and ethical dilemmas of teaching. It is a useful guide for forming a personal conception of ethics in teaching and for making ethical behavior part of day-to-day decision making in the classroom.

Thorndike, E. L. (1906). *The principles of teaching: Based on psychology.* New York: A. G. Seiler.

A study of teaching that blends scientific principles and practical classroom applications. See Chapter 1 for a discussion of teaching as an art.

Thorndike, E. L. (1923). *Education: A first book.* New York: Macmillan.

An introductory study of education featuring a nontechnical account of the aims, means, methods, and results of education. See Chapters 2 and 3 for a discussion of the aims of education.

Thorndike, E. L., & Gates, A. I. (1929). *Elementary principles of education.* New York: Macmillan.

A thorough study of the principles of education as a guide for dealing with the daily classroom needs of the teacher. See Chapter 11 for a discussion of teaching methods.

CHAPTER 2
♦ ♦ ♦ ♦ ♦ ♦ ♦

Learning

INTRODUCTION

Teaching is not learning. Teaching and learning are two different yet closely related processes. Remember this distinction. A serious weakness often found in inexperienced teachers is their inattention to the learning process. Many inexperienced teachers spend most of their time and efforts on finding out about or practicing various teaching techniques. All these efforts are to no avail, however, unless equal attention is given to developing a basic understanding of what it takes and what it means to learn.

The most effective way to understand the learning process is to be actively involved in learning and to reflect on the process as you experience it. To be effective as a teacher it is not sufficient merely to study learning theory and become familiar with the latest research on learning. The teacher must also be able to identify with the learning process through firsthand experience. Only then can he or she understand the difficulties and subtleties of learning. The teacher must always remain a student at heart. Reflecting on one's own efforts to learn is an important step in understanding the meaning of such concepts as cognitive learning style or readiness for learning as they apply in practice. It is a mistake for the teacher to think, Now that I have my degree and teaching certificate I will concentrate all my energy on teaching my subject. The person thinking along these lines will soon lose touch with what students are going through in order to learn. So, what are some effective ways for the teacher to be involved in the learning process?

A list covering a broad range of areas for continued learning is presented in Table 2.1. In each area some particularly useful learning activities to be involved in and think about are mentioned as a way to better understand the learning process. As Russell, who considered a person's continuing involvement in learning important, pointed out,

TABLE 2.1 *Areas for Continued Learning*

AREAS	LEARNING ACTIVITIES
School	*Classroom research*
	Learn about the effectiveness of various teaching strategies and materials
	Learn about the various needs and abilities of every student
Formal study	*Graduate study*
	Enroll in an advanced degree program or take courses in a particular subject area (i.e., major area or other area of education, such as administration)
Informal study	*Self-designed study*
	Stay current on what others are doing in the field through visitations, discussions, seminars, workshops, professional journals
	Carry out research projects related to a particular subject area and/or to teaching in general utilizing a variety of resources (e.g., university libraries, interviews with experts in the field)
Daily life	*Everyday events*
	Learn from day-to-day experiences in different areas (intellectual, social, emotional, physical)
	Develop a keen awareness of life and the events going on around (home, community, nation, world)

The more a man has learnt, the easier it is for him to learn still more—always assuming that he has not been taught in a spirit of dogmatism. . . . No doubt the word "intelligence" properly signifies an aptitude for acquiring knowledge rather than knowledge already acquired; but I do not think this aptitude is acquired except by exercise, any more than the aptitude of a pianist or an acrobat. . . . The desire to instil what are regarded as correct beliefs has made [teachers] too often indifferent to the training of intelligence. . . . For this purpose I shall consider only the aptitude for acquiring knowledge, not the store of actual knowledge which might legitimately be included in the definition of intelligence. (1926, pp. 58–59)

Knowing how to make learning understandable to students is directly related to and dependent upon first making that learning understandable to ourselves. Understanding and imparting understanding are part of the same process.

Thus far our discussion has focused on becoming familiar with the learning process, or the "how" of learning. It is equally important to consider the "what" of learning. Because the teacher takes on a great responsibility in leading students in the areas of intellectual, social, emotional, and spiritual growth, determining what they learn must be done with utmost care and understanding. As Bolton said,

The true educator [teacher] must be concerned not only with adjusting John and Mary to particular niches in life, but he must look to the development of higher ideals for the whole human race and the conscious striving for and attainment of these ideals. (1911, p. 14)

In terms of his or her subject, the teacher must be continually learning in order to enrich the curriculum and bring alive classroom instruction. Learning cannot occur in a vacuum. The teacher must have something to teach—something that has captured his or her interest and to which he or she has given much thought. In short, the teacher must be as interested in and excited about a subject as he or she hopes students to be.

This chapter focuses primarily on the how of learning. The active and cyclical nature of the learning process is first described. Principles and recommended practices for determining readiness for learning are then examined. The chapter concludes with a discussion of what to look at and when for effective assessment of learning.

BASIC THEORIES

♦ The Learning Process

This section focuses on developing an understanding of learning both as an active and a cyclical process.

Learning as an Active Process

In Table 2.2 the three main elements (effort, attention, and habit) of learning as an active process are defined. An examination of these elements reveals their interrelatedness. For example, it is hard to imagine being able to pay careful attention without making an effort or having developed the habit of paying attention. Similarly, effort without proper attention to what is to be learned is aimless. Examination of each element reveals that it originates in the learner, requiring his or her active involvement for its development. This is fully in keeping with the highest ideals of education, in which learning is considered to be one's interest in and "aptitude for acquiring knowledge rather than knowledge already acquired" (Russell, 1926, p. 58). Because it is an active process, learning cannot be predetermined, predigested, and delivered in a neat package to the learner. Quite the contrary, students learn most effectively when they are interested in a subject and make continued efforts to learn it.

The process of learning begins with perception. Perception is defined as an awareness of elements or stimuli in the environment. Without perception there is no possibility of conception, and thus of internalizing learning. The teacher's first task, therefore, is to maximize the likelihood that students perceive instructional activities fully and accurately. The key to succeeding in this task is the teacher's ability to gain and hold students' attention.

The capacity to pay attention is always there in the students. Observe any adolescent absorbed in a video game or transfixed by an engaging movie. The teacher's task, therefore, is not to create attention but to direct it. Close observation of students in a class reveals that inattention to classwork often means attention to something else. The teacher can secure students'

TABLE 2.2 *Learning as an Active Process*

THREE MAIN ELEMENTS	DEFINITION IN TERMS OF LEARNING	RELATED AREAS OF CHARACTER DEVELOPMENT
Effort	Involves paying attention to what is being taught and participating in learning activities	Commitment
Attention	Involves focusing on a particular learning activity or stimulus	Self-discipline
Habit	*Active:* Involves thought, invention, and initiative in applying capacities attained to new learning	Will
	Routine: Involves developing certain behavioral tendencies through numerous repetitions of those behaviors	

attention with demands and threats of punishment. But to do this is a short-term solution. If the students' genuine interest is not aroused, through appropriate content and method of instruction, they will not be motivated to pay attention in the future. Steady attention because of interest and the habit of work is the desideratum. It is not enough simply to have students' attention; attention must be to the right thing and with the right intention.

All too often the teacher attempts to solve the attention problem by using any of a number of devices, such as threats, busy work, and special effects (i.e., striking language, videos), regardless of whether or not they focus students' attention on the facts or ideas to be learned. Attention gotten in this way is useless and may even have a negative effect. Rather than requiring students to make the necessary mental effort and exert the necessary self-discipline, the teacher settles for the mere appearance of attention. The importance of attention to the growth of students should not be minimized. "The faculty of voluntarily bringing back a wandering attention, over and over again, is the very root of judgment, character and will. . . . An education which should improve this faculty would be the education par excellence" (James in Montessori, 1917, p. 155). The goal is to develop the ability of steady attention in the students through a careful balance between interests (i.e., motivation) and good work habits (i.e., self-discipline).

In Chapter 5 motivation is examined as a way of gaining students' attention; in Chapter 7 the relationship between self-discipline and attention is discussed.

By developing the capacity to pay attention, students can increase the quantity and quality of their perceptions and thus derive more meaning from classroom learning experiences and maximize retention of what they learn as the basis for continued interest and further understanding.

Even if classroom instruction is made interesting to students and results in their paying attention, it is crucial that the students also develop good habits for the future. When we think of a habit we usually associate it with some action that has become routine, if not automatic, due to numerous repetitions over time. Routine habits help us maintain a balance in carrying out daily activities in our environment. Another type of habits, called active habits, is less associated with automatic responses and more with intelligent action and reason.

Although routine habits are valuable for building stability, active habits are the key to meaningful and continued learning in that they require thought, creativity, and initiative in applying knowledge and capacities already attained to new experiences. Learning is impeded when routine habits are emphasized too much or at the wrong time. For example, a student's ability to make progress in a general science course would be hampered if he or she used a routine habit, such as memorizing basic scientific principles, for activities that require the active habit of deriving principles from observations of experiments.

A careful study of both routine and active habits as they apply to learning reveals that they are organized in hierarchies or patterns. Simply, routine habits precede and pave the way for more complex, active ones. Thus, forming bad or inappropriate habits initially can block further development and learning.

Learning as a Cyclical Process

The word *cyclical* is used here to characterize learning as a process that repeats itself over and over again, each time at a higher and deeper level of understanding. The learner is viewed not as a passive receiver of information but as an active participant in discovering knowledge. Thus, learning is considered an evolutionary process in which new information, ideas, and experiences are continually integrated with previous learning.

In the discussion above, the importance of students' ability to pay attention in the classroom so that their perceptions of what is being taught are as complete and accurate as possible was emphasized. In considering learning as a cyclical process, however, it is important to understand the influence students' preconceptions have on their actual perceptions.

> Not all perceptions are correct, even if careful attention has been given to them. The senses do not deceive us, but our interpretations may be erroneous. We view all phenomena with glasses colored by all our previous experiences. Our world is what past experience makes it. (Bolton, 1911, p. 459)

Figure 2.1 shows a cycle of learning that includes the three levels of cognition: perception, registering stimuli from the environment; conception, grouping the meaning of stimuli for comprehension; and ideation, forming ideas from the meanings derived. Each succeeding level of cognition reached, from perception to conception to ideation, marks an increased awareness of stimuli from the environment and thus a higher level of cognition. To say that a student has knowledge of a particular theory, for

FIGURE 2.1 *The Cycle of Learning*

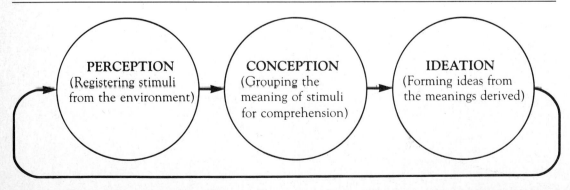

instance, can have several meanings depending upon the level of cognition being referred to. That is, he or she might have memorized the theory (perception), comprehended the meaning of the theory (conception), or thought of creative ways of applying the theory (ideation).

The task then is how to develop instructional materials and structure classroom activities that take into account the different stages of learning so that clear perception can give rise to conception and culminate in the formation of creative ideas. Whitehead describes three stages of learning (Figure 2.2) that coincide precisely with the three levels of cognition:

1. **The Stage of Romance.** The stage of romance is the stage of first apprehension and as such addresses the need for clear perception based on attention and interest. In this stage, subject matter should have the vividness of novelty, holding within itself unexplored connections with possibilities half-disclosed by glimpses and half-concealed by the wealth of material. In this stage, knowledge is not dominated by systematic procedure.

2. **The Stage of Precision.** The stage of precision also represents an addition to knowledge, but one in which initial perceptions coalesce and take on collective meaning. In this stage, interest, though still necessary, is channeled toward the discovery of meaning (i.e., conception). New facts are added, but they are facts that fit into the analysis. It is evident that a stage of precision is barren without a previous stage of romance: Unless there are facts that have already been vaguely apprehended in their broad generality, the previous analysis is an analysis of nothing. It is simply a series of meaningless statements about bare facts, produced artifically and without any further relevance.

3. **The Stage of Generalization.** The stage of generalization represents a synthesis; concepts derived in the preceding stage become unified through the formation and classification of ideas. As such it is a return to romanticism with the added advantage of classified ideas and relevant

---

FIGURE 2.2 *Whitehead's Three Stages of Learning*

---

1. Romance (Perception)
   - Vividness, novelty
   - Facts seen in their broad generalities

2. Precision (Conception)
   - Analysis, exactness
   - Relationships disclosed through systematic discovery

3. Generalization (Ideation)
   - Classification (of ideas), relevant technique
   - Renewed search based on knowledge and aptitudes acquired

---

Source: Based on material from *The Aims of Education and Other Essays* (pp. 27–31) by A. N. Whitehead, 1929, New York: Macmillan.

technique. It is the fruition that has been the goal of the precise train-ing. It is the final success. (1929, pp. 27–31)

These three stages of learning, referred to by Whitehead as "the rhythm of education," are similar to the processes of acquisition, transformation, and evaluation found in what Bruner (1960) calls "learning episodes" (Fig-ure 2.3). The learning episode is characterized by initial acquisition, where information is presented to the learner with the aim of adding to or replacing previously held information. Acquisition is followed by transformation, where the information acquired is analyzed, given meaning, and put to use. In this sense it follows the stage of precision and marks the beginnings of the stage of generalization as well. Finally there is evaluation, where the learner is required to examine the usefulness of meanings that have been derived as a preparation for wider and varied applications—in short, a full flowering of the stage of generalization.

> A learning episode can be brief or long, contain many ideas or a few. How sustained an episode a learner is willing to undergo depends upon what the person expects to get from his efforts, in the sense of such external things as grades but also in the sense of a gain in understanding. (Bruner, 1960, pp. 48–49)

Learning episodes are seen by Bruner to naturally form a "spiral curriculum" in which basic ideas and information on the subject are presented repeatedly, each time building upon the student's level of understanding until a com-mand of the subject has been attained.

In Figure 2.4 the three basic characteristics of the spiral curriculum are outlined, and their correspondence with the stages of the learning episode and the three levels of cognition is noted.

A significant mistake many teachers make is to carry out instruction as though it were a linear process with learning being merely additive and one-dimensional. In Table 2.3 learning as a cyclical process and learning as a linear process are compared. In the instructional program of Teacher

---

FIGURE 2.3 *Three Stages of the Learning Episode*

1. Acquisition (Romance)
   - ♦ Replacing or adding to previous information
2. Transformation (Precision)
   - ♦ Making information fit new tasks
3. Evaluation (Generalization)
   - ♦ Checking whether uses of information are adequate to the task

---

Source: Based on material from *The Process of Education* (pp. 48–49) by J. S. Bruner, 1960, Cambridge, MA: Harvard University Press.

FIGURE 2.4 *Three Basic Characteristics of the Spiral Curriculum*

1. Design and teach subject material with scrupulous intellectual honesty and clarity
   ♦ Perception (Acquisition)
2. Emphasize students' initiative, grasp of concepts, and application of those concepts
   ♦ Conception (Transformation)
3. Use learning activities that require students to use ideas in progressively more complex forms
   ♦ Ideation (Evaluation)

Source: Based on material from *The Process of Education* (pp. 48–49) by J. S. Bruner, 1960, Cambridge, MA: Harvard University Press.

A, note that topics (and related concepts) were initially introduced at one level of difficulty and then repeatedly presented at increasingly sophisticated levels of understanding, not as isolated bits of learning to be stored up, but fully integrated with other topics. Teacher B, on the other hand, clearly delineated the sequence and scope of the topics to be covered and then proceeded to introduce one topic after another until all were covered. Teacher B made no plan for relating the information, concepts, or ideas

TABLE 2.3 *Cyclical versus Linear Learning*

TEACHER A—CYCLICAL PROCESS				TEACHER B—LINEAR PROCESS		
Time Allotment	**Areas**	**Topics**		**Time Allotment**	**Areas**	**Topics**
Week 1	Decimals	a		Week 1	Decimals	a, b
Week 2	Percents	a		Week 2	Decimals	c, d
Week 3	Decimals	b		Week 3	Percents	a, b
	Percents	b				
Week 4	Decimals	c		Week 4	Percents	c, d
	Equations	a				
	Percents	c				
Week 5	Equations	b, c		Week 5	Equations	a, b
	Decimals	d				
Week 6	Percents	d		Week 6	Equations	c, d
	Equations	d				
	Decimals	d				

Note: The letters a, b, c, and d represent topics of increasing difficulty to be covered under each area of this Math 7 course.

between topics for purposes of reinforcing or deepening students' understanding of the subject as a whole.

Wittrock (1974) proposed a model of "generative learning" focusing on various types of comprehension gained from instruction. This model of learning is similar to the cyclical process used by Teacher A in Table 2.3, in which "teaching and instruction are designed to help the learner to transfer memories of previous experiences to the comprehension of new information" (Wittrock & Lumsdaine, 1977, p. 427). In the model of generative learning, as with other cognitive models, the student is an active participant and catalyst for learning rather than a passive onlooker.

> Even when learners are given the information they are to learn, they still must discover its meaning. In the process they use their information-processing strategies, memories, and attentional and motivational mechanisms to organize and understand it. (Wittrock, 1978, p. 26)

Effective use of cognitive models of learning and instruction requires much more than mere intellectual understanding of how such models are constituted and why they are used. The teacher needs to take on "a new and more important role in instruction" (Wittrock, 1978, p.27). He or she must learn to develop creative curriculum and to rely much less on ready-made materials (e.g., textbooks, commercial materials). In addition, he or she must learn to become a keen observer in the classroom, detecting just how the various materials and instructional practices used affect student learning.

◆ Readiness for Learning

The first question the teacher must ask is, How ready are the students for various types and levels of learning experiences?

> Since learning is developmental, it follows that one learns better when one is ready to learn. The principle of readiness has confused both teachers and laypeople. Psychologically it can have many ramifications, but for our classroom purposes it can be defined quite simply. Readiness is a combination of maturity, ability, prior instruction, and motivation. (Clark & Starr, 1986, p. 43)

Readiness to learn is indicated by the student's ability to benefit from specific learning experiences. Lack of readiness on the cognitive level can be due to incomplete or incorrect perception, inability to understand concepts, or inability to form ideas about the material presented. Thus, the main task in addressing student readiness for learning "is to manipulate the learning situation to take into account and optimal advantage of existing cognitive capacities [i.e., perception, cognition, and ideation] and mode of assimilating ideas and information" (Ausubel, 1963, p. 30).

To address the important aspects of readiness for learning, learning styles and the dynamic nature of learning are examined, followed by a discussion of the impact classroom learning experiences have on student readiness for learning.

In Table 2.4 three broad areas are outlined to show the developmental nature of readiness for learning in terms of physical, intellectual, and social/emotional growth. The three areas of readiness are called developmental because in each area a gradual growth or unfolding occurs in each student over time. Thus, an important task of the teacher is not only to accurately assess readiness for learning but to plan and carry out instruction in a way that fosters the developmental process of readiness as well.

Learning Styles

Style of learning refers to the mode of learning a student tends toward and the one in which he or she naturally learns most effectively. Cognitive development is an important factor in determining and addressing student learning styles. An examination of learning styles reveals that many differences found among students can be traced to how they perceive, conceptualize, and form ideas about stimuli (in the form of learning experiences) presented to them.

Classroom learning tasks, therefore, should be designed to account for students' various levels of cognitive development as seen in their abilities to perceive, conceptualize, and form ideas inasmuch as "learning often depends upon the congruence between the task and the learner's ability and cognitive style" (Wittrock & Lumsdaine, 1977, p. 436). For example, stress on perceptual aspects in a particular learning activity (e.g., recognition or recall of facts) is boring and counterproductive for students who have a more reflective approach to learning. These students would benefit

---

TABLE 2.4 *Readiness for Learning*

AREA OF READINESS	DESCRIPTION
Physical	Physical development and coordination, and control and use of senses (perception of learning)
Intellectual	Mental capacity and prior experiences, including habits developed and knowledge attained (assimilation of learning)
Social/Emotional	Self-confidence, openness to people and ideas, and interest in participating in a group-learning environment (utilization of learning) (cooperation in learning)

more from learning tasks involving analysis and application of information and ideas. Spending extended time, however, on developing perceptual skills (i.e., ability to focus on and register stimuli accurately) is necessary with students having language problems to prepare them for more conceptually or ideationally oriented activities. Although it is helpful to design learning activities to suit specific learning styles, students should also have opportunities to develop the ability to successfully handle tasks requiring different styles. Achieving a balance between tailoring learning activities to students' learning styles and using learning activities to modify or broaden students' learning styles is necessary to maximize their readiness for continued learning.

Familiarity with characteristics of the students in each of the three areas listed in Table 2.4 is also helpful in understanding students' different learning styles. When planning and carrying out daily classroom lessons, the teacher sometimes forgets to consider the stage of students' physical development and the implications this may have on their ability to learn. In certain subjects, such as instrumental music, physical education, art, and various other technically oriented subjects, the need for physical readiness is apparent because specific muscular development and coordination are needed to learn and perform tasks properly.

In a more subtle yet no less important way, however, students' abilities to use all their senses to perceive stimuli from the environment must also be considered in terms of physical readiness to learn and should be addressed in all subject areas. For example, some students may have difficulty learning in a particular teacher's class because that teacher speaks too fast for them to take adequate notes. Although these students may possess the muscular development necessary to write quickly and hear clearly, they may not be able to coordinate the use of both senses after a certain point. Similarly, if material is placed on the board or on a worksheet without considering how it will look to students, failure to learn may result. This applies not only to cluttered or illegible writing but also to material so unorganized that students cannot fully comprehend what is before them. As a result the students either form misconceptions or become frustrated by their inability to comprehend the material presented. It is hard to say which students are in a worse position. Students who believe they have accurately perceived the material when in fact they have not form misconceptions and remain unaware of what they do not know, while students who simply cannot comprehend the material at least know that they do not know.

The question arises, How does the teacher appropriately take into account students' physical readiness to learn? The answer to this question generally applies to all areas of student readiness to learn. To address student readiness to learn requires most alert and careful observation of each student's actions and work as he or she proceeds through various instructional activities. To be useful, this must be supplemented by frequent use of well-chosen questions to students during lessons, timely use of quizzes, tests, and other diagnostic instruments, and conferences with students, parents, other teachers, and other school personnel (e.g., grade counselors). A thorough discussion of assessing learning will be presented in the next section and in Chapter 8.

Intellectual readiness refers to students' mental capacity to interpret and process what is being taught. Readiness in this area is closely associated with learning habits that have been established and previous learning that has occurred.

Guilford classifies five levels of primary mental abilities (i.e., "structure of the intellect") that need to be kept in mind when attempting to make instructional decisions that address intellectual readiness to learn.

1. Cognitive abilities are those that allow discovery, recognition, and comprehension of information.
2. Memory abilities are those that permit the storage and retention of information.
3. Convergent production is the generation of specific (right answer) information from other information.
4. Divergent production is the generation of varied ideas based on given (or known) information.
5. Evaluation abilities are those employed when a decision must be made about accuracy, appropriateness, or suitability of information. (In Grambs & Carr, 1979, pp. 201–202)

Social/emotional readiness to learn concerns self-image, confidence, and interest and ability to work with others. Adolescents are at a delicate yet volatile stage of social and emotional development, in which seemingly small events can have a significant and lasting impact on their future behavior and growth. Therefore, the teacher must become sensitive to the potential impact various activities and comments may have on students. One particularly valuable skill to develop to foster social/emotional growth is that of creating a nonthreatening atmosphere in which students not only feel comfortable participating in class discussions but also feel a natural camaraderie with each other. This type of environment helps students reach a state of emotional balance that is crucial for mental health and thus for learning unencumbered by undue stress, strain, and fear.

To understand the role learning styles play in both determining and fostering readiness for learning requires an understanding of the dynamic nature of learning.

The Dynamics of Learning

The term *dynamics* is used here to describe the causal and forceful nature of learning. An examination of the dynamics of learning in relationship to student readiness to learn focuses on the principles of apperception and deutero-learning.

Apperception. Apperception refers to students' ability to proceed from the known to the related unknown. For example, a teacher can profitably begin instruction on algebraic functions only if students already understand basic arithmetic.

> What any [student] thinks or feels or does on any occasion depends upon what he has thought and felt and done in the past and upon the present "set" or tendency of his mind [i.e., preconceptions]. . . . A mind's past experience and present content determine its responses. . . . If the knowledge or power needed as a preparation for the task in hand is lacking, the teacher's first duty is to secure it. This is the law of apperception. (Thorndike, 1906, p. 42)

In brief, apperception is the aspect of learning that looks at the dynamic connection of past experience with present learning. In this sense the law of apperception fits very well into the notion of learning as a cyclical process in which new information, ideas, and experiences are continually integrated with previous learning. This dynamic aspect of learning also demonstrates that student readiness for learning is not something simply to be measured by sophisticated statistical means. Rather, it requires careful observation and planning. "The idea of 'readiness' is a mischievous half-truth. It is a half-truth largely because it turns out that one teaches readiness or provides opportunities for its nurture, one does not simply wait for it" (Bruner, 1966, p. 29).

Cognitive psychologists similarly look at readiness for learning in terms of "conceptual frameworks" (Nussbaum & Novick, 1982) or "schemata" (Piaget in Wadsworth, 1971) to describe the mental processes involved in linking past with present learning. Students' existing conceptual frameworks, or the way they view ideas and information in relation, are important in determining what they are able to learn and how they understand what they learn.

In this sense, students' conceptual frameworks, or preconceptions, have a prismlike effect on knowledge as it is transmitted to them. This sometimes interferes with intended learning goals because what filters through the prisms of their minds (i.e., their conceptual frameworks) may be very different from what is presented. For example, various students in a class participating in the same learning activity may come away with very different perceptions or interpretations of the material presented. Additionally, many of the students' perceptions and interpretations may even conflict with what the teacher was trying to convey. Situations such as these are problematic and indicate a failure to consider and plan adequately for students' readiness to learn. The difficulty in remedying situations like these is that the dynamics of what is actually happening often go undetected both by teacher and student. Thus, each student feels he or she has learned what the teacher intended to teach, while the teacher remains unaware of how his or her teaching has been perceived or understood.

Frequently when students' understanding of a particular learning experience is checked and found wanting, it is attributed to their inability to learn. In reality they may have understood but in a different way. To solve this problem, instructional activities, especially those used to introduce new material or topics, should be designed so they provide opportunities for students to explain the ideas presented in their own words, not merely to parrot what the teacher has said. Put concisely, as a necessary first step to determining and developing readiness for learning, stimulate thought and feeling in the students and then listen closely to their voices.

To stimulate thought and feeling in students about learning activities so their inner voices can find a means of expression, instruction must serve to set their internal learning processes in motion. Gagne suggests this can be accomplished by using a thirteen-step instructional procedure (Table 2.5) that begins by creating an expectancy of learning through motivation and follows by using verbal directions to focus attention and perception and to enhance recall of essential information and concepts. Additional verbal directions are then given to outline the basic structure inherent in the material so information and concepts can be understood. At this point in the procedure, with the foundation for understanding set, "performance of the learner is called for, followed by reinforcement. The transferability of the newly learned skill is tested, again with suitable feedback informing the learner of success in achieving a new capability" (Gagne, 1977, p. 299). The teacher, therefore, must play an active role not only by assessing readiness but also by using well-planned learning experiences and materials to create conditions that serve to increase students' readiness to learn.

Deutero-learning. Deutero-learning as a dynamic aspect of learning is closely related to the law of apperception. Whereas apperception deals with the effects of previous learning on readiness for present learning, deutero-learning deals with the effects of present learning on future learning. Specifically, deutero-learning involves developing the ability of learning how to learn. Sustaining, retaining, and transferring learning are the three factors essential to deutero-learning.

> For instance, if we are teaching a [student] methods of solving arithmetic problems, when we have once clearly conveyed the method of solving one type of problem, the student is not only adept at that method but is also prepared to learn more rapidly than before how to solve a second type of problem, and so on. (Metraux, 1959, p. 28)

The principle of deutero-learning also takes into account the spontaneous wish to learn that is so evident in the young child's efforts to walk and talk, and in the adolescent's continuous quest to accomplish goals. The task, therefore, is to structure learning so that "learning one thing permits [the student] to go on to something that before was out of reach, and so on toward such perfection as one may reach" (Bruner, 1966, p. 30).

TABLE 2.5 *Thirteen-Step Instructional Procedure to Support Learning**

INSTRUCTIONAL EVENT	FUNCTION
1. Teacher directs attention to clouding of windows on a cold day or the ring of water left by breathing on a mirror, then questions students about why these events happen.	1. Establishment of achievement motivation, based on curiosity and the desire to display knowledge to other children and to parents.
2. Children are given tin cans and ice cubes.	2. Providing stimulus objects.
3. Students are told to put the ice cubes in the cans and to watch what happens to the outside of the cans.	3. Completion of stimulus situation. Directions to focus attention, selective perception.
4. Students are asked to describe what they see: "Fog"; "drops of water"; "large drops running down"; "ring of water at base of can."	4. Verbal directions to stimulate recall of previously learned concepts.
5. Students are asked what they can infer from their observations: "Liquid is water from the air."	5. Learning of a rule by discovery; for some students, this may be recall. Feedback provided.
6. Other alternatives are pointed out to students. "Could it be some other liquid?" "Could it come from the metal of the can?" "How can one test an inference?"	6. Verbal directions to inform the learners of the expected outcome of instruction (how to test this inference). Establishing an expectancy.
7. "How can we tell whether this liquid is water?" ("Taste it.")	7. Requiring recall of previously learned rule.
8. "If the water comes out of the metal, what should happen when it is wiped off?" ("Can should weigh less.")	8. Requiring recall of previously learned rule.
9. Students are asked, "If the water comes from the air, what should happen to the weight of the can after the water collects on it?" ("Can should increase in weight.") Direct observation is made of increase in weight of can by ice, by weighing on an equal-arm balance.	9. Requiring recall of previously learned rules.
10. Students are asked to recall that steam consists of water droplets and water vapor (an invisible gas). Air can contain water vapor.	10. Required recall of previously learned rules.
11. Students are asked to state (a) what they observed; (b) what they inferred; and (c) how they checked their inference.	11. Verbal guidance to suggest encoding for concepts of observation and inference; and of rules for checking inferences. Feedback provided.
12. Students are asked to make and test inferences in two or three other new situations and to describe the operations	12. Additional examples of the concepts and rules learned, for the purpose of ensuring retention and learning transfer.

TABLE 2.5 *(Continued)*

INSTRUCTIONAL EVENT	FUNCTION
and reasoning involved. These might be (a) water evaporation; (b) the extinguishing of a candle in a close cylinder; (c) the displacement of water by gas in an inverted cylinder.	
13. Another new situation is presented to the students and they are asked to describe it in terms of (a) what they observed; (b) what they inferred; (c) how they checked their inference.	13. Appraisal providing feedback.

*Instructional procedure for an exercise on inferring the presence of water vapor in air

Source: From *The Conditions of Learning* (3rd ed.) (pp. 301–302) by Robert M. Gagne. Copyright © 1977 by Holt, Rinehart and Winston. Reprinted by permission of Holt, Rinehart and Winston, Inc.

Thus, with the principle of deutero-learning in view, a major concern of the teacher is to help students make sustained effort to learn as instruction proceeds. Collateral learning, sometimes referred to as the "hidden curriculum," and the goals of learning are the two key areas involved in achieving sustained student learning.

Most teachers are aware of what they are explicitly, or consciously, trying to teach. The principle of collateral learning addresses the question, What are students learning *implicitly* from classroom instruction? Teachers are not always fully aware of the consequences their teaching has on student learning.

> Perhaps the greatest of all pedagogical fallacies is the notion that a person learns only the particular thing he is studying at the time. Collateral learning in the way of formation of enduring attitudes, of likes and dislikes, may be and often is much more important than the spelling lesson or lesson in geography or history that is learned. (Dewey, 1938, p. 49)

The desire to learn is the most important attitude a student can form. Therefore, kindling this desire must be one of the primary goals of all instructional activities. This attitude cannot be kindled where the teacher's understanding of the subject is limited, because students are likely to get only a narrow view of the subject and will probably not feel encouraged to develop an interest in or seek a deeper understanding of it. Further, where the teacher lacks enthusiasm for the subject, students merely go through the motions of learning just as the teacher merely goes through the motions of teaching. It is unfortunate when teachers fail to be enthusiastic about teaching their subject and thus fail to engender the desire to learn, not only because students lose interest in the subject itself, but because enthusiasm is a noble, life-giving quality that can and should be passed on to adolescents who are naturally searching for models and directions to follow.

To summarize, factors affecting collateral learning include:

♦ Teacher's understanding of the subject
♦ Teacher's enthusiasm for teaching the subject
♦ Teacher's interest in reaching the students
♦ Teacher's ability to involve students in learning activities
♦ Teacher's understanding of the cyclical nature of the learning process
♦ Teacher's understanding of learning as an active process
♦ Teacher's awareness of the consequences of his or her teaching on the students

The goals set for learning also play a dynamic role in sustaining learning. As a guiding principle, the goals of learning should appear to the students to be both worthwhile and reachable.

> Research demonstrates that students will work harder, longer, and more successfully when they know the goal of their efforts, when they understand the reasons for seeking the goal, when they believe that the goal can be reached, when they want to reach the goal, and when they are promptly informed of the degree of success resulting from their efforts. (Alcorn, Kinder, & Schunert, 1970, p. 54)

This implies that goals need to be stated clearly, capture students' interest, and take into account their learning capacities. To summarize, goals should have the following characteristics if they are to sustain learning:

♦ Goals should be clearly communicated and considered to be worthwhile and reachable.
♦ Goals should involve creative thinking, the hallmark of self-sustaining, self-nourishing activity.
♦ Goals should be stated in terms of acts or conduct so they communicate precisely what is to be attained, thus allowing students to direct their efforts purposefully and to measure their progress.
♦ Goals should be stated with a degree of specificity sufficient for clarity and subsequent effort. Over-specificity, however, can limit the adaptability of goals to classroom needs and thus be dysfunctional to learning. The teacher should guide students to make specific goals increasingly more specific according to their rate of progress, degree of understanding, and learning needs.
♦ Whenever possible select and represent goals as a series of integrated sub-acts both to make the overall goal more understandable and to convey that incremental progress toward attainment of the goal is possible.

♦ Select some goals that are not immediate but rather require sustained effort over a relatively long period of time to be realized. Goals such as these provide opportunities for the adolescent to develop the mature outlook of commitment to and effort toward something that is not immediately attainable.

To sustain learning the principle of connectedness or continuity must be considered in planning and presenting instructional sequences. This principle involves the structural and inherent connectedness found in the material to be learned. The structural aspect of connectedness focuses on a holistic view of an instructional sequence in which each step in the development of the material fits into preceding as well as subsequent steps to form a unified whole. Often continuity in learning is disrupted because an instructional sequence consists of an eclectic array of ideas and activities presented more or less in miscellaneous order rather than as a coherent progression of learning experiences. The inherent aspect of connectedness focuses on how the design and presentation of an instructional sequence maintain both balance and consistency between the learning experiences and "the basic orientation of the learner as revealed in his enduring motivation" (Phenix, 1964, p. 292). Therefore, the progression of learning experiences must account for students' existing range of experiences while presenting new problems that have the potential to stimulate new ways of understanding, all toward the development of further experience. "Connectedness in growth must be [the teacher's] constant watchword" (Dewey, 1938, p. 90).

Retention of learning is another essential factor in deutero-learning. Retention of knowledge, skills, and understanding is a necessary precondition for continued readiness to learn. Learning that is retained serves as an ever-widening foundation for the derivation of new meanings and creation of new ideas. This is apparent in Figure 2.5, which depicts the cyclical nature of cognitive development. For example, within one cycle (i.e., perception to conception to ideation) initial perceptions must be retained to a degree as the basis for conception, and conceptions derived likewise need to be retained as the basis for forming ideas. Thus from one cognitive cycle to another retention serves a facilitating function as readiness for subsequent levels of growth is directly dependent upon retention of what has been previously attained.

Retention of learning, therefore, means much more than being able to recite numerous facts or bits of information. True retention of learning means that one can use what has been learned in a meaningful way.

Two basic areas come into play concerning students' ability to retain what they have learned: (1) use of appropriate review techniques by the teacher, and (2) development of appropriate study habits by the students. In Table 2.6 a list of important factors in each of these areas is provided as a guide to increasing students' retention of learning. Keep in mind that review and study should not mean merely drill or repetition. A review of

FIGURE 2.5 *Cyclical Nature of Cognitive Development*

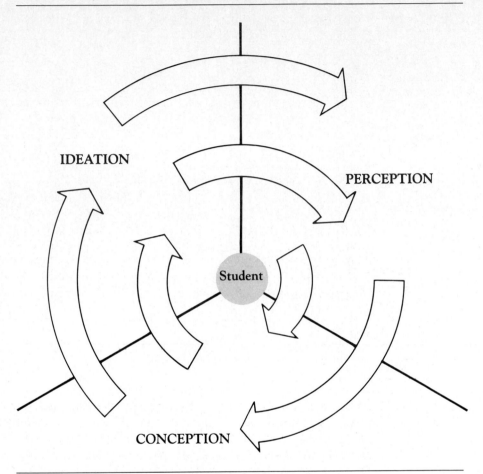

material is most productive when it is connected with new work or new ideas. Similarly, to be most efficient, study should represent the student's attempt at self-teaching. Done in this way, review and study address the cyclical, dynamic nature of the learning process.

Transfer of learning is a third important factor in deutero-learning. When review and study are done in a way that maximizes retention, the student's ability to transfer learning from one area to another increases.

> The teaching and learning of structure, rather than simply the mastery of facts and techniques, is at the center of the classic problem of transfer. There are many things that go into learning of this kind, not the least of which are supporting habits and skills that make possible the active use of the materials one has come to understand. (Bruner, 1960, p. 12).

TABLE 2.6 *Factors Influencing Students' Retention of Learning*

TEACHER'S REVIEW TECHNIQUES	STUDENTS' STUDY METHODS
1. Providing review spaced at increasing intervals.	1. Various skills in reading, such as reading rapidly to get the main idea, skimming to review, reading selectively to find the answer to a question, reading precisely to master directions, and so on.
2. Referring to related sources in class for new ideas and for initiating discussions to reinforce old and new ideas.	2. The habit of studying with some aim.
3. Working through a quiz; including review, quiz, and follow-up.	3. The habit of recalling from time to time the important facts previously covered and relating them to the present material.
4. Providing opportunities for students to think through the implications of the material presented.	4. The habit of putting questions to oneself.
5. Using the knowledge gained by students as a stepping-stone to more advanced learning.	5. The habit of problem solving, of finding and bringing to bear on any problem the relevant facts.
6. Making learning meaningful by relating it to students' in- and out-of-school experiences.	6. The habit of thinking of possible applications of new facts and principles to various fields.
7. Making students conscious of the importance of remembering the material learned (e.g., pointing out instances when students will have to put learning to use).	7. The habit of recording in useful form facts acquired during reading and study (taking notes).

The likelihood of students successfully transferring earlier learning to new situations is significantly increased when the teacher understands the structure of the subject, determines how this structure can be clearly communicated, and develops an awareness of the structure actually formed in students' minds. In addition, transfer of learning is facilitated by orienting learning experiences with advance organizers or focusing elements to give students "guidance as to the mental connections they should make both between the new ideas, and between the new ones and the old" (Phillips & Soltis, 1985, p. 53).

In essence there are two ways the student can demonstrate successful transfer of learning. One way, often referred to as *specific transfer of training,* involves the student's ability to apply what has been learned in one area to another similar area. For example, the student who has learned how to use the classroom resource area to get information for a report will be better able to learn how to use the library for the same purpose. The second way is frequently called *nonspecific transfer* because it is the learning of a general idea that is transferred rather than that of a specific skill. This general idea or principle then serves as the basis for understanding and learning from new situations and information. For example, the student who has learned the principle that cooperation is a higher value than competition will be better able to understand why a particular society has no word in their language for "war." The teacher's job is to design the instructional program so that students continually have the opportunity to transfer the skills and ideas they have learned. This requires considerable thought on the part of both teacher and student. In fact, there is no better way for students to develop critical thinking skills than to be constantly looking for opportunities to transfer the skills or principles they have already learned. "Transfer is the basis of all creativity, problem solving and the making of satisfying decisions. In addition to these important functions, transfer can dramatically shorten or lengthen the time it takes to acquire new learning" (Hunter, 1982, p. 107). The value of the ability to transfer learning is that it opens up the possibility of continuing progress, because each instance of learning sets the stage for further learning. In short, students acquire the habit and skill of learning—they learn to learn.

Developing in students the ability to transfer the ideas and skills they learn in one area to other areas is at the heart of the entire educational process. It is often said that teachers have a key role in building for the future and that much of the product of their labor remains forever unknown to them as their students leave and go through life. For the most part, the "product" referred to in this statement is the ability teachers have developed in their students to transfer what they learn to the many and varied experiences and situations in life.

Learning Experiences

Although the teacher may plan for and provide specific learning experiences for a class on a given day, the resulting learning experiences of the students may be quite different from what was intended. Furthermore, because of the students' different learning styles and general readiness for certain kinds of learning, the teacher's single set of planned learning experiences might result in a variety of unintended experiences among the students. Failure to pay attention to this phenomenon leads to the erroneous assumption that all students get the same learning experience from the material presented. From this we can understand that the term *learning experience* is neither the material planned for presentation in a lesson nor even the activities students take part in during a lesson. Rather, it is the interaction of the students and the prevailing conditions in the classroom at any given time that determine the learning that is experienced by the students.

> Essentially, learning takes place through the experiences which the learner has; that is, through the reactions he makes to the environment in which he is placed. . . . It is possible for two students to be in the same class and for them to be having two different experiences. (Tyler, 1950, p. 41)

For example, a teacher of a seventh-grade math class may make a thorough and organized explanation of how to do two-step equations. The students who have a firm grasp of how to do one-step equations (the previous topic) will get something quite different out of this learning experience than those who never quite understood how to do one-step equations.

> This places considerable responsibility upon the teacher, both to set up situations that have so many facets that they are likely to evoke the desired experience from all the students or else the teacher will vary the experiences so as to provide some that are likely to be significant to each of the students in the class. (Tyler, 1950, p. 42)

The challenge for the teacher is to develop a wide range of creative possibilities in planning the work for a particular class. The teacher's first step in meeting this challenge is to accurately assess each student's readiness for learning. The degree to which this step is accomplished successfully determines the eventual effectiveness of the next step, which is to plan a variety of learning experiences so that the various abilities, learning styles, and interests of the students are taken into account.

To stimulate learning and foster readiness, learning experiences should be designed and presented in a way that captures students' interest and at the same time challenges them to a degree. This combination of interest and challenge creates fertile conditions for students' active involvement in learning because it taps their natural desire to find meaning in the world around them and to meet other challenges that come their way. For example, in a learning activity on the topic of nutrition, instead of telling students that grains and vegetables in the diet lessen the possibility of certain types of cancer, interest and perplexity can be evoked by asking what effect grains and vegetables might have on the body when taken as a regular part of the diet. This method of presenting the topic makes students think and search for answers and thus actively involves them in learning.

Effective learning experiences are based on substance, that is, what the students actually have to do to learn, not simply on what they appear to be doing. Therefore, it is important to understand that reception learning, where subject material is presented in more or less final form, need not be mere rote learning. Rather, direct presentation of material that takes into account what the students already know and that encourages integration of new learning with what has been learned previously can be characterized as "meaningful learning" (Ausubel, 1963). On the other hand, discovery learning, usually considered the height of meaningful learning, is little more than rote learning when students mechanically follow formulas or sequences of steps without understanding or thinking about what they are doing.

◆ Assessing Learning

In this section, we discuss what to assess in student learning. (Chapter 8 examines the specifics of how to measure student progress and achievement in learning and interpret the information obtained.) To gain a clear understanding of the areas related to student learning that require timely and accurate assessment, it is necessary first to look at some basic considerations for assessment, then to understand how to focus assessment, and finally to understand how assessment must consider not only cognitive styles and development but all three aspects of consciousness—cognition, conation, and affection.

Basic Considerations for Assessment

Effective assessment of learning requires an awareness of what to assess and when, provision for ample student involvement in learning activities, a balance between breadth and depth of coverage of course material, and an understanding of students' self-perceptions.

An awareness of what to assess and when in terms of student learning is a basic consideration for the teacher and cannot be minimized if classroom instruction is to be effective. For teachers, the most reliable guide to planning and carrying out daily lessons is found in students' actions and work. The way students respond to questions, comments, and ideas, the way they display interest and attention to what is being taught, and the degree of understanding they exhibit in terms of being able to apply and transfer what they have learned are all indicators that can help teachers make relevant and effective decisions concerning classroom instruction. As noted in Chapter 1, the teacher's work in this area can appropriately be called classroom research, in that it requires continuous, disciplined observation and analysis focused on all the daily happenings in the classroom.

Providing students with frequent and timely opportunities to actively participate in classroom activities is the key to effective assessment for learning. All too often teachers carry on instruction for weeks and months completely oblivious to how much and in what way the material presented is being understood. In Table 2.7 classroom observations necessary for effective assessment of learning are listed according to general areas of student work involved.

The teacher must assess not only student work but also whether instruction maintains a balance between expanding and extending student learning. Thus a third basic area to consider in assessing student learning concerns the maintenance of a balance between the breadth of subject material covered and the depth to which it is covered. This can be called the *principle of expansion and extension,* where expansion refers to the breadth of coverage for each topic of a particular subject and extension refers to the depth of coverage. This balance is upset when the teacher fails to plan and carry out instruction that considers student learning needs or when quantity rather than quality takes precedence as the goal of learning. "The ideal of education is not necessarily to teach the maximum but to help students learn to learn and to help them maintain the desire to continue to develop as lifelong learners" (Piaget in Heck & Williams, 1984, p. 59).

TABLE 2.7 *Observations Necessary for Effective Assessment of Learning*

AREA OF STUDENT WORK	FOCUS OF OBSERVATIONS
In a variety of learning activities	Observing/assessing students as they work on individual assignments and projects, work in small group tasks, respond to or ask questions, participate in discussions, communicate with others, and take quizzes and tests.
In learning a variety of topics	Observing/assessing students as they learn a variety of topics covering material deemed important to understand the subject.
In learning at a variety of levels	Observing/assessing students in learning activities that require the ability to recall and understand basic facts and ideas, to analyze and interpret ideas and information, to apply principles and transfer learning, and to think carefully and solve problems.

For example, the teacher who tries to cover so many facets of a particular topic in a tenth-grade biology class that the students do not have the time or opportunity to think about or apply what is being taught has failed to maintain this balance. On the other hand, the teacher who plans numerous activities and uses a considerable amount of time to cover a few aspects of a particular topic while slighting coverage of other topics runs the risk of boring the students and of providing them with too narrow a conception of the subject. Thus, an imbalance toward either expansion or extension negatively affects student learning.

Another area for the teacher to consider in assessing learning involves students' perceptions of themselves. (See Chapter 5, in the section "Students as Adolescents," for a discussion of student self-perceptions.)

> Teachers need to help students develop the attitude "I'm great because I am!" not "I'm great only when I get A's," or "when I help the basketball team win," or "when I'm elected class president." Too often, value is associated with outstanding achievement. Those who are not able to achieve begin to feel negatively about themselves and tend to minimize their overall value. (Heck & Williams, 1984, p. 65)

The teacher has to constantly keep in mind the sensitive emotional nature of adolescents and help them look objectively at their own and others' strengths and weaknesses. This can only be done if teachers set a good example for the students by carrying out, communicating, and utilizing assessments of student learning with objectivity, fairness, and sensitivity.

Focusing Assessment

To be effective, assessment of learning needs to focus on the students, on the instructional program, and on the classroom environment. In focusing on the students, assessment of learning styles and readiness are the two most important tasks to consider. Dunn and Dunn suggest the following elements for assessing learning styles and readiness as the basis for effective instruction:

1. *Time.* When is the student most alert? (In the early morning, at lunch time, in the afternoon, in the evening, at night?)
2. *Schedule.* What is the student's attention span? (Continuous, irregular, short bursts of concentrated effort, forgetting periods, etc.?)
3. *Type of work.* How does the student work best? (Alone, with one person, with a small task group, in a large team, a combination?)
4. *Motivation.* What helps motivate the student? (Self or teacher expectation, deadlines, rewards, recognition of achievement, internalized interest, etc.?)
5. *Place.* Where does the student work best? (Home, school, learning centers, library, media corner?)
6. *Assignments.* On which type of assignments does the student thrive? (Teacher-selected tasks, totally self-directed projects, etc.?)
7. *Perception.* How does the student learn most easily? (Visual materials, sound recordings, printed media, tactile experiences, multimedia packages, combinations of these?) (1972, pp. 29–30)

In focusing on the instructional program to assess learning, the teacher needs to determine whether the materials and activities chosen for the daily lessons match the students' learning styles and readiness for learning. A good indicator of whether or not students are learning the subject with the desired depth of understanding is the amount of "cramming" they do, or need to do, to prepare for tests or quizzes. In the proportion that students have to cram for exams, that is the measure of the failure of the classroom instructional program. The teacher should be planning and carrying out instruction so that students are learning all along, assimilating information and ideas. If students find it necessary and, worse yet, possible to cram for exams, even if they manage to score well, a very wrong conception of learning has been conveyed to them. Something is seriously wrong when it is possible to assess student learning and find good exam scores even though no real learning has taken place. Therefore, using assessment merely to look at relatively trivial aspects of a subject and at memorization or recognition of disconnected ideas and facts should be avoided. Rather, assessment should be used to ascertain each student's understanding of the basic principles and concepts of a subject to both determine and plan for continued cognitive development. Even when it is necessary at times to assess students' knowledge of particular details and facts about a subject, the emphasis should be on their ability to recognize the connectedness between those details and facts and not simply to remember information.

In principle, when assessing learning "the knowledge which is acquired should appear in the [student's] mind as skill, just like skill in games or gymnastics" (Russell, 1926, p. 192). For example, a general science teacher presenting the basic principles of the experimental method has to continually assess not only how well students remember what was said (i.e., perception) but how well they have internalized what was said based on how successfully they use the principles either in discussion or practical application (i.e., conception and ideation). Thus, it is important to provide a variety of activities and exercises that require using the skills and concepts involved in learning so students can demonstrate the degree to which they have internalized an understanding of the subject.

To determine whether the classroom environment fosters learning, it is first necessary to determine if students feel at ease interacting with each other and participating in classroom activities. To foster learning, a classroom environment must provide students with a feeling of confidence and security. The room should be well-organized with a relatively stable daily routine to minimize stress and confusion. In addition, remember that even though there are many students in a single classroom, the individual represents the basic unit of learning. It is necessary, therefore, to let students have "a feeling of ownership of an individual space" (Heck & Williams, 1984, p. 32).

The recommendations listed in Table 1.5 for developing a positive classroom environment can also be used as a guide for assessing the extent to which a particular classroom environment fosters student learning and growth. To do this, make the determining elements the focus of the assessment and the requirements listed the criteria against which the results obtained are measured.

Usually assessment of learning focuses on cognitive development, that is, perception, conception, and ideation. However, cognitive development, or cognition (registering and understanding the environment), is only one of the three interrelated aspects of consciousness involved in learning; the other two aspects are conation (willing and acting purposefully in the environment) and affection (inner feeling leading to self-modification). Because learning involves a person's total consciousness, it is necessary to assess conative and affective development as well as cognitive development to obtain a meaningful account of students' learning needs, accomplishments, and progress. The conative and affective aspects cannot be ignored simply because their roles in learning and personal growth are not easy to understand, especially in relation to cognitive development. The fact remains that the three aspects of consciousness are at work in different degrees in every act of learning and thus must be understood and accounted for if assessment is to be effective with respect to all students' needs. Figure 2.6 illustrates how the three aspects of consciousness relate to each other and depicts the cyclical nature of the overall growth of consciousness.

The cognitive, conative, and affective aspects of consciousness as they relate to learning are described here in the form of a knowing, willing, feeling model of assessment. In this model knowing, willing, and feeling

FIGURE 2.6 *Cyclical Nature of the Growth of Consciousness*

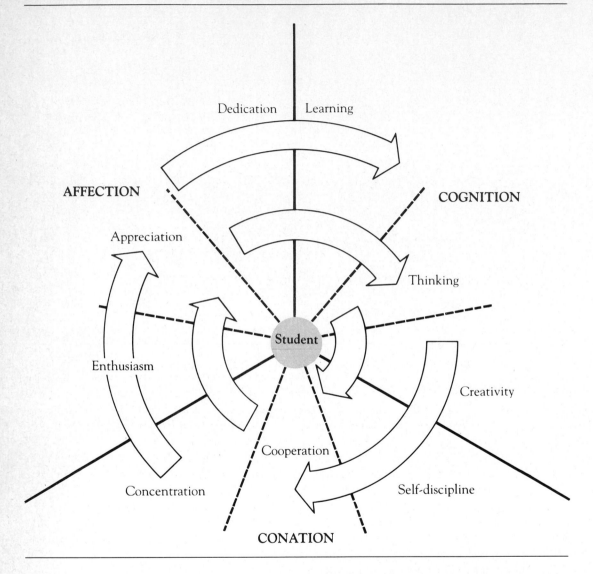

refer, respectively, to the cognitive, conative, and affective aspects of students' consciousness. Some combination of these three aspects is at work
in every student thought and action. In a given student one or two of the
aspects are usually dominant, leading to difficulties in learning. Therefore,
it is important to accurately assess the degree to which each student has
the knowledge, will, and feeling to participate in various classroom learning
experiences. To give you an idea of how this model may be used for assessing
learning, consider these three problem cases:

1. *Case 1.* If a student has the knowledge (i.e., intellectual awareness or necessary information) needed for a particular learning experience and a feeling (i.e., interest) for participating but lacks the will (i.e., ability or habit of applying the mind fully) to carry through, the chances of successful learning are poor, because the student will not have the necessary mental discipline.
2. *Case 2.* If a student has the knowledge needed for a particular learning experience and the will to carry through but lacks the feeling for participating, the chances of successful learning are poor because the student's heart won't be in the work.
3. *Case 3.* If a student has the feeling for participating in a particular experience and the will to carry through but lacks the knowledge needed for the learning experience to be meaningful, the chances of successful learning are again poor because the student will not be able to grasp what is being presented.

The student in each of the three cases is prepared for learning according to two of the aspects but is lacking in the third. These three suggestions are presented as possible steps to remedy the problem seen in each case:

1. *Suggestion for Case 1.* When a student has the knowledge and feeling but lacks the will (i.e., ability to act in and upon the environment), the teacher can try to overcome the student's inertia, which may be caused by lack of proper habits or laziness, by helping him or her develop an effective, organized approach to completing a particular task or by making clear the sanctions involved if a particular task is left undone. In short, train and empower the student to act.
2. *Suggestion for Case 2.* When a student has the knowledge and will but lacks the feeling (i.e., desire to change) the teacher can try to show how others have gained from completing a similar task or how much he or she can benefit from completing the task. In short, interest the student in self-growth.
3. *Suggestion for Case 3.* When a student has the will and the feeling but lacks the knowledge (i.e., ability to clearly perceive and understand), the teacher can try to present various explanations, demonstrations, and activities until proper understanding is reached for completing a particular task. In short, guide the student to comprehend the environment.

In Figure 2.7 a basic framework for assessing each student's capabilities according to the knowing, willing, feeling aspects of consciousness at work in every act of learning is presented. With this guide, teachers can better utilize classroom observations and other diagnostic information to decide where students need counseling, additional activities, special projects, or tutoring to bring the three aspects into balance and toward the "excellent" level.

FIGURE 2.7 *Knowing, Willing, Feeling Assessment Framework for Assessment of Learning*

ASPECTS OF CONSCIOUSNESS AT WORK IN LEARNING	DEGREE EACH ASPECT OF CONSCIOUSNESS IS EVIDENT IN A STUDENT FOR A GIVEN LEARNING ACTIVITY				
	None	Little	Moderate	Good	Excellent
Knowing (Cognition)					
Willing (Conation)					
Feeling (Affection)					

SUMMARY

In this chapter several points about learning were presented:

1. The most effective way for the teacher to understand the learning process is to be actively involved in learning. The teacher, therefore, must have a passion for learning—remaining always a student at heart.

2. Learning is an active process in that it requires effort, attention, and the development of proper habits, and as such, requires the active involvement of students for growth to occur.

3. Learning is considered an evolutionary process in which new information, ideas, and experiences are continually integrated with previous learning. To address the cyclical nature of learning, the basic ideas and information about a subject should be presented repeatedly, each time building upon the student's level of understanding.

4. Cognitive development is characterized by three levels—perception, conception, and ideation—with each succeeding level representing increased awareness of stimuli from the environment.

5. An important task of the teacher is not only to accurately assess readiness for learning but also to plan and carry out instruction in a way that fosters the developmental process of readiness.

6. Students' readiness for learning depends upon their individual learning styles, their existing conceptual framework, their previous learning experiences, and the extent to which they have learned how to learn in terms of sustaining, retaining, and transferring learning (i.e., deutero-learning).

7. To accurately assess student learning the teacher must create an environment where each student can be observed in a variety of learning activities, involving various aspects of the course material, and requiring various levels of understanding.

8. Because learning involves a student's total consciousness, it is necessary to assess cognitive, conative, and affective development. Thus, it is important to accurately assess the degree to which each student has the knowledge, will, and feeling for participating successfully in various classroom activities.

Learning is the key to growth for the individual. The teacher can significantly influence the habits, attitudes, interests, and capabilities for learning that students form and thus can play a major role in their lives. The responsibility is enormous. Therefore, it is essential that the teacher helps students realize that real learning, that is, being able to apply in life what they have learned, is the way for them to achieve all that they may want in life. As Vivekananda so wisely pointed out:

> Education [learning] is not the amount of information that is put into your brain and runs riot there, undigested all your life. We must have life-building, man-making, character-making, assimilation of ideas. If you have assimilated five ideas and made them your life and character, you have more education than any man who has got by heart a whole library. If education were identical with information, the libraries would be the greatest sages in the world. (1964, p. 6)

♦ ♦ ♦ ♦ ♦ ♦ ♦

PRACTICAL MODEL 2.1   A Vertical/Continuous Learning Plan

Introduction   This practical model represents the efforts of a high school teacher who has four sections of the same Spanish, level II, class to handle the dilemma of having to adhere to department guidelines that specify which textbook to use and what material to cover on the one hand, and the need to address the different learning abilities that exist within and between his four classes on the other.

Submitted by   Stephen Carlin, high school Spanish teacher, foreign languages department chairman, Mission Hills, California

Purpose   To develop daily instructional plans that will accommodate the varied learning abilities of individual students as well as the varied speeds at which different classes progress

Setting   High school in a multiracial community; 1985–1986 school year; Spanish (level II); four classes of approximately thirty-four students each

♦ **Rationale**

Because of the nature of the subject matter I teach and the particular environment in which I teach it, I have developed my own method of allowing for differences in student learning rates and abilities. I teach four classes of second-year Spanish and one class of first-year Spanish. To accommodate the varied learning abilities of individual students as well as the varied speeds at which different classes progress, I have developed what I refer to as a "vertical/continuous learning plan." I will describe the main features of this plan as it is used for my four Spanish, level II, classes.

At Alemany High School, where I am chairman of the foreign languages department as well as a Spanish instructor, students change teachers after each semester as well as upon completion of each course. This situation demands a certain uniformity among all teachers who are teaching the same course. We therefore adhere to the use of one specific text and try to keep our classes at more or less the same pace as we progress through the text.

The vertical/continuous learning plan allows me to set a particular standard with my slower classes that keeps them on track with the other classes. It also allows me to progress at a much faster rate with my more advanced classes. In the same way, the plan can also be used to address the learning differences among students within a single class. The following five steps outline the vertical/continuous learning plan (see Figure 2.8 for a diagrammatic representation of these five steps):

1. *Step 1: Listing basic categories.* This step entails extracting the material presented in each lesson of the text and dividing it into different activity categories. The text I use is divided into ten units. I chose to consolidate these units to form five categories that I thought would be most manageable and suitable for my classes.
2. *Step 2: Eliminating unimportant material.* In this step I eliminate material that is relatively unimportant or unnecessary considering the type and amount of material I feel will be needed to cover each topic properly.
3. *Step 3: Integrating original material.* In this step I integrate original material wherever the text seems to be weak or lacking in coverage of a particular topic, or where I have some especially effective ideas or materials to use.
4. *Step 4: Ordering topics across categories.* This step entails vertically listing all the material to be presented in the course in the order it will be presented. To do this, material is drawn from each of the five categories to form a sequence of activities, materials, and concepts that is most effective for learning the various topics of the course.
5. *Step 5: Using the plan.* In this step I put the plan to use in each of the four Spanish II classes. For example, I keep a separate copy of the vertical/continuous learning plan for each class. Then after each period I draw a line across each class's copy of the plan to indicate exactly how far they have progressed in the material. Instruction for each class begins from where they left off the previous day. In this way all classes cover the same material but at different rates. I find this method to be much more effective and organized than using a single daily lesson plan for all four classes. It becomes very complicated and messy to try to

bend one prepared lesson to the needs of four different classes. This plan allows me to be fully prepared, flexible, and up to date as I address the different rates of learning of each class.

♦ ♦ ♦ ♦ ♦ ♦ ♦
CASE STUDY 2.1   Learning as an Active Process

Orienting
Questions   As you read this case study ask yourself these questions:

Specific
♦ To what extent has this teacher succeeded in arousing genuine interest in the day's work?
♦ Does it appear that this teacher provides for the development of active habits?

General
♦ What points in this lesson stand out as indicators of this teacher's strengths and/or weaknesses?
♦ What recommendations would you make for addressing the problems this teacher seems to have?

Setting   *School* – Junior high school in an inner-city area

Subject – Math 7, level II (forty-five minutes)

Teacher – Mr. Cardenas, emergency-credentialed teacher

Students – Thirty-six seventh-grade students who are on the slow track in math

Topic – One-Step Equations

Lesson   *Note:* Under Time Frame the numbers represent the minutes that elapse as the period progresses. Under Dialog the names of the students and the teacher appear as they speak. The symbol ► represents a brief description of a particularly noteworthy action or observation.

Time Frame	Dialog
0 to 5	► Mr. Cardenas turns on the overhead projector so the day's warm-up appears on the wall. The warm-up includes three division problems and six simple (one-step) equations.
	Mr. C.: Begin the warm-up and I'll come around to see how you are doing. First, let me quickly take attendance. Those who were absent yesterday please remember to look at the assignments log posted near my desk to find out what you need to make up.
5 to 8	► Mr. Cardenas goes to the back of the room and watches for about two minutes as the students work on the warm-

FIGURE 2.8 A Vertical/Continuous Learning Plan

STEPS	DESCRIPTION OF PLAN (WORK FOR APPROXIMATELY 5–8 DAYS)				
	Reading Activities	Vocabulary Activities	Grammatical Explanation	Grammatical Reinforcement	Application Activities
1. Listing basic categories and extract material from text	276 #1 276 #2 276 #3 277 #1 277 #2	278 #1 278 #2 278 #3	278 #4 278 #5 278 #6 278 #7 278 #8	279 #1 279 #2 279 #3	279 #4 280 #1 280 #2 280 #1
2. Eliminating unimportant and unnecessary material	276 #1 276 #3 277 #1	278 #2 278 #3	278 #4 278 #7 278 #8	279 #1 279 #3	280 #1 280 #2
3. Integrating original material	276 #1 Worksheet A 276 #3 277 #1 Script A	Game A 278 #2 Overhead A Review A 278 #3 Handout A	Worksheet B 278 #4 Review B 278 #7 278 #8 Overhead B	Overhead C 279 #1 Review C Handout B 279 #3	280 #1 Project A Discussion A 280 #2 Skit A

4. Ordering topics across categories

Overhead A	280 #2
276 #1	Handout B
Worksheet B	278 #2
280 #1	Script A
278 #4	Review B
279 #1	277 #1
Game A	Discussion A
276 #3	Overhead B
Handout A	278 #8
278 #7	279 #3
Worksheet A	Review C
Review A	Skit A
Project A	278 #3
Overhead C	

5. Using the plan for Spanish II,* 3rd Period

			Progress
	Overhead A	276 #1	Worksheet B
Day 1	280 #1		Progress
	278 #4	279 #1	Game A
Day 2	276 #3		Progress
	Handout A	278 #7	Worksheet A
Day 3			Progress
	Review A	Project A	Overhead C
Day 4			Progress
	280 #2	Handout B	278 #2
Day 5	Script A		Progress
	Review B	277 #1	Discussion A / Overhead B
Day 6	278 #8		Progress
	279 #3	Review C	Skit A
Day 7	278 #3		Progress

*Each Spanish II class has a plan like this for recording the day-to-day progress.

Time Frame	Dialog	
		up. He then asks those who are having difficulty to raise their hands so he can assist them.
8 to 14	Mr. C.:	As I go around I'm noticing that you are confused about when to add and when to subtract. Remember, if there is a plus in the equation you should subtract and if there is a minus you should add. The rule is to do the opposite function from what's given. In solving equations we reverse the whole process.
	►	Luis raises his hand. Mr. Cardenas goes over to Luis.
	Mr. C.:	Luis, let's see what you did in number one. You apparently don't understand how to get x alone on one side. You need to subtract "three" from both sides of the equation.
	Luis:	Do you always subtract "three"?
	Mr. C.:	No. It's "minus three" here because we have a "plus three" in the problem.
	►	Most students have gotten to do only three of the four warm-up problems when Mr. Cardenas announces that the first three problems are going to be put on the board.
14 to 22	Mr. C.:	Who will put numbers one, two, and three on the board? Okay, Jerry, Maria, and Tony.
	►	Jerry, Maria, and Tony quickly put their work on the board.
	Mr. C.:	Let's look at number one (he quickly checks Jerry's work). Very good, Jerry. Maria, number two is fine. Any questions on numbers one or two? Remember, in regular computations we do the addition/subtraction functions first and then multiplication/division. But when we are doing equations we reverse the process. Tony, number three looks fine.
22 to 40	►	Mr. Cardenas puts a new set of problems on the overhead.
	Mr. C.:	Up until now we have been doing one-step equations. This is all you really need to know how to do as a level II class. However, let's see how far we can go. I'd like us to try some more complicated problems that require two steps. Let me give you an example.
	►	Mr. C. goes through a two-step equation to show the students the method to use.
	Mr. C.:	Class, following the rules I just showed you, do the nine problems on the overhead. I'll come to you if you raise your hand.

Time Frame	Dialog	

► Rosemarie has quickly finished the first three problems. A close look shows that she doesn't know what needs to be isolated in the equation. Several students do remember that they need to add or subtract a number from both sides of the equation; but when asked they can't say why this is done.

Mr. C.: Remember, it's the method of how to do these problems that's important. Later on when the problems have three or four steps you'll have less difficulty if you learn to apply the method correctly now.

► The students continue to do the nine two-step equations. Mr. Cardenas goes around assisting those students who have raised their hands. Most students are going very slowly, either because they are confused about how to apply the method or because their basic skills in division and multiplication are not good.

40 to 45   **Mr. C.:** I want to remind you that this afternoon we have our first math club meeting for anyone interested in coming. Also, remind your parents to come to open house tonight because I have many nice things to say about all of you.

► For the last few minutes most students sit quietly. A few begin the homework assignment. When the bell rings they all look at Mr. Cardenas for the signal that they can get up and leave.

Brief *Key Facts* – List three key facts verbatim that characterize the main positive and/or negative aspects of the lesson.

Strengths/Weaknesses – Briefly explain how the key facts selected indicated strengths and/or weaknesses in the teacher's performance.

Recommendations – Briefly describe what the teacher could have done to alleviate or avoid the problems that were seen.

♦ ♦ ♦ ♦ ♦ ♦ ♦

CASE STUDY 2.2   Readiness for Learning

Orienting Questions   As you read this case study ask yourself these questions:

Specific
♦ Is there any indication that this teacher designs instruction to allow for students' varying levels of cognitive development?

♦ Does this teacher take into account students' preconceptions or conceptual frameworks to make instruction more effective?

General
♦ What points in this lesson stand out as indicators of this teacher's strengths and/or weaknesses?
♦ What recommendations would you make for addressing the problems this teacher seems to have?

Setting   *School* – High school with students from a variety of socioeconomic levels

Subject – English (fifty minutes)

Teacher – Ms. Jones, third-year teacher

Students – Thirty-three freshmen

Topic – The Five Elements of the Short Story

Lesson

Time Frame	Dialog	
0 to 5	►	The bell for fourth period has rung and students begin filing in for class in an orderly fashion. On the upper lefthand corner of the board is printed, "Wednesday, Journal: Describe in detail (paragraph form) one characteristic of a good friend." Directly below this is written, "Homework: Define literary terms — give an example from one of the stories. STUDY FOR THE QUIZ!"
5 to 10	►	The second bell rings . . . class has begun.
	Ms. J.:	Good morning, class . . . let's settle down, the bell has rung. You all have your journals so let's get busy with today's entry.
	►	Five minutes or so are spent with the students writing a daily entry into their journals. This exercise calms them down and gives Ms. Jones time to take roll and gather her lesson notes.
10 to 15	Ms. J.:	Okay, let's put the journals away. Please finish the entry tonight if you haven't already finished.
	►	There appears to be a good rapport between students and teacher.
	Ms. J.:	Now, it seems from the looks of yesterday's test we don't have a clear understanding of the five elements of the short story or of some of the literary terms I had on the board. Frankly, I'm disappointed in the test scores. I have been explaining these elements throughout each of

Time Frame	Dialog	
		the three short stories we've read, and I've also explained and given examples for the test. Now, either you didn't study for the test, or I didn't teach the material well. I'm willing to take responsibility for my part in this class, but you have to take responsibility for yours. If you still don't understand the terms after I've explained them, you've got to tell me or see me after class for help. When I ask, "Do you understand?" and you nod your heads, I tend to believe you.
	►	The students listen attentively to Ms. Jones's comment and offer no disagreement. Many have failed the test and have not handed in homework. They look on rather sheepishly as Ms. Jones continues.
	Ms. J.:	However, the fact remains that a good number of you don't know the material and we must learn it before we can move on. So, I will take this class time to explain or clear up any difficulties you have with the terms and we'll have a quiz tomorrow. This is a second chance not only to learn the material but to raise your grade. Now, take out some paper for notes.
	►	The students follow Ms. Jones's directions.
15 to 45	Ms. J.:	For those who got C's or above on the test, you can get a jump on tomorrow night's homework. Start working on that while I review with those who got lower grades.
	►	Thursday's homework assignment is written on the board right under Wednesday's assignment. The students get their paper, books, and so on and begin working.
	Ms. J.:	Now, it seems some of you had trouble even remembering the five elements! So, a helpful hint might be this sentence: "Carly Simon's pink parrot talks."
	►	Ms. Jones shows how the first letter of each word of this sentence will be useful to the students by writing the following on the board: "C = Characters, S = Setting, P = Plot, P = Point of view, and T = Theme."
	Ms. J.:	Let's repeat the sentence a few times.
	►	The students repeat the sentence three times.
	Ms. J.:	Now, does that help?
	►	The students say "yes" and seem pleased to have a "trick" to learn the material.
	Ms. J.:	Okay, you seem to get the idea behind characters, plot, and setting, but you're missing the bus when it comes to theme and point of view.

Time Frame	Dialog

► The students agree and voice their confusion by saying, "It's hard," "I don't understand," and so on.

Ms. J.: Okay, Okay, settle down. Let's look at theme. The theme is the main or general idea behind a story. For example, you all saw *Top Gun* . . .

► Ms. Jones uses the movie as an example, asking the students what the main idea behind it was. She also asks them about some songs they are all familiar with. The students begin to see how the terms being discussed relate to their own experiences.

Ms. J.: Now, let's go back to *Top Gun* and look for examples of foreshadowing, irony, suspense, climax, and internal/external conflict.

► Ms. Jones explains each term and writes it on the board. She then proceeds to direct the students to remember specific incidents in the movie that exemplified the terms. The students seem to be getting a grip on the material now.

Ms. J.: Now, these terms apply to works in literature, not just in *Top Gun*. So, I want you to write the terms tonight and know what the definitions are. On the same paper, after each term, give me an example from one of the short stories we've discussed so far in this unit. Spend some time on it tonight so you know the material tomorrow. Don't forget, there will be a quiz tomorrow!

45 to 50   ► The last few minutes of class are spent copying the assignment from the board, putting books away, and so on. The bell rings.

Ms. J.: Class dismissed. Have a good day, and please study tonight.

Brief   *Key Facts* – List three key facts verbatim that characterize the main positive and/or negative aspects of the lesson.

Strengths/Weaknesses – Briefly explain how the key facts selected indicate strengths and/or weaknesses in the teacher's performance.

Recommendations – Briefly describe what the teacher could have done to alleviate or avoid the problems that were seen.

◆ ◆ ◆ ◆ ◆ ◆ ◆

CASE STUDY 2.3   Assessing Learning

*Orienting
Questions*   Ask yourself these questions as you read this case study:

Specific
◆ Does this teacher encourage student participation in classroom activities in a way that makes effective assessment of learning possible?
◆ Does it seem possible that the students in this class can achieve satisfactory grades and yet lack an understanding of the basic principles of the subject?

General
◆ What points in this lesson stand out as indicators of this teacher's strengths and/or weaknesses?
◆ What recommendations would you make for addressing the problems this teacher seems to have?

Setting   *School* – Private high school in middle-income area

Subject – Algebra 2A (fifty minutes)

Teacher – Mr. Dennis, first-year teacher

Students – Forty ninth-grade students who scored low on the last state-wide standardized math exam

Topic – Adding Like Terms

Lesson

Time Frame	Dialog	
	►	The bell to start class has rung. All students except two are sitting in their seats. The teacher is standing at the podium taking roll using a seating chart.
1 to 5	**Mr. D.:**	David and Lisa, I am marking you both tardy. David, that's the second one this week for you.
	David:	I am not late. My locker was stuck.
	Mr. D.:	Regardless, you weren't in your seat when the bell rang.
	►	The students are talking among themselves. Some are quite loud.
	Mr. D.:	All right, let's begin with a quick drill. Whose turn is it to answer first today? Mark, is it yours?
	Mark:	(Looking surprised) Who, me? I went first on Monday. It's Jeff's turn (pointing to Jeff).
	Mr. D.:	Jeff, is it your turn? (Jeff nods yes, looking a bit nervous.)

Time Frame	Dialog

     ►   Jeff recites two formulas correctly from memory. This is followed by similar recitations by Stephanie and Miguel.

5 to 20   **Mr. D.:** Okay, tomorrow's drill will be on the definitions of the glossary words on page fifty-eight in the text. Remember, Roberto, you will be first. Get out your homework so we can go over it.

    Julie: Mr. Dennis, I left it in my other notebook in my locker. Can I go get it? (As she is walking toward the door)

    Mr. D.: Yes, but make it fast. We're not waiting for you. The rest of you exchange papers so we can correct the homework.

    ►   Most students switch papers with the person next to them.

    Mr. D.: All right, Kim, let's start with your row and go down. Read the problem and then the answer.

    ►   After about ten students have read and given answers there is a pause and some rustling is heard at the end of the row.

    Mr. D.: Nick, number fourteen please.

    ►   Nick turns around and grabs the paper of the person behind him.

    Mr. D.: Nick, what's the problem? Do you have the answer to number fourteen?

    Nick: I do, but I have Lois's paper and she didn't get that far. So I was going to read what I have on my paper.

    Mr. D.: (A little irritated) Nick, just read the answer.

    ►   As they are going up and down the aisles reading answers some students are switching papers and whispering answers to each other as their turns come up. Mr. Dennis, realizing that it is taking too long to correct the homework, begins to read the answers to them.

    Mr. D.: Are there any questions?

    ►   Debbie, sitting in the back, raises her hand.

    Mr. D.: Yes, Debbie.

    Debbie: Could you put number twenty-four on the board? How did you get $4ac + 2b$? I got $6abc$.

    ►   Mr. Dennis begins to answer her question but stops to stare at two students who are talking. He stares at them until they stop talking. Then he looks back at Debbie.

    Mr. D.: To answer your question, Debbie, (which he does without writing on the board) $4ac$ and $2b$ are not like

Time Frame	Dialog	
		terms, so you can't add them. Remember, we are adding, not multiplying. Okay, pass your homework up.
20 to 40	►	As the students are passing their papers up there is a lot of talking going on. Mr. Dennis begins to talk louder than the class.
	Mr. D.:	Turn to section six, part two.
	►	A girl in the back blurts out, "What page is that?" Mr. Dennis fumbles through his book until he finds section six, part two.
	Mr. D.:	Page 112. The page after last night's homework.
	►	Mr. Dennis reads the introduction to the section. He then puts two problems on the board. A student who has been working on other class work asks, "Do we have homework tonight?"
	Mr. D.:	Yes, you are going to have to do the odd-numbered problems on page 114.
	►	A number of students turn to page 114 in their book and begin to work on the homework assignment.
	Mr. D.:	Okay, let's do a few more examples. How about number three? Jess, can you tell me how to do number three?
	►	Jess, flipping back to where number three is, asks Mr. Dennis which one he wanted again.
	Mr. D.:	I said number three. Had you been paying attention you would know what number we're on.
	►	After three or four more examples the students seem to understand the lesson.
40 to 50	**Mr. D.:**	All right, you have ten minutes to get started on your homework. If you have any problems raise your hand and I will come to you.
	►	A student in the second row stands up and starts moving his desk.
	Mr. D.:	Alex, what are you doing?
	Alex:	I don't have my book. Can I share with Elena?
	Mr. D.:	Yes, but be quiet and do your own work.
Brief		*Key Facts* – List three key facts verbatim that characterize the main positive and/or negative aspects of the lesson.
		Strengths/Weaknesses – Briefly explain how the key facts selected indicate strengths and/or weaknesses in the teacher's performance.

Recommendations – Briefly describe what the teacher could have done to alleviate or avoid the problems that were seen.

◆ ◆ ◆ ◆ ◆ ◆ ◆

CHAPTER PROJECT   **Carry Out a Service Study (Teacher-Directed Classroom Research) on Student Readiness for Learning**

Goals
1. To determine student readiness for learning in a particular class, using ideas and principles discussed in this chapter (e.g., learning styles, dynamics of learning).
2. To make a learning readiness profile for the students in a particular class.
3. To outline a learning plan to address student readiness for learning, using ideas and principles discussed in this chapter as well as your own ideas and experience (e.g., a plan that addresses various cognitive styles and levels of development in terms of perceptual, conceptual, and ideational aspects of learning).

Phases
One, two, or three phases (i.e., planning, partial implementation, full implementation) of the chapter project can be completed as is deemed appropriate to student needs and the design of the course.

Planning
1. Select a class you have ample opportunity to observe as the focus for this project.
2. Develop a learning matrix that lists the major areas of readiness for learning to be assessed down the lefthand column (e.g., perceptual, conceptual, ideational levels of development or physical, intellectual, social/emotional growth) and course material covered or specific instructional activities across the top.

Partial Implementation
1. Observe the students in the class you have selected for at least five class sessions.
2. Record the learning characteristics of individual students in the class on the learning matrix you have developed.

Full Implementation
1. Write a brief analysis of what you have been able to discern about the students' readiness for learning from the information recorded on the learning matrix.
2. Outline a plan of action you would recommend to address the students' readiness for learning the material of the particular course observed and for learning in general.

◆ ◆ ◆ ◆ ◆ ◆ ◆

REFERENCES

Alcorn, M. D., Kinder, J. S., & Schunert, J. R. (1970). *Better teaching in secondary schools* (3rd ed.). New York: Holt, Rinehart and Winston.

Ausubel, D. P. (1963). *The psychology of meaningful verbal learning: An introduction to school learning.* New York: Grune & Stratton.

Bolton, F. E. (1911). *Principles of education.* New York: Charles Scribner's Sons.

Bruner, J. S. (1960). *The process of education.* Cambridge: Harvard University Press.

Bruner, J. S. (1966). *Toward a theory of instruction.* Cambridge: Harvard University Press.

Clark, L. H., & Starr, I. S. (1986). *Secondary and middle school teaching methods* (5th ed.). New York: Macmillan.

Dewey, J. (1938). *Experience and education.* New York: Macmillan.

Dunn, R., & Dunn, K. (1972). *Practical approaches to individualizing instruction: Contracts and other effective teaching strategies.* West Nyack, NY: Parker.

Gagne, R. M. (1977). *The conditions of learning* (3rd ed.). New York: Holt, Rinehart and Winston.

Grambs, J. D., & Carr, J. C. (1979). *Modern methods in secondary education* (4th ed.). New York: Holt, Rinehart and Winston.

Heck, S. F., & Williams, C. R. (1984). *The complex roles of the teacher: An ecological perspective.* New York: Teachers College Press.

Hunter, M. (1982). *Mastery teaching.* El Segundo, CA: TIP Publications.

Metraux, R. (1959). Anthropology and learning. In A. Frazier (Ed.), *Learning about learning* (pp. 21–37). Washington, DC: Third ASCD Research Institute.

Montessori, M. (1917). *Spontaneous activity in education.* New York: Schocken.

Nussbaum, J., & Novick, S. (1982, December). Alternative frameworks, conceptual conflict and accommodation: Toward a principled teaching strategy. *Instructional Science, 11*(3), 183–200.

Phenix, P. H. (1964). *Realms of meaning: A philosophy of the curriculum for general education.* New York: McGraw-Hill.

Phillips, D. C., & Soltis, J. F. (1985). *Perspectives on learning.* New York: Teachers College Press.

Russell, B. (1926). *On education.* London: George Allen & Unwin.

Thorndike, E. L. (1906). *The principles of teaching: Based on psychology.* New York: A. G. Seller.

Tyler, R. (1950). *Basic principles of curriculum and instruction.* Chicago: University of Chicago Press.

Vivekananda, S. (1964). *Education.* Coimbatore, India: Sri Ramakrishna Mission Vidyalaya.

Wadsworth, B. J. (1971). *Piaget's theory of cognitive development: An introduction for students of psychology and education.* New York: David McKay.

Whitehead, A. N. (1929). *The aims of education and other essays.* New York: Macmillan.

Wittrock, M. C. (1974). Learning as a generative process. *Educational Psychologist, 11,* 87–95.

Wittrock, M. C. (1978). The cognitive movement in instruction. *Educational Psychologist, 13,* 15–29.

Wittrock, M. C., & Lumsdaine, A. A. (1977). Instructional psychology. *Annual Review of Psychology, 28,* 417–459.

◆ ◆ ◆ ◆ ◆ ◆ ◆
ANNOTATED READINGS

Brown, G. I., Phillips, M., & Shapiro, S. B. (1976). *Getting it all together: Confluent education.* Bloomington, IN: Phi Delta Kappan Educational Foundation.
> *An overview of the concept of confluent education, an integrative approach that recognizes the need to design classroom experiences that account for students' affective as well as cognitive readiness and needs.*

Bruner, J. S., Oliver, R. R., Greenfield, P. M., et al. (1966). *Studies in cognitive growth: A collaboration at the center for cognitive studies.* New York: John Wiley & Sons.
> *A compilation of studies concerned with how humans increase their mastery in achieving and using knowledge. See Chapters 1 and 2 on cognitive growth.*

Eisner, E. W. (1985). *The educational imagination: On the design and evaluation of school programs.* New York: Macmillan.
> *A book stressing the importance of context in making educational decisions, especially in the area of curriculum development. See Chapter 3 for a discussion of curriculum in terms of learning experience.*

Giroux, H. A., Penna, A. N., & Pinar, W. F. (Eds.). (1981). *Curriculum and instruction: Alternatives in education.* Berkeley, CA: McCuthan.
> *This book includes a study of the relationship of curriculum theory to practice. See Chapter 12 for a guide to using a mastery learning approach.*

Goodlad, J. I. (1968). *The future of learning and teaching.* An Occasional Paper of the Center for the Study of Instruction. Washington, DC: National Education Association.
> *The printed version of an address at the inaugural ceremonies of the Institute for Development of Educational Activities (IDEA).*

Gregorc, A. F., & Butler, K. A. (1984, April). Learning is a matter of style. *VocEd, 59,* 27–29.
> *A useful and interesting conception of student learning styles to consider for designing classroom learning experiences. Four specific categories of learning styles (i.e., concrete sequential, abstract sequential, concrete random, and abstract random) are defined and discussed in terms of their implications for classroom instruction.*

Hoover, K. H. (1977). *Secondary/middle school teaching: A handbook for beginning teachers and teacher self-renewal.* Boston: Allyn and Bacon.
> *A text consisting of six learning modules featuring classroom simulations. Each module can be used for small-group activities or for self-instruction. See Module 5 for a description of fundamental approaches to learning.*

Joyce, B. R. (1978). *Selecting learning experiences: Linking theory and practice.* Washington, DC: Association for Supervision and Curriculum Development.
> *A booklet examining the relationship between various models of teaching (i.e., social-interaction, information-processing, personal and behavior modification, and cybernetic models) and student learning styles as a guide to selecting and creating learning experiences.*

Krishnamurti, J. (1953). *Education and the significance of life.* New York: Harper & Row.

An excellent study of the role education plays throughout life. See Chapter 3 for a discussion of learning in terms of intellect, authority, and intelligence.

Montessori, M. (1914). *Dr. Montessori's own handbook.* Cambridge, MA: Frederick A. Stokes.

A thorough guide to Montessori's method of sensory education. See the section on language and knowledge of the world as it relates to the principles of learning.

National Association of Secondary School Principals' Learning Style Task Force. (1986). *Strategies for improving achievement within diversity.* Paper presented at the meeting of the International Intervisitation Programme in Educational Administration, Hawaii.

This paper presents the "Learning Style Profile," a twenty-three scale instrument that attempts to help determine secondary school students' learning styles in terms of their cognitive skills, perceptual responses, study preferences, and instructional preferences.

Phillips, D. C., & Soltis, J. F. (1985). *Perspectives in learning.* New York: Teachers College Press.

A comprehensive look at theories of learning. See Chapters 1–7 for an examination of various areas of learning and Chapter 8 for numerous classroom cases and related dialogues.

Russell, B. (1948). *Human knowledge: Its scope and limits.* New York: Simon and Schuster.

A book dealing with philosophical questions related to knowledge and learning. See Part 3 for a discussion of science and perception.

Russell, B. (1972). *In praise of idleness and other essays.* New York: Simon and Schuster.

A book containing essays on the connection between education and important social questions. See Chapter 2 for a discussion of "useless knowledge."

Soltis, J. F. (1978). *An introduction to the analysis of educational concepts* (2nd ed.). Reading, MA: Addison-Wesley.

An introductory text to effective ways of thinking about education. See Chapter 4 for a thorough discussion of learning, explaining, and understanding.

Thelen, H. A. (1981). *The classroom society.* New York: John Wiley & Sons.

This book focuses on the life of students in the classroom in conjunction with the policy-making efforts of those responsible for carrying out and supporting the educational process. See Chapter 7 for an examination of the classroom as a microsociety and a discussion of how classwork can be used to integrate the psyche-, socio-, and task aspects of the classroom.

Wadsworth, B. J. (1971). *Piaget's theory of cognitive development: An introduction for students of psychology and education.* New York: David McKay.

An introduction to the major concepts of Jean Piaget's theory of cognitive development as they relate to learning. This volume can serve as an excellent preparation for a direct review of Piaget's original works. See Chapter 2, "Cognitive Development and Other Factors," and Chapter 7, "Cognitive Development and Adolescence."

CHAPTER 3

Planning for Instruction

INTRODUCTION
BASIC THEORIES
◆ Instructional Objectives
◆ Curriculum Planning
◆ Curriculum Research and Development
◆ Curriculum Model
SUMMARY
PRACTICAL MODEL 3.1   Framework for Classroom Planning
CASE STUDIES
◆ 3.1   Instructional Objectives
◆ 3.2   Curriculum Planning
◆ 3.3   Relating Instructional Objectives to Planning
CHAPTER PROJECT   Develop a Complete One-Semester Course of
                   Instruction
REFERENCES
ANNOTATED READINGS

INTRODUCTION

The phrase *back to basics* is frequently heard in education. This phrase is usually understood to mean a return to emphasizing English, math, and science in the school curriculum. However, as Goodlad notes,

> If a predominance of rote learning, memorization, and paper-and-pencil activity is what people have in mind in getting the school back to basics, they probably should rest assured that this is where most classrooms are and always have been. (1984, p. 358)

In his comprehensive survey of American education, Goodlad found that essentially the same amount of time is now spent on the "basics" as during any previous period of this century. Yet a feeling persists among parents, educators, and society as a whole that some aspects of education are not as they should be.

One of the ways educators can make education more "as it should be" is to offer a curriculum that meets not only the "basic" needs of students but their needs on every level. The teacher's part in this process involves mastery of the subject being taught and, further, his or her ability to carry out continuous, disciplined inquiry to enrich the classroom curriculum. Increasing the amount of classroom time spent on the "basics" has little positive effect if the teacher does not have the understanding and skill to develop effective short- and long-range plans. Thus, going back to basics must involve not only the material being presented to the students but the teacher's grasp of the material as well.

> A curriculum is not a mass of material, any more than an automobile is a mass of metal. It is an active instrument for bringing about a flexible, creative, progressive adjustment to the institutions of society. Its purpose may be defeated just as surely by putting it together in the wrong way, as by making it out of unworkable stuff. (Mursell, 1934, p. 388)

The goal of the curriculum is to provide a resource and a means of growth for students both as individuals and as members of society. The curriculum, therefore, must be much more than material organized into a series of lessons leading merely to tests and grades. Simply because students are able to pass a series of examinations does not mean they are educated. The curriculum should be imbued with the highest values and ideals and should be the result of a penetrating and creative exploration of a subject. Thus, the skill and care with which the curriculum is developed is crucial in determining the effectiveness of classroom instruction.

Ideally, curriculum planning should involve the teacher in developing a complete course curriculum, not only course units or daily lesson plans. Although the ability to develop and work with course units and daily lesson plans is essential to teaching, the quality and effectiveness of unit and lesson plans rest largely with the teacher's creative involvement with and understanding of the curriculum as an integrated whole from which the units and plans derive.

The task of planning a classroom instructional program primarily involves the teacher in the role of curriculum developer. This role requires the vision, perseverance, and sense of materials that any architect needs to build a great edifice. The "edifice" the teacher constructs in the form of the classroom instructional program has to address the needs, abilities, and interests of many students. Because the instructional program that is constructed can have profound and lasting effects on many young lives, merely understanding the subject and principles of curriculum development alone are not enough to successfully complete this task. The teacher has to take a broader view of the curriculum by fully integrating his or her efforts in this area with efforts in the areas of instruction, research, guidance/counseling, and school/community relations—in short, with all areas essential to his or her roles and responsibilities as a teacher. Emphasis on, or skill in, one area alone is not sufficient. For example, a well-planned instructional program is rendered virtually useless by the teacher who, failing to carefully observe the effect instruction has on each student from day to day, loses sight of the need for classroom research. The results will be similar for the teacher who neglects his or her role as instructor and thus does not strive to discover the most effective teaching strategies for carrying out the instructional plan. Although more attention to one particular area may be necessary at any given time, failure to make effort in and see the relationship between all the areas eventually weakens the instructional program.

In this chapter numerous ideas, theories, and examples are presented on how to effectively plan a classroom instructional program in a way that recognizes the relationship between the teacher's role as curriculum developer and his or her roles in other areas.

BASIC THEORIES

♦ Instructional Objectives

The selection of effective instructional objectives is of utmost importance. This section focuses on how to select and state objectives and how to relate them to learning activities so that they may be used as a guide to effective instructional planning.

Before beginning to make an intelligent instructional plan, the teacher must decide on a focus to give the plan meaning in terms of student growth. This focus is comprised of the set of instructional objectives students must reach to grow in the ways desired. At the outset of planning, then, the teacher must thoughtfully select the objectives the instructional plan aims to reach.

The selection of instructional objectives plays an indispensable role in curriculum development.

If an educational program is to be planned and if efforts for continued improvement are to be made, it is very necessary to have some conception of the goals that are being aimed at. These educational objectives become the criteria by which materials are selected, content is outlined, instructional procedures are developed and tests and examinations are prepared. All aspects of the educational program are really means to accomplish basic educational purposes. (Tyler, 1950, p. 3)

How to Select and State Objectives
As a general rule, the selection of instructional objectives should be based on sound principles and theories of learning. For example, objectives should be appropriate to student age levels, should address the varied student

learning styles, and should take into account students' previous learning experiences. Clark and Starr suggest nine elements to consider when selecting objectives:

1. The nature and structure of the subject
2. The needs of the students
3. The readiness of the students
4. The interests, abilities, attitudes, and other characteristics of the students
5. The larger educational goals and general objectives
6. [The teacher's] philosophy, inclinations, and capabilities
7. Community expectations
8. The feasibility of the objectives, for example, the facilities, equipment, supplies, and time available
9. Other elements of the curriculum (1986, p. 142)

In selecting and stating objectives we often hear of the need for using behavioral objectives, or of stating objectives behaviorally. Unfortunately, the concept of behavioral objectives is frequently associated with a programmed, mechanistic approach to classroom instruction. And, even more unfortunately, this is likely to be how behavioral objectives are used. Ralph Tyler, one of the guiding forces in this century in the use of instructional objectives as an essential part of curriculum development, has clearly expressed what the behavioral aspect of instructional objectives should really signify. Tyler's words point out the proper use of instructional objectives and refute many of the misuses of the term:

> Education is a process of changing the behavior patterns of people. This is using behavior in the broad sense to include thinking [cognition] and feeling [affection] as well as overt action [conation]. When education is viewed in this way, it is clear that educational objectives, then, represent the kinds of changes in behavior that an educational institution seeks to bring about in its students. A study of the learners themselves would seek to identify needed changes in behavior patterns of the students which the educational institution should seek to produce. (1950, p. 4)

Two main ideas emerge from these words. First, behavioral objectives must be concerned with all aspects of student growth (i.e., intellectual, social, emotional, and spiritual) if they are going to help in developing an effective instructional plan. Second, the ability to identify the most effective behavioral objectives is based primarily on the teacher's care and perseverance in observing the effects of instruction on students. The question then arises, Once careful classroom observations have been made, how should the teacher go about selecting and stating instructional objectives?

Objectives must be selected to take into account the dynamic nature of the learning process. Their individual worth as well as the combined effect attaining a series of objectives may have on students over a period of time must be considered. Skillful planning in terms of sequencing and integrating learning objectives is necessary to maximize the cumulative effect of several objectives on learning. In connection with selecting and stating each objective the teacher should also consider how the learning that is to be achieved can be used in subsequent activities both within and outside the classroom. Objectives must not be viewed as isolated entities but as integral parts of a much larger plan.

Because it is what students actually do in the classroom that determines what they learn, objectives should be expressed in terms of conduct or behavior expected in relation to the subject matter, concepts, ideas, skills, or values involved.

For example, the objective "Explain how the Treaty of Versailles contributed to the outbreak of World War II" indicates the subject material involved (i.e., the Treaty of Versailles) and the kind of behavior desired (i.e., explaining). Stating objectives for a course in this way ensures that the instructional plan not only covers all the essential material (i.e., information, concepts, ideas, skills, and values) to be learned but also specifies the level of understanding (i.e., recall, interpretation, analysis, application, and evaluation) at which the material must be learned. In addition, selecting and stating objectives in a way that clearly describes the subject material in relation to the behavior desired makes a focused and accurate assessment of student progress and achievement possible.

Performance objectives, which state the performance levels expected of students for a particular learning activity, are not always interchangeable with behavioral objectives. Looking only at performance levels (e.g., test scores) to determine progress toward objectives leads to overemphasizing aspects of learning that are readily quantifiable at the expense of assessing the quality of learning. For example, although high test scores may satisfy the teacher and student interested primarily in performance, they alone are not enough for the teacher and student interested in attaining meaningful behavioral changes, such as learning to think carefully or focus attention, that contribute to those high test scores.

Tyler suggests a way of clearly depicting the objectives for a course that takes into account both the content and behavior aspects of instruction:

> Since a clearly formulated objective has the two dimensions of the behavioral and the content aspect, it is often useful to employ a graphic two-dimensional chart to express objectives concisely and clearly. An illustration of such a chart is presented herewith [Figure 3.1]. This is an illustration of the use of a two-dimensional chart in stating objectives for a high school course in biological science. It is not assumed that this course is an ideal course nor that these are ideal objectives. The purpose of the chart is to show how the chart can more compactly indicate the objectives that are being sought and how each objective is defined more clearly by the chart in terms both of the behavioral aspect and the content aspect. (1950, pp. 30–31)

FIGURE 3.1 *Tyler's Illustration of the Use of a Two-Dimensional Chart in Stating Objectives for a High School Course in Biological Science*

CONTENT ASPECT OF THE OBJECTIVES	BEHAVIORAL ASPECT OF THE OBJECTIVES						
	1. Understanding of Important Facts and Principles	2. Familiarity with Dependable Sources of Information	3. Ability to Interpret Data	4. Ability to Apply Principles	5. Ability to Study and Report Results of Study	6. Broad and Mature Interests	7. Social Attitudes
A. Functions of Human Organisms							
1. Nutrition	X	X	X	X	X	X	X
2. Digestion	X		X	X	X	X	
3. Circulation	X		X	X	X	X	
4. Respiration	X		X	X	X	X	
5. Reproduction	X	X	X	X	X	X	X
B. Use of Plant and Animal Resources							
1. Energy relationships	X		X	X	X	X	X

2. Environmental factors conditioning plant and animal growth	X	X	X	X	X	X
3. Heredity and genetics	X	X	X	X	X	X
4. Land utilization	X	X	X	X	X	X
C. Evolution and Development	X	X	X	X	X	X

Source: From *Basic Principles of Curriculum and Instruction* (pp. 32–33) by Ralph Tyler, 1950, Chicago: University of Chicago Press. Copyright © 1950 by The University of Chicago Press. Reprinted by permission.

The behavioral aspect of the objectives in Figure 3.1 describes actions students should be involved in and areas where changes should occur, while the content aspect relates these actions and areas to specific course topics. This form of matrix is a valuable aid for developing objectives to guide and represent the instructional plan. The objectives listed under the behavioral aspect of objectives in this figure can be changed to reflect other focuses. For example, a teacher concerned with student cognitive growth might choose to relate the content aspect of the objectives to the areas of perception, conception, and ideation. Another teacher interested in student readiness for learning may wish to define the behavioral aspect of the objectives according to physical, intellectual, and social/emotional capacities. One other particularly useful way to define the behavioral aspect of objectives on this matrix would be in terms of the cognitive, conative, and affective areas as they relate to learning. (See the knowing, willing, feeling model of assessment in the "Assessing Learning" section in Chapter 2.)

The definition of objectives and course content on this matrix can also become more detailed by delineating each area of behavior into a series of integrated sub-acts and each course topic into a list of constituent subtopics. Defining the objectives and content in such detail provides an excellent framework for planning daily lesson activities and for constructing quizzes and tests. Considerable thought, both about the subject content and about the changes to be brought about in student behavior, is required to successfully reach this level of specificity; such thought is essential for effective instructional planning. This last point has extremely important implications for planning an instructional program in that the teacher's selection and statement of instructional objectives becomes the map that guides instruction. This map tells both teacher and students where they are headed, how they might get there, and whether they have succeeded. However, no matter how well the map for guiding classroom instruction is worked out, its value will be limited if objectives are not selected and stated with a broad view of the subject and an understanding of the dynamic nature of learning. All too often the curriculum and related objectives of a subject are "determined largely by the editorial staffs of publishing houses and the subject-matter specialists and writers chosen by them" (Goodlad, 1984, p. 290).

The traditional behaviorist's use of objectives only concerns behavior that is directly observable, without attention to what might be going on in the mind of the learner. "The behaviorist (or stimulus-response) approach to learning—as developed from the work of Spence and Skinner—focuses on how presentation of material influences behavior" (Weinstein & Mayer, 1986, p. 316). Completely opposite to this, the cognitive approach seeks to develop objectives that provide scope to understanding and addressing the way in which students perceive, conceptualize, and form ideas about stimuli presented to them in the form of learning experiences. Tyler's conception of instructional objectives, which relies so heavily on the conscious efforts of students to find meaning and purpose, is worlds apart from that of the behaviorists. To judge the effectiveness of instructional objectives on the basis of observable student behavior alone is to fail to appreciate the importance of the learning process going on inside the student.

To successfully select and state instructional objectives for a particular class, the teacher should understand and use what is called here the *standard of learning* to ensure that the total consciousness of the student (i.e., cognition, conation, and affection) is addressed. In Table 3.1 the main areas and qualities crucial to maintaining a high standard of learning are described in relation to the cognitive, conative, and affective areas of consciousness.

One way to use the standard of learning for selecting and stating objectives is to create a two-dimensional chart similar to the one in Figure 3.1. The nine main areas under cognition, conation, and affection in Table 3.1 would be the behavioral aspect of the objectives. Objectives pertaining to various aspects of the course content could then be developed according to any or all of the nine main areas of the standard of learning. The information and ideas in Table 3.1 can also be useful in developing student-learning profiles.

Reaching a high standard of learning means much more than attaining a high grade-point average or high test scores. Test scores do indicate a facet of student performance, and they do have a place in developing objectives. But in developing instructional objectives to address the total well-being of students, much more than test scores must be considered. As

TABLE 3.1 *Areas and Qualities Denoting the Standard of Learning*

MAIN AREAS	QUALITIES TO DEVELOP
Cognition	
Thinking skills	Thinking through problems, including analyzing, interpreting, applying, and evaluating concepts and ideas
Learning skills	Carrying on and integrating learning through all activities and experiences in and out of school
Creativity	Forming original and imaginative ideas
Conation	
Self-discipline	Attending to the work at hand and persevering until tasks are completed
Cooperation	Working well with others, including giving and receiving help
Concentration	Applying the mind fully to an activity or task
Affection	
Enthusiasm	Taking interest in learning and personal growth
Appreciation	Recognizing and aspiring to what is valuable, healthy, and life-giving
Dedication	Being committed to the attainment of goals

students develop the qualities indicative of a higher standard of learning (as described in Table 3.1), higher test scores and grades will be a natural consequence. By approaching learning from a standard-of-learning perspective, achievement becomes the direct result of developing qualities in essential areas of human growth rather than through using superficial or narrow means such as cramming, teaching to the test, cheating, memorizing without understanding, or manipulating behavior. This concept of the standard of learning also communicates the idea that the highest learning objectives are those that foster an understanding that cooperation, not competition, is the principle to follow and that all people have the right to grow and learn, at whatever rates and in whichever ways are suited to them.

Although teachers may spend considerable time developing sets of instructional objectives for their courses, they should remember that "there is no such thing as a fixed and final set of objectives, even for the time being or temporarily. Each day of teaching ought to enable a teacher to revise and better in some respect the objectives aimed at in previous work" (Dewey, 1929, p. 75).

◆ Curriculum Planning

No matter what the teacher's goals are, a course of action for guiding students to those goals is needed. The teacher can develop this course in two ways. One way involves setting a personal example, an example that can profoundly affect students' lives. The second way, discussed here, involves the instructional program. Without a well-planned curriculum, one the teacher has a direct role in creating, the best intentions may be unrealized and the effectiveness of instruction may be severely hampered.

This section focuses on initial steps in planning, factors that limit planning, and principles of effective planning.

Initial Steps in Planning

Chapter 2 provided insights into understanding the learner. This chapter emphasizes understanding subject matter in relation to the learner through active and creative involvement in curriculum planning. The teacher stands at the middle and pivotal point of a triadic relationship between those taught (students) and what is taught (subject matter). To bring students and the subject together so that learning and growth occur requires not only understanding each separately, but also understanding their relationship to each other.

Thus at the outset of planning a course curriculum, four questions need to be considered concerning the relationship between the objectives to be achieved and the learning experiences required to reach those objectives.

1. What educational purposes or objectives should the school or course seek to attain?

2. What learning experiences can be provided that are likely to bring about the attainment of these purposes?
3. How can these learning experiences be effectively organized to help provide continuity and sequence for the learner and to help him in integrating what might otherwise appear as isolated learning experiences?
4. How can the effectiveness of learning experiences be evaluated by the use of tests and other systematic evidence-gathering procedures? (Tyler, 1950, pp. 1–2)

These four questions form a cyclical pattern: the determination of objectives leads to the selection of learning experiences, then to the integration of learning experiences, and finally to the evaluation of the learning achieved, which leads back to reconsideration of the original objectives, and so on.

Because the focus of instruction is the learner, initial planning of objectives and learning experiences must always proceed from an understanding of the learner's characteristics and needs. Therefore, an integrated approach to planning requires that four curricular decisions (Bloom, 1956) that specifically address the learner's needs be made in conjunction with the four questions mentioned above (Table 3.2).

Factors That Limit Planning

Four major factors tend to limit the teacher's role in planning the instructional program:

TABLE 3.2 *Four Curricular Decisions*

DECISIONS	DESCRIPTION IN TERMS OF STUDENT LEARNING
How much knowledge should be required learning?	Reaching a balance between all the knowledge the students may conceivably learn and only the knowledge most basic to a particular subject
What degree of precision should be required?	Introducing knowledge at a general but accurate level, gradually making finer and finer distinctions until the students reach the more detailed and precise level of the expert
What is the best organization of knowledge to facilitate learning?	Fitting the organization of knowledge in a subject to the internal state of the learners at their particular stage of development. Thus, realizing that the organization the specialist finds most useful is not necessarily best for the student's learning
How does the curriculum relate to the immediate as opposed to the future needs of the students?	Communicating the importance of a body of knowledge to the students so they can become interested in learning whether or not they find an immediate use for this knowledge

Source: Based on material from *Taxonomy of Educational Objectives: The Classification of Educational Goals. Handbook I: Cognitive Domain* (pp. 336–337) by B. Bloom (Ed.), 1956, New York: Longmans, Green.

1. Lack of expertise in the subject area
2. Required adherence to school and department guidelines and plans
3. State and district testing programs
4. Lack of available instructional resources (in and out of school)

Lack of Expertise in Subject Area. Teachers who are not well-versed in the subject they teach find it difficult to identify major and minor topics to cover in the course and to decide on the scope and sequence of presentation for these topics. It is not unusual for a teacher lacking subject-area expertise to start the crucial first weeks of the school year without a clear idea of exactly what to teach, for how long, and with what emphasis. To bring out the inherent cyclical and dynamic nature of the learning process in the instructional plan requires knowledge of and careful thought about all aspects of the subject (i.e., information, concepts, ideas, skills, values) and how these various aspects relate to each other and to the learner.

Students benefit when instruction is presented in an organized fashion, and they benefit even more when the instructional plan provides opportunities to learn the material at increasingly higher levels of understanding. Thus on the teacher's part considerable knowledge and understanding of a particular subject is required even to begin to design an intelligent plan that is relevant to students and conducive to learning. Planning classroom instruction without understanding all aspects of the subject results in a waste of valuable classroom time through misplaced emphasis and ineffective sequencing of course material. For example, the teacher who has not determined the scope and sequence of topics for a course may spend the first week covering a particular topic and then later in the semester come to the rude awakening that the students do not understand many key concepts because information and ideas presented initially were not adequately emphasized. Although this may be a rude awakening it is an awakening nonetheless, and the teacher can at least begin to rectify the problem. In many cases, however, the teacher in this situation never realizes what has gone wrong and assumes that the students' inability to learn is due either to ineffective teaching methods or to the students themselves.

School and Department Guidelines and Plans. In some instances school and department guidelines and plans allow for little opportunity or incentive for the teacher to actively participate in planning the instructional program. Rather than creatively planning the curriculum, adherence to guidelines becomes the main goal whether or not the guidelines address students' actual learning needs. School and department plans may also require the teacher to rely heavily on a specific text rather than on originally developed material for many daily activities and assignments. An example of this is a junior high school where the history department adopts a particular series of texts (e.g., History I, History II, and History III) put out by a publisher for use in grades seven, eight, and nine, respectively, and builds the course syllabi and major exams around these texts. Where this is the case, opportunities to develop and practice the decision-making and leadership skills involved in instructional planning are considerably limited and most definitely discouraged. In the next section, on curriculum research and planning, school and department guidelines and plans as well as textbooks are discussed as effective aids to planning when used in conjunction with a variety of other resource materials.

State and District Testing Programs. As the use of various standardized tests to measure student achievement and teacher effectiveness proliferates, there is a corresponding increase of pressure on districts, schools, and teachers to align their instructional programs with these tests. The phrase that aptly describes such alignment is "teaching to the test." Unfortunately, teaching under these conditions severely limits flexibility in deciding the scope and sequence of instruction for a particular course and, worse, does not allow the teacher to make any of the four curriculum decisions essential to effective and relevant instruction (Table 3.2). On the one hand, the teacher's understanding of the subject and of the particular students being taught may lead to a feeling that certain topics need to be included or emphasized in the instructional plan. On the other hand, the teacher, realizing that the students need to do well on a particular district- or state-wide test in the subject, may feel compelled to plan instruction according to the demands of the test even if it means developing plans that are not really adequate to meeting the students' learning needs.

Lack of Available Instructional Resources. Even if the teacher finds the school environment supportive and conducive to instructional planning, all efforts will have limited success if necessary resources are not available. For example, a teacher who is encouraged by the principal or department chairperson to revise a course of instruction needs access to relevant books, journals, college and university libraries, and computer search facilities as well as time for interclass and interschool visitations and consultation with other experts and practitioners. The teacher's work in revising the course of instruction will be facilitated to the extent that such materials and time are available. The mere availability of materials and time alone, however, cannot assure effective instructional planning. The teacher must have some guidance and skill in using these resources.

Table 3.3 describes how deductive and inductive methods of defining objectives can be used to overcome or lessen the factors that limit the teacher's ability to plan the instructional program.

Principles of Effective Planning

The true test of knowledge is found in its application. Thus, regardless of how conversant a teacher is with the principles and techniques of planning, a certain depth of understanding and interest in the subject as well as a sincere desire to learn are needed before these principles can be put into practice.

TABLE 3.3 *Using Deductive and Inductive Methods of Defining Objectives*

LIMITING FACTORS	OBSERVATIONS	RECOMMENDATIONS	DESCRIPTION
Teacher's lack of expertise	Teacher has minimal knowledge and training in the subject area	Teacher should use the deductive method of defining objectives	Teacher reviews and selects objectives from authoritative sources such as state frameworks, district guides, department handbooks, or texts as the basis for reducing these objectives to specific classroom activities appropriate to a particular course
Lack of available resources	Few and inadequate resources for curriculum research		
Requirements of school and department guidelines	Course curriculum has been clearly defined by school or department guidelines	Teacher should use the inductive method of defining objectives	Teacher derives objectives from a classification of the specific activities performed by students in the classroom to adapt a predetermined curriculum to meet student needs
Pressure of state and district testing programs	Considerable pressure to align curriculum to the requirements of standardized tests		

Only through pursuing a subject well beyond the introductory level can the student gain a coherent picture of the subject, get a glimpse of the vast reaches of knowledge, feel the cutting edge of disciplined training, and discover the satisfactions of the scholarly habit of mind so that if he or she becomes a teacher, he or she can communicate something of this spirit to others. (Conant, 1963, p. 106)

The three basic principles presented below should be followed and used as criteria for measuring the effectiveness of instructional planning (Table 3.4).

1. *The results of planning must be practical and usable.* To meet this criterion, the instructional plan must be based much more on the internal classroom situation than on any external factors. For example, the planning for a given course becomes more relevant when it takes into account the particular students in the class, the school and department objectives and mode of operation, and the teacher's expertise and capabilities. Planning is less useful when priority is given to external factors, such as district guidelines, prescriptions derived from research, commercially prepared materials, or standardized tests. Although these external factors cannot be completely ignored, they should be allowed to influence the instructional plan only after the classroom situation has been fully taken into account.

2. *Planning must be realistic in terms of time.* Instructional planning must be within the realm of possibility considering all the demands on the teacher's time. The teacher who fails to accurately assess the amount of

TABLE 3.4 *Three Principles for Planning the Classroom Instructional Program*

PRINCIPLES	DESCRIPTION
1. The results of planning must be practical and usable.	The instructional plan is based much more on the classroom situation (i.e., type of students, department objectives, and teacher's capabilities) than on external factors (i.e., district guidelines, prescriptions derived from general research, or standardized tests).
2. Planning must be realistic in terms of time.	The scope of instructional planning is based on an accurate assessment of the amount of time and resources available to the teacher. (This also means that an organized approach must be used for planning so that optimal use is made of available resources.)
3. Planning should result in better teaching.	The instructional plan should provide a viable means for helping students (i.e., fully assimilating exemplary information and ideas to address the practical needs of the classroom).

time available for planning becomes frustrated at being unable to do the job with the thoroughness desired. Because so little time is usually available for planning, it is essential that an intelligent and well-organized approach be used for curriculum planning. The comprehensive curriculum development method presented in the next section represents one such approach.

3. *Planning should result in better teaching.* Although comprehensive instructional planning requires a considerable amount of subject-area research, scholarship, which is indicative of such research, is only one of the factors that contributes to effective instructional planning. When planning becomes overly complicated or merely an academic exercise it lessens the effectiveness of instruction. Continual reevaluation of all the ideas, material, and information in a course in terms of how these can be fully assimilated into day-to-day classroom lessons is needed to create an instructional plan that provides a viable means for student learning and growth and to strike a natural balance between scholarship and the practical needs of the classroom.

In addition to understanding these three basic principles of planning, it is important to understand the role of what can be called *spontaneous planning.* As pointed out in the discussion on teacher as artist in Chapter 1, the teacher must be able to address the needs of students impromptu as new situations arise. Spontaneous planning refers to those instances where the teacher finds it necessary to modify the instructional plan during the lesson. For example, in the midst of a lesson the teacher may realize that the concepts and related information for a given topic should be presented in a sequence much different than the one originally planned. This teacher would then change the order of presentation accordingly and might even find it necessary to add or delete material to make the modified plan work. The teacher who does not carefully observe the effects of instruction on students, or who lacks a depth of understanding of the subject, is in no position to plan spontaneously in this way. As in music, sports, and many other fields, in teaching the ability to successfully improvise is based on an understanding of the subject and a keen awareness of the immediate environment. In Table 3.5 some requirements for successful spontaneous planning are listed.

◆ Curriculum Research and Development

The importance of the teacher's efforts in curriculum research and development and a method for carrying out comprehensive curriculum research to develop a classroom instructional program are the focus of this section.

Because of the proliferation of ready-made instructional plans and materials and the emphasis on standardized tests and related curriculum frameworks, the importance of the teacher's efforts in curriculum research and development is not adequately recognized or encouraged. One of the best

TABLE 3.5 *Requirements for Successful Spontaneous Planning*

REQUIREMENT	DESCRIPTION
Keen awareness of the environment	Careful observation of student responses, questions, attentiveness, attitudes, and interest ♦ To understand the effects of instruction on student learning and growth ♦ To effectively modify the instructional plan as needed
Thorough understanding of the subject	In-depth study of all aspects of the subject area from a variety of perspectives ♦ To think of ideas and information to enrich classroom instruction ♦ To think of various ways of presenting and explaining material to students ♦ To show students how various concepts and facts throughout the course relate to each other

ways for the teacher to be firmly in touch with the learning process is to be actively involved in learning. There is perhaps no better way for the teacher to do this than to be involved in disciplined subject-area research for the purpose of planning the course of instruction.

The goal of such research is much more than what is commonly called *subject-area expertise.* The teacher must constantly be thinking of how to best utilize his or her knowledge and understanding of the subject to design an instructional plan that provides experiences that address the needs and interests of the learner. The comprehensive curriculum method presented here represents a teacher-directed, carefully organized approach to increasing understanding of a subject area while at the same time maintaining a sharp focus on curriculum development as it relates directly to effective daily classroom instruction.

Comprehensive Curriculum-Development Method

This method is designed to deepen the teacher's understanding of the subject as a means to enrich classroom learning experiences. The process requires the teacher to assume the role of curriculum developer and decision maker through every step of the process. The goal is the development of a complete course of instruction that can stand on its own, using textbooks, teaching guides, and curriculum frameworks only as supplemental resources for further enrichment. This method provides scope for creative and intimate involvement with every aspect of the course curriculum so that the subject becomes a living, dynamic entity rather than a prepackaged, secondhand body of information to be delivered by the teacher to the students. It can be used effectively by the novice and experienced teacher alike. For the novice it provides an orientation to a world of possibilities for continued planning and growth. And for the veteran it provides an opportunity for refinement of existing materials and for professional self-renewal.

The emphasis, therefore, is on first developing the capability of constructing an overall course curriculum to serve as the foundation and wellspring for planning and carrying out daily classroom lessons. In Chapter 6 several ideas and recommendations for planning and carrying out the daily lesson are presented. Viewing daily classroom instruction in its broader context of the full curriculum coincides perfectly with the notion that daily lessons and learning activities are effective when they are based on an understanding of the nature and structure of the subject and on an awareness of the various instructional materials available.

In addition, the perspective obtained through creative involvement with curriculum development on the scale described here makes it possible to understand the content of a subject in relation to other subjects and to the same subject during earlier and later grade levels. Such an understanding is particularly useful because it accounts for students' actual day-to-day and year-to-year situations concerning their school subjects. The twelve steps that constitute the method are introduced and explained below. Key terms are italicized when they are introduced.

1. **Step 1.** Select a *course* (one semester) to develop. Because this method involves the teacher in a major curriculum project, the course selected for development should have special importance. For example, a high school English teacher who has always wanted to teach a semester course on poetry could use this method to construct an original course of instruction, such as Poetry as a Literary Form. The experienced junior high school Spanish teacher who has taught Spanish II classes for many years could use this method to enrich and update his or her understanding of the subject as a means of rejuvenating a stagnating instructional plan. The result of carrying out this project is a well thought out and organized instructional plan and related materials to draw upon for day-to-day instruction. For those about to assume their first teaching position, this method is especially useful for instilling confidence in and control over instructional plans and activities, thus permitting them to begin their classroom duties from a position of strength. Beginning the school year firmly in control of the instructional plan is very important because students are quick to sense how prepared and enthusiastic the teacher is concerning the subject.

2. **Step 2.** List *own ideas* concerning the major *elements* of the course (Figure 3.2). In this step the teacher breaks the course into major divisions (i.e., elements) before referring to any sources or materials for ideas so that the project starts solely with the teacher's current understanding of the subject. Thus, from the very outset of the curriculum-development process the teacher's role as decision maker is emphasized. For example, a junior high school math teacher who develops a course on elementary algebra

FIGURE 3.2 *Course Title and Own Ideas*

COURSE: SEVENTH-GRADE LIFE SCIENCE

Own Ideas

1. The Scientific Method and Characteristics of a Good Scientist
2. Good Scientific Techniques
3. The Basic Cell
4. Animal versus Plant Cells
5. Organizations of Cells
6. Specialization of Cells (Animal and Plant)
7. Green Leaf Structure/Photosynthesis

would have to think deeply about the subject to determine what major areas to cover. To address the needs of the learner this thinking must look not only at the subject in an academic sense but also at how the subject should be presented to students. In this first step, it is important for teachers to reflect on their understanding of the subject so that their involvement in and control of the process are firmly established immediately. As research proceeds, the teacher has to constantly keep in mind that the ideas and information reviewed for the various designated course elements must provide the basis and substance for worthwhile classroom learning experiences. This process requires creative involvement coupled with enormous concentration and perseverance. Although carrying out this project demands considerable time and effort, it is a valuable undertaking for any teacher who aspires to excellence.

3. *Step 3.* Locate and review *key guiding materials* to survey the subject area. By this point considerable thought has been given to what the major divisions (elements) of the course should be. In this step the aim is to locate and review materials (key guiding materials) that cover the subject to find out what experts in the field think the major divisions for the subject should be. Among the key guiding materials that can be particularly useful are highly recommended textbooks, course outlines obtained from reputable teachers of the subject, department and district guidelines, state curriculum frameworks, books on the subject, and discussions with experts in the particular field. The research in this step remains general because the goal is only to determine what the field suggests the major divisions of the course should be. The quality, not the quantity, of the key guiding materials reviewed ultimately determines the value of the ideas discovered and thus the effectiveness of this crucial step (Figure 3.3). The less experienced teacher especially should exert considerable effort and care in locating key guiding materials for the dual purpose of determining course elements and becoming conversant with new and important ideas and materials in the subject area. The more experienced teacher should regard this step as an

FIGURE 3.3 *Key Guiding Materials*

KEY GUIDING MATERIALS: SEVENTH-GRADE LIFE SCIENCE

Biology I Course Syllabus. Maria Fernandez, science teacher at Hawthorne High School, 1986.

Guidelines for Instruction: Secondary School Science. Los Angeles Unified School District, 1985.

Joint Science Department Curriculum Outline. St. Monica's High School, 1986.

Perkins, O., & Stranger, R. (1981). *Life science.* New York: Globe Book Company.

Science Department Curriculum Handbook. Cerritos High School, 1986–1987.

Science Framework Addendum. California Public Schools, 1985.

Sherman, I., & Sherman, V. (1979). *Biology: A human approach.* New York: Oxford University Press.

WASC Committee Recommendations for Biology I at St. Joseph's High School. Western Association of Schools and Colleges, 1985.

opportunity to become familiar with the most recent research and trends in the subject area and to look at ideas he or she has not been able to explore before.

4. *Step 4.* Decide on a final list of elements for the course. In this step the teacher's own conception of the subject outlined in Step 1 is combined with ideas obtained from various key guiding materials. Although later steps call for more extensive research, the determination of the overall structure of the course completed in this step sets the foundation for the entire instructional plan. It is crucial, therefore, that careful thought be given to deciding this final list of elements. For the person who has not had much training in the subject it is likely that the key guiding materials will have more influence in determining the major course elements than for the more experienced and trained person, for whom it would be significant if the review of key guiding materials effects even a few changes in his or her original (own) ideas. In either case, the selected elements should constitute a workable broad outline of the course to serve as the basis for further research and planning (Figure 3.4).

5. *Step 5.* Divide each course element into *topics.* The initial choice of topics made here is likely to be modified as research proceeds and becomes refined. Up to this point course elements have been identified based on the teacher's understanding of the subject in combination with ideas from key guiding materials. In this step careful thought is given to determine the specific topics for instruction that are contained in each element. Division of the elements into topics serves two main purposes. First, it

FIGURE 3.4 *Elements and Topics*

COURSE: SEVENTH-GRADE LIFE SCIENCE

Elements*

1. Methods of Science
2. The Basic Unit of Life
3. Classification of Organisms
4. Specialization of Cells
5. Plant Specialization
6. Animal Specialization

Elements and Topics

1. Methods of Science
    a. Scientific method
    b. Scientific techniques
2. The Basic Unit of Life
    a. Cell structure
    b. Cell processes
    c. Cell division
    d. Exchange of materials
    e. Animal/plant cell differences
3. Classification of Organisms
    a. Protists
    b. Animals
    c. Plants
    d. Fungi
    e. Monera
4. Specialization of Cells
    a. From cells to organisms
5. Plant Specialization
    a. Structure of the leaf, root, stem
    b. Photosynthesis
6. Animal Specialization
    a. Respiratory system
    b. Digestive system
    c. Circulatory system
    d. Nervous system
    e. Endocrine system
    f. Reproductive system
    g. Skeletal system

*After reviewing the key guiding materials, notice how these elements differ from the major course divisions listed in Figure 3.2 that were based on the teacher's own ideas.

requires a consideration of the fundamental structure of the subject, particularly as it relates to classroom instruction. Second, it provides the detail and needed focus for carrying out the research called for in the following steps (Figure 3.4).

For example, a junior high school science teacher developing a life science course for a seventh-grade class may decide that one of the topics under the element The Basic Unit of Life should be cell structure. He or she can then proceed with the more extensive and focused research required in the next step, looking for information and ideas related to cell structure (and all other topics delineated) in the various resource materials to be selected for review in Step 6.

6. *Step 6.* Identify and select *basic sources* to serve as a comprehensive set of reference materials for carrying out the necessary research on all course topics. The quality of the course curriculum is directly related to the quality of the resource materials used for obtaining insights, ideas, and materials related to the subject area. This means a thorough search must be made for a wide variety of materials from many sources. As this search is conducted, a keen sense of discrimination should be exercised so that only the most useful information and ideas are culled from resource materials. In brief, the aim is to find basic sources of the highest quality and to select from these sources information and ideas deemed most useful and relevant to the envisioned instructional plan. The range of basic sources to consult is limited only by the teacher's knowledge and imagination. Some very useful basic sources include books that cover the subject fully or partially (i.e., covering anywhere from all course elements to a particular topic under one element), exemplary textbooks, journal articles, course materials of reputable teachers, department handbooks, school and district guides, state curriculum frameworks, formal and informal discussions with experts in the field, observations of other classes, originally and commercially developed materials, and materials distributed by professional associations (e.g., National Association of English Teachers). Some places to look for basic sources include college and university libraries, school district and county professional reference centers, teacher education program curriculum inquiry centers or labs, recommendations of colleagues, school district instructional materials centers and textbook review areas, publishing houses, reputable teachers at the college and secondary school levels, and professional associations. Throughout all phases of the research a bibliographic list of the materials selected should be maintained to serve as a ready reference to guide further research (Figure 3.5).

7. *Step 7.* List *source reference points* for each topic under each element. This step involves systematically reviewing each basic source, using topic titles (e.g., Cell Structure) to pinpoint and make note of the specific sections and pages in the basic sources where material relating to the various topics can be found. Looking in tables of contents and indices of the various basic sources, where applicable, greatly facilitates finding the material desired. For example, in Figure 3.6 note that information or ideas relating to Topic A of Element 1 are found on pages 106–121 of Book 2, and so on through each basic source and for each topic. The resulting list of source

FIGURE 3.5 *Basic Sources*

BASIC SOURCES: SEVENTH-GRADE LIFE SCIENCE

Anderson, H. O. (1969). *Readings in science education for the secondary school.* New York: Macmillan.

(1982, January). Biology notes. *School Science Review,* 63(225), 678–696.

Brandwein, P., Burnett, R., & Stullberg, R. (1968). *Life, its forms and changes.* New York: Harcourt, Brace, and World.

(1976). Course and curriculum improvement materials: Elementary, intermediate, and secondary. Washington, DC: National Science Foundation.

DeVito, A., & Krockover, G. H. (1976). *Creative sciencing: A practical approach.* Boston: Little, Brown.

Flanagan, J. D., Mager, R. F., & Shanner, W. M. (1971). *Science behavioral objectives: A guide to individualizing learning.* Palo Alto, CA: Westinghouse Learning Press.

Freshman Science Faculty. (1985). *Teacher resource units in biology.* The Bronx High School of Science, New York City Schools.

Joint Department Work. (1986). *Life science curriculum guide.* St. Monica's High School, Santa Monica, CA.

Kirk, D., Taggart, R., & Starr, C. (1978). *Biology, the unity and diversity of life.* Belmont, CA: Wadsworth.

Kormondy, E. J. (1984, September). Human ecology: An introduction for biology teachers. *American Biology Teacher,* 46(6), 325–329.

Mandell, A. (1974). *The language of science.* Washington, DC: National Science Teacher Association.

Pauling, L. (1964). *The architecture of molecules.* San Francisco: W. H. Freeman.

Sherman, I., & Sherman, V. (1979). *Biology: A human approach.* New York: Oxford University Press.

Szent-Gyorgyi, A. (1960). *Introduction to submolecular biology.* New York: Academic Press.

Szent-Gyorgyi, A., & Hayashi, T. (1966). *Molecular architecture in cell physiology.* Englewood Cliffs, NJ: Prentice-Hall.

Tilling, S. (1984, Winter). Keys to biological identification: Their role and construction. *Journal of Biological Education,* 18(4), 293–304.

Wilson, E., Eisner, T., & Briggs, W. (1978). *Life on earth.* Sunderland, MA: Sinauer Associates.

reference points provides a complete index to the compendium of basic source materials gathered for developing the course. Thus, by referring to the source reference points, research on any topic under any element can be immediately directed to the appropriate place(s) in the appropriate

FIGURE 3.6 *Source Reference Points*

| BASIC SOURCES | SOURCE REFERENCE POINTS FOR ELEMENT 1 | | | |
	Topic A	Topic B	Topic C	Topic D
Book 1	17–20	1, 17, 29	—	—
Article 1	7	21–40	—	—
Book 2	106–121	12	2, 4–6	71–78
Book 3	—	3–5, 12–14	—	106–109
Article 2	3–15	—	—	—
Handbook 1	4–20	25–31	32–40	107–130
Syllabus 1	1	—	2–3	5
Text 1	35–80	1–34	110–140	81–109
Text 2	1–21	65–96	22–64	122–140

source(s). Because this curriculum development method requires consulting many basic sources on numerous topics, the listing of these source reference points is an essential step in organizing and focusing all subsequent research.

8. *Step 8.* Take *preliminary notes* for each topic under each element using the source reference points as a general index to material in the basic sources. This step represents the major research that is to be carried out for developing the course curriculum. The goal is to review all the source reference points so that the best material from the basic sources can be clearly identified for eventual use in planning classroom learning experiences. To read all the basic sources, all the while taking copious notes or highlighting material, is a considerable waste of time and effort. Research conducted in this fashion requires only minimal thought and usually results in a plethora of indiscriminate notes or markings far exceeding what is needed. The researcher merely uses enough thought to decide that certain material seems to look good, while little or nothing is decided about why the material looks good or, more important, how it may be used in the course or to address the needs of learners. Add to this the time it takes to copy many notes and the uselessness of having dozens of pages with highlighted material and it becomes apparent that this method is hardly adequate for the comprehensive and reflective research needed to complete this curriculum-development project.

The key to effectively carrying out this step lies in developing the ability to take concise, telegraphic notes and, even more important, to add spontaneous ideas as the basic sources are reviewed. For example, in Figure 3.7 notice that under "Comments" for this particular set of preliminary notes for Topic A, all the comments are very brief (i.e., telegraphic), and in some instances they have a note in brackets (i.e., spontaneous notes). The

FIGURE 3.7 *Preliminary Notes*

PRELIMINARY NOTES FOR ELEMENT 1 (TOPIC A)	
Page/ Paragraph	Comments
Book 1	
17/3–6	Good idea on *xyz* process
20/1	See diagram of *abc* theory [*Note:* Use this diagram to introduce Topic D later on]
Article 1	
7/4	Excellent point to discuss on issue *y*
Book 2	
111/3–5	Cull general points on value of theory *a*
114/2	Good list of definitions [*Note:* Use to develop word games]
Article 2	
5/2, 6/3	Seven criteria for measuring completeness of *xyz* process
15	See footnote 3 for good book to look up
Handbook 1	
4/1	Thorough explanation of inhibiting factors
9/3, 10/1	Steps for analyzing density [*Note:* Use on overhead and in study guide]
20/1	See Figure 2 and description [*Note:* Adapt figure to form a matrix of causes and effects]
Syllabus 1	
1	Notice recommended sequence of objectives and types of classroom activities
Text 1	
40–42	Summarize ideas from these ten modes of operation
50/3–5	Key point on what research has to say about *abc* theory
79–80	Select from this listing of questions and projects

preliminary notes listed indicate that when the first source reference point in the basic source, Book 1, was reviewed, the teacher found useful material on the *xyz* process on page 17, paragraphs 3–6. Rather than copying all the material, a concise, telegraphic notation was made so that a record of the relevant and potentially useful material in Book 1 was maintained. Thus, when the preliminary notes are subsequently reviewed, a clear message concerning how the material may be used is quickly conveyed by the telegraphic note that has been taken. For each telegraphic note, therefore, the teacher must not only determine what material is worth citing but must also capture the essence of the material. Original and creative ideas (i.e., spontaneous notes) should be added wherever possible to facilitate the concluding steps of the curriculum-development process.

In the set of preliminary notes in Figure 3.7 there is also an indication that a worthwhile citation for Topic A on page 20, paragraph 1, of Book 1 was found. For this particular citation the teacher made a further determination in the form of a spontaneous note that the material cited would be useful for introducing another topic in the course (i.e., Topic D). Spontaneous notes should be added where material found in the basic sources brings to mind other connections or original and creative thoughts. Spontaneous notes may include sudden insights, comments on the author's viewpoint or reasoning, ideas on how the material might be effectively used in a lesson (i.e., for planning activities, teaching methods, or associated resource materials, ideas for linking the material with previous or subsequent course topics, and indications of how the material can address students' various interests and learning styles. To add spontaneous notes throughout as research proceeds requires exercising a degree of intensity in thought clearly indicative of creative and intimate involvement in developing the course curriculum and continued learning in the subject area. In addition, a record of very useful ideas is maintained.

To summarize briefly, preliminary notes are taken by referring to the source reference points that indicate where each basic source addresses each topic of the various course elements. Successful completion of this step signifies a thorough and thoughtful investigation of the subject. It also demonstrates that even the new teacher can be in control of the curriculum rather than being controlled or confused by it, which fosters confidence and paves the way for continued development of curricular and instructional materials.

9. *Step 9.* Review preliminary notes to select citations and original ideas (i.e., telegraphic and spontaneous notes) that can be effectively used to develop instructional plans. Up to this point the teacher has located and reviewed all the basic sources, reviewed all the source reference points, and taken a complete set of preliminary notes. In this step, the teacher needs to go back over all the preliminary notes to select citations and notes he or she considers to be of the highest quality and potentially of the greatest value to classroom instruction. This review of preliminary notes continues the process of selecting the "best of the best" that is characteristic of each step in this method. For example, in Figure 3.8 notice how the teacher, after looking over all the preliminary notes for Topic A, determined that the citation dealing with the *xyz* process on page 17, paragraphs 3–6, of Book 1 was not as thorough or clearly explained as another citation dealing with the *xyz* process found on pages 5–6 of Article 2. All the preliminary

FIGURE 3.8 *Reviewing Preliminary Notes*

PRELIMINARY NOTES FOR ELEMENT 1 (TOPIC A)	
Page/ Paragraph	**Comments**
	Book 1
~~17/3–6~~	~~Good idea on xyz process~~
20/1	See diagram of *abc* theory [*Note:* Use this diagram to introduce Topic D later on]
	Article 1
7/4	Excellent point to discuss on issue y
	Book 2
~~111/3–5~~	~~Cull general points on value of theory *a*~~
114/2	Good list of definitions [*Note:* Use to develop word games]
	Article 2
5/2, 6/3	Seven criteria for measuring completeness of *xyz* process
15	See footnote 3 for good book to look up
	Handbook 1
~~4/1~~	~~Thorough explanation of inhibiting factors~~
9/3, 10/1	Steps for analyzing density [*Note:* Use on overhead and in study guide]
20/1	See Figure 2 and description [*Note:* Adapt figure to form a matrix of causes and effects]
	Syllabus 1
1	Notice recommended sequence of objectives and types of classroom activities
	Text 1
40–42	Summarize ideas from these ten modes of operation
50/3–5	Key point on what research has to say about *abc* theory
79–80	Select from this listing of questions and projects

notes are reviewed in a similar fashion with the goal of selecting material and ideas that most effectively and adequately cover all the course topics delineated.

The wisdom of taking preliminary notes in telegraphic form and including spontaneous ideas becomes clear at this point. Much material that was considered promising at first is eventually eliminated once the citations from all the basic sources have been reviewed.

If the teacher has effectively completed all the steps of the project to this point, the best ideas and information from the best sources available, covering all topics deemed important to the subject, will have been culled. In addition, the continuous and concentrated thought that has been applied will have creatively immersed the teacher in the course material and in the curriculum-development process.

10. *Step 10.* Sequence the preliminary notes that have been selected for each course topic according to their projected use in the instructional plan. Once the most useful material has been identified through a review of the preliminary notes, it is necessary to consider when and where in the overall instructional plan the material selected and the related original ideas should be presented to best account for both the inherent structure of the subject and student learning needs. A comparison of Figure 3.8 with Figure 3.9 illustrates how reviewed preliminary notes (Figure 3.8) are placed into a projected sequence for classroom presentation (Figure 3.9). Sequencing the selected material in this way requires further consideration of the ideas and information, keeping in mind both day-to-day and long-range plans and needs.

11. *Step 11.* Log *final notes.* The citations that have been selected should be put into final form in one of two ways, depending on the time available or the teacher's preference. If time allows and the teacher prefers, all the selected citations can be systematically written out, paraphrased, or photocopied and filed by element or topic for easy reference. If time does not allow and the teacher prefers, the location of all the selected citations can be carefully noted as a guide for retrieving information and ideas from the basic sources as needed for planning instructional purposes. (The lists of sequenced preliminary notes can serve this function.)

12. *Step 12.* Develop a *filing system.* In the final step of the process, a filing system should be developed to organize all the course materials. A simple yet effective filing system could consist of large (legal-size) folders to hold all the materials related to each element, and within each large folder could be a set of one-third tab (letter-size) folders for the final notes selected for each topic. In addition, within each of the large element folders, binders could be used to hold other course materials such as tests, quizzes, handouts, study guides, vocabulary lists, overhead transparencies, assignments, projects, activities, bibliographic lists of materials, and special notes and ideas (all filed according to element and topic). The filing system that is developed should be viewed as part of a dynamic and ongoing curriculum-development process and thus should be organized so that new and creative ideas and materials can be readily incorporated and accessible for use in lesson planning and instructional activities.

In Figure 3.10 the twelve steps of the comprehensive curriculum development method are summarized and presented in abbreviated form.

FIGURE 3.9 *Sequencing Preliminary Notes*

PRELIMINARY NOTES FOR ELEMENT 1 (TOPIC A)	
Page/ Paragraph	Comments
	Syllabus 1
1	Notice recommended sequence of objectives and types of classroom activities
	Article 2
5/2, 6/3	Seven criteria for measuring completeness of *xyz* process
	Book 2
114/2	Good list of definitions [*Note:* Use to develop word games]
	Handbook 1
20/1	See Figure 2 and description [*Note:* Adapt figure to form a matrix of causes and effects]
	Book 1
20/1	See diagram of *abc* theory [*Note:* Use this diagram to introduce Topic D later on]
	Text 1
50/3–5	Key point on what research has to say about *abc* theory
	Article 1
7/4	Excellent point to discuss on issue y
	Article 2
15	See footnote 3 for good book to look up
	Text 1
40–42	Summarize ideas from these ten modes of operation
	Handbook 1
9/3, 10/1	Steps for analyzing density [*Note:* Use on overhead and in study guide]
	Text 1
79–80	Select from this listing of questions and projects

◆ **Curriculum Model**

In this section an outline of a model that suggests how the curriculum of a given subject can be enriched by and related to material in other curriculum areas is presented.

FIGURE 3.10 *Summary of the Twelve Steps of the Comprehensive Curriculum Development Method*

1. Select a course (one semester) to develop.
2. List *own ideas* concerning the major *elements* of the course.
3. Locate and review *key guiding materials* to survey the subject area.
4. Decide on a final list of elements for the course using own ideas and ideas gotten from key guiding materials.
5. Divide each course element into *topics*. (The choice of topics is likely to be modified after further research.)
6. Identify and select *basic sources* to serve as a comprehensive set of reference materials (i.e., covering all topics fully) for developing the course.
7. List *source reference points* for each topic under each element.

Example

BASIC COURSES	SOURCE REFERENCE POINTS FOR ELEMENT 1			
	Topic A	Topic B	Topic C	Topic D
Book 1	17–20	1, 17, 29	—	—
Article 1	7	21–40	—	—
Book 2	106–121	12	2, 4–6	71–78

8. Take *preliminary notes* for each topic under each element using the source reference points as a general index to material in the basic sources. (Note: the brackets in the example below are used to indicate spontaneous ideas.)

Example

PRELIMINARY NOTES FOR ELEMENT 1 (TOPIC A)	
Page/ Paragraph	Comments
	Book 1
17/3–6	Good idea on *xyz* process
20/1	See diagram of *abc* theory [*Note:* Use this diagram to introduce Topic D later on]
	Article 1
7/4	Excellent point to discuss on issue *y*

9. Review preliminary notes to select citations and original ideas (i.e., telegraphic and spontaneous notes) that can be effectively used to develop instructional plans.
10. Sequence the preliminary notes that have been selected for each topic according to their projected use in the instructional plan.
11. Log *final notes* either by writing them out, paraphrasing them, or photocopying them or by carefully noting where the references can be found for

FIGURE 3.10 *(Continued)*

quick use at the appropriate point in developing daily and long-range instructional plans. (The lists of sequenced preliminary notes developed in Step 10 can serve this function.)

12. Develop a *filing system* consisting of various sizes of folders and organized by elements and topics so that new and creative ideas and materials are readily accessible for use in instructional planning and activities.

McNeil's Alternative Organizational Patterns

In this model four alternative organizational patterns for enriching the curriculum of a given course are proposed. Each organizational pattern involves expanding the students' opportunities for understanding and discovery across several disciplines:

1. *Unified or concentrated.* Major themes serve to organize the subject matter from various disciplines. The concept of energy, for example, can be studied from biological, physical, chemical, and geologic perspectives.
2. *Integrated.* Skills learned in one subject area are used as tools in another field. Mathematics, for instance, is taught for the solving of scientific problems.
3. *Correlated.* Disciplines retain their separate identities, but students learn how concepts in one discipline are related to those in another. For example, history, geography, and English may be taught so as to reinforce one another.
4. *Comprehensive problem solving.* Problems may be drawn from current social interests such as consumer research, recreation, and transportation. Students must draw on skills and knowledge from the sciences, social sciences, mathematics, and art in the attempt to optimize a solution. (McNeil, 1985, p. 71)

Successfully integrating the knowledge of different disciplines to enrich students' learning in a particular course requires considerable skill and confidence. There are, however, no shortcuts to gaining such skill and confidence. It requires consistent and thoughtful effort to gain the level of understanding of a subject needed to effectively integrate material of several disciplines in a form that addresses students' learning needs. An unquenchable interest in learning, one of the teacher's greatest assets, is the basis for successfully making such effort.

SUMMARY

In this chapter several main points about planning for instruction were presented.

1. The goal of the curriculum is to provide a resource and a means of growth for students both as individuals and as members of society.

2. The basis of successful curriculum development is the teacher's mastery of the subject and ability to carry out continuous, disciplined inquiry in the subject.

3. To focus planning, the teacher must carefully select objectives that clearly indicate the aims of the instructional plan in terms of student growth.

4. Sequencing and integrating learning objectives is necessary to maximize the cumulative effect of several objectives on learning.

5. Four factors that limit effective planning are lack of expertise in the subject area, required adherence to school/department guidelines, state/district standardized testing programs, and lack of available resources.

6. In developing instructional plans the teacher should understand and employ a standard of learning that ensures the three aspects of consciousness (i.e., cognition, conation, and affection) are addressed.

7. Effective planning is based on three principles: the results of planning must be practical and usable; planning must be realistic in terms of time; and planning should result in better teaching.

8. The teacher can get to know the subject as a living and dynamic entity by carrying out comprehensive curriculum development to construct a complete course of instruction.

9. An effective way to enrich the curriculum plan is to provide students with opportunities for understanding and discovery across several disciplines.

10. By using a classroom planning framework the teacher can effectively translate curriculum research into daily lesson plans.

11. The true test of knowledge is found in its application. Thus, regardless of how conversant a teacher is with the principles and techniques of effective planning, a certain depth of understanding and interest in the subject as well as a sincere desire to learn are needed before these principles can be put into practice.

In the fullest sense, knowledge of the subject means the ability to carry out research in a variety of resources and then to organize what has been found into effective daily lessons. Successful teaching is impossible without this knowledge. To be successful, the teacher must have the ability as well as an interest in reaching the students. Knowledge of the subject (as defined above) is a primary component of this ability.

♦ ♦ ♦ ♦ ♦ ♦ ♦
PRACTICAL MODEL 3.1   Framework for Classroom Planning

Introduction   The type of detailed planning outlined in this practical model is a logical extension of the comprehensive curriculum-development method presented in this chapter. It shows how the exemplary ideas and materials that have been gathered can be transformed into specific instructional plans and learning experiences.

FIGURE 3.11 *Flow Chart*

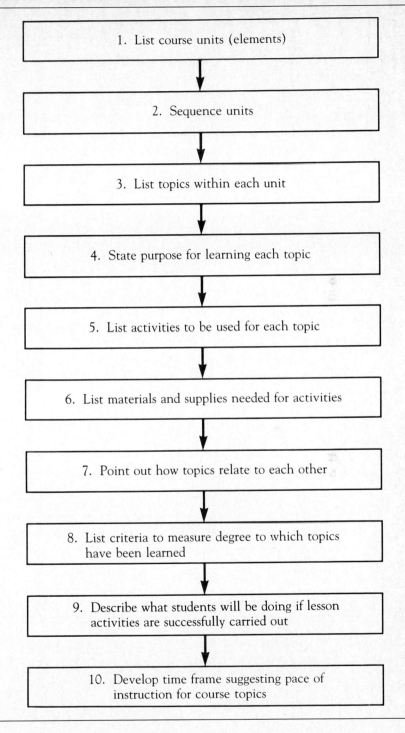

1. List course units (elements)

2. Sequence units

3. List topics within each unit

4. State purpose for learning each topic

5. List activities to be used for each topic

6. List materials and supplies needed for activities

7. Point out how topics relate to each other

8. List criteria to measure degree to which topics have been learned

9. Describe what students will be doing if lesson activities are successfully carried out

10. Develop time frame suggesting pace of instruction for course topics

Submitted by   Dr. Joel Levine, former secondary school music teacher in New York City and Los Angeles

Purpose   To provide teachers with a framework for planning classroom instruction so that the topics covered in a particular course can be effectively sequenced and related to one another

Setting   Junior high school; four sections (seventh grade); general music program

◆ Narrative

The classroom planning framework presented here consists of four major parts: (1) flow chart (planning outline), (2) list of course units (elements), (3) process plan for determining the scope and sequence of topics to cover within each unit, (4) program planning guide plan for writing daily lessons.

1. *Flow chart.* This is the important first stage in which the major aspects of the classroom plan are outlined. Figure 3.11 is an example of a flow chart showing how the process moves from the most general to the most specific level of planning.
2. *List of course units (elements).* In this stage the major areas (units) to be covered by the course are determined, as well as the sequence of presentation of the units (Figure 3.12).
3. *Process plan.* In this stage the topics to be covered within each unit are listed according to the order they will be presented (Figure 3.13).
4. *Program planning guide.* This stage is the most detailed and represents the development of a well-organized resource for planning the daily classroom lessons. In Figure 3.14 the extent and nature of the detail involved in this stage are shown. Next to each topic the following information is listed: a concise rationale stating the role of the topic in the overall scheme; a list of basic lesson activities describing how the topic should be covered in a given lesson; where applicable, a brief

---

FIGURE 3.12 *Units and Sequence of Presentation*

GENERAL MUSIC UNITS (ELEMENTS)

1. Introduction to Rhythm
2. Percussion Instruments
3. African Music
4. Instruments of the Orchestra
5. Folk Music of the World
6. Musical Styles and Forms
7. The Guitar
8. The Keyboard and Note Reading
9. Performing in an Ensemble

FIGURE 3.13 *Process Plan*

GENERAL MUSIC UNITS AND TOPICS

1. Introduction to Rhythm	2. Percussion Instruments	3. African Music	4. Instruments of the Orchestra	5. Folk Music of the World	6. Musical Styles and Forms	7. The Guitar	8. The Keyboard and Note Reading	9. Performing in an Ensemble
Beat	Defining Percussion (pitched and unpitched)	Use of Music in Daily African Life	Introduction to the Four Families of Instruments	Map of the World	Melody and Harmony	Introduction to the Guitar	Reading the Notes of a C-scale	Musical Score
Conductor/ Conducting	Xylophone (bells)	Map of Africa	Instrument Fingering Charts	Listening to Recordings of Folk Music	Phrasing and Cadences	Playing by Fret Numbers	Locating Notes on the Keyboard	Performing from a Score on Rhythm Instruments
Basic Rhythms	Drum Rudiments	Record: The Music of Africa	Woodwind Instruments	Styles and Characteristics of Different Folk Music	Motive	Locating Note Names	Three-Step Process to Playing Piano Music	Composing for Two or More Instruments
Time Signatures	Drum Set Playing	Record: Negro Spirituals and Folksongs	Brass Instruments	Instruments from Around the World	Ternary Form	Playing from Notation	Playing Melodies on the Piano	Class Concert of Performing Ensembles
Rhythm Instruments		Polyrhythms: Olatunji Record	String Instruments		Playing Melodies on the Piano		Composing Melodies	
Ostinato Patterns		African Culture			Composing Melodies		Chords	
Rhythm Score					Chords		Playing Scales	
					Program Music			
					Electronic Music			
					Jazz, Classical Rock, Disco			

FIGURE 3.14 *Program Planning Guide*

UNIT 6: MUSICAL STYLES AND FORMS

Topics	Rationale	Activities	Resources	Related	Criteria	Narrative	Time (minutes)
Melody and Harmony	The two essential building blocks of music compositions	1. Teacher demonstrates difference between melody and harmony on the piano (also shown on music staff).	Piano Music staff (on blackboard)				25
		2. Students identify melody and harmony in examples played by teacher.			Students can differentiate between melody and harmony.	Students will be able to correctly identify at least five of seven examples of melody and harmony as they are played.	25
		3. Students compose short seven-note melodies on staff paper using only whole notes.	Dittoed staff paper	Link: With rhythm values (U-1, t-3) Ask students what seems to be missing from the melodies	Students can place notes on the lines and spaces of a staff to make a melody.	Students will be able to place at least five different notes on the music staff to form a short melodic line.	30
		4. Teacher plays a recording demonstrating a melodic line accompanied by a bass line.	Record player and recording of Vivaldi's Trio for Flute, Oboe, and Bassoon	Link: With classical music (U-6, t-10)			20
		5. Students identify melody lines and bass lines in examples played by teacher.		Link: With the guitar (U-7, t-5)	Students can distinguish melody line from bass line (harmony).	Students will be able to identify melodic line and bass line in four of five examples played.	20

Concept	Activities	Resources	Links	Objectives	Evaluation	Time
Ternary (ABA) Form						
Basic "song-form" used in most musical compositions	1. Teacher plays a recording demonstrating ABA form.	Recording of Wagner's Prelude to Act III of *Lohengrin*				15
	2. Students draw a picture on a piece of paper describing what they learn in the recording.		Link: With musical score (U-9, t-1)	Students can identify changes (of some sort) as they occur in music.	Students will be able to correctly indicate changes that occur (loudness, speed, instruments) in three of five musical examples.	30
	3. Students list the names of the instruments they hear on the recording.		Link: With instruments of the orchestra (U-4, all)	Students can identify the different families of instruments by their characteristic sounds.	Students can successfully identify when the brass, woodwind, or string families are playing in four of five examples.	20
	4. Teacher plays a tape of a song demonstrating typical "song-form" (i.e., verse-chorus-verse).	Cassette tape player and tape of the Beatles' song "Yesterday"				10
	5. Students identify verse-chorus-verse as they are played.	Song sheets		Students can identify the melodic pattern of a "song-form" composition.	Students can successfully differentiate between the verse and chorus sections in at least three out of five songs.	25

note pointing out how topics relate to each other; a statement of the criteria suggesting the standards for measuring students' understanding of the topic; a narrative, stated as behavioral objectives, describing what the students will be doing if the activities are successfully carried out; and a time frame suggesting the pacing of activities for each topic.

This framework for classroom planning should be used once all twelve steps of the comprehensive curriculum-development process have been completed so that all ideas and materials that have been identified can be used for planning of and incorporating into daily classroom learning activities.

◆ ◆ ◆ ◆ ◆ ◆ ◆
CASE STUDY 3.1   Instructional Objectives

Orienting
Questions   As you read this case study ask yourself these questions:

Specific
◆ Do the students appear to know what the objectives for this lesson are?
◆ Has the teacher set objectives for this lesson that provide scope for cognitive development (i.e., development of perceptual, conceptual, ideational abilities)?

General
◆ What points in this lesson stand out as indicators of this teacher's strengths and/or weaknesses?
◆ What recommendations would you make for addressing the problems this teacher seems to have?

Setting   School – Port-of-entry high school in a large urban school district

Subject – U.S. history (fifty-five minutes)

Teacher – Mrs. Carrie, emergency-credentialed teacher

Students – Twenty-five remedial students (ESL students)

Topic – Characteristics of the Early Settlements

Lesson   Note: Under Time Frame the numbers represent the minutes that elapse as the period progresses. Under Dialog the names of the students and the teacher appear as they speak. The symbol ► represents a brief description of a particularly noteworthy action or observation.

Time Frame	Dialog
1 to 5	► The students noisily enter the classroom, take their seats without taking out their notebooks or texts, and wait for instructions. Mrs. Carrie quickly adds a few thoughts to the day's lesson plan and then takes attendance using her roll book.

Time Frame	Dialog	
5 to 9	**Mrs. C.:**	I'll be with you in a minute. Today we are going to talk about the early settlements in the United States.
	Felipe:	(Coming late to class) Hi, Mrs. Carrie. I didn't hear the bell, sorry I'm late.
	Mrs. C.:	Felipe, you have to come on time. You always have some excuse. Okay, go ahead and sit down. (To the class) First thing, if you remember, we are going to have a quiz.
	►	Almost in complete unison the students shout, "You never told us about a quiz today." A few students very quietly say, "Yes she did."
	Mrs. C.:	I'm sure I told you, so get out a piece of paper and write a definition for each of the words I dictate to you. Don't worry about spelling. Write the words as best you can. It's very important for me to see how you do on these quizzes so I know how to help you.
9 to 18	►	Mrs. Carrie dictates ten words that relate to the topic being studied (such as "colony" and "settlement"). Most students had not remembered the quiz and either leave blanks on their papers or make up definitions at the spur of the moment.
18 to 35	**Mrs. C.:**	Now let's begin today's topic. Who can tell me where some of the early settlements were located?
	►	Two students call out the answer and Mrs. Carrie says "That's right." She then starts writing some facts on the board about the religious and social practices in the settlements.
	Mrs. C.:	Copy these notes and study them at home so you will do better on the next quiz. Do you think the settlements were run democratically?
	►	There is no response from the class. Mrs. Carrie then explains how the settlements could, in some ways, be considered democratic, and in other ways, undemocratic. While explaining, she is writing notes on the board.
	Rosa:	What do these words "intolerance to divergent philosophies" on the board mean?
	Mrs. C.:	Basically, these words mean that sometimes the people in these settlements didn't accept people with ideas different from their own.
	Rosa:	Why was that?
	Mrs. C.:	Copy these notes now so we get through this material. We will discuss them further, later.

Time Frame	Dialog	
35 to 45	**Mrs. C.:**	I've planned a little different activity for us today. We are going to do research. Get out your texts. Henry, give everyone a copy of this handout sheet.
	Carlos:	I left my book in homeroom. (A few other students also don't have their texts.)
	Mrs. C.:	We better get into groups to do this research. The following students go to sit near each other. (She then divides the class into five groups of five each, trying to have at least one text in each group and at least one "good" student in each group who can serve as the group leader.)
	►	The students seem a bit confused but finally get settled in their respective groups.
45 to 55	**Mrs. C.:**	Here is what I want you to do. Each group is to do research on one of the early settlements. For the settlement I assign you, look up all the information you can find about it in our text and in the handout sheets I've given you. Then answer these three questions: (1) What were the religious practices in the settlement? (2) What was the relationship of the settlement with neighboring settlements? (3) What person(s) played the most important leadership role(s) in the settlement?
	John:	(To the other members of his group) What settlement are we looking up?
	Alva:	I don't know.
	Carlos:	Mrs. Carrie wrote the instructions over there on that board. Let's try to figure out which is our settlement.
	►	All but one group seem to be lost about what to do. The one group that is getting it has several strong students. None of the students are referring to the index in the text or to the table of contents in the handout sheets to locate relevant information.
	Mrs. C.:	(As the bell rings) All right, we'll start tomorrow right away with our group research again. I'll see you then.
Brief	*Key Facts* – List three key facts verbatim that characterize the main positive and/or negative aspects of the lesson.	
	Strengths/Weaknesses – Briefly explain how the key facts selected indicate strengths and/or weaknesses in the teacher's performance.	

Recommendations – Briefly describe what the teacher could have done to alleviate or avoid the problems that were seen.

◆ ◆ ◆ ◆ ◆ ◆ ◆

CASE STUDY 3.2   Curriculum Planning

Orienting Questions   As you read this case study ask yourself these questions:

Specific
◆ Does this teacher appear to have considered how learning experiences should be organized to provide the students with a sense of continuity and order?
◆ Do this teacher's plans seem to be influenced more by external factors (i.e., district or department guidelines) or by her own perception of student needs?

General
◆ What points in this lesson stand out as indicators of this teacher's strengths and/or weaknesses?
◆ What recommendations would you make for addressing the problems this teacher seems to have?

Setting   School – High school with predominantly Hispanic and Asian students
Subject – Reading (fifty minutes)
Teacher – Ms. Jung
Students – Twenty-four freshmen
Topic – Mark Twain (a week-long unit)

Lesson

Time Frame	Dialog
	DAY 1
1 to 5	► The bell rings. The students are seated and class is brought to order. The students begin working on the daily vocabulary exercise while Ms. Jung takes roll, counts out some magazines, and organizes her lecture notes and study guide sheets.
5 to 15	**Ms. J.:** Good morning, class. This week we are going to depart from our usual routine a little bit to study a great American author, Mark Twain. It is the one hundred and fiftieth anniversary of his birth. In the issue of *Scholastic Magazine* you will get are three short stories by

Time Frame	Dialog	
		Mark Twain. I would like us to read the first one today in class and discuss your ideas about the story. But first, let me give you a little background on just who Mark Twain was.
	Delia:	Oh, we've read some of his stories already.
	Antonio:	Yeah, I've read *Tom Sawyer*.
15 to 45	►	The students are alert and appear confident that they know all about Mark Twain.
	Ms. J.:	Good! You seem to know something about Mark Twain. Tell me what else you know and I'll fill in any of the blanks.
	►	The students relate their information and Ms. Jung adds explanations as needed.
	Ms. J.:	Now that we all know who Mark Twain was, let's silently read the introduction to the story and then go on to read the rest of the story. Please notice the homework questions on the study guide that I'm passing out.
	►	The introduction contains basically the same information that Ms. Jung has just discussed with the class. The study guide questions cover biographical material on Mark Twain along with discussion questions on the first story.
45 to 50	**Rafael:**	Ms. Jung, what are these other questions for on the study guide?
	Ms. J.:	Well, I can't tell you now. Tomorrow I hope to surprise you. Now, before the bell rings, are there any questions about the story we read today or about the assignment?
	►	The bell rings.
	Ms. J.:	All right, class dismissed. I'll see you all tomorrow.

DAY 2

1 to 5	►	Class begins in the usual manner. The students notice a TV/video recorder set-up in the front of the room. They are excited about the movie and Ms. Jung brings them to order. She takes roll, sets up the video equipment, and pulls the shades while the students work on the daily vocabulary words.
5 to 10	**Ms. J.:**	Well, I'm sure you've guessed the surprise. I have a movie based on the story by Mark Twain called "The Prince and the Pauper." And I don't mean Prince from *Purple Rain*.
	►	The students laugh.

Time Frame	Dialog	
10 to 25	**Ms. J.:**	Before we begin the film, let's briefly go over the study guide questions from yesterday.
	►	The students take out their study guides and begin discussing and correcting their work. The movie is a ninety-minute video. Ms. Jung has planned to show the first fifteen minutes or so during this lesson to spark their curiosity. The bulk of the movie will be shown the next day, and the remaining thirty minutes will be shown on the third day.
25 to 45	**Ms. J.:**	(Reviewing the previous day's work) All right. We left off yesterday with . . .
	►	The students review the story read the previous day and are ready to see the movie. Ms. Jung then shows the film for seventeen minutes, jotting down the locater number so they can start the next day from where they left off.
45 to 50	**Ms. J.:**	How do you like the movie so far?
	►	The students say they really like the movie.
	Ms. J.:	We don't have a lot of time now to discuss the movie, but I'd like to draw your attention to the board for the assignment. Please note that you should do the next study guide questions for homework tonight.
	►	The bell rings.
	Ms. J.:	Class dismissed. Tomorrow we will finish the movie and discuss it.

DAY 3

Time Frame	Dialog	
1 to 45	►	Day 3 progresses in a similar fashion to the previous two days. The movie is set and shown. With the remaining fifteen minutes, Ms. Jung reviews the main points of the movie and gets the students' opinions of the movie and the story in more detail than she did the previous two days.
45 to 50	**Ms. J.:**	Please note the homework assignment on the board. Finish the questions pertaining to the movie. We'll go over them tomorrow. Class dismissed.

DAY 4

Time Frame	Dialog	
1 to 30	►	Class begins in the usual manner. Ms. Jung uses the first half of class to discuss and correct the students' study guides.

Time Frame	Dialog
30 to 50	**Ms. J.:** For the remaining class time, please read the second story by Mark Twain in your *Scholastic Magazine*. Please note that the remaining study guide questions are due tomorrow. These questions cover the story you are now going to read.

DAY 5

1 to 30	► Class begins as usual. The majority of the class time is spent discussing and correcting the study guide questions for the last story.
30 to 47	**Ms. J.:** Now that we've completed our unit on Mark Twain, I'd like your opinions. Write a paragraph about what you liked most about either the movie or the stories we've read.
	► The students begin writing.
47 to 50	**Ms. J.:** Please take your study guides home over the weekend because, as you may have guessed, there will be a short test on Monday on Mark Twain. All the material you need to know should be in the study guide.
	► The bell rings.
	Ms. J.: Class dismissed. Remember, test on Monday!

Brief   *Key Facts* – List three key facts verbatim that characterize the main positive and/or negative aspects of the lesson.

Strengths/Weaknesses – Briefly explain how the key facts selected indicate strengths and/or weaknesses in the teacher's performance.

Recommendations – Briefly describe what the teacher could have done to alleviate or avoid the problems that were seen.

◆ ◆ ◆ ◆ ◆ ◆ ◆
CASE STUDY 3.3   Relating Instructional Objectives to Planning

Orienting Questions   As you read this case study ask yourself these questions:

Specific
♦ Does this teacher incorporate creative ideas or material into the instructional plan to enrich instruction?

◆ What basic sources do you think this teacher primarily uses to develop instructional plans?

General

◆ What points in this lesson stand out as indicators of this teacher's strengths and/or weaknesses?

◆ What recommendations would you make for addressing the problems this teacher seems to have?

Setting   *School* – Junior high school in a multiracial lower- and middle-class community

Subject – General life science (forty-five minutes)

Teacher – Mrs. Barney, a teacher for seven years

Students – Thirty-five seventh-grade students

Topic – Basic Life Processes

Lesson   *Note:* Mrs. Barney had discussed three life processes on the previous day. She now wants to review these briefly and then introduce the remaining five processes. She also wants to assign homework based on all eight life processes.

Time Frame	Dialog
1 to 15	► The students enter the classroom in single file and take their assigned seats. Mrs. Barney moves toward the chalkboard at the front of the room. She quickly glances around to make sure the students are settled before she begins.
	Mrs. B.: Yesterday we began our discussion on the basic life activities. What do I mean when I say "life processes"?
	► There is a large show of hands to answer the question.
	Mrs. B.: Yes, Mark, what does it mean?
	Mark: Well, to be considered alive you have to do them.
	Mrs. B.: Okay, you're on the right track. Anyone else have any ideas?
	► Again, a large show of hands.
	Mrs. B.: Maria, what do you think?
	Maria: We talked about motion yesterday. You said that all living things had to move.
	Mrs. B.: But just move?
	Maria: No, we mentioned a couple of things besides moving.
	Mrs. B.: Can you remember any of the other examples, Maria?
	► Maria shuffles to find the correct page in her notebook. Mrs. Barney looks around and sees a few students wanting to answer.

Time Frame	Dialog	
	Mrs. B.:	Let's get some ideas from someone else. Bobby, what do you think?
	Bobby:	(As he checks his textbook) We went over movement, growth, and nutrition.
	Mrs. B.:	Good, Bobby. Now, what did we say about growth?
	Greg:	(Without raising his hand) When someone gets bigger.
	Mrs. B.:	Greg, raise your hand and I will call on you next time. What did we say about nutrition?
	►	Mrs. Barney calls on a student who is not raising her hand and not paying full attention to the lesson.
	Mrs. B.:	Susie, what did we say nutrition is?
	Susie:	(After hesitating) Eating good foods? I think that's what you said.
	►	Hands start waving back and forth.
	Mark:	(After being called on) No, that's wrong. Nutrition is a big name for a few processes, like getting food and digestion.
15 to 20	►	Mrs. Barney congratulates Mark on his answer and then spends the next few minutes reviewing nutrition.
	Mrs. B.:	Is anyone not clear about this life process? If you're still confused read pages eighty-nine to ninety-seven in your textbook again.
	►	No hands go up.
20 to 26	**Mrs. B.:**	Okay, let's go on to the next one.
	►	Mrs. Barney starts writing on the board and the students start writing the words in their notebooks. Mrs. Barney explains and writes at the same time.
	Mrs. B.:	Number 4 of the life processes is reproduction. (She writes the definition on the board.)
	Nancy:	But Mrs. Barney, my sister can't have kids and I usually consider her to be alive.
	►	There is laughter and conversation throughout the room. It takes a minute to settle down.
	Mrs. B.:	Well, reproduction doesn't have to be on an individual level. It can be on a species level also.
	John:	What does "species" mean?
26 to 30	►	Mrs. Barney takes a few minutes to explain "species."
30 to 38	**Mrs. B.:**	Now, getting back to the life processes. Number 5 is respiration. (She writes the definition on the board.) After reading this definition, who will try to explain the difference between breathing and respiration?
	►	No hands go up. Mrs. Barney picks Maria again.

Time Frame	*Dialog*

                            Maria: (Hesitatingly) Breathing is like using your lungs. Mrs. Barney, I'm still writing down respiration in my notebook so I'm not sure.

                        Mrs. B.:   Come on, people, you have to think.

38 to 45   ►   Mrs. Barney realizes she is running out of time and so she tells the students to look up the rest of the definitions in their books and copy them into their notebooks.

                        Mrs. B.:   Please answer the questions on page fifty-five of the text for homework. These questions are based on the life processes. If you have any more questions, we'll go over them tomorrow.

        Brief   *Key Facts* – List three key facts verbatim that characterize the main positive and/or negative aspects of the lesson.

             Strengths/Weaknesses – Briefly explain how the key facts selected indicate strengths and/or weaknesses in the teacher's performance.

             Recommendations – Briefly describe what the teacher could have done to alleviate or avoid the problems that were seen.

◆ ◆ ◆ ◆ ◆ ◆ ◆

CHAPTER PROJECT   Develop a Complete One-Semester Course of Instruction

        Goals   1. To become familiar with the major aspects of comprehensive curriculum development.
                 2. To carry out continuous, disciplined research in a particular subject area.
                 3. To develop the thinking and decision-making skills needed to progress through the various steps of the curriculum-development process. For example, think about and decide on the scope and sequence of topics to be covered for the entire course and within each element (unit) of the course and the resource materials, information, and ideas to incorporate into the instructional plan.
                 4. To develop confidence and self-sufficiency in the area of curriculum development so that the textbook and other instructional guidelines can be utilized as supplementary materials for the course.

Phases   To carry out each phase of this project it will be necessary to refer to the discussion and examples provided in the "Comprehensive Curriculum-Development Method" section of this chapter.

Planning
1. Select a *course* (one semester) to develop.
2. List *own ideas.*
3. Locate *key guiding materials.*
4. Decide upon *elements.*
5. Delineate *topics.*

Partial Implementation
1. Identify *basic sources.*
2. Locate and list *source reference points.*
3. Take *preliminary notes.*

Full Implementation
1. Review and select preliminary notes.
2. Sequence preliminary notes.
3. Log *final notes.*
4. Develop a *filing system.*
5. For extra credit, outline a classroom planning framework similar to the one in Practical Model 3.1 as a way of utilizing the ideas and material gathered in this project.

◆ ◆ ◆ ◆ ◆ ◆ ◆
REFERENCES

Bloom, B. (Ed.). (1956). *Taxonomy of educational objectives: The classification of educational goals. Handbook I: Cognitive domain.* New York: Longmans, Green.

Clark, L. H., & Starr, I. S. (1986). *Secondary and middle school teaching methods* (5th ed.). New York: Macmillan.

Conant, J. B. (1963). *The education of American teachers.* New York: McGraw-Hill.

Dewey, J. (1929). *The sources of a science of education.* New York: Horace Liveright.

Goodlad, J. I. (1984). *A place called school: Prospects for the future.* New York: McGraw-Hill.

McNeil, J. D. (1985). *Curriculum: A comprehensive introduction* (3rd ed.). Boston: Little, Brown.

Mursell, J. L. (1934). *Principles of education.* New York: W. W. Norton.

Tyler, R. (1950). *Basic principles of curriculum and instruction.* Chicago: University of Chicago Press.

Weinstein, C. E., & Mayer, R. E. (1986). The teaching of learning strategies. In M. C. Wittrock (Ed.), *Handbook of Research on Teaching* (3rd ed.). New York: Macmillan.

◆ ◆ ◆ ◆ ◆ ◆ ◆
ANNOTATED READINGS

Alcorn, M. D., Kinder, J. S., & Schunert, J. R. (1970). *Better teaching in secondary schools* (3rd ed.). New York: Holt, Rinehart and Winston.

A comprehensive text designed to help beginning teachers solve the complex problems of teaching. See Chapters 4, 5, and 6 for discussions of the major aspects of planning.

Bruner, J. S. (1960). *The process of education.* Cambridge, MA: Harvard University Press.

A landmark book on curriculum development focusing not only on coverage but also on the structure of a subject. See Chapter 2 for a discussion on the importance of structure of the subject in developing the curriculum plan.

Cooper, J. M. (Ed.). (1977). *Classroom teaching skills: A workbook.* Lexington, MA: D. C. Heath.

A workbook providing practice in major teaching skill areas through analytical exercises as well as guidelines and suggestions on how these skills may be practiced in microteaching. See Chapter 2 on instructional planning.

Eisner, E. W. (1985). *The educational imagination: On the design and evaluation of school programs.* New York: Macmillan.

Stresses the importance of context in making educational decisions, especially in the area of curriculum development. See Chapter 6 for a discussion of educational aims and objectives and Chapter 7 for a discussion of curriculum planning.

Giroux, H. A., Penna, A. N., & Pinar, W. F. (Eds.). (1981). *Curriculum and instruction: Alternatives in education.* Berkeley, CA: McCuthan.

This book includes a study of the relationship of curriculum theory to practice. See Chapter 3 for an essay relating the structure of disciplines to curriculum development.

Gronlund, N. E. (1971). *Measurement and evaluation in teaching* (2nd ed.). New York: Macmillan.

A thorough introduction to the principles and procedures of evaluation that are essential to good teaching. See Chapter 18 for an examination of the role evaluation plays during the planning stages of teaching.

Heck, S. F., & Williams, C. R. (1984). *The complex roles of the teacher: An ecological perspective.* New York: Teachers College Press.

A book focusing on the dynamic interactive contexts within which teaching and learning take place. See Chapter 8 for an interesting study of the teacher as administrator (focusing on the teacher's role in planning).

Henson, K. T. (1981). *Secondary teaching methods.* Lexington, MA: D. C. Heath.

A basic text in secondary school teaching emphasizing practical applications of the principles of teaching. See Chapters 8, 9, and 10 for discussions on the essential aspects of planning.

Kim, E. C., & Kellough, R. D. (1974). *A resource guide for secondary school teaching: Planning for competence.* New York: Macmillan.

An excellent workbook featuring an organization of basic resource materials designed to improve secondary school teaching. See Part II for a wide array of exercises, discussion questions, and bibliographic references on instructional planning.

Mager, R. F. (1975). *Preparing instructional objectives* (2nd ed.). Belmont, CA: Fearon.

A practice-oriented book aimed at helping teachers in developing instructional objectives that clearly state the intended results of instruction. A procedure for developing instructional objectives is described along with guided practice exercises and opportunities for readers to periodically test their understanding of the material.

McNeil, J. D. (1976). *Designing curriculum: Self-instructional modules.* Boston: Little, Brown.

Four useful modules intended to help the teacher decide what should be taught to particular learners and how to develop the most appropriate learning activities. See Module 3 for excellent pointers and exercises on how to select educational objectives.

Orlich, D. C., Harder, R. J., Callahan, R. C., Kravas, C. H., Kauchak, D. P., Pendergrass, R. A., & Keogh, A. J. (1985). *Teaching strategies: A guide to better instruction* (2nd ed.). Lexington, MA: D. C. Heath.

Presents a broad spectrum of instructional methodologies, techniques, and approaches tailored to the secondary school classroom. See Chapter 2 for a thorough examination of the role objectives play in planning for instruction.

Phenix, P. H. (1964). *Realms of meaning: A philosophy of the curriculum for general education.* New York: McGraw-Hill.

Examines curriculum from a philosophical perspective that sees human nature rooted in and directed toward fulfillment of meaning. See Chapters 21 and 22, respectively, for a discussion of scope and sequence of the curriculum.

Walker, D. F., & Soltis, J. F. (1986). *Curriculum and aims.* New York: Teachers College Press.

Presents basic theoretical approaches to curriculum, emphasizing practical applications within the context of personal, pedagogical, and moral educational issues. See Chapter 4 on procedures for curriculum making.

Whitehead, A. N. (1929). *The aims of education and other essays.* New York: Macmillan.

A book by one of the foremost philosophers of the twentieth century on the purpose of education.

CHAPTER 4
◆ ◆ ◆ ◆ ◆ ◆ ◆

Procuring, Developing, and Using Instructional Resources

INTRODUCTION

A well thought out and organized instructional plan that specifies what students should achieve is the basis for intelligent selection of teaching methods and learning experiences for classroom instruction. Instructional resources are the supportive materials essential for putting these teaching methods and planned learning experiences into practice. In this sense they are the materials and aids for enriching daily classroom lessons.

This chapter will explain how a variety of instructional resources can be effectively incorporated into the classroom instructional plan. The focus is on the teacher's active role in selecting and adapting instructional resources to use in day-to-day classroom activities and on creating materials when appropriate ones are not available.

The principal aspects of instructional resource procurement, development, and use involve identifying existing resources available, reviewing various materials for potential use in the instructional plan, becoming familiar with new and creative uses of various materials, developing and adapting various materials to address student learning needs, and developing an understanding of the interrelationship between teaching method, resource materials, and subject matter as the basis for planning effective learning activities.

BASIC THEORIES

◆ Types and Uses of Instructional Resources

This section will examine the three major categories of instructional resources. The first category, printed materials, includes textbooks, collateral materials (i.e., books, journals, magazines, and newspapers), workbooks, and duplicated materials. The second category, audiovisual materials, includes overhead transparencies, films, filmstrips and slides, video and tape cassettes, chalkboards, bulletin boards, graphic materials (i.e., charts, graphs, posters, maps, and models), and computers. The third category, community resources, includes field trips and resource persons.

Printed Materials

Textbooks, collateral materials, workbooks, and duplicated materials are the major printed materials available to teachers and students.

Textbooks. Textbooks represent the primary instructional resource in this category. Too often the teacher uses the textbook as a substitute for an instructional plan and for knowledge of the subject. In fact, the text should be used only as one of many resources for classroom instruction.

The teacher can use the textbook as an effective resource in four particular ways (Table 4.1):

1. *As a source of ideas for organizing course contents.* Used in this way it serves as one of the key guiding materials called for in the comprehensive curriculum-development method presented in Chapter 3. A good textbook is the culmination of a significant amount of research on a particular subject. Teachers should utilize this considerable research for their instructional planning, but not as a substitute for an instructional plan or their own knowledge of the subject. A narrow view of the subject results when teachers go beyond using the text as a guide and use it as a substitute for their own

TABLE 4.1 *Effective Use of Texts*

USE	DESCRIPTION
To suggest organization of course contents	Use the textbook as one of the key guiding materials called for in comprehensive curriculum development.
To suggest activities, strategies, and questions	Adapt the activities, teaching strategies, and questions suggested in the text to suit students' specific learning needs.
To suggest further readings and related materials	Identify firsthand sources to examine by reviewing the lists of references, readings, and related materials that served as resources to writing the text.
To provide a basic source for student research	Design exercises and assignments requiring students to use the various parts of the text (e.g., index, charts) and to think about (e.g., apply, evaluate) the ideas and information presented in the text.

research and thought. Textbooks should serve primarily as summaries of the material presented by the teacher and of the material found in collateral materials used in conjunction with the course.

2. *As a source of activities, strategies, and questions for enhancing classroom instruction.* In addition to surveying a particular subject, most textbooks suggest classroom activities and teaching strategies for presenting specific material to students. The teacher should keep in mind that these activities, strategies, and questions are based on general principles of the learning process, which may not be applicable to a particular classroom situation. As such, these recommendations are better regarded as general guides to be adapted to students' specific needs in terms of previous learning, varying abilities, and other individual characteristics.

3. *As a source of references, readings, and other materials on the subject.* Because a text represents comprehensive research in a subject area, the teacher can often find in it a list of the many references, readings, and other related materials that served as its resources. Firsthand reading of such references affords the teacher an opportunity to examine the primary sources available on his or her subject. For example, a high school biology teacher preparing instructional material on Darwin's theory of evolution will gain a much better understanding of the theory of evolution by making the effort to read Darwin's *Origin of Species* than by reading a summary of this theory in a biology textbook.

4. *As a basic source for student research.* Because the textbook represents a comprehensive treatment of a particular subject, it can be an excellent source for students to learn fundamental research methods. The teacher should design exercises and assignments requiring students to use the various parts of the textbook (e.g., index, charts, tables, table of contents) and to think about (e.g., apply, evaluate) the ideas and information presented in the textbook.

Using the textbook in these four ways requires an understanding of its contents including the scope, sequence, and quality of treatment for each topic and the organization of headings, subheadings, readings, introductions, summaries, exercises, questions, assignments, projects, and glossaries.

If the teacher relies on the textbook too much, the problem of superficial treatment of the subject will arise. Instead of conducting subject-area research and curriculum development, the teacher adopts the textbook as the instructional plan. The teacher who assigns little importance to firsthand research in his or her subject will find it difficult to present the material with the imagination and enthusiasm needed to interest students in the subject. Some schools or departments require strict adherence to the textbook. An example is the high school history department that bases all its courses of instruction and related assessment instruments on the material contained in a specific series of textbooks. Practical Model 2.1, "A Vertical/ Continuous Learning Plan" (Figure 2.7), demonstrates how a teacher in such a situation may incorporate original ideas and research to enhance textual material.

Overreliance on textbooks also affects student learning, in that textbooks provide little opportunity to use critical thinking skills. Because they typically present information and ideas that have already been thought out and organized, textbooks assist mainly with the perceptual aspect of cognitive development. They do not encourage or lead the learner to use reasoning faculties (conception) or to creatively form ideas (ideation). In addition, they provide no scope for exercising the conative aspect of consciousness in terms of action in and upon the environment and only minimal scope for developing the affective area of consciousness. Textbooks, therefore, cannot address all student needs for learning and growth. They must never be used as the primary source of planning and carrying out instruction but rather as a useful resource to draw upon.

The way teachers can overcome the limitations of textbooks is to rely less exclusively on them. The text should be only one among many resources used to develop the instructional plan.

Below, several ways to avoid weaknesses of the text are suggested:

1. Become really familiar with the textbook before you use it.
2. Use the textbook in your planning as a source of structure if it seems desirable to do so, but do not let yourself become chained to the book.
3. Use the text as only one of many materials and activities. Use other readings, simulation, role playing, discussion, films, and pictures.
4. Use problem-solving approaches in which the text is but one source of data.

5. Use only those parts of the book that seem good to you; skip the other parts; rearrange the order of topics if you think it desirable. In other words, adapt the text to your pupils and their needs.
6. Use additional or substitute readings to allow for differences in pupils.
7. Provide help for pupils who do not read well.
8. Teach pupils how to study the text and to use the parts of the text, such as table of contents, index, headings, charts, graphs, and illustrations.
9. Use the illustrations, charts, graphs, and other aids included in the textbook in your teaching. Build lessons around them; study them.
10. Encourage critical reading. Compare the text to source materials and other texts. Test it for logic and bias.
11. Teach vocabulary.
12. Incorporate the textbook into a multiple-text teaching strategy. (Callahan & Clark, 1982, p. 391)

Selecting an appropriate textbook is one of the teacher's most important decisions. Before an informed selection can be made, the teacher must have a clear idea of both the topics to be covered and the objectives to be reached in the course. Obviously, the best textbook would be the one containing the largest number of satisfactory treatments of the largest proportion of subject topics. Unfortunately, teachers rarely devote the time needed to select a text.

In brief, the process of selecting a textbook should include a comparison of the scope and sequence of material presented, a comparison of the major features (e.g., exercises, projects) and formats (e.g., graphics, introductions/ summaries) used, and an assessment of how the material and major features and formats address student needs and readiness for learning. In Figure 4.1 a guide for selecting a text is presented.

Because students often do not know how to use their textbooks intelligently, the teacher should plan early in the year to give them instruction and practice in the proper use of the textbook. The time set aside to introduce students to the textbook is time well spent, because the textbook may be the one source they take home that will clarify and reinforce information presented in the classroom. As follow-up to instruction in textbook use, the teacher must design lessons and assignments to encourage students to use the textbook correctly. The teacher should demonstrate the use of the textbook, of the table of contents, index, glossary, and bibliography sections and, depending on the nature of the course, also instruct them in the use of charts, tables, graphs, and maps.

To render such instructions more than idle information soon forgotten, students should receive a text assignment requiring them to apply what they have learned about using the textbook. For example, an American History teacher can divide students into several groups of five and have each group briefly research "The Meaning of Democracy" and write a short report on their findings. Each group could receive a guide sheet listing

FIGURE 4.1 *Guide for Selecting a Textbook*

CHECKING OBJECTIVES AGAINST CRITERIA FOR TEXTS

Objectives of a Course						Desired Content and Form of Text Materials
IA	IB	IIA	IIB	IIC	IIIA	
X	X		X			Adequacy of topic coverage
X	X	X	X		X	Biographical information
X	X	X	X		X	Quality of writing
X	X	X		X		Correlation with other subjects
						Sequence of subject matter within a grade determined by
X	X	X	X		X	a. Circumstances of pupils' needs and interests (i.e., provision made for flexibility)
X		X				b. Progress from grade to grade and within grade
X		X			X	c. According to differences in pupils' needs
	X		X		X	Effective utilization of pupils' experiences—material introduced through situations familiar to the children
X	X	X	X	X	X	Course of study so organized as to provide for individual differences in ability, interest, and so on
X		X		X	X	Arrangement and gradation of material according to difficulty (i.e., within grade)
X		X			X	Suggested use of varied forms of activities, projects, and so on, such as dramatization, debate, and so forth
	X		X	X		Respect for the judgment and initiative of the teacher with provision for flexibility of arrangement so as to give the teacher some choice as to subject matter, method, and so on
	X		X			Helpful suggestions and directions for making oral reading effective (i.e., audience reading)
			X			Suggestions for directing and testing pupils' silent reading abilities and habits
X			X		X	Suggested standards for checking results of teaching (knowledge tests, indications of attitude formation, habits of study, and so on)
X		X	X	X	X	Use made of scientific studies in determining methods and materials
X		X	X		X	References, basic and supplemental, for pupils' use
X		X	X	X	X	References to experiments, magazines, and books treating of theory and method—teachers' references

Source: Based on material from *Research Methods and Teachers' Problems: A Manual for Systematic Studies of Classroom Procedures* (pp. 170–171) by D. Waples and R. W. Tyler, 1930, New York: Macmillan.

important events, major personalities, and key terms related to the development of democracy in the United States. Such an assignment requires research beyond one particular section of the text. Thus students will find it necessary to use the table of contents and index to locate information about the listed important events and key personalities, and they will need to look up key terms in the glossary. Making this assignment a group activity encourages students to share ideas about using the textbook and allows the teacher to spend time assisting each group. The assignment can also be used to train students in note-taking methods, organizational skills, and the decision-making process.

Although mindful use of a textbook will provide the teacher and students with a valuable instructional resource, it cannot and should not replace the teacher as the principal source of information and ideas. The responsibility for presenting ideas clearly resides with the teacher, not with the textbook. The teacher's task, then, is to take the relatively abstract ideas and information in the textbook and make them clear and alive to students through creative and interesting illustrations and activities.

Collateral Materials. Collateral materials such as encyclopedias, dictionaries, atlases, world almanacs, journals, magazines, newspapers, and books are excellent for enriching curriculum and enhancing classroom instructional activities. These materials should serve as the teacher's main resource for subject-area research and subsequent curriculum planning. Gathering basic sources, as called for in the comprehensive curriculum-development method presented in Chapter 3, represents an effective use of collateral materials.

Collateral materials suggested by the teacher are also particularly beneficial to students, encouraging them to explore ideas or topics from many viewpoints and to delve into the subject as a scholar rather than as a casual, disinterested learner. Examining original sources for firsthand information is always more invigorating than reading someone else's digested version of the material. When investigating a variety of sources, students attain control over their own learning process and a sense of responsibility for their work. The teacher who fosters such efforts will achieve increased student interest in and understanding of the subject. Heck and Williams describe how a particular collateral material, the daily newspaper, can be effectively used:

> The daily newspaper is an excellent means for applying problem-solving skills to local, state, national, and international problems. Environmental, cultural, social, and technological issues can be studied in terms of their problem-solving implications. . . . The problem-solving skills of describing, comparing, contrasting, analyzing, and evaluating [i.e., the six levels of understanding defined by Bloom in his taxonomy of objectives in the cognitive domain] can be reinforced by debating controversial dilemmas such as the need for nuclear energy versus the hazards of waste disposal, the economy of strip-mining of coal versus preservation of our natural landscape,

and the demand for lower school taxes versus the high cost of good education. (1984, p. 80)

Assignments that require research in a variety of collateral materials are an excellent way to help students develop proficient study habits like those listed in Figure 2.5. One such assignment for a tenth-grade biology class is to have students investigate the medicinal uses of vitamin C by reviewing portions of selected journal and newspaper articles and books on the subject. To assure disciplined research, a study guide that enumerates the basic steps required by the assignment and includes a list of recommended sources with related research questions and a glossary of key terms should be handed out. It should be made clear to students that successful completion of the assignment requires study with a particular aim in mind, the organized recording of information, correlation of previously learned facts to newly discovered ones, and thinking of possible applications of the ideas reviewed.

Workbooks. Workbooks are a valuable addition to classroom instruction. They afford students drill in specific skill areas, problems to solve, pertinent questions to answer, self-assessment quizzes to take, and vocabulary words to learn.

> In subjects which possess a basic structure the worksheet [workbook] can show the way. In certain cases they can provide a prop for the child who has been absent or works at a totally different pace from the rest of the class. Particular skills like using the library, or working a tape recorder, can often be communicated efficiently through the worksheets. (North, 1976, p. 69)

Some helpful features of workbooks include:

♦ Exercises that supplement material presented in the textbook and in classroom lessons, through review exercises that reinforce learning and through questions that require students to apply what they have learned
♦ Practice in working independently, during which time students can pace themselves while the teacher can provide for individual differences among them
♦ A change of pace from large-group activities
♦ An opportunity to create or adapt materials compatible with classroom instruction

A chief benefit of workbooks is the time they give the teacher to help individual students. Time thus spent is precious, because an individual student's learning needs, misunderstandings, inabilities, and unique ways of thinking often become clear to the teacher in a one-to-one session. Additionally, the student experiences the teacher's personal interest in his or her academic progress.

Workbook exercises often fail to facilitate either individualized instruction or learning.

> Where even the best written worksheets so often fail is in their extreme itemization and codification of complex phenomena. Many, I regret to say, are not well written. Apart from the typographical atrocities they inflict upon the eye, they often contain vocabulary, language structures and conceptual frameworks which are beyond the understanding of their readers. (North, 1976, pp. 69–70)

Perhaps the most negative effect worksheets can have on learning is their tendency to convey to students a conception that learning is mechanical, requiring little use of the imagination. Teachers should address this shortcoming by creating original worksheets that are not only relevant to classroom instruction but that require the use of conceptual and ideational faculties as well.

The following uses of workbooks should be avoided if at all possible to maintain the effectiveness and integrity of the instructional program:

♦ Using the workbook for busy work where students mechanically follow a set of directions, requiring minimal thought and originality
♦ Using workbook exercises that focus on material unrelated to textbooks or the course curriculum

The teacher also has to consider what to do once the students have completed their workbook assignments.

> As with anything else, assignments in workbooks and locally produced materials must be followed up. . . . In no case should you leave the workbook work completely unchecked until you can find a propitious moment at some later time to collect and correct it. (Clark & Starr, 1986, p. 412)

Effective review of workbook assignments can be accomplished by working through all, or at least selected, problems in class with allowance for discussion of the work, or through supervised small-group activities where students help each other work through and understand the material with the guidance of the teacher.

The most effective workbooks are those developed by the teacher because they can be tailored to the course material and to student learning needs. (See Figure 4.2 for a description of an originally developed workbook used for a high school science course.) Such workbooks represent the teacher's active involvement in curriculum development.

Duplicated Materials. Duplicated materials include supplementary readings, exercises, assignments, vocabulary lists, and study guides. From the discussions above it is apparent that all types of printed materials can be duplicated to serve these purposes. One particularly effective use of

FIGURE 4.2 *Student Handbook for a Unit on the Scientific Method*

INTRODUCTION

The purpose of this booklet is to accompany prepared lesson plans when teaching students about the scientific method. The booklet can be used as a master for the teacher and copies can be made of the activities to be used as supplements, or the booklet can be copied and distributed to each student and used as the lesson plan permits. The graphics (some cartoon clippings, some computer printouts) have been used to make the booklet attractive and interesting to students.

The activities included are from an array of alternative sources. Some of the activities, such as the optical illusions, come from standard psychology texts. Other activities, dealing with magic tricks, are rewritten from books on that subject.

The booklet also has photocopied segments from textbooks and various collated materials on the scientific method. This section of the booklet could easily be modified by inserting materials from other sources and at other levels as the teacher deems necessary.

Overall, preparing a student handbook such as this to accompany lesson plans is very profitable and provides the opportunity to have well thought out activities for students to carry out and relevant information to enhance students' understanding of the subject.

TABLE OF CONTENTS

duplicated materials is the resource packet. A resource packet is a compendium of information culled from various sources and could include quotations, diagrams, figures, and suggested activities. There are three principal criteria in selecting material for the resource packet:

1. It should represent the most interesting and enlightening information on the subject.
2. It should help organize the students' approach to learning the many elements of the subject.
3. It should correspond with the classroom instructional plan.

The resource packet should serve as a potent resource for the teacher and as a trusty course guide for students. An example of a resource packet used for a unit of a high school science course is presented in Figure 4.2.

Because of the growing use of duplicated materials, teachers need to become familiar with duplicating processes available in their school. Photocopying (xeroxing), mimeographing, and thermofaxing are the three duplicating processes most often used. Each process has both advantages and limitations depending on the nature and quantity of material needing duplication. Instructions for using these duplicating processes are listed in Table 4.2.

Audiovisual Materials

Chapter 2 emphasized the crucial role of attention in the learning process. Anything that increases student attention to instruction can be considered a boon to the teacher. Audiovisual materials, which send stimuli to several senses simultaneously, are very effective for gaining student attention.

> For most students audiovisual materials seem immediate, authentic, and involving. For certain types of learners—language-handicapped, ear-oriented, visual-oriented, deaf or nonreaders—audiovisual materials can convey information far more effectively than print materials. For the general run of students, these materials may be most valuable for effective education. (Woodbury, 1978, p. 34)

The principal audiovisual materials used for classroom instruction are overhead transparencies, films, filmstrips and slides, video and tape cassettes, chalkboards, bulletin boards, graphic materials, and computers.

Overhead Transparencies. The overhead projector is second only to the chalkboard as the most used audiovisual aid. It functions on a simple optical system consisting of four main parts: the light source, the stage, the projector head, and the transparency to be projected. Light emanating from a powerful bulb carries the image depicted on a transparency up to the projector head. The projector head is, in fact, a lens positioned to deflect

TABLE 4.2 *Instructions for Using Three Major Duplicating Processes*

PROCESS	CHARACTERISTICS	STEPS TO FOLLOW	SUGGESTIONS FOR USE
Photocopying (xeroxing)	Automatic, rapid copying Simple to control (dial settings and paper loading) Collating often available Copies letter- and legal-size paper Copying through photographing	1. Lift document cover and place original face down. 2. Close the cover and set dial to number of copies desired. 3. Press start button (watch controls for indication of problems in the system).	1. Remove staples and paper clips before copying. 2. Check originals for irregularities (e.g., dark copy, off size, or tissue-thin paper, bent or torn originals). 3. Run one copy first when making many copies of a document to ascertain best copying position. 4. Learn how to deal with problems (i.e., loading paper, clearing stuck paper, stopping printing). 5. Learn how to use special features (i.e., collating, printing on two sides, adjusting for light and dark originals).
Mimeographing	Automatic, rapid copying Consists of four main elements: stencil, ink, paper, and mimeograph machine Stencils are handwritten, typed, drawn, or electronically produced Duplicates letter- and legal-size paper Copying through ink printing	1. Prepare stencil appropriately according to method used (i.e., handwritten, typed, drawn, electronically produced). 2. Check ink supply. 3. Clamp stencil face down to revolving drum with the backing sheet face up. 4. Tear off backing sheet and clamp lower portion of stencil to drum. 5. Load paper supply by adjusting paper feeder and make the run.	*Typing Stencils* 1. Shift typing ribbon so keys strike stencil directly (if no stencil setting, remove ribbon). 2. Place a cushion sheet between stencil and backing sheet with wax stencil side face up. 3. Align stencil and set margins within markings printed on stencil face. 4. Apply correction fluid to make corrections.

Thermofaxing

Automatic, rapid copying

Consists of three main elements: heat stencil, thermagraph machine, mimeograph machine

Inexpensive method for making multiple copies of charts, drawings, articles, and complex illustrations

Copying through imprinting and ink printing

1. Place material to be copied face up between the backing and carbon sheets of the spirit master.

2. Remove the slip (protective) sheet.

3. Insert the prepared stencil into the thermagraph machine (in a few seconds the heat will cause a transfer of carbon to the master).

4. Carefully peel the master from the carbon sheet.

5. Attach the now imprinted master to the mimeograph machine.

6. Set the mimeograph machine and run the copies.

1. Make sure original material that is to be copied is clearly printed (preferably in dark black print).

2. Become familiar with the lightness and darkness settings on the thermagraph machine. This is the key to producing masters that will copy well.

3. Place used masters in a folder, face down on the smooth slip sheet for future use.

Running Stencils

1. Run a few trial copies to check for quality.

2. Stay near machine to fix paper jams or add ink when necessary.

3. Remove stencil and place in a folder for future use.

the image on the transparency to the screen, and the image is focused either by moving the lens toward or away from the screen or by changing the distance of the projector head from the transparency.

The overhead projector has several advantages. It saves time. The entire process of positioning the transparency, switching on the machine, and focusing the image takes less than twenty seconds. Whereas using a chalkboard takes up class time as the teacher writes lists or diagrams on the board, transparencies can be prepared in advance and presented to the class without interrupting instruction. However, if the teacher so chooses, transparency material can be created during the lesson, with students contributing at appropriate points. Unlike movie or filmstrip projectors, the overhead projector, with its powerful light source and close-to-screen projection, can be used in a lighted room, permitting students to take notes without difficulty. The main advantage of the overhead projector is that it allows the teacher to face the class as material is presented. The importance of maintaining eye contact with students cannot be minimized. Many control and motivation problems spring from the teacher's failure to establish eye contact and other manifestations of direct involvement with students. In addition, facing the class provides more opportunities to observe the students and thus stay attuned to their needs.

The teacher may encounter some problems when using the overhead projector. Because classrooms often have low ceilings, teachers sometimes find it difficult to focus the image at normal eye level. This problem can usually be avoided by orienting transparencies horizontally rather than vertically. Another advantage of using the horizontal format is that it lessens the incidence of the "keystoning effect," a distortion of the projected image in which it appears wider at the top than at the bottom. The following is a set of guidelines to help teachers avoid additional problems when using the overhead projector:

1. Use a good transparency pencil or transparency pen (not an ordinary felt pen).
2. Check the best position in the classroom for projection so that all students can see the projection clearly.
3. Face students when speaking to them (you don't have to turn around every time as you would do when using the chalkboard).
4. Any transparent models or objects such as plastic rulers, protractors, ripple tanks, and test tubes can be projected vividly.
5. Tracing charts or drawings on construction paper or on the chalkboard can be easily done by simply projecting the original transparency.
6. When you do not want to show the entire transparency, cover up the portion of the contents with paper (masking tape).
7. When you want to add or correlate the contents simultaneously, simply add on another transparency, in what is known as an overlay technique. (Henson, 1981, p. 127)

Overhead transparencies are particularly effective at the beginning of a class session. The teacher can routinely display important information not available in the textbook for the students to copy as attendance and other business are taken care of. Later in the lesson, the transparency can be shown again as information is explained in depth. Such use of overhead transparencies creates an opening activity to focus student attention, a way of upgrading the content and organization of student notebooks, the convenience of increased chalkboard availability, and time to take attendance.

Films. Through films students are exposed to a galaxy of people, events, processes, and experiences they might never otherwise see. Further, films can be used to address and overcome learning problems by permitting perception and understanding of many objects, processes, and actions not observable under normal visual conditions through a variety of techniques. These techniques include animation, slow- and stop-motion, photomicrography (i.e., making microscopic objects visible), and telescopic photography (i.e., bringing distant objects near).

In addition, films can include numerous special effects including "montages, flashbacks, fades, cuts, close-ups, quick and slow pans, and dissolves to enhance meaning and build interest" (Brown, Lewis, & Harcleroad, 1983, p. 241). For example, students with poor reading skills can benefit significantly from viewing films that entice them to explore the world of words and ideas, what has been so captivatingly presented on the screen, thus fostering understanding of course-related material and an interest in developing reading skills.

To derive maximum benefit from films the teacher should follow these eight basic guidelines:

1. Select films directly related to classroom instruction. A film may be entertaining, but it should not serve as a diversion, irrelevant to classroom instruction.
2. Preview the film to ascertain its quality and contents instead of selecting a film based on the title alone.
3. Determine the instructional aim of the film and how this aim specifically relates to the instructional plan. This formulated aim should be expressed to the students before the film is shown. A focused instructional aim results in optimal learning, whereas an overly generalized or broad aim minimizes learning.
4. Prepare the students for the film by holding discussions guided by the instructional aim. Distribute study guides and a glossary of terms to focus student attention on the salient features of the film and to help them grasp its meaning.
5. Check all viewing equipment ahead of time so that preparation time is not wasted if the projector is found to be defective.
6. Prepare for the actual running of the film. Make sure that the room is sufficiently darkened and that the screen is situated so that all students can see the film clearly. In addition, the teacher should sit where all the students can easily be seen.

7. Plan follow-up activities to the film. Learning derived from the film is reinforced by brief written or oral assignments and reports and discussions, or by reading reference materials pertaining to the film (e.g., books, magazines, maps, atlases). On occasion, a second showing may help clear up misunderstandings or help give a deeper understanding of the film.
8. Evaluate the effectiveness of the film. Quizzes, worksheets, and question-and-answer sessions are the best ways to assess what students have learned from the film. Additionally, such activities make students aware of their accountability for the material in the film.

Filmstrips and Slides.   The filmstrip is essentially an elaboration of the slide. A slide is made of a two-by-two inch piece of 35-millimeter photographic film on a glass, plastic, or cardboard mount. In the filmstrip these individual frames are joined together in a series on one strip of the same 35-millimeter film. Because of their similarity it is often possible to show filmstrips and slides on the same machine. However, the difference between the two must be considered to determine which one is more appropriate for a given learning activity and situation.

> The filmstrip has the advantage of having been put together by an expert in a ready-made sequence. Slides are more versatile, but using them requires more careful planning by the teacher. Just one slide out of order or upside down can throw a well-conceived lesson out of step. (Clark & Starr, 1986, p. 406)

There are three kinds of slides and filmstrips: those with recorded commentary and sound effects, those with captions, and those projecting the images alone (i.e., plain slides and filmstrips). When using plain slides and filmstrips the teacher has to take complete responsibility for a major part of the presentation—the commentary. Although the meaning of some frames may be self-evident, most require explanation to be fully understood. The teacher, therefore, needs to review the slides or filmstrip carefully to determine what remarks to make during presentation. For efficiency, an original commentary and sound effects can be prerecorded, synchronized to the sequence of slides or filmstrip frames to be shown. An alternative to making such a prerecording is to narrate extemporaneously or from a brief outline as the presentation is made. This method works, however, only when the teacher is fully acquainted with the slides or filmstrip.

In general, the eight principles for showing a film apply equally to showing filmstrips or slides. In addition, the following rules should be applied when showing filmstrips or slides:

♦ Locate the beginning and ending frame to avoid projecting a reversed or inverted image. Often there is a title frame at the beginning and a frame that says "The End."

- Face the screen and hold the first frame up so that it appears upside down and reads right to left. Inserting the filmstrip this way ensures correct projection.
- Take special care not to damage the sprocket holes on the filmstrip. These holes have to join with the sprocket teeth to advance the filmstrip.
- Prepare either a prerecorded commentary or notes to guide a commentary for slide and plain filmstrip presentations.
- Assign a number and title to each slide and frame in case one or more is to be deleted. Do this for slides, particularly, to assure the intended order of loading for presentation.
- Encourage interest and thought during viewing by asking questions or requesting comments about various frames. For practice in writing, students can record their answers or comments in a few brief sentences.
- Integrate other instructional resources (e.g., maps, charts, worksheets) with the presentation to maximize learning.

Although teacher discretion over the sequence of presentation is usually associated with slide presentations, the same can be accomplished with filmstrips by rearranging the sequence of frames.

> It is possible, with very little trouble, to skip ahead or to review earlier frames without showing any of the intervening ones. When skipping frames, place your hand in front of the lens and count frame clicks. When you reach the desired frame, quickly withdraw your hand to project the image. Practice a few times to improve your skill in synchronizing the movement involved. (Brown et al., 1983, pp. 201–202)

Simplicity of operation and portability make slide and filmstrip projectors effective for individual or small-group study. Often schools have media centers for this purpose. Without much difficulty, however, the teacher can set up screening carrels in the back of the classroom for such viewing. Individual or group work with slides and filmstrips can be used for remedial practice, enrichment study, report preparation, or to guide book reading. Guidelines must be established and clearly communicated to students to ensure proper use of equipment and study time.

Video and Tape Cassettes. Videocassettes can perform all the same functions as films in classroom instruction. The difference between the two is technological, with the videocassette allowing greater flexibility. For example, a high school physics teacher showing a videocassette of an experiment illustrating Bernoulli's principle can easily rewind or fast-forward to clarify particularly complex points. Videocassettes are very easy to use and less expensive than films. Now that videocassette recorders and cameras are standard equipment in schools, it is possible to plan a variety of interesting productions to enrich the instructional program. For example, students' oral reports can be videotaped, enabling them to get a rare and objective view of their performance. Because television (i.e., the screen from which video images emanate) is such a powerful and clear medium of communication, classroom video productions allow students to recognize their problems and strengths where even prolonged explanations fail. Besides providing students with a glimpse of themselves, classroom-produced videos involve active learning in terms of the planning, taping, and viewing phases of production.

In addition, a classroom videocassette library can be established containing commercial, educational, and class-produced videos as well as selected teacher lessons and demonstrations. All these videocassettes can be used effectively for whole-class or individualized learning activities. Also, because most students have videotape machines at home, videocassettes can be taken home and parents can be encouraged to join their children in viewing, thus creating a unique and valuable learning experience.

The limitation of video presentations is that the projected image is only as large as a television screen. Although excellent for individual or small-group viewing, it is often too small for a full class. Figure 4.3 outlines recommendations for using the video recorder.

The cassette tape recorder, among instructional resources available to the teacher, is probably the most familiar to students. It can be used in two ways: (1) to prerecord material that would ordinarily be presented live to the students, and (2) to provide audio materials for independent, self-paced study away from the teacher or classroom.

Examples of the first use are prerecorded filmstrip and slide-show commentaries, quizzes, and drills. Examples of the second are recorded exercises that accompany worksheets or flash cards; audio versions of reading material; study guides that summarize and define the key concepts and terms of a particular topic; directions for a project; and recordings of classroom discussions, comments on teaching materials, and student responses to questions.

The teacher can set up a cassette audio center in the classroom by setting aside an area and equipping it with tape recorders and earphones and by collecting an assortment of tapes and related instructional materials.

The best use of the cassette tape recorder is for independent study, because it allows for self-paced study and bypasses students' learning disabilities. Students can review or skip material at will by merely pressing the rewind or fast-forward control. Reading a book while listening to an audio version of it teaches correct inflection, phrasing, and pronunciation, helping students to better grasp the meaning of the material.

Chalkboards. The chalkboard, the most valuable instructional resource available to the teacher, is rarely used to its full advantage. The teacher should become familiar with all possible uses of the chalkboard to increase the success of classroom instruction. Alcorn, Kinder, and Schunert list several of these values:

1. It is both a group and an individual device.
2. It fits the tempo of any presentation.

FIGURE 4.3 *Using the Video Recorder*

  I. Advantages of the video recorder
   A. Portability
      1. Can be shown anywhere
      2. Small, lightweight
      3. Very easy to hook up
   B. Easy to use
      1. Push-button operation
         a. stop; start
         b. play; record
   C. Availability
      1. Video rental centers in most communities
      2. Almost all films now come in videotape
      3. Numerous educational videotapes available
   D. Technologically advanced
      1. Excellent detail of audio and video
      2. Special effects
         a. freeze frame
         b. step-by-step operation
 II. How to use VCRs in the classroom
   A. Hook up
      1. TV antenna to RF out on VCR
      2. Tune to "signal channel" on TV
   B. Common classroom use
      1. Insert tape
      2. Push play
      3. Rewind as desired
      4. Remove tape without rewinding (if tape to be continued)
      5. Use counter to find place on tape for use from period to period
III. Special uses of the video recorder
   A. Recording directly from television
      1. Tune to channel broadcasting program to be recorded
      2. Check start and stop time
      3. Program the video recorder to start and stop automatically
   B. Recording off camera
      1. Prerecording lectures and labs
      2. Recording student presentations
   C. Audio video dubbing
   D. Special effects
      1. Slow motion
      2. Freeze frame

---

   3. No special talent is required for its use.
   4. Teachers of practically all subject content as well as all grade levels use chalkboards.
   5. Pupils' errors can be quickly and easily corrected for all to see.
   6. It is possibly the cheapest of all instructional materials.
   7. The chalkboard encourages note-taking.

8. Neatness, orderliness, and graphic skills add new values.
9. Where certain forms or designs are used repeatedly, as in music [the staff], stenography, bookkeeping, logarithms, and the like, permanent rulings save time. (1970, p. 269)

The teacher should not be fooled by the simplicity of the chalkboard. Its optimal use requires thoughtful preparation. The teacher needs to plan ahead of time how the board will be used during the lesson. Specific notes to be copied by the students should be determined before the lesson and put neatly on the board as those ideas are discussed. Other information and supplementary material should be placed on the board beforehand for ready reference during the lesson. Few things break the rhythm of a lesson as does the teacher turning away from the students for several minutes and writing on the board. The following principles should be followed if the chalkboard is to be used effectively:

♦ Designate each area of the chalkboard for a specific purpose. For example, have one area for homework assignments, one for daily notes, one for vocabulary words, and one for special announcements. This helps organize the teacher's use of the board and the students' attention to where information will appear on the board.

♦ Use the chalkboard to conduct a seminar-style class in which individual students put their work on the board as the teacher and fellow students comment. Among the oldest and most efficient teaching techniques, this helps students realize that they can learn as much from others' work as from their own. In addition, having to work in front of the class helps students develop speaking skills and self-confidence.

♦ Board notes that are clear and visually appealing naturally attract student attention. For clarity, write legibly and avoid clutter. For visual appeal, vary the size of letters and use underlining, boxes, and simple diagrams. In addition, rotating the chalk while writing keeps line width uniform.

♦ Face the class and use a pointer when referring to information on the board. Standing at a forty-five degree angle to the board, it is possible both to use the pointer and to maintain eye contact with students. Because the pointer directs students' eyes back and forth between the teacher and the board, it helps focus their attention on the material discussed.

Bulletin Boards. The bulletin board visually enhances instruction and adds to the attractiveness of the classroom environment. To make the bulletin board an effective and motivating means of communication the following guidelines should be taken into account:

♦ Place bulletin boards so they are visible to all students.
♦ To enliven bulletin boards, use dynamic layouts, color schemes, and

bold titles and captions to broadcast the theme of the display. Always frame bulletin boards for a neat, finished appearance.

♦ Decide on the purpose for each bulletin board. For example, some displays can present ideas or information related to a particular course topic; others can present illustrations and graphic materials (i.e., charts, graphs); and others can present exemplary student work, such as reports, letters, and quizzes.

♦ Involve students in the planning and construction of bulletin board displays. This teaches them to work cooperatively and fosters interest in the topic being studied.

Most classrooms come equipped with the usual wood-fiber wall board, felt, or cork bulletin boards. Where bulletin board space is insufficient, five devices can be used to create or increase the existing space:

1. *Easel-type boards.* Movable easels (with either fixed or folding legs, as desired) multiply classroom display opportunities.
2. *Corrugated paper.* Display materials can be attached to corrugated board, which is available in a variety of colors, textures, and sizes and will stand on a low shelf or cabinet or hang over unused chalkboard or wall space.
3. *Room dividers.* By assembling panels on stand legs, you can make a bulletin board that implements room arrangement for work areas and also provides two-sided displays.
4. *Temporary bulletin boards.* A Celotex or wood-fiber panel set on the chalk tray or hung on the map rail or frame adds extra display space. Wallboard or similar panels may be painted, sprayed, or covered with paper.
5. *Pegboard.* Excellent display boards result from mounting pegboard panels wherever a suitable surface is available. Commercial hooks or homemade devices can be used to fasten materials. (Brown et al., 1973, p. 73)

Graphic Materials. The most common graphic materials in the classroom are charts, posters, graphs, and maps and globes. With graphic materials, as with the chalkboard and bulletin board, the cardinal rule in the selection of materials is the relevance of the material to classroom instruction. Instructions on the use of graphic materials are listed in Table 4.3.

Computers. Computers, especially microcomputers because of their relatively small size, are the most technologically advanced instructional resource available. Being a two-way communication medium, they are among the most captivating of instructional aids. While books, films, and cassette tapes provide a wealth of information, they cannot respond to the user. The computer, by contrast, as an interactive medium, can provide students with immediate feedback on their performance. Multifaceted and interactive as the computer may be, its effective use requires as much planning and forethought as a field trip or a slide presentation.

TABLE 4.3 *Using Graphic Materials*

GRAPHIC MATERIAL	TYPES	RECOMMENDATIONS FOR USE
Charts	Flow charts depict sequences of events or work relationships and responsibilities. Tabular charts depict lists of items in sequential order for chronological comparisons. Experience charts consist of stories, behavior standards, health principles, and class plans. Flip charts consist of sheets that can be flipped over to reveal new material.	Make certain the language and symbols used are fully understood by students. Emphasize one main idea clearly for each chart. Use words the students understand and leave sufficient space between letters and words to assure readability. Use overlays (thin transparent sheets covering the chart) to increase student participation by allowing them to add information without damaging the chart.
Posters	Student- and teacher-made posters are developed in conjunction with course topics, current issues, or school activities. Commercially produced posters are useful for decorating the classroom and for supplementing the instructional program (i.e., posters providing specific subject-area information). Solid, pasted, and laminated paperboards are the types commonly used for posters.	Design posters so they capture attention immediately and communicate their messages quickly. Make posters attractive so they enhance the classroom environment. Change or update posters periodically so they remain relevant.
Graphs	Circle or pie graphs are used to show how parts relate to the whole. Bar graphs are used to show comparisons of similar entities as they are affected by common elements over time. They are particularly useful for comparing large amounts of information. Line graphs, also known as two-scale graphs (i.e., horizontal and vertical scales), are used for showing time and amount relationships. Information on one scale has a corresponding value on the other scale.	Use graphs to depict quantitative and qualitative relationships. Use graphs to give meaning to large amounts of complex information. Make symbols used self-explanatory. Keep the design used and display of information clear and simple.

TABLE 4.3 *Continued*

GRAPHIC MATERIAL	TYPES	RECOMMENDATIONS FOR USE
Maps and globes	Chalkboard outline maps clearly depict a wide variety of information and are best used for group instruction.	Determine each student's ability to read maps before assigning individualized work with such material.
	Atlases are flat maps usually found in book form and best used for individual study.	Explain how the markings and symbols on different types of maps and globes are to be interpreted.
	Outline maps allow students to record and fill in various kinds of data.	Use maps and globes in conjunction with other materials such as pictures, slides, or films.
	Globes are portable and useful for showing relationships in location and surface features.	Store maps and globes so they are easily accessible and ready for use.

> First, certain global or strategic decisions must be made—what is to be communicated, to whom (that is, what is the audience's background), and how (what sequence of ideas is to be presented, what actions are to be solicited). From this global point of view, planning a computer-based presentation differs little from planning a speech, an article, a film, or a personal tutoring session. (Nievergelt, Ventura, & Hinterberger, 1986, p. 22)

An understanding of the fundamentals of computer technology, however, is necessary before attempting to incorporate computers into the instructional plan.

The two main aspects of computer technology are hardware and software. Hardware refers to the equipment and its capabilities (e.g., display of text and graphics, disk drive set-up, printer accommodations) and its compatibility with various programs (i.e., software). The piece of the hardware most important to instruction is the display. "If the quality of display is poor, or if response time to trivial tasks is too long, the rational user will decide to study the same material more efficiently through another medium" (Nievergelt et al., 1986, p. 64). In addition to being clear and easy to read, displayed instructions should be simple to follow.

Computer software, also known as computer programs, are the types of disks and cartridges that adapt the hardware to instructional use. Below is a list of some types of software available:

- Utility software, which functions as a tool for recordkeeping, allows for the creation of materials (e.g., spreadsheets, data bases) for use in any subject area.
- Tutorial software, which leads students through the steps of a learning sequence, is available for a variety of subjects.

◆ Drill and practice software reinforces particular skills through exercises or problems.
◆ Problem-solving software requires students to reason logically and improve their skills in analysis and evaluation.
◆ Simulation software presents real-life situations to analyze, evaluate, and respond to.
◆ Word-processing software allows students to create and edit written material.

Because each type of software is best suited for a particular purpose, determining which type to use and when requires careful planning. Matching types of software to course topics and objectives is the most organized method of selection (Table 4.4).

Each piece of software selected requires firsthand examination to ascertain its quality and usefulness for classroom instruction. The teacher should ask the following questions when selecting software:

1. Does the program mesh with your content and teaching approaches? Does it aim at important objectives? Are the concepts clearly developed? Are the style, content, and educational philosophy compatible with yours?
2. Is the program motivating? Will it appeal to students? Remember, dull, dry computer programs can be just as ineffectual as any other method of teaching.
3. Will the program open up students' creativity, imagination, and thinking? Will it encourage logical thought?
4. For whom is the program designed? For individuals? For small groups? For large groups? What ability levels? Is it suitable for the ability levels of your students? Is the reading level suitable? What prerequisites are necessary?
5. Is the program usable? Are the instructions easy to follow? Are the responses clear and appropriate? Is the screen formatting well done? Does it have adequate support materials? How long does it take to run?

TABLE 4.4 *Integrating Computer Software into the Instructional Plan*

TYPE OF SOFTWARE	COURSE TOPICS				
	A	B	C	D	E
Utility (tool-type)	X				
Tutorial		X			
Drill and practice	X	X			
Problem-solving				X	
Simulation	X			X	
Word-processing			X		

6. Is the program friendly, supportive, and encouraging or is it threatening? Does it help students who make errors or does it react harshly? Does it provide for constructed responses?
7. Does the program allow for teacher management? How much teacher supervision is necessary?
8. What does the program cost? Does it seem durable? Will the suppliers give it proper support and backup? Is it worth the expense? (Clark & Starr, 1986, p. 419)

Additional criteria to consider include:

♦ Program instructions should be clearly displayed, preferably double spaced, in a vocabulary understandable to the particular grade level. They should indicate which section or chapter of the program the student is in, the next step to perform, and how to get help when needed.
♦ Programs should make apt use of graphics and sound to motivate and help students accomplish the educational goals.
♦ Programs should call for student control and should provide feedback to students.
♦ A software program should not replace instructional activities better performed by direct teacher instruction, textbooks, workbooks, or other traditional instructional methods.
♦ The speed and number of items presented and the level of difficulty should be adjustable to the needs of different groups of students.
♦ The teacher may need to edit a program to suit the needs of students. A good program should be flexible to accommodate such editing and should possibly provide instructions for editing.
♦ Documentation should include complete operation instructions, a teacher's guide, a statement of objectives, a summary of the program, suggestions for classroom use, and suggested activities.
♦ Programs should provide a branching function (i.e., some form of subprogram) that offers remedial exercises featuring different approaches to solving problems. For example, where a student does not understand the concept "continent" in a geography program, the software should identify the problem and automatically use the branching function to provide a tutorial on continents.
♦ Programs should be "crash proof," meaning it should not be possible to halt a program's operation merely by hitting a wrong key or responding incorrectly.
♦ Loading time and response time should be reasonable so students will not be frustrated or lose a sense of continuity in their work with the program.

Sources to consult in the software evaluation process include school district offices of computer instruction, state education department offices of computer instruction, professional journals, periodicals, educational association reviews, printed software reviews, and other teachers experienced in computer program use.

The teacher needs to plan the gradual, step-by-step introduction of students to computers and to the particular software selected. The first step is to develop students' basic understanding of computer operations skills, such as knowing how to turn on the computer, load the disk or cartridge, and follow screen instructions. Use these guidelines to prepare a classroom for computer activities:

♦ Learn all the peculiarities of the program by running through it as a student might do.
♦ Make support material, such as instruction and assignment sheets, related software, printed material, and other instructional resources (e.g., charts, filmstrips, workbooks), available.
♦ Become familiar with the computer hardware layout. Know the precise location of each machine, all attachments and accessories, electrical outlets, and the way all three are interconnected.
♦ Decide whether students are to work individually, in small groups, or in large groups. Schedule the use of the computer(s), noting both user and purpose on the schedule. Such a schedule both organizes student use of the computer and reserves blocks of time for the class if the computer has to be shared with other classes.
♦ Prepare students for computer operation by reviewing the basic rules for use, such as "never open the disk drive door when the red light is on."
♦ Check that all equipment in the computer work area is set up and functioning properly.

As with any instructional resource, computers are used to best advantage when incorporated into the instructional plan with clear statements of the objectives they are helping the students reach along with methods, materials, and assessment procedures to use. In Table 4.5 a useful description of a specific instructional application of a computer program developed by the California State Department of Education is presented.

Routine classroom computer use does not require that the teacher develop programming expertise. Rudimentary familiarity with a programming language such as BASIC or LOGO, however, is recommended, because the teacher may need to help resolve the numerous decision possibilities presented by a typical computer program.

Interactive systems [computers] have many commands. It is not easy to count them since one single command with many parameters can always be traded for many simple commands. But if we count each command with multiplicity of the parameters it has, that is, the number of distinct decisions that the user may have to make, the total easily reaches a hundred. (Nievergelt et al., 1986, p. 41)

TABLE 4.5 *Instructional Application of a Computer Program*

AREAS	DESCRIPTION
Curriculum objectives	Students will be able to use a word-processing program to prepare a research report, including footnotes and a bibliography.
	Students will be able to access on-line data bases.
Instructional objectives	Students will use a word-processing program to set margins, tabs, and line spacing; to move paragraphs; and to edit text.
	Students will use a modem and appropriate communications software to connect with on-line encyclopedias.
Instructional methods	Demonstration of word-processing software operations; hands-on use by students
	Demonstration of techniques for searching an on-line encyclopedia
Instructional materials/ equipment	Word-processing software and instructional manuals
	Computer lab with no more than three students per computer
	A large-screen monitor for demonstrating to the entire class
	Modem and communications software
	Large-screen monitor for viewing by the entire class
	Handouts describing steps in connecting to a data base and describing searching techniques
Assessment measures	Students will prepare a one-page essay in which margins, tabs, and spacing are set as required.
	Students will demonstrate the ability to move paragraphs.
	Students will access a specific on-line database and obtain information through appropriate searching techniques.

Source: From *Computer Applications Planning* (p. 26) by the California State Department of Education, 1985, Sacramento, CA: California State Department of Education.

In summary, computers can be used to develop mental skills and reinforce learning in almost any subject area. Computers, however, cannot replace the teacher, and their capabilities cannot replace the mental effort of the student. They cannot accomplish the combination of the teacher's carefully planned curriculum and teaching by personal contact. Also, computers cannot replace the human being's capacity to integrate and apply learned information, because they are merely advanced mechanical data storage machines that fall far short of the human brain. Computers, like other instructional resources, can only serve as adjuncts to teaching and learning.

Community Resources

One of the teacher's main goals is making instruction relevant to students' lives. Classroom learning occasionally needs to be juxtaposed with community activities. Field trips and resource persons are two ways of fulfilling this goal, because they provide opportunities for linking classroom instruction with the reality students come into contact with every day.

> Children live in houses, belong to families and share in the life of the community. All of this they bring with them into the classroom. Too often the activity of that classroom is centered on the recreation of a pale image of that real world which exists out there beyond the school gate. The representation of the real world inside the classroom can so easily become unrelated to that world as it exists. (North, 1976, p. 69)

Field trips and resource persons are two ways of teaching students the application of academic ideas to their community and the world at large.

Field Trips. Few experiences equal the well-planned field trip in stimulating student interest in learning. A field trip focuses students' attention on the applicability of course material to circumstances existing in their immediate surroundings. For example, an empty field or lot becomes a geological site as the science teacher leads students on a dig for various kinds of rocks; or a visit to a produce market familiarizes students with an array of foods from countries around the world, bringing to life classroom discussions on climate, location, and culture. In such excursions the everyday experiences of students take on new meanings. Field trips not only advance learning of a subject but also heighten students' awareness of the surrounding world.

Carrying out a field trip is similar in ways to most other instructional activities in that students need to be introduced to the activity, oriented on what to look for, and given an opportunity for discussion to summarize the experience. Some aspects of field trips, however, involve special consideration, including obtaining parental permission, arranging for transportation and necessary expenses, and coordinating schedules.

The teacher should follow these principles when taking the class on field trips:

- ◆ Take field trips to fulfill a specific instructional goal.
- ◆ Plan each detail of the field trip with a view to increasing students' awareness of their environment and its relation to classroom subject matter.
- ◆ Make clear to students what they are to learn from the experience, and include them in making trip preparations.
- ◆ Be aware of the legal responsibilities of going on the trip.
- ◆ Advise and ask for the assistance of school administration and, if needed, of other teachers.
- ◆ Set standards of safety and conduct for the trip.
- ◆ Conduct teacher-led discussions and student reports as a follow-up to the trip.

Alcorn et al. (1970) recommend five basic steps for planning and carrying out a field trip (Table 4.6).

The most effective field trips are those that naturally grow out of some aspect of classroom instruction. For example, a visit to a publishing company that includes a tour of the facilities, demonstration of the equipment, and question-and-answer sessions with editors, authors, and technicians can be a stimulating way to both explain and encourage written forms of communication and expression. A similar purpose can be served by a trip to a newspaper plant. Either of these two field trips can be easily followed up. For instance, the classroom can temporarily become a mini publishing house or newspaper plant where students assume the various roles of editor, technician, journalist, and so on as they work toward the creation of a very short book or class newspaper. Thus, these field trips result in engaging and creative writing activities that can be related to many topics and subject areas and, above all, provide an opportunity for students to experience the joy of cooperative work.

The previous example provides a glimpse of how properly conducted field trips can heighten students' consciousness. Understanding takes on new meaning (cognition) through cooperative action in a new environment (conation) and with a keen sense of enthusiasm and appreciation (affection) for the work observed and subsequently undertaken. In short, the field trip that is well planned from the preparation phase through the follow-up is one of the most effective resources available for raising students' standard of learning.

Resource Persons. Throughout their years of schooling, students hear and read about occupations and roles of people in society. They derive most of their understanding of these occupations and roles from television, movies, and magazines. Their conception of how a musician, store owner, lawyer, or professional athlete works and affects the community remains incomplete at best. Media-inspired stereotypes can be dispelled through direct contact with representatives of different professions in a setting that encourages thoughtful questions and meaningful dialog. There is nothing like seeing the real thing—not on television, but in real human interchange. Visits of resource persons to the classroom, or of the students to different work places, provide a forum for such interchange. Besides giving students a clearer picture of their environment, resource persons provide role models who exemplify character and excellence in action. Adolescent students naturally search for direction in their lives. They have many questions and seek many answers. Meeting those who have found their way in life is both reassuring and enlightening.

To invite resource persons to the classroom, take the following seven steps:

1. Prepare a list of potential resource persons and inquire about their availability.

TABLE 4.6 *Five Steps for Planning and Carrying Out a Field Trip*

STEP	DESCRIPTION
1. Teacher preparation	The teacher should: ♦ Consult the authorities of the area to be visited. ♦ Visit the area; go over details. ♦ Arrange for transportation. ♦ Check on safety, restroom facilities, and so on. ♦ Obtain approval from school authorities. ♦ Notify parents; obtain consent; if this is in order, issue invitations for selected parents to accompany class on trip. ♦ Schedule the trip on the school calendar. ♦ Make arrangements with other teachers regarding absences.
2. Class preparations for the trip	Teacher and students should: ♦ Discuss the reason for the trip. ♦ Write questions to be answered; list things to be checked. ♦ Work out ways to document the trip, such as taking notes, taking pictures, recording sounds, sketching, interviewing, writing. ♦ Plan pretrip reading, study, film previewing. ♦ Discuss behavior standards for the group. ♦ Discuss appropriate dress. ♦ Plan for and appoint committees as needed.
3. At the site	Students should: ♦ Arrive on time at scheduled meeting place. ♦ Stay with assigned groups or guides. ♦ Show an active interest. ♦ Procure samples, specimens, booklets, and so on, to take back to the school with permission of hosts. ♦ Be courteous at all times. ♦ See that lunch scraps and papers are neatly disposed of if lunches are carried. ♦ Check to see that no belongings are left behind.
4. The follow-up	Members of the group should: ♦ Review the objectives of the trip. ♦ Discuss individual and committee findings. ♦ Discuss unexpected problems. Why did they arise? ♦ Draft a thank-you letter to the hosts. ♦ Display any specimens brought back along with any pictures taken or sketches made on the trip. ♦ Discuss the benefits of such a trip for future classes. ♦ Test the sentiment for other field trips. ♦ Share the fruits of the trip with other classes through student reports, newspaper accounts, and so on.
5. Evaluation	The teacher should: ♦ Prepare a written evaluation of the trip to be filed with the school principal and/or the instructional materials center. (This

TABLE 4.6 (*Continued*)

STEP	DESCRIPTION
	report may be written by teacher or students, preferably by both.) ♦ Answer the questions, Was the trip worthwhile? Was it worth what it cost in time, money, and extra effort?

Source: Based on material from *Better Teaching in Secondary Schools* (3rd ed.) (pp. 263–264) by M. D. Alcorn, J. S. Kinder, and J. R. Schunert, 1970, New York: Holt, Rinehart and Winston.

2. Define and state the main purpose of the visit at the first contact so the resource person focuses his or her presentation accordingly.
3. Prepare the invited resource person for the audience. Provide information on the grade level, nature, and size of the class, and include a list of questions students have asked about the topic. Confirm the purpose, date, and time of the visit in a letter that also includes travel directions.
4. Determine the need for any special equipment or facilities, such as filmstrip projectors, maps, or charts, and arrange for their availability on the date and hour of the presentation.
5. Brief students about the resource person and his or her area of expertise. Such classroom discussion helps focus their attention during the actual presentation.
6. During the presentation, maintain an orderly classroom environment and stay alert to any possible needs of the speaker.
7. Follow up and reinforce what has been learned in the presentation with activities that will move students to ponder how the presentation may affect their lives. Essays, classroom discussions, and research projects serve this purpose well.

Visits to and from the community greatly enrich classroom instruction but require careful thought and planning on the part of the teacher to have their optimal result.

♦ **Organizing Instructional Resources**

This section focuses on the organization of instructional resources by means of the classroom library, instructional materials file, and resource matrix.

Classroom Library
It is one thing to tell students about the virtues of reading and good study habits; it is another to maintain a classroom environment that fosters those virtues. A classroom library, set up as a resource center where inter-

esting and instructive materials are available, creates just such an environment. It enhances classroom instruction, providing introductory, background, or follow-up material on numerous topics; activities and exercises that reinforce learning; independent study resources that allow students to work at their own pace; and materials for research under the teacher's guidance. Such research, while enlightening students on a particular topic, teaches them initiative and responsibility for their learning. A diversity of materials encourages students to view a topic from a variety of perspectives. The classroom library, appropriately used, becomes a center of independent study where students work on assigned projects at their own pace and level, while teacher guidance remains within easy reach. Additionally, the proximity facilitates the transition from large-group activities to independent study.

An effective classroom library is characterized by four main elements—high-quality instructional materials, equipment, study guides, and work and storage space—that require thought in their selection and preparation.

High-Quality Instructional Materials. Appropriate instructional materials must be available: books, periodicals, resource packets, workbooks, articles, pamphlets, brochures, filmstrips and slides, audio and videocassette tapes, and computer software. Sources for locating these materials include other teachers, school libraries or resource rooms, school district instructional materials centers, professional educational associations, and publishers of educational materials.

Equipment. The equipment needed to use the above instructional materials might include filmstrip and slide projectors, audio and videocassette recorders, and microcomputers. Almost all schools possess such equipment, which can be requisitioned through the appropriate channel from the school district authority. A clearly written request to the school principal, outlining the need and plans for using such equipment, could convince him or her to allocate funds for such a purchase. Creative ways of obtaining equipment not available through school channels include grant proposals to federal, state, and private agencies; grants or donations from companies that manufacture educational equipment; and fund-raising events to collect money.

Study Guides. Well-written study guides are essential to successful independent study. The many possible formats for study guides are characterized by the following six features:

1. A statement of purpose
2. Background information on the subject of the study
3. Step-by-step directions on how to begin, develop, and complete the project, detailing the required activities and exercises to complete, problems to solve, questions to answer, and ideas to think about
4. A list of necessary materials

5. An annotated list of suggested readings
6. Recommended follow-up activities

Work and Storage Space. The size of the classroom library depends upon the available space and materials. The ideal classroom library contains the following materials:

1. Signs or flow charts in key locations to help students find their way in the library area
2. A quick-reference card catalog of materials on hand
3. A file of study guides, worksheets, and assignments
4. A few small desks for individual study and a table that accommodates three or four students
5. A study carrel with partitions for viewing filmstrips or slides
6. A microcomputer with its necessary attachments and accompanying software
7. Audiocassette recorders and tapes
8. A video recorder and viewer with videocassettes
9. Materials shelves containing books, periodicals, and materials developed both commercially and by teachers

Instructional Materials File

An instructional materials file would be the natural result of the comprehensive curriculum-development method described in Chapter 3. The well-organized curriculum library described above helps put into logical order the plethora of materials, many of which are misused or not used at all, that accumulate in the classroom. Unorganized or disorganized instructional materials are little better than no materials. Well-organized instructional materials, however, facilitate learning activities because they are always retrievable for use in conjunction with various topics.

The best filing system is alphabetical by subject with a cross-reference index according to type of material (e.g., filmstrip, computer software, newspaper article), designated use (e.g., independent study, homework assignment, small-group project), and level of difficulty (e.g., reading grade level, prerequisites).

The teacher should start a materials file at the time he or she enters a teacher-preparation program so that when he or she begins student teaching a useful collection of materials is already available. Developing the materials file should be a process that continues throughout one's teaching career.

A continuous search for effective instructional materials deepens the teacher's knowledge of the subject and of how to bring it alive for students. Other teachers are the best source of suggestions for instructional materials to add to the collection. Discussions with other teachers draw on their experiences in selecting materials and adapting them to student needs and generate new ideas for improving classroom instruction.

Resource Matrix

The resource matrix can be used effectively for developing, implementing, and evaluating the instructional program. Its use requires careful attention to the availability of various resource materials and their possible use in the classroom.

Program Development. There are five steps involved in using the resource matrix to develop the instructional program (Figure 4.4):

1. *Step 1.* Take inventory of resources already on hand, listing them by type and amount.

FIGURE 4.4 *Using the Resource Matrix in Developing the Instructional Program*

STEP 1: INVENTORY RESOURCES ON HAND

Type of Resource	Amount on Hand	Comments

STEP 2: REVIEW INSTRUCTIONAL PLANS TO PROJECT RESOURCE NEEDS

Topic/Unit	Types of Resources Needed	General Purpose

STEP 3: REVIEW LISTS OF RESOURCES AVAILABLE

Sources	Types of Resources Listed	Comments

STEP 4: PROCURE NEEDED RESOURCES

Sources	Types of Resources Procured	Amount	Comments

STEP 5: ASSESS EFFECTIVENESS OF RESOURCE PROCUREMENT PROCESS

Types of Resources	Maintenance of Inventory	Timeliness of Procurement	Procurement According to Plan

2. *Step 2.* Project additional resource needs in accordance with the instructional plan.
3. *Step 3.* Identify the best sources of instructional resources, such as school district instructional resource centers, federal and state education departments, publishers, and producers of educational materials. Draw upon past experience, recommendations of other teachers, resource material catalogs, and new research. (See "Sources of Instructional Resources" below for places to contact for obtaining catalogs and materials.)
4. *Step 4.* Procure needed resources after reviewing catalogs and materials from the sources identified in Step 3.
5. *Step 5.* Assess the effectiveness of resource procurement by asking three questions: Is the resource inventory up to date? Does the procurement of resources synchronize with the instructional plan? Are resources procured according to plan?

Program Implementation. There are two steps involved in using the resource matrix for program implementation (Figure 4.5):

1. *Step 1.* Develop a detailed plan for allocating resources according to planned activities within course topics. The statement of how each resource is to be used should indicate whether the resource will be used by a whole class, small group, or for individual instruction, and the statement of purpose should indicate the level of learning involved (e.g., recall of information, application of concepts).
2. *Step 2.* Maintain an account of how resources are actually used for classroom instruction.

FIGURE 4.5 *Using the Resource Matrix in Implementing the Instructional Plan*

STEP 1: DEVELOP DETAILED PLAN FOR USING RESOURCES

Topic/ Unit	Activity	Type of Resource	Amount	Purpose: 1. Level of Learning Involved	2. Individual, Small-, or Large- Group Use

STEP 2: ACCOUNT FOR RESOURCE ALLOCATIONS AND USES

Topic/ Unit	Activity	Type of Resource	Amount	Purpose: 1. Level of Learning Involved	2. Individual, Small-, or Large- Group Use

Program Evaluation. There are three steps involved in using the resource matrix for program evaluation (Figure 4.6):

1. ***Step 1.*** Monitor how resources used for classroom instruction affect student readiness for learning (i.e., interest and ability to learn).
2. ***Step 2.*** Assess effectiveness of resource use according to purpose fulfilled and student learning achieved.
3. ***Step 3.*** Modify resource use (i.e., change in type, amount, specified use, and purpose) based on assessment of their effectiveness for classroom instruction. This step, leading once again to the program development phase, denotes the cyclical nature of the resource planning process.

◆ Sources of Instructional Resources

Instructional resources play an important role in fostering in the students a spontaneous sense of involvement that is fundamental to learning in any subject area. Despite this significant role in classroom instruction, only

FIGURE 4.6 *Using the Resource Matrix in Evaluating the Instructional Plan*

STEP 1: MONITOR HOW RESOURCES USED ARE AFFECTING STUDENT READINESS FOR LEARNING

Resource Used	Amount	Purpose	Effects on Student Interest and Ability to Learn

STEP 2: ASSESS EFFECTIVENESS OF RESOURCE USE

Topic/ Unit	Activity	Resource Used	Amount	Degree Purpose Fulfilled	Student Learning Achieved

STEP 3: MODIFY USE OF RESOURCES

Topic/ Unit	Activity	Type of Resource	Amount	Purpose	Comments

limited funds are usually available for their purchase. The teacher, therefore, must make a thorough search for resource materials, select wisely among those discovered, and become aware of sources that can provide relatively inexpensive or free materials of high quality.

The practical suggestions and examples below provided by Davida Shipkowitz, president of the local chapter of the California Association of Resource Specialists, Simi Valley, California, give an idea of how the lists of sources presented in this section can be effectively used for procuring instructional resource materials.

Where to Look for Material

Lists of Available Publications. Invaluable are those time-honored lists of available publications (see pages 177–178) that provide lists of a rich variety of materials for all subject areas. Equally useful are lists of resource materials from company catalogs that not only list items but also categorize and describe them. If desired, many of the items listed may be group purchased and used by several teachers on a rotational basis. Criterion-referenced charts pinpoint objectives and make particularized choices relatively simple. In addition, it is not unusual for publishers to continuously send issues of updated listings to keep teachers informed of the latest resource materials available.

Trade Books. Books are available that list library selections categorically. For example, *Reading, New Edition: A Booklist for Junior High and Middle School* (Christiansen, National Council of Teachers of English, Urbana, IL) is one of numerous volumes indicating appropriate resource selections by topic and reading level. Another list of materials by Jim Trealise in *Read-Aloud Handbook* (New York: Penguin Books) includes a delightful text directed to both parents and teachers based on the author's philosophy of reading aloud to young people of all ages. The *American Library Association Booklist* (Chicago), is a bimonthly magazine that updates various publications and educational software.

Vendor Displays. Often, useful and inspiring material can be found at vendor displays at professional conferences. Among the materials to look for are creative instructional units that dovetail to form a larger learning segment and groups of "collectibles" from varied sources to use in a multifaceted approach for a unit in a particular subject area.

Where to See Instructional Resources Demonstrated

Conference Sessions. Unique and skillful uses of resource materials can be seen at sessions of annual or regional conferences of various professional associations. Included in such sessions are recommended strategies for employing the materials along with access to related publications and materials that can be reviewed for planning and subsequent adoption for school and classroom libraries.

Workshop Courses. Extended six-week, quarter, or semester workshop or "mini" courses can suggest a range of useful instructional resource choices and uses. For example, an intensive introduction and in-depth exploration of the critical thinking strategies found in Reuven Feuerstein's *Instrumental Enrichment* (Baltimore, MD, 1979) was given at California Lutheran University. Resource packets were available throughout the workshop series to demonstrate how such materials could be effectively employed.

Factors to Consider When Selecting
Instructional Resource Materials

Teaching Strategies and Models. Current teaching strategies and models influence the selection of resource materials. For example, for mastery learning groups there are resources that provide extensive suggestions for a variety of activities including reteaching, expansion, and retesting of material. A good example of this is *Math Around Us* with its accompanying teacher's resource books (Menlo Park: Addison-Wesley, 1986). An excellent selection of a worktext for cooperative learning groupings is *Developing Key Concepts for Solving Word Problems* by Panchyshyn and Monroe (New York: Barnell Loft, 1986). This "story problems" soft-cover text is visually well designed with extremely clear directions, sufficient practice examples, reviews, practice tests, final tests, and well-paced units that gradually increase in difficulty as the book proceeds.

Student Learning Styles. Because instruction needs to apply to student learning styles, resource materials should be selected and used to stimulate learning through different modalities, including auditory, visual, and tactile (i.e., hands-on) channels.

Standardized Tests. Standardized tests also influence the choice of resource materials. Various curriculum alignment and criterion-referenced resource materials that have been developed to strengthen skill and other learning deficiencies indicated by certain standardized test scores are available. For example, useful lists of resource materials to refer to that focus on learner behavior can be found in the *WISC Compilation: What to Do When You Know the Score* (Whitworth & Sutton, Novato, CA: Academic Therapy, 1978).

The Need to Strengthen Social Behavior. Resource materials should also be selected to strengthen social behavior. For example, to address trends toward violence, drugs, and suicide, resource units are available that provide forums for classroom discussions and preventive presentations. Among the materials available are the *Sunburst Catalogue* (Pleasantville, NY: Sunburst,

1987) and selections from bibliotherapeutic lists that assist in selecting readings directed to help understand and deal with emotional crises and intercultural experiences.

Changing the Pace of Instruction. On the lighter side, there are resources, such as *Games for Middle Schools* (Weickert & Bell, Littleton, CO: Libraries Unlimited, 1981), that contain carefully selected subject-oriented games to provide a change of pace from usual instructional strategies. These materials help meet the need for variety in the classroom as well as for occasional relaxation in the daily pace of instruction.

Selected Sources for Procuring Resource Materials
Resource materials or lists of such materials can be acquired from the following selected sources:

Argus Communications, Niles, IL (posters)
BFA Educational Media, New York, NY (interactive videos and videocassettes)
Educational Images, Elmira, NY (slides, filmstrips, and computer software)
Educational Materials and Equipment Company, Pelham, NY (slides, videocassettes, and computer software)
Educational Media Laboratories, Ellensburg, WA (media in general)
Encyclopedia Britannica Educational Corporation, Chicago, IL (overhead transparencies, films, and filmstrips)
Hammond, Inc., Maplewood, NJ (maps, globes, and overhead transparencies)
National Audio-Visual Association, Fairfax, VA (films and filmstrips)
National Geographic Society, Washington, DC (maps, globes, films, and filmstrips)
New York Times, School Services Department, New York, NY (collateral reading materials and filmstrips)
Rand McNally & Company, Chicago, IL (maps and globes)
Sunburst Communications, Pleasantville, NY (computer software)
Time-Life Films, New York, NY (films and filmstrips)

General Sources for Procuring Resource Materials
Resource materials or lists of such material can be found in the following general sources:

College or university curriculum inquiry centers
College or university education libraries
County professional education reference centers
Education or public relations departments of newspapers and periodicals
Professional education associations
School district curriculum materials centers
School district instructional publications units

School district teacher development centers
School district textbook annexes

Organizations Listing Sources of Instructional Materials

The following organizations are useful sources for finding instructional materials:

Agency for Instructional Technology, Bloomington, IN
American Library Association, Chicago, IL
Association for Supervision and Curriculum Development (ASCD), Washington, DC
Clearinghouse on Teacher Education, American Association of Colleges for Teacher Education, Washington, DC
Education Products Information Exchange (EPIE), Teachers College, Columbia University, New York, NY
Eastman Kodak Company, Rochester, NY
Educational Film Library Association (EFLA), New York, NY
Educators' Progress Service, Randolph, WI
George Peabody College for Teachers, Nashville, TN
Mount St. Mary's College Teacher Education Program, Los Angeles, CA
National Audio-Visual Center, Washington, DC
National Educational Association (NEA), Washington, DC
National Information Center for Educational Media (NICEM), Albuquerque, NM
R. R. Bowker Company, New York, NY
U. S. Government Printing Office, Washington, DC
Westinghouse Learning Corporation, New York, NY

Educational Journals

The following educational journals are good sources of instructional materials:

Booklist
Classroom Computer
The Computer Teacher
Educational Technology
Instructional Innovator
Learning
The Learning Media Magazine
Media and Methods
Media Review
School Tech News
Today's Education

Other journals published by various subject-area associations are also available.

SUMMARY

In this chapter several main points about procuring, developing, and using instructional resources were presented.

1. Instructional resources, including printed, audiovisual, and graphic materials, and community resources are the supportive materials essential for putting teaching methods and planned learning experience into practice.
2. The principal aspects of instructional resource procurement, development, and use include identifying existing resources available, reviewing various materials for potential use in the instructional plan, becoming familiar with new and creative uses of various materials, developing and adapting various materials to address student learning needs, and developing an understanding of the interrelationship between teaching method, resource materials, and subject matter as the basis for planning effective learning activities.
3. Prudent selection of instructional materials requires a knowledge of reputable sources and existing materials, their use by colleagues, and firsthand thoughtful review of materials by the teacher.
4. The textbook can be effectively used as a guide for organizing course contents as a source of activities, strategies, and questions; as a source of references and readings; as a basic source for student research; and as a source to use in conjunction with material derived from original research.
5. Collateral materials such as encyclopedias, dictionaries, atlases, world almanacs, journals, magazines, newspapers, and books on a particular subject enrich curriculum and instructional activities.
6. Teacher-made and commercial workbooks provide students with drill in specific skill areas, problems to solve, questions to answer, self-assessment quizzes to take, and vocabulary words to learn.
7. Audiovisual materials such as overhead transparencies, films, filmstrips and slides, video and audio tape cassettes, chalkboards, bulletin boards, graphic materials, and computers increase students' interest in and attention to classroom instruction.
8. The computer, especially the microcomputer because of its relatively small size, is the most technologically advanced instructional resource available. Being a two-way communication medium, it is among the most captivating of instructional aids.
9. The use of community resources, such as field trips and visits from resource persons, helps students apply ideas learned in the classroom to their community and the world at large. Field trips are most effective when they naturally grow out of some aspect of daily classroom instruction.
10. The teacher can organize instructional resources by setting up a classroom library and a materials file and using a resource matrix in conjunction with instructional planning.

11. Because only limited funds are usually available for the purchase of instructional resource materials, the teacher must make a thorough search for resource materials, select wisely among those discovered, and become aware of sources that can provide relatively inexpensive or free materials of high quality.

Instructional resources serve "to help the [students] solve a problem by reflective thinking or to provide the sort of practice necessary in acquiring a given skill" (Waples & Tyler, 1930, p. 269). Selecting instructional resources to accomplish these two purposes requires careful planning coupled with imaginative experimentation.

The keynote is flexibility. Students should be confronted with a wide range of resources, some open-ended, some structured, some employing demanding language and concepts, others providing a basic understanding. Learning is a complex process. There are no sure guides or easy paths. Motivation and comprehension are as important as structure and effort. (North, 1976, p. 70)

◆ ◆ ◆ ◆ ◆ ◆ ◆
_____

PRACTICAL MODEL 4.1   How to Utilize a Teacher's Aide

Introduction   Teacher's aides, if used wisely, can be a valuable resource in the classroom. They can, however, be just another burden and wasted resource if no serious thought is given to how they can be best employed in the classroom. This practical model provides advice on how to best use the many skills a teacher's aide can bring to your classroom.

Submitted by   Felipe Caceras, math teacher in East Los Angeles, California

Purpose   To provide teachers with a guide on how to productively utilize a teacher's aide to enhance classroom management and instruction

Setting   Junior high school in a large urban school district; several sections of seventh-grade students, most of whom are performing below grade level

◆ **Rationale**

Teachers who have planned well for their classes often do not think to make plans for the most effective use of their teacher's aides. A teacher's aide is a valuable resource who is often used merely to correct papers, make photocopies, or handle an array of paperwork. Although these tasks should be performed by a teacher's aide from time to time to lessen the teacher's administrative burden, his or her primary role should be as a resource for the students to help them with learning activities. Another reason for planning how to best utilize the teacher's aide is that occasionally you may have one who has his or her own agenda for what he or she feels needs to be done. Thus, instead of the teacher's aide being a resource for you and the students, he or she may actually begin to tell you how to organize important aspects of the classroom environment. This unfortunate situation can come about if ample thought is not given to determining how the teacher's aide can best serve your particular students and teaching/learning environment.

♦ Recommendations

The following ten recommendations will help make your association with your teacher's aide a useful and productive one.

1. Outline the duties and expectations you have for your teacher's aide and go over this outline with him or her.
2. Use your teacher's aide to work with students one on one. He or she can help students who you may not have time for every day. It may be necessary, however, to spend some time before, during, or after class to train the teacher's aide in how to work effectively with individual students.
3. A key rule to ask teacher's aides to follow is not to interrupt you while you are teaching. Sometimes students will try to use the teacher's aide to disrupt a lesson or particular activity. The teacher's aide may not realize this is going on until you point it out.
4. Sometimes it is beneficial to give a teacher's aide a small group, consisting of two to four students who are behind the rest of the class, to work with. This can best be done by having the teacher's aide take the students either outside the room (e.g., to an empty room, the library, or a patio) or to an area of the classroom set aside for small-group work. This allows the teacher's aide and the small group of students to interact without disrupting or being disrupted by the rest of the class.
5. Always have the teacher's aide remain in the classroom for the first five to ten minutes of each period to get a feel for the material you are going to cover that day and for how you are going to cover it. Also, in case of an emergency, the teacher's aide can be left to cover the class or go to the main office.
6. Try to keep open and clear channels of communication between you and your teacher's aide. Tension often occurs when plans and procedures are not fully discussed and understood.
7. A disciplinary problem with one student that can ruin your whole day can sometimes be effectively dealt with by having the teacher's aide take the student to an appropriate area for individual tutoring. Beware, however, of the problem student who uses this to avoid doing the work at hand. In addition, you must judge whether the teacher's aide has the training and experience needed to work constructively with the particular student under the prevailing circumstances.

8. Designate a special place in the classroom for the teacher's aide to sit and work. This will establish his or her importance and authority in the eyes of the students as well as his or her own sense of self-worth.

9. Address the teacher's aide in front of the students as you would any other member of the faculty or administration (i.e., Mr., Mrs., Ms.). This conveys the desired respectful, professional image of the teacher's aide to the students.

10. Get to know the strengths and weaknesses of the teacher's aide by observing how he or she handles various duties and situations. Also, notice how he or she understands directions and is able to spontaneously improvise as circumstances may demand.

♦ ♦ ♦ ♦ ♦ ♦ ♦
_____

CASE STUDY 4.1   Combining Instructional Resources

Orienting Questions   As you read this case study ask yourself these questions:

Specific
♦ How has this teacher related the instructional resources used in this lesson to the planned instructional objectives?
♦ Do the teacher and students have a clear idea of how the resource materials involved are going to be used in this lesson?

General
♦ What points in this lesson stand out as indicators of this teacher's strengths and/or weaknesses?
♦ What recommendations would you make for addressing the problems this teacher seems to have?

Setting   *School* – Junior high school in lower-middle-class, multiethnic community

Subject – English (fifty-five minutes)

Teacher – Mr. Wells, English department chairman

Students – Thirty-seven eighth graders of average ability

Topic – Writing Paragraphs

Lesson   *Note:* Under Time Frame the numbers represent the minutes that elapse as the period progresses. Under Dialog the names of the students and the teacher appear as they speak. The symbol ► represents a brief description of a particularly noteworthy action or observation.

Time Frame	Dialog
−5 to 5	► The students enter the room quickly and quietly. As they take their seats they open their notebooks and copy the notes being shown on an overhead transparency. Mr. Wells has a seating chart out and is taking attendance.

Time Frame	Dialog	
5 to 9	**Mr. W.:**	Make sure you have the proper heading and date on today's notes. We will be referring to them later in this lesson, as usual.
	Andy:	Could you read us the last line of number 2? It's a little squished.
	Mr. W.:	It reads, "Outline clearly the ideas you plan to include in each paragraph."
	Andy:	Thanks.
	Mr. W.:	We have three things to do today that will help us write clear, well-structured paragraphs.
	►	Mr. Wells then writes the three headings on the board: Activity A—Outlining a Story from a Picture; Activity B—Reading Paragraphs with Accompanying Audio Version; Activity C—Workbook Writing Exercise.
	Mr. W.:	This is how we will proceed: Rows 1 and 2 start with Activity A, rows 3 and 4 with Activity B, and rows 5 and 6 with Activity C. After about ten minutes we will switch activities so that by the end of the period everyone will have participated in all three activities.
9 to 13	►	Mr. Wells gives each set of rows the materials appropriate to its assigned activity.
13 to 25	**Carla:**	(A student doing Activity A) Mr. Wells, what do we do with this picture?
	Mr. W.:	Carla, I'll be right there to help you.
	►	Mr. Wells is answering individual students' questions about what to do while passing out the materials.
	Mr. W.:	(Going over to Carla) Look at the two columns of words beneath the picture and select the ones that best outline your story and describe what's happening. (Addressing the whole class) Everyone, when you outline a story from a picture, remember to make up a title first. This will help focus your thinking when you write a paragraph from the outline you've developed.
	►	Mr. Wells has spent the past ten minutes working with the students in rows 1 and 2, who are doing Activity A.
	John:	(A student in row 5 who is doing Activity C) Mr. Wells, would you take a look at my worksheet.
	Mr. W.:	I'll be right there, John. (Looking over John's work) John, don't you remember what we learned last week about adding "ing" to words? I thought we all understood that. (Addressing the whole class) Class, look here for a second. Will someone tell John the rule for adding "ing" to words.

Time Frame	Dialog	
	►	A student reads the rule for adding "ing" from her notes. Mr. Wells then asks the students to get ready to change activities.
	Mr. W.:	Finish now whatever you are doing and take out the material I gave you for your next activity.
25 to 36	►	Rows 1 and 2 work on Activity C, rows 3 and 4 work on Activity A, and rows 5 and 6 work on Activity B. Again, Mr. Wells spends almost all his time with the students doing Activity A.
36 to 41	Mr. W.:	(Putting on the overhead transparency shown at the beginning of class) I want to spend a few minutes talking about the principles listed here because they relate to all three activities we are doing today.
	Lupe:	Mr. Wells, I can't see the first two sentences. Would you move the transparency down a little?
	►	Immediately, two students on the other side of the room yell out that then they won't be able to see.
	Mr. W.:	Cool down. I'll focus it so everyone can see it.
	Lupe:	Thank you.
	Mr. W.:	(Explaining the first principle) Each paragraph should have an opening sentence that gives an idea of what the paragraph is going to be about. We call this a topic sentence.
	►	Mr. Wells calls on a few students to read a short paragraph from their textbooks and then tell whether it has a good topic sentence.
41 to 52	Mr. W.:	Okay, let's get back to our activities. This time I'm going to work with those doing the workbook exercise.
	►	Mr. Wells circulates among the students doing Activity C, observing their problems and giving assistance.
	Mr. W.:	(Speaking to a student doing her workbook exercise) Gina, it would really help if you had your dictionary and writing skills packet out to refer to.
	Tim:	(A student who has just overheard what Mr. Wells has told Gina) That's a great idea, Mr. Wells. (He then tells the student sitting behind him about this idea for completing the workbook exercise.)
	Quan:	(Speaking to his neighbor) Larry, what page are we supposed to be reading?
	Larry:	Who knows? I'm just listening to the cassette anyway.
	Quan:	(Looking around at the other students doing the reading and listening activity) Hey, everybody else seems to be only listening too. Let's ask Mr. Wells what to do.

Time Frame	Dialog

Larry: Forget it. I'd rather just listen. Reading is boring.

Mr. W.: (Pointing to several mistakes on a student's workbook exercise) Ravi, look at your answers to questions 1, 4, 5, and 9. What is each of those questions about?

Ravi: They all ask something about sentences.

Mr. W.: Right. What does each sentence have to have to be considered complete?

Ravi: I'm afraid I'm not sure. I know it has to be a thought.

Mr. W.: Look in your writing skills packet and review the notes we took today from the overhead transparency. I'll look at your answers again after that.

52 to 55   **Mr. W.:** Class, I guess time has run out. We'll start tomorrow where we left off. You each have one more activity to do. Carefully pass in the materials so I can pass them out quickly tomorrow.

Brief   *Key Facts* – List three key facts verbatim that characterize the main positive and/or negative aspects of the lesson.

Strengths/Weaknesses – Briefly explain how the key facts selected indicate strengths and/or weaknesses in the teacher's performance.

Recommendations – Briefly describe what the teacher could have done to alleviate or avoid the problems that were seen.

◆ ◆ ◆ ◆ ◆ ◆ ◆

CASE STUDY 4.2   Showing a Filmstrip

Orienting Questions   As you read this case ask yourself these questions:

Specific
◆ Does this teacher appear to have a good plan for using the filmstrip?
◆ How effectively does this teacher use the filmstrip to get across the concepts presented in the lesson?

General
◆ What points in this lesson stand out as indicators of this teacher's strengths and/or weaknesses?
◆ What recommendations would you make for addressing the problems this teacher seems to have?

Setting   School – Parochial junior high school in an economically disadvantaged
            neighborhood

Subject – Science (forty-five minutes)

Teacher – Mr. Palmer

Students – Thirty-two eighth graders

Topic – Chemical and Physical Changes

Lesson

Time Frame	Dialog	
−5 to 0	►	The students enter the room in an orderly manner and take their seats before the second bell rings. On the overhead is the direction, "Do the following review exercise in your science notebooks: Make up an example of a physical and a chemical change. (Be original. Do not use one from the book.)"
0 to 5	**Mr. P.:**	Say "present" when Angie calls your name.
	►	Attendance is taken from the roll book as the students are busy doing their examples. Mr. Palmer walks around the room reminding students of the classroom rules and monitoring their progress.
5 to 20	**Mr. P.:**	Please put your pens down. Heather, please read your example of a chemical change.
	Heather:	When wood is on fire it turns into ashes.
	Mr. P.:	How many of you agree with Heather's example? Just raise your hands.
	►	Most of the students raise their hands.
	Mr. P.:	(Calling on a student who did not raise her hand) Cathy, why do you disagree with Heather's example?
	Cathy:	I don't know.
	Mr. P.:	Cathy, open your book and copy the definition of a chemical change ten times in your notebook. I am very disappointed that you did not do your homework last night.
	Cathy:	But I did do it.
	Mr. P.:	Your homework was to memorize the definition of a chemical change; obviously, you did not do it. Heather's example is an excellent one. Why is wood burning into ashes a chemical change, Mary?
	Mary:	(Startled) The wood molecules change into the element carbon.
	Mr. P.:	Excellent! Mary, would you read your example of a physical change?

Time Frame	Dialog

Mary: Ice cream melts on a hot day.

Mr. P.: How many agree that this is an example of a physical change?

► Everyone raises their hand.

Mr. P.: Excellent! That's a terrific example. Now we are going to watch a filmstrip about the various types of chemical and physical changes. These examples may help you visualize the concept. After the filmstrip you will be given a worksheet to complete. For now, I would like you to watch and listen to the filmstrip. Do not take notes during the presentation. We will discuss the important points afterwards, or tomorrow if we run out of time today. Does anyone have a question before I start the filmstrip?

► The projector, filmstrip, and tape with tape recorder are all arranged at the back of the room and ready to go.

Mr. P.: No questions? Then I'll start the machine. Hubert, would you turn off the lights, and would Margaret press the button when the tone is heard on the tape. Thank you.

► When the first frame is projected, Mr. Palmer realizes he forgot to rewind the filmstrip after showing it earlier in the day.

Mr. P.: I have to rewind the filmstrip. Judy, will you read your example of a physical change?

Judy: I can't read it in the dark.

Mr. P.: Hubert, please turn the lights on again. Thank you. Now, please read your example, Judy.

Judy: The rust on a nail.

Mr. P.: How many agree that this is an example of a physical change? Raise your hands.

► No hand is raised.

Mr. P.: Terry, why is that not a good example of a physical change?

Terry: The rust molecules are different from the molecules of the nail. Therefore, it is an example of a chemical change.

Mr. P.: That is correct. Can you see the difference, Judy?

Judy: Uh huh.

Mr. P.: Good. The filmstrip is all rewound now. Hubert, please turn off the lights. Thank you.

20 to 35 ► The lights are turned off and the filmstrip begins. The lights go on at the end of the filmstrip.

Time Frame	Dialog
35 to 43	**Mr. P.:** The examples in that filmstrip were excellent. Does anyone have any questions as to why the examples shown were physical and not chemical changes or chemical and not physical changes?
	► No responses from the students.
	Mr. P.: Okay, if there are no questions, here are the worksheets. You have the rest of the time to complete them. If you do not finish, complete it for homework tonight.
	► The students quietly work on the worksheet.
43 to 45	**Mr. P.:** I expect these worksheets to be completed for tomorrow's class discussion. You are dismissed.

Brief   *Key Facts* – List three key facts verbatim that characterize the main positive and/or negative aspects of the lesson.

Strengths/Weaknesses – Briefly explain how the key facts selected indicate strengths and/or weaknesses in the teacher's performance.

Recommendations – Briefly describe what the teacher could have done to alleviate or avoid the problems that were seen.

♦ ♦ ♦ ♦ ♦ ♦ ♦
CASE STUDY 4.3   Using the Overhead Projector

**Orienting
Questions**   As you read this case study ask yourself these questions:

Specific
♦ Does this teacher appear to have thought through her presentation on the overhead projector?
♦ Could this teacher have used the overhead projector to better advantage for this particular project?

General
♦ What points in this lesson stand out as indicators of this teacher's strengths and/or weaknesses?
♦ What recommendations would you make for addressing the problems this teacher seems to have?

Setting	*School* – High school in middle-class community
	Subject – Biology (fifty-five minutes)
	Teacher – Ms. Barr, second-year teacher
	Students – Forty tenth graders of above-average ability
	Topic – The Digestive System
Lesson	

Time Frame	Dialog	
1 to 5	►	The second bell has rung as the last students enter the room. Ms. Barr is busy setting up an overhead projector. She plans to use a transparency to illustrate the digestion of food, from chewing to elimination, and then to show a ten-minute film on what happens in the body during digestion.
5 to 15	**Ms. B.:**	All right. Would everyone please take their seats. We're going to go over the digestive system today in class. Mike, if you will plug in the projector we will get started.
	►	Ms. Barr turns on the overhead projector. The class begins to giggle as Ms. Barr discovers that the screen has not been pulled down and the picture is being projected on the chalkboard.
	Ms. B.:	Randy, would you pull the screen down. Everyone else be quiet.
	Randy:	I can't reach it.
	Nick:	(Jumping out of his seat) Here, I'll get it.
	►	Ms. Barr turns on the projector again and places the transparency on it. The picture is too big and does not focus on the screen.
	Ms. B.:	(Pointing to the students sitting on the lefthand side of the room) Would this whole row move to the right?
	►	The six students in the row all move their desks as Ms. Barr moves the overhead projector up and back until the image fits on the screen.
15 to 29	**Ms. B.:**	Now, follow me as I point out the parts of the digestive system and what is taking place where.
	►	Ms. Barr very quickly describes each part of the system in succession. As she does so, the students are writing as fast as they can, their heads bobbing up and down almost nonstop in order to see what Ms. Barr is pointing to as well as to get the notes down.

Time Frame	Dialog	
	Diane:	(Pointing to the lower righthand portion of the screen) What is that thing down there?
	Ms. B.:	(Pointing to something on the transparency in that general area) You mean that thing there?
	Diane:	No, over more.
	Ms. B.:	That?
	Diane:	(Getting up to touch the board) This!
	Ms. B.:	Oh, that's the appendix. It doesn't have any particular function in the body. Mark, would you go to the library to get a film projector. I'll leave this transparency on so you can finish copying the diagram.
29 to 45	►	As the students finish copying the diagram, Ms. Barr searches for the short film to put on the projector. After a few minutes Mark returns without a projector.
	Mark:	Mrs. Robinson said there aren't any projectors left because other teachers have already signed them out for today. But she said that Mrs. Harper, next door, has one.
	Rick:	Ms. Barr, do you want me to see if she is finished using it?
	Ms. B.:	No. Mark, would you ask Mrs. Harper if she is finished with the projector and if we can borrow it? Tell her that I will return it at the end of this period.
	►	Mark returns with a projector. Ms. Barr unplugs the overhead and moves it out of the way as Mark sets up the film projector.
	Ms. B.:	This film should answer any questions you still have about the digestive system, so pay attention.
45 to 55	►	The film is shown, minus the last minute or so.
	Ms. B.:	(As the dismissal bell rings) Your homework for tonight is on the board.

Brief   *Key Facts* – List three key facts verbatim that characterize the main positive and/or negative aspects of the lesson.

Strengths/Weaknesses – Briefly explain how the key facts selected indicate strengths and/or weaknesses in the teacher's performance.

Recommendations – Briefly describe what the teacher could have done to alleviate or avoid the problems that were seen.

◆ ◆ ◆ ◆ ◆ ◆ ◆

CHAPTER PROJECT   Develop a Workbook for a Particular Course of Instruction

Goals
1. To create a resource to supplement the activities and materials used for daily classroom lessons.
2. To increase the teacher's understanding of a subject through the research necessary to develop a workbook.

Planning
1. Determine the scope of the workbook (i.e., will it cover one particular unit or the entire course?).
2. Make a prospective list of materials to include in the workbook (i.e., activity sheets, exercises, guide sheets, collateral readings, quizzes, projects, and reference lists).
3. Prepare a list of sources (e.g., school district curriculum centers, college or university education libraries, or publishers of educational materials) for locating materials to include in the workbook.

Partial Implementation
1. Use the prepared list of sources to carry out research for finding ideas and materials to include in the workbook.
2. Review the selected materials, indicating the possible instructional uses for each (e.g., drill exercises, collateral readings, projects, or quizzes.

Full Implementation
1. Coordinate the selected workbook materials with the course instructional plan.
2. Develop a table of contents for the workbook, indicating when and how the materials are to be used. (See the discussion on the resource matrix in this chapter for suggestions on planning the use of instructional resource materials.)
3. Assemble the workbook in final form for duplication and decide whether it will be given to the students as a whole or sheet by sheet over a period of time.

◆ ◆ ◆ ◆ ◆ ◆ ◆

ALTERNATIVE CHAPTER PROJECT   Review and Compare Four Textbooks in a Particular Subject Area

Goals
1. To design an effective method for reviewing and comparing textbooks.
2. To become familiar with several exemplary textbooks in a particular subject area.
3. To write a brief report comparing the textbooks reviewed and recommending one for adoption.

Planning
1. Review publisher's textbook catalogs and state and school district approved textbook listings; consult with other teachers of the subject concerning textbooks.
2. Select and procure four exemplary textbooks in a particular subject area.

Partial Implementation
1. Design a framework for reviewing and comparing textbooks (e.g., to determine the scope and sequence of contents, quality of graphics, and reading grade level of writing). Use this framework as the basis of textbook analysis.
2. Review each textbook using the above framework as a guide.

Full Implementation
1. Write a report comparing the four reviewed textbooks.
2. Include in the report a section of recommendations as follows: a ranking of the four textbooks according to overall quality and appropriateness for a particular course of instruction; a description of how the effectiveness of the top-ranked textbook can be increased by using parts of the other textbooks and other supplementary materials.

◆ ◆ ◆ ◆ ◆ ◆ ◆
REFERENCES

Alcorn, M. D., Kinder, J. S., & Schunert, J. R. (1970). *Better teaching in secondary schools* (3rd ed.). New York: Holt, Rinehart and Winston.

Brown, J. W., Lewis, R. B., & Harcleroad, F. F. (1973). *AV instruction: Technology, media and methods* (4th ed.). New York: McGraw-Hill.

Brown, J. W., Lewis, R. B., & Harcleroad, F. F. (1983). *AV instruction: Technology, media and methods* (6th ed.). New York: McGraw-Hill.

California State Department of Education. (1985). *Computer applications planning.* Sacramento, CA: California State Department of Education.

Callahan, J. F., & Clark, L. H. (1982). *Teaching in the middle and secondary schools* (2nd ed.). New York: Macmillan.

Clark, L. H., & Starr, I. S. (1986). *Secondary and middle school teaching methods* (5th ed.). New York: Macmillan.

Heck, S. F., & Williams, C. R. (1984). *The complex roles of the teacher: An ecological perspective.* New York: Teachers College Press.

Henson, K. T. (1981). *Secondary teaching methods.* Lexington, MA: D. C. Heath.

Nievergelt, J., Ventura, A., & Hinterberger, H. (1986). *Interactive computer programs for education: Philosophy, techniques, and examples.* Reading, MA: Addison-Wesley.

North, P. (1976, Spring). Learning resources in the mixed ability classroom. *Forum for the Discussion of New Trends in Education, 18*(2), 69–70.

Waples, D., & Tyler, R. W. (1930). *Research methods and teachers' problems: A manual for systematic studies of classroom procedure.* New York: Macmillan.

Woodbury, M. (1978). *Selecting instructional materials.* Bloomington, IN: Phi Delta Kappa Educational Foundation.

♦ ♦ ♦ ♦ ♦ ♦ ♦
ANNOTATED READINGS

Aubrey, R. H. (1978). *Selected free materials for classroom teachers* (6th ed.). Belmont, CA: Fearon-Pittman.
> *An excellent source book listing a wide variety of useful resource materials available for no cost to classroom teachers.*

Caissy, G. A. (1984, December). Evaluating educational software: A practitioner's guide. *Phi Delta Kappan, 66*(4), 249–250.
> *A concise guide assessing the quality and suitability of computer software packages for classroom instruction.*

Ellington, H. (1985). *Producing teaching materials: A handbook for teachers and trainers.* London: Kagan Page.
> *One of the few comprehensive works describing how teachers can develop their own high-quality instructional resource materials.*

Film and video finder. (1987). Albuquerque, NM: National Information Center for Educational Materials (NICEM).
> *A complete listing of film and video resource materials put out by this nationally acclaimed resource information center.*

Free things for teachers. (1982). New York: G. P. Putnam's Sons.
> *A comprehensive list of free instructional resource materials for teachers.*

Freedom, F. B., & Berg, E. L. (1971). *Classroom teachers' guide to audio-visual materials.* Philadelphia: Chilton.
> *A guide to a multitude of audiovisual materials available for use in classroom instruction.*

Grady, M. T., & Gawronski, J. D. (1983). *Computers in curriculum and instruction.* Alexandria, VA: Association for Supervision and Curriculum Development.
> *Numerous practical ideas for integrating computer technology into daily classroom instructional plans.*

Horn, R. E., & Cleaves, A. (Eds.). (1980). *The guide to simulation/games for education and training* (4th ed.). Beverly Hills, CA: Sage.
> *One of the most comprehensive guides to simulation games available to teachers.*

Information America. (1985). New York: Neal-Schuman.
> *A directory containing hundreds of sources for finding various kinds of instructional resource materials.*

Kepner, H. S. (Ed.). (1982). *Computers in the classroom.* Washington, DC: National Education Association.
> *Useful suggestions for understanding and using computer technology as an effective resource for classroom activities.*

McCluhan, M. (1964). *Understanding media: The extensions of man.* New York: McGraw-Hill.
> *A classic work on the impact of media on the human mind, containing valuable insights into how to avoid negative influences of various media.*

Micro-courseware PRO/FILE and Evaluation. (1986). New York: Education Products Information Exchange (EPIE).
> *An excellent description and assessment of computer software available for classroom instructional programs.*

Minor, E. O. (1978). *Handbook for preparing visual media.* (2nd ed.). New York: McGraw-Hill.
>   *A comprehensive and practical guide for using a variety of visual media in the classroom.*

Papert, S. (1980). *Mindstorms: Children, computers and powerful ideas.* New York: Basic Books.
>   *A major study raising questions on the role computers can, do, and will play in educating children.*

Satterthwaite, L. (1980). *Graphics: Skills, media, and materials.* Dubuque, IA: Kendall-Hunt.
>   *A book presenting many excellent suggestions and guidelines for using different kinds of graphics as effective instructional aids.*

Taggart, D. T. (1975). *A guide to sources in educational media and technology.* Metuchen, NJ: Scarecrow Press.
>   *A comprehensive listing of sources for obtaining instructional resources using various media and technologies.*

Wittich, W. A., & Schuller, C. F. (1979). *Instructional technology: Its nature and use* (6th ed.). New York: Harper & Row.
>   *A book discussing the major issues and concerns facing teachers as they attempt to incorporate a variety of instructional technologies into their classroom programs.*

CHAPTER 5
♦ ♦ ♦ ♦ ♦ ♦ ♦

Reaching the Students

INTRODUCTION

The rapid rate of change in society, particularly of its younger members, presents modern-day classroom teachers with a dilemma. The longer they teach, the more likely they are to lose touch with the coming generations of adolescents. What they remember of their adolescence, or even what they experienced as teachers of adolescents in the past, cannot always explain the nature, needs, and problems of the current and future generations of adolescents with whom they must work. In search of a solution to this dilemma, Mead (1950, p. 34) asks, "How can we set up some pattern which will enable the teacher to grow through the years, instead of becoming stunted and distorted, affrighted by the increasing gap between herself and her pupils?"

This chapter attempts to answer this question and to guide the teacher in reaching adolescent students.

> On the one side, it is [the teacher's] business to be on the alert to see what attitudes and habitual tendencies are being created. In this direction he must, if he is an educator, be able to judge what attitudes are actually conducive to continued growth and what are detrimental. He must, in addition, have that sympathetic understanding of individuals as individuals which gives him an idea of what is actually going on in the minds of those who are learning. (Dewey, 1938, p. 32)

To reach students requires understanding their distinctive natures as members of particular age groups, as individuals, and as products of their environment. Such understanding should then serve as the basis for addressing their needs and problems, for preparing them as members of society, and for motivating them to realize their full potential. In this chapter, ideas and recommendations are presented for understanding, dealing with, and motivating students in ways that meaningfully touch their lives.

BASIC THEORIES

♦ Understanding Students

It is essential to understand your students; you cannot reach someone you know nothing about. This section will focus on understanding the general characteristics of students as adolescents, as individuals, and as products of their environment.

Students as Adolescents

In looking at the adolescent it often seems as though the previously innocent child has become uncontrollable and, to a degree, destructive. In actuality adolescence does not represent a regression but rather an awakening of tremendous energy and new awarenesses that have yet to be harnessed and tempered by the maturity gained through experience and understanding. Adolescence denotes a growth of consciousness. Cognition, conation, and affection expand as new and varied perceptions are possible. And with this expansion comes concomitant changes in the adolescent's understanding of the world around as well as in his or her ways of dealing with the environment and the feelings and upheavals within. The growth of the adolescent in this way is natural and is to be considered neither good nor bad. During this period of rapid growth in consciousness and physical development, it is essential to give constructive direction so the emerging young adult forms a sense of purpose and sobriety and an affinity with his or her fellow humans.

Adolescence is the period of life when one is too young to be considered an adult but too old to be treated like a child. The adolescent seeks independence yet at the same time needs guidance and security. Adolescence is a time of rapid physical and intellectual development, with the corresponding personality changes and emotional turbulence. Students at this age feel great pressure to demonstrate that they are individuals worthy of respect. Acceptance by parents, teachers, and especially peers, is crucial to them. Adolescents feel increasing responsibility for what they do. This sense of responsibility, coupled with the search for identity and acceptance, makes adolescence one of the most difficult periods of life.

Working with adolescents can present great difficulties, but it can also present great opportunities. Teachers who meet this challenge and make the effort to understand and deal with students throughout the turbulence of adolescence can influence the direction of their lives as no one else can.

> Adolescence is a time when cooperative work and mutual understanding predominate. At the beginning of adolescence social life enters a new phase of increasing collaboration which involves exchange of viewpoints and discussion of their merits before joint control of the group is possible. (Beard, 1969, pp. 97–98)

This new phase of cooperative effort and consideration of varied perspectives opens up adolescents to new patterns of thinking. Their conception of the world changes, their imagination reaches new realms, and their creative energy is at its highest level yet. Adolescents are a force—a force needing direction through constructive activities, experiences, and examples.

Adolescents around the ages of ten to thirteen (later for those who develop more slowly) have limited capacity for abstract thought. In school, however, adolescents often find themselves confronted with large quantities of information they cannot relate to their own experiences. It is important, therefore, to plan instructional activities and examples with which students can readily identify. Such concrete learning experiences provide the transition to more abstract thinking. For example, when beginning a lesson on finding the area of various geometrical forms, the junior high school math teacher should first let students experiment by constructing and measuring cardboard boxes. Only after these experiments should formulas for finding area be introduced. Working with the boxes will set students' minds searching for the solution to a tangible problem, thus capturing their interest and preparing them for the abstract thought needed to understand and apply the mathematical formulas that will help them solve their problem. To develop the capacity for logical thinking, adolescents also need to be actively engaged in discussions and cooperative tasks in which their assumptions and ideas can be examined and different viewpoints reconciled.

To give you an idea of the various levels of development found within the adolescent age range, developmental units measured in terms of chronological time from ages ten to sixteen are listed in Table 5.1. The charac-

TABLE 5.1 *Developmental Units of Adolescence*

DEVELOPMENTAL UNITS	CHARACTERISTICS
Ten year olds (fifth grade)	They like school and learning.
	Their teachers are important to them and they often respect their word as law even more than that of their parents.
	They like their teachers to schedule their time and activities for them.
	They like to memorize but have difficulty connecting two facts.
Eleven year olds (sixth grade)	The teacher is probably the most important single factor of their school life.
	One of their greatest weaknesses is in seeing relationships; they understand best if the teacher imparts knowledge through a story.
	They are keen on competition of any sort.
Twelve year olds (seventh grade)	Their one outstanding characteristic is enthusiasm.
	They like to get to school early, and they show interest in doing homework.
	They are ready to be demanded of by the teacher but take liberties with a teacher who is "soft."
	They have many interests and need help channeling their energy and expressing themselves.
	They need firmness and control, but when their freedom is too curtailed they become frustrated.
Thirteen year olds (eighth grade)	They organize their time better, sustain concentration more, and are more self-controlled.
	Their eagerness to learn is overtly less enthusiastic while being more organized and sustained.
	They are calmer, more inhibited, and conscientious.
	They are interested in trying new things and feel a sense of accomplishment after solving a word problem.
	They enjoy a broadened outlook of world affairs as well as discussions and debates.
Fourteen year olds (ninth grade)	Their contemplation of their own personality is becoming less uneasy, dissatisfied, and defensive, and is becoming more calm and judicious.
	They intermingle well, are more respectful, and have ideals.
	They tend to spread themselves too thin and thus fail to spend time and energy on school work.

TABLE 5.1 *Continued*

DEVELOPMENTAL UNITS	CHARACTERISTICS
	They have a readiness for change and a capacity for leadership.
	They like to evaluate both their subjects and teachers.
Fifteen year olds (tenth grade)	They want to define their thoughts, philosophy, and place in life.
	If they cannot find their place or some expression through activity, they are in danger of dropping out.
	They have a tendency to rebel, so it is very important to plan for them as individuals.
	They learn quickly in new fields and like the stimulus of fresh material or a new slant on some topic.
	They are responsive to group loyalty and like to participate in class projects.
Sixteen year olds (eleventh grade)	They are more tolerant of the world in general.
	They are very interested in people and build many friendships.
	They are more solidly oriented to the future than they were at fifteen.
	They can be receptive and may even like criticism because of their interest in improving as a person.

Source: Based on material from *Youth: The Years from Ten to Sixteen* by A. Gesell, F. L. Ilg, and L. Ames, 1956, New York: Harper and Brothers.

teristic manifestations of each unit are completely accurate for very few if any students, and they are best employed as a general guide to understanding the developmental trends that occur during the adolescent years.

Students enter junior high school as children and leave high school as young adults. Their interests and capabilities change so much between the ages of twelve and eighteen that classroom instruction can be relevant only if it addresses these changes as they occur.

Students as Individuals

Each student is a unique individual who has unique strengths and weaknesses, needs and problems. Therefore it is crucial when working with adolescents to develop the capability to recognize and the willingness to preserve their inherent qualities, and to tolerate their shortcomings long enough so that they may be gradually corrected rather than summarily rejected. Of all the possible difficulties an adolescent faces, rejection, especially by his or her teacher, can be the most devastating.

Because the secondary school program is divided into specialized subject areas, the student often goes through these years without being seen as a person, but only as a student in a variety of subjects in which he or she is considered either a success or a failure. Unfortunately, the tendency in most schools is to teach students as though they were all alike by minimizing differences and overemphasizing whatever similarities exist. As a result, many teachers employ a uniform method for dealing with all students and fail to deal with each one as a unique individual.

Each student within each developmental unit has a unique style and rate of growth:

> Every individual has a distinctive style of growth which is revealed when the progressive course of development is viewed in perspective. Some individuals, for example, develop in a smooth, gradual, step-by-step fashion; others seem to move in spurts, hardly changing for long periods of time, then acquiring new behaviors in a sudden flood. Again, some individuals show wide swings of behavior as they proceed from stage to stage of maturity, highlighting the extremes of each phase, while others, by contrast, show only a slight gravitation toward the prototypes of behavior along their overall course. Growth patterns such as these are often characteristic of the individual from earliest infancy throughout life. (Gesell, Ilg, & Ames, 1956, p. 31)

Students generally are of three different types—intellectual, active, and emotional, corresponding to the cognitive, conative, and affective aspects of consciousness, respectively. Each type clearly has implications for the teacher's selection of instructional strategies and classroom activities. Further, individual students at different times may tend toward any one of the three types as situations change and growth continues. It is important to help students function in all three modes and thus develop a balanced approach to learning. But the teacher must first understand clearly each student's particular type so that weak areas can be developed and strengths built upon.

Students' ability to understand concepts is determined not only by their age or by the information presented to and retained by them but also by the unique experiences they have in life. The more vivid the experience, the deeper the understanding it creates. For example, most adolescents can understand the concept "Waste not, want not" in an intellectual sense, but cannot understand it experientially and have a hard time applying it to their own lives. The child who has experienced prolonged hunger, however, will understand the concept all too well.

Students' individual natures and qualities must be accurately determined if instructional activities are to be of any value to them.

> The child comes to school with his own ideas about space, time, causality, quantity, and number. His ideas are, however, incomplete in comparison with those of adults. The concept of education must, therefore, be broad-

ened to encompass aiding children in the modification of their existing knowledge in addition to helping them to learn new material. (Elkind, 1981, p. 108)

Equating intellectual development with age, failing to take into account each student's unique experiences or rate of growth, is likely to result in classroom instruction that will neither interest students nor further their capacity to learn. Discerning each student's interests and capabilities requires constant and careful observation as well as great perceptivity.

Students as Products of the Environment

Learning about students' cultural backgrounds aids the teacher in understanding and appreciating their behavior so he or she can better determine their strengths and weaknesses and assist them in their growth.

> A culture is the fabric of ideas, ideals, beliefs, skills, tools, aesthetic objects, methods of thinking, customs, and institutions into which each member of society is born. . . . Perhaps it is not too much to say that the basic personality structure of the individual is shaped by the culture into which he is born and grows to maturity. (Smith, 1957, pp. 4–5)

Because their cultural backgrounds largely determine their capacity to comprehend and expand their perceptions, knowledge of students' cultural backgrounds provides a key to the influences that shape their values, personality, and interests. For example, students brought up in a certain cultural environment may find aggressive competition alien. Knowing this, the teacher can avoid creating a competitive atmosphere that might make these students feel left out. To understand each student's cultural experience, it is necessary to look at his or her capacities for such experience.

Cross, Baker, and Stiles suggest four sets of capacities common to all people that should be taken into account in order to accurately assess their capacities for cultural experience (Figure 5.1):

FIGURE 5.1 *Capacities for Cultural Experience*

1. *Congenital.* Capacities that are developed from the effects of the environment on native capacities.

2. *Inherited.* Capacities that are developed due to characteristics that emerge from generations within the family setting.

3. *Acquired.* Capacities that are developed as one moves out of one's inherited setting into a fuller social world.

4. *Attained.* Capacities that are developed by one's reaching out beyond what is normally available.

Source: Condensed from *Teaching in a Multicultural Society* (pp. 122–125) by D. E. Cross, G. C. Baker, and L. J. Stiles (Eds.), 1977, New York: Free Press.

1. *Congenital capacities.* Although our congenital capacities are almost totally hereditary, physical environmental conditions both in the womb and from infancy on greatly affect which native capacities will be accessible to development.
2. *Inherited capacities.* Our biological inheritance, or inherited capacities as persons, is not simply derived from isolated physical properties such as eye color and bone structure. To a considerable extent, these characteristics emerge from the family setting.
3. *Acquired capacities.* Each of the four categories overlaps with the others in actual experience, if for no other reason than that each begins early. Nonetheless, it is a sign of cultural growth that individuals move out of their inherited setting into a fuller, less narrowly controllable social world and acquire further capacities for relationships there.
4. *Attained capacities.* The etymology of the word *acquire* refers to a process of gaining for oneself by seeking things from the outside world. In contrast, *attain* refers to a process of gaining some end by reaching out, as if to touch, and by one's own distinctive efforts. (1977, pp. 122–125)

At the root of understanding students' diverse cultural backgrounds is an acceptance of their many differences and characteristics.

Teachers need to view each student as a unique individual who possesses a rich cultural heritage. . . . What a teacher perceives as a deficiency may be a value that is part of the traditional culture of the student—a value that needs to be recognized and legitimized in its own right. (Heck & Williams, 1984, pp. 53–54)

Culture in the sense of recognizing the value of students' diverse backgrounds is an understanding and appreciation of the world around us. "An educated person is continually seeking to understand more fully, oneself, other human beings, and the world in which one lives in order to live more intelligently" (Tyler in Mickler, 1985, p. 28). This must be the guiding principle if acceptance, and with it understanding, of students' cultural backgrounds is to be realized.

Although it is important for the teacher to become familiar with students' cultural backgrounds as a means of understanding them, it is also important that he or her share this knowledge with students so they can grow as members of a multicultural society. A multicultural approach seeks to impart knowledge of the values and ways of various cultures. It is invaluable for widening students' perspectives on life, and it helps them learn to value cooperation and tolerance.

The multicultural approach in teaching takes its direction from these basic tenets; it aims to create within the school a sensitivity to cultural diversity by creating a model of a healthy multicultural society and helping students to develop and accept diverse perspectives. (Cross et al., 1977, p. 15)

A multicultural approach embraces the concepts and ideals of brotherhood, justice, and freedom.

As part of the classroom instructional program, the study of other cultures can help students learn the ways of other peoples while providing an excellent opportunity for an interdisciplinary approach to learning. For example, one such cultural unit would discuss the language and literature, art, music, history, economics, and science of a particular culture. Because no one teacher has the knowledge to cover all these areas competently, it is also an opportunity for collaborative planning, something usually missing in most secondary schools. Through such studies students can come to appreciate the common problems of life faced by people the world over and the variety of ways these problems are dealt with. Thought-provoking discussions often result as the students attempt to answer questions such as, Why have particular types of educational systems developed in other cultures? or Are we solving our problems in particular areas more wisely than people in other cultures?

Without adequate information and understanding of other cultures students have no frame of reference from which to look out on the world. Much of their information about other cultures comes from the media, which treats these subjects both superficially and unrealistically and perpetuates numerous stereotypes. Dispelling prejudice so students can appreciate the qualities of all peoples is a primary goal of cultural instruction.

An example of a useful series of multicultural learning activities can be developed by considering the following five questions as they apply to various cultural groups:

1. What expectations and values are evident in this culture? How might these affect the frame of reference of members of the society?
2. How are trust and authority perceived and communicated in this culture?
3. In this culture what are considered important goals to aspire to and personal qualities to develop?
4. How do people of this cultural heritage attempt to assimilate other cultures? What problems have they encountered in doing this?
5. What variations in characteristics seem to exist within this particular cultural group as related to regional, language, and socioeconomic differences?

These questions can effectively guide the study of any cultural group and are likely to result in discussion that provides many insights for increasing social awareness and tolerance.

Table 5.2 contains a list of objectives Cross et al. developed for teachers to increase understanding and consequently improve teaching of students from various cultural backgrounds.

TABLE 5.2 *Multicultural Objectives for Teachers*

GENERAL AREAS	OBJECTIVES
Knowledge	To expand teachers' knowledge of their own and other cultures
	To deepen and increase teachers' awareness of their own cultural identity
	To help teachers develop a better understanding of various ways to expand their contacts with other cultural groups and to become acquainted with their own cultural roles
Philosophy	To develop teachers' capacities for humane, sensitive, and critical inquiry into the nature of cultural issues, particularly as these may relate to education
	To study the aesthetic, epistemological, and ethical interrelationships of cultural life in the United States and elsewhere through their psychological, social, economic, and political dimensions
	To increase teachers' capacities for examining their own cultural attitudes and values in the light of history and current situations
	To augment teachers' abilities for envisaging future developments and engaging in planning for cultural interchange within an emerging world society
Methodology	To help teachers develop the ability to plan and conduct multicultural learning experiences by
	◆ Investigating, developing, and testing suitable teaching strategies for a multicultural curriculum
	◆ Increasing skills for locating, developing, and using instructional resources for multicultural education
	◆ Learning to assess the effectiveness of a multicultural curriculum

Source: Based on material from *Teaching in a Multicultural Society* (pp. 133–134) by D. E. Cross, G. C. Baker, and L. J. Stiles (Eds.), 1977, New York: Free Press.

◆ Dealing with Students

To effectively deal with students it is necessary to address their needs and problems, prepare them as members of society, and understand the main areas that must be considered in working with them.

Addressing Students' Needs and Problems

Adolescents see their world as full of problems to solve. They try to figure out the world around them and how to deal with it. Table 5.3 lists some of the more important problem areas confronting adolescents along with the crucial factors that must be considered in helping them deal with these areas.

The development of positive values in school depends more than anything else on hope and love in the school atmosphere. Children who

TABLE 5.3 *Problem Areas Confronting Adolescents*

PROBLEM AREAS	FACTORS TO CONSIDER
Personal	
Rapid growth and search for identity	Provide guidance to give direction and meaning
Social	
Need for acceptance by peers, teachers, and parents	Show caring attitude to foster confidence and sobriety
Educational	
Pressure to succeed and need to develop mental discipline	Instill good habits to foster discipline and motivation
Vocational	
Increasing responsibility and need to prepare for adult life	Set example to give purpose and build character

experience love and acceptance from adults around them are likely to become reliable, thoughtful, and self-confident teenagers. Thus, reaching students' hearts and minds is directly related to the degree they feel their interests are being taken seriously. Words and gestures alone are not convincing—corresponding actions must exemplify the words and gestures. A sincere effort to create a positive classroom environment (see Table 1.5) clearly demonstrates an interest in students' well-being.

A sensitive teacher can make all students feel like an important part of the class. "The classroom belongs to each learner" (Heck & Williams, 1984, p. 66). This feeling of belonging not only fosters a sense of security but one of trust as well. Trust is the basis for a close relationship with students. Because secondary school students are keenly aware of others' feelings about them, any disrespect or mistrust from the teacher brings a similar response from them, closing off the possibility of mutual effort toward classroom goals.

The nature of the classroom environment greatly influences both character development and intellectual readiness to learn. "The intellectual development of the child is no clockwork sequence of events; it also responds to influences from the environment, notably the school environment" (Bruner, 1960, p. 39). The teacher should not wait for students to reach higher levels of cognitive development before introducing various ideas and materials, but instead should be continuously striving to create and maintain a mode of classroom operation that facilitates such development (e.g., providing challenging, engaging, and creative classroom experiences).

Purkey (1978) suggests that the teacher's verbal and nonverbal communication with students serves either to invite or disinvite students to learning and, as such, is a determining factor in creating a supportive classroom environment. He also notes that invitations or disinvitations to learn are each of essentially two types: intentional and unintentional (Table 5.4).

Adolescents are seeking a direction in life. They are constantly asking, What is important? What should I be doing? The example the teacher sets is an important factor in their growth. It is natural, therefore, that one of the primary factors serving to stimulate students to learn is their relationship with teachers who themselves are engaged in and thus exemplify a quest for learning. On the other hand, nothing dampens student desire to learn more than teachers for whom learning is a thing of the past and instruction a mere formality.

Adolescents are constantly bombarded with messages from television and movies that glamorize violence and glorify greed. And they spend more time watching television or movies in a given year than they spend in school! Add to this the adolescent's quest for emancipation from authority at home, and the importance of the teacher's role in constructively directing the adolescent's energy is seen not only as desirable but as imperative.

Being at a very impressionable stage of life, the adolescent is open to many other destructive influences, such as gang violence, drug taking, and various illegal activities. The teacher, who occupies the strategic position of "custodian of the gateway to culture" (Mead, 1950, p. 13), can use this impressionability to encourage constructive activities, such as learning new ideas in a particular subject area, tutoring less able students, and participating in school events and community projects. In addition, the teacher can foster a more mature outlook on life by directing students to see their own needs in relation to others' needs.

TABLE 5.4 *Inviting and Disinviting Students to Learn*

INVITATIONS TO LEARN	DISINVITATIONS TO LEARN
Unintentionally Inviting	**Unintentionally Disinviting**
Teachers functioning at this level are characterized by a natural interest in students, a charismatic and friendly personality, and an enthusiasm for teaching.	Teachers functioning at this level are characterized by lack of expertise in their subject area and in teaching methods and by an inability to assess or cope with differences.
Intentionally Inviting	**Intentionally Disinviting**
Teachers functioning at this level have the same characteristics of unintentionally inviting teachers but make conscious plans to invite students to learn.	Teachers functioning at this level are characterized by a judgmental and negative nature, a narrow perspective on life, and a lack of interest in helping students.

Source: Based on material from *Inviting School Success: A Self-Concept Approach to Teaching and Learning* by W. W. Purkey, 1978, Belmont, CA: Wadsworth.

"[The teacher] is also in a strategic position as a respected neutral bystander to ease the tensions between parents and their adolescent children that are incidental to the struggle for emancipation" (Ausubel, Montemayor, & Pergrouhi, 1977, p. 428). Thus the teacher can extend his or her influence beyond the classroom and into the home, where many essential learning experiences occur.

In 1977 the National Education Association conducted a study of ninety-five secondary school students, asking them what might be done to improve schools and schooling (Shane, 1977, pp. 68–69). The responses revealed that students' major concerns centered around their social and emotional well-being. Their three major concerns were these: (1) they wanted help in learning how to cope with a frustrating, frightening world; (2) they wanted schools that care about them as people; and (3) they wanted school to teach them how to communicate their feelings, hopes, and concerns. The students said little or nothing about hiring better teachers, placing more emphasis on certain subjects, or spending more money for schools. This can be attributed to students' overwhelming concern with their emotional and personal growth, indicating that the teacher should be particularly sensitive to student needs in these areas.

Preparing Students as Members of Society

The teacher should plan not only academic learning experiences but also those that foster the understanding and assimilation of higher human values such as justice, cooperation, and perseverance.

> The school years are crucial in the development of positive attitudes toward self, others, and society. Students need to be aware and accepting of themselves in order to live with other students and with adults, to learn from their environment, to enjoy the present, to prepare responsibly; in a word, to be total human beings. (Heck & Williams, 1984, p. 60)

Teaching values and developing character must be at least as high on the agenda as imparting information and ideas of particular subject areas. The success attained in educating adolescents directly measures the future well-being of our society. The secondary school teacher has the great responsibility of setting an example of honesty, tolerance, service, and self-discipline. Further, the teacher must guide students to discover the higher values in life and to make these values their own.

> At this time the studies ought to be directed toward humanity, toward human life, and particularly toward the men who have helped civilization advance. Until he is twelve years old, nature ought to constitute the child's primary interest. After twelve years, we must develop in the child the feeling of society, which ought to contribute to more understanding among men and, as a result, more love. Let us develop admiration and understanding for work and for the life of man to this end. We put particular emphasis

on the practical exercises. We have the child participate in social work of some kind. We help him intellectually, by means of study, to fathom man's work in society in order to develop in him the understanding and solidarity which are so sorely needed. (Montessori, 1948, p. 96)

What a person values determines to a large extent where his or her time and energy will go, which in turn measures his or her worth to society. Thus, it is important to understand what a particular value system can mean to the adolescent.

1. It supplies the individual with a sense of purpose and direction.
2. It gives the group a common orientation and supplies the basis of individual action and of unified, collective action.
3. It serves as the basis for judging the behavior of individuals.
4. It enables the individual to know what to expect of others as well as how to conduct himself.
5. It fixes the sense of right and wrong, fair and foul, desirable and undesirable, moral and immoral. (Smith, 1957, p. 61)

In this sense the development of values should be considered more important than, but not apart from, what one knows. Knowledge that remains only information, touching no vital point in one's life, does little to further personal growth. Values, on the other hand, largely determine one's actions and relationships with others and thus can be considered a higher aspect of knowledge and intelligence. Therefore, healthy values, ideals, attitudes, and tastes are more important than the accumulation of information.

Helping students develop high values requires a close link with their home and community situations and an understanding of their day-to-day problems. Without this specific knowledge, talk of developing values and character would seem to students like empty preaching. To counterbalance any negative effects of difficult experiences, the teacher must first demonstrate to students that he or she takes a personal interest in their lives—in and out of school. Discussions with students, either as a group or individually, can be particularly effective in helping them appreciate new ideas and see problems from a wider perspective. In addition, the teacher "can furnish students with literature, including stories, novels, drama, essays, and poetry, that illuminates ethical issues and helps students understand and feel the significance of courage in acting in accordance with conscience" (Tyler, 1975, p. 13). The selection and the timing of the use of such materials requires the specific knowledge and understanding of each student's home and community life.

Much learning occurs indirectly through various social relationships. It may be necessary for the teacher to help students understand and deal with these often complex social interactions. Dewey outlines three special functions of the school in a complex society:

1. *Simplifying the environment.* A complex civilization is too complex to be assimilated in toto. It has to be broken up into portions, as it were, and assimilated piecemeal, in a gradual and graded way.
2. *Establishing a purified medium of action.* It is the business of the school environment to eliminate, so far as possible, the unworthy features of the existing environment from influence upon mental habitudes.
3. *Balancing the various elements of the social environment.* To see to it that each individual gets an opportunity to escape from the limitations of the social group in which he was born, and to come into living contact with a broader environment. (1928, pp. 22–27)

Main Areas to Consider
There are six main areas to consider when working with adolescents:

1. *Expectations.* Do not expect more of adolescents than they can do. They are not yet mature in understanding and experience. Expectations that realistically challenge them, however, will help them grow.
2. *Firmness.* Carefully set out rules for study and behavior, considering well before making absolute prohibitions. Once you say "No" you should mean it and should not be swayed or provoked.
3. *Guidance.* Students need guidance in forming views of the world around them. Do not force your own views; rather, lead them to appreciate the worth of your views.
4. *Self-respect.* Be sensitive to their feelings and need for self-respect. They are very self-conscious as well as peer conscious. Do not unnecessarily speak ill of them before their peers; it could injure their self-respect. Help them develop self-respect as a preliminary asset to character building.
5. *Character.* The teacher, through example, can teach students honesty, sincerity, a sense of responsibility, love of work, good habits, and good manners. These traits manifested in the teacher can greatly influence students' character development.
6. *Careful observation.* Constant and careful observation is essential to the execution of the above guidelines. Watch how your actions affect students and modify your subsequent actions accordingly.

Although they are very much preoccupied with their own needs, adolescents are at the impressionable stage of development where they can learn to care about others. The teacher, through his or her own example and by object lessons, can demonstrate that focusing on others not only leads to greater personal joy but also puts one's problems in perspective. Discussing people who have sacrificed personal comfort for ideals can be valuable to this end. The teacher's personal example, however, will influence students the most.

The teacher's love and concern for each student lie at the heart of his or her role as guide and model. They are the very basis of effective teaching. Russell asserts that this love and care are what make service possible:

Neither character nor intelligence will develop [in the student] as well or freely where the teacher is deficient in love; and love of this kind consists essentially in feeling the child as an end. We all have this feeling about ourselves; we desire good things for ourselves without first demanding a proof that some great purpose will be furthered by our obtaining them. . . . Parents want their children to grow, to be strong and healthy, to do well at school, and so on, in just the same way in which they want things for themselves; no effort of self-denial and no abstract principle of justice is involved in taking trouble about such matters. This parental instinct is not always strictly confined to one's own children. In its diffused form, it must exist in anyone who is to be a good teacher. (1926, pp. 46–47)

◆ Motivating Students

Motivation is the inner force that moves a person to take action toward a specific end. In terms of the teacher's role, motivation involves "getting students to move towards instructional goals, move into academic learning, and move forward in the acquisition of skills and values" (McDaniel, 1985, p. 19). The sources of motivation range from purely physical needs such as hunger and thirst to the highest human ideals of selfless service and love. The aim of the teacher should be to motivate students to increasingly higher aspirations. Students should be taught that personal fulfillment most often comes when motivated by ideals such as dedication to their chosen work, empathy and respect for their fellow humans, and moral courage in the face of hardship or danger. At a certain stage, efforts to motivate students focus on their need to develop self-discipline and confidence. Once these qualities are achieved and the students have gained stability and strength, sources of motivation can include a wider sphere in which the well-being of others becomes a primary factor.

Adolescents need to be motivated to fulfill their potential in life. Being emotionally immature and having limited experience, they do not know in which directions to apply their energies and capabilities and often channel them into unproductive and even self-destructive activities. The success of the teacher in motivating a student can make the difference between a productive and fulfilled life and a life of uselessness and failure. Motivation is a function of teaching values and character development. Students learn about the value of positive action and gain an understanding of the consequences of inaction or negative action. The key principle in motivation toward positive behavior patterns is whether the end result, or goal, is considered desirable and worth the effort.

The effectiveness of a teacher's motivational efforts is measured by what students actually do in the classroom. The teacher's actions and words serve as a catalyst, directing and stimulating students to self-sustained effort.

Nothing motivates students like a teacher who is alive with enthusiasm for the subject. Such enthusiasm must be the result of his or her own sincere interest in learning and in the extensive search for ideas and materials described in Chapter 3 for carrying out comprehensive curriculum development.

Effective motivation can awaken students to surmount the limitations of their local environments. "If [the students] depend only on what the community can teach, [learning] is going to be provincial, and there is going to be bias rather than a more objective examination of our social institutions" (Tyler in Mickler, 1985, p. 25). The school, therefore, must expand students' horizons to encompass a larger reality—that of the human family. Furthermore, courses and related schoolwork and exams have to represent more than simply a means of accumulating credits on the way to graduation. The overall goal to be achieved through the curriculum developed and instructional activities carried out is the realization that one never does, nor need want to, graduate from learning and growing.

Adolescents have great difficulty relating to anything too remote from their current condition. Motivational activities are more effective if the purpose of learning is clear and immediate to their lives. A balance must be maintained between their immediate interests and what is the best for their long-term growth. It may sometimes be necessary to engage in learning activity that is not interesting and that does not have immediate results but is nonetheless essential to understanding a subject or developing discipline in study habits. Students can be shown that applying themselves to activities that do not have immediately discernible results can have beneficial long-term results.

The following steps should be taken for investigating problems in motivation:

1. Determine the personal traits that the teacher should express in order to secure the cheerful cooperation of the given class.
2. Identify the dominant interests of the class as a whole or of individual pupils within the class.
3. Find classroom activities pertinent to the work that provide sufficiently for pupils' self-expression.
4. Identify the items of prescribed or supplementary subject matter that are most intrinsically appealing to the class.
5. Identify methods of directing group work to which the class best responds.
6. Identify the particular rewards or penalties that offer the strongest incentive to individual pupils. (Waples & Tyler, 1930, pp. 313–314)

Students are very quick to gauge how demanding a particular teacher is and will adjust their efforts accordingly. If sufficiently stimulated by the teacher's high expectations, they will rise to the challenge and accomplish the tasks set before them. When backed up by teacher support, such high expectations motivate students.

Setting low standards may make for temporary or short-term success but results in less learning over time.

Therefore, those teachers who respond to lack of achievement in a given subject or section of the curriculum by significantly simplifying the learning material content, by literally resorting to "spoon-feeding" in the case of all complex issues and concepts, are hardly doing themselves justice. (Markova, 1986, p. 64)

Classroom instruction carried out in this manner brings only temporary success at best. At worst, it can cripple students in terms of their readiness for continued and future learning. Besides, activities and material that present no challenge soon become boring and thus stifle rather than motivate interest in learning. In the long run, students find that studying undemanding learning material is a boring and onerous business that, naturally enough, does nothing to increase motivation toward learning activity.

In Table 5.5 the factors indicating the teacher's expectations for students that are listed need to be considered to obtain an accurate assessment of what students may actually feel is being expected of them.

Students whose hopes have been dashed often give up on life and move more or less aimlessly from situation to situation. Motivating students means at times restoring and boosting their sense of self-worth. In so doing, however, the teacher must be careful to appeal to the constructive rather than

TABLE 5.5 *Factors Indicating the Teacher's Expectations for Students*

FACTORS	INDICATIONS TO LOOK FOR
Nature of learning activities	Are many levels of learning addressed or is information just memorized?
Nature of teaching methods used	Are the methods used primarily teacher-directed (e.g., lecture) or are student-directed (e.g., independent study) and interactive (e.g., discussions) methods used as well?
Nature of resource materials used	Are there many different instructional resources used to provide insights into the subject from many perspectives, or is a single text the only resource used?
Nature of motivation evident	Are the students motivated to learn through extrinsic means such as fear of punishment and competition or through intrinsic means such as interest in the subject and personal growth?
Nature of the teacher's attitude toward students	Is the teacher's attitude toward the students characterized by respect, trust, and encouragement or by disinterested neglect?
Nature of assessment techniques used	Do the assessment techniques used provide information about student interest and readiness for learning, or do they provide information about a narrow range of mechanical skills?

destructive forces within students. "It is an easy way out merely to appeal to a person's desire for approval and recognition. Such motivation in excess can lead to exaggerated egoism and personal ambition that could ultimately become destructive forces for both the individual and the community. Instead, the teacher must use a balance of motivational methods" (Einstein, 1950, p. 197).

Love is the ultimate motivator. There are no secrets for understanding students, no psychology texts to read or courses to take for sure-fire techniques. Dedication, patience, and a sincere interest in students' well-being are the only methods that work.

SUMMARY

In this chapter several main points about reaching students were presented:

1. To reach students requires understanding their distinctive natures as members of particular age groups, as individuals, and as products of their environment.
2. Adolescence is the period of life when one is too young to be considered an adult but too old to be treated like a child. The adolescent seeks independence yet at the same time needs guidance and security.
3. In looking at the adolescent it often seems as though the previously innocent child has become uncontrollable and, to a degree, destructive. In actuality adolescence is not a regression but rather an awakening of tremendous energy and new awarenesses that have yet to be harnessed and tempered by experience and understanding.
4. Because each student is a unique individual, it is important for the teacher to develop the capability to recognize and the willingness to preserve his or her inherent qualities and to tolerate his or her shortcomings long enough that they may be gradually corrected rather than summarily rejected.
5. Students' ability to understand concepts is determined not only by their age or by the information presented to and retained by them but also by the unique experiences they have in life.
6. Knowledge of students' cultural backgrounds provides a key to the influences that shape their values, personality, and interests. At the root of understanding students' diverse cultural backgrounds is an acceptance of their many differences and characteristics.
7. Imparting a knowledge of the values and ways of various cultures is invaluable for widening students' perspectives on life and gives them a sense of the value of cooperation and tolerance.
8. Being at a very impressionable stage of life, the adolescent is open to many destructive influences, such as gang violence, drug taking, and various other illegal activities. The teacher, who occupies the strategic position of "custodian to the gateway of culture," can use students'

impressionability to encourage constructive activities and growth and to direct them to see their own needs in relation to others' needs.

9. Because values are at the heart of character development, the teacher should plan not only academic learning experiences but also those that foster the understanding and assimilation of higher values such as justice, cooperation, and perseverance.

10. The teacher's love and concern for each student, which lie at the heart of his or her role as guide and model, are the basis of effective teaching.

11. The success of the teacher in motivating a student can make the difference between a productive and fulfilled life and a life of uselessness and failure.

12. The aim of the teacher should be to motivate students to increasingly higher aspirations.

Minimizing personal needs and aspiring to serve are prerequisites for being able to reach students.

> A man who is to educate really well, and is to make the young grow and develop into their full stature, must be filled through and through with the spirit of reverence. . . . The teacher without reverence easily despises the child for [its] outward inferiorities. He thinks it is his duty to "mold" the child: in imagination he is the potter with the clay. And so he gives to the child some unnatural shape, which hardens with age, producing strains and spiritual dissatisfactions, out of which grow cruelty and envy, and the belief that others must be compelled to undergo the same distortions. The man who has reverence will not think it his duty to "mold" the young. He feels in all that lives, but especially in human beings, and most of all in children, something sacred, indefinable, unlimited, something individual and strangely precious, the growing principle of life, an embodied fragment of the dumb striving of the world. . . . The outward helplessness of the child and the appeal of dependence make him conscious of the responsibility of a trust. His imagination shows him what the child may become, for good or evil, how its impulses may be developed or thwarted, how its hopes must be dimmed and the life in it grow less living, how its trust will be bruised and its quick desires replaced by brooding will. All this gives him a longing to help the child in its own battle. . . . The man who feels this can wield the authority of an educator without infringing the principle of liberty. (Russell, 1927, pp. 90–91)

◆ ◆ ◆ ◆ ◆ ◆ ◆

PRACTICAL MODEL 5.1 A Guide for Motivating Secondary School Students

Introduction This practical model provides advice for motivating students by fostering self-esteem and creating a nurturing classroom environment through mutual respect.

Submitted by Jane Rudolph, high school English teacher, Los Angeles, California

Purpose   To provide secondary school teachers with a guide to the aspects of classroom instruction to consider for motivating students

Setting   Secondary school

♦ **Rationale**

An effective teacher comes to class well prepared. If a teacher is knowledgeable and enthusiastic about teaching a particular subject and uses creative methods to reach students, it is likely he or she will succeed in gaining and holding their attention. The following suggestions cover many aspects of classroom instruction and are presented as a guide to motivating students.

1. Promise students a successful year at the beginning of the school year. Invite success! Communicate clearly your high expectations and intention to see them do well in your class.
2. Get students involved in the assignments. Give homework and classwork that provide students with opportunities to learn and grow. Hold them accountable for their work and give them as much credit as is feasible for all the work completed. Before collecting the work, have students share some of their ideas with each other. Vary the assignments and give students a variety of options so they feel involved in making some decisions.
3. Use a variety of teaching methods and instructional activities in one class period. Students' attention spans are short, so you have to be flexible and creative to engage and maintain their interest.
4. Create activities, projects, and lessons that provide opportunities for all students to succeed so they can develop a sense of self-confidence.
5. Plan for activities that allow students to work cooperatively in small groups. Hold students accountable for their participation and contributions to the group through occasional cooperative evaluations at the conclusion of a particular group activity.
6. Allow for active student involvement and concrete learning experiences. Research shows that students who are actively involved in solving problems through such experiences learn better.
7. Plan for field experiences. Students can be assigned to a long-term project that requires interviews and work in the community. Such activities keep students alert to what is happening around them as it relates to what they are learning in the classroom.
8. Recognize when students are slumping and attempt to identify the causes so quick action can be taken to set them moving in the right direction.
9. Assign credit to many different activities to show students that all their work and participation in class is recognized and rewarded.
10. Give personal attention to the "do nothing" student. A plan for helping such a student should be developed based on his or her abilities. Because lack of self-confidence may be a cause of this student's problem, have

him or her work on only one assignment or project at a time. Formulate precise, meaningful goals that can be realistically accomplished and then assure success by providing support and opportunities for reinforcement as the student proceeds toward the goals.

11. Return work promptly with helpful comments so students know that you care about their efforts. If papers, quizzes, projects, and assignments are returned only after a long time students will not do their work carefully.

12. Check the grade book every week to see how each student is doing. Intervene immediately if a student is performing poorly. Conferences should be held with such students because personal, immediate attention is often helpful.

13. Give positive rather than negative attention to students as much as possible. Assign "difficult" students tasks that require taking responsibility, thereby redirecting their energies and giving them a sense of self-worth.

14. Encourage parents to support their children by maintaining a home environment conducive to learning. Individual conferences and workshops are useful for informing parents about how they can help their children develop good study habits and a sense of responsibility.

◆ ◆ ◆ ◆ ◆ ◆ ◆

CASE STUDY 5.1   Motivating Students

Orienting Questions   As you read this case study ask yourself these questions:

Specific
- ◆ Does this teacher tend to appeal more to the constructive or destructive forces within the students?
- ◆ What is the relationship between this teacher's conception of motivation and the students' needs to reach their potential for learning?

General
- ◆ What points in this lesson stand out as indicators of this teacher's strengths and/or weaknesses?
- ◆ What recommendations would you make for addressing the problems this teacher seems to have?

Setting   *School* – Magnet high school drawing students from all parts of a large urban center

Subject – Reading (sixty minutes)

Teacher – Mrs. Doan, experienced history and reading teacher

Students – Eighteen eleventh-grade students of average to above-average ability

Topic – Individualized Reading Practice

Lesson	*Note:* Under Time Frame the numbers represent the minutes that elapse as the period progresses. Under Dialog the names of the students and the teacher appear as they speak. The symbol ▶ represents a brief description of a particularly noteworthy action or observation.

Time Frame	Dialog	
0 to 5	▶	As the students enter the room they take their seats and immediately look at the board to see their assignment for the day.
	Mrs. D.:	Before we all start on our individual assignments let's get out our books and do ten minutes of silent reading.
	Leroy:	Mrs. Doan, I didn't bring my book, so can I borrow one for today?
	Mrs. D.:	Sure. (Pointing to a pile of paperback books on a table near her desk) Take one of these books. They're pretty easy to read and kind of interesting.
5 to 16	▶	Most students are reading their chosen books. Some students are merely turning pages, and a few students have decided to get a head start on their individualized assignments.
	Gene:	(One of the students who has begun her worksheet early, speaking to the girl next to her) Marcie, how did you finish your word-problem worksheet so fast yesterday? I'm jealous.
	Marcie:	Dummy! Just spend a few seconds on each question and don't worry so much about right answers. You can always correct anything you have wrong when Mrs. Doan reads the answers.
16 to 35	**Mrs. D.:**	Okay, it's time for our daily timed reading test so please get out your pencils.
	▶	Mrs. Doan hands out a mimeographed sheet having four paragraphs on it for the test. The students have two minutes to read the material and then two minutes to answer three vocabulary and three comprehension questions.
	Thanh:	(To no one in particular) Man, I don't ever finish reading this thing. I must be slow in the brain!
	Mrs. D.:	Let's see if some of our slowpokes can speed it up today. We would like to show Mr. Johnson (the assistant principal overseeing the school's remedial reading program) that this class can compete with anyone.
	▶	Most students are nervously looking at the clock as they complete the timed reading test, but a few, like Thanh,

Time Frame	Dialog	
		seem to have given up any hope of improving their speed.
	Mrs. D.:	I'm putting the answers to the timed test on the board, so quickly score your papers and pass them up. I've been very pleased with your progress on these tests.
	►	Most students honestly score their papers, but some take the liberty of inserting correct answers to boost their scores.
	Mrs. D.:	For the remaining time I want each of you to pick up where you left off on your individualized exercises. Remember, those who don't get up to level 4 in their exercises by next Tuesday will only be eligible for a B at best on the next report card.
	►	The students take out their individualized learning "menus" that list sequences of exercises contained in a variety of commercially prepared reading skills workbooks.
35 to 60	Mrs. D.:	Beverly, Joanne, and Lisa, you go to the round table and do the advanced dialogs. I'll be coming over to work with you in a few minutes. Everyone else get to your menus and work fast. We want to be the first class to complete all the exercises up to level 4.
	►	Everyone is busily working on their worksheets, while keeping one eye on the clock.
	Thanh:	Mrs. Doan, I'm stuck on this vocabulary exercise. Which words do they want us to know?
	Mrs. D.:	(Going over to Thanh's desk) Oh, this is a bit unclear isn't it? Let's see, I think they want you to match each underlined word with a word from this other column that can serve as an acceptable substitute. Work a little quicker, Thanh, you're always lagging behind. I know you can do it.
	►	Mrs. Doan sits down with the three girls at the round table to observe how well they read the dialog and answer the summary questions.
	Joanne:	Mrs. Doan, I hope I'm getting an A now that I've finished all the level 4 exercises.
	Mrs. D.:	That was the agreement. You've got an A.
	Beverly:	(Pointing to the word "palatial") How do you pronounce this word, Mrs. Doan?
	Mrs. D.:	Look at the bottom of the page. They give pronunciations of the difficult words.

Time Frame	Dialog

Beverly: It's not there.

Mrs. D.: Oh. Look in your dictionary then. I'll take up your part in the dialog so we don't lose any time. When you find the pronunciation let us know.

► The bell rings to end the class.

Mrs. D.: Wait a second, everyone. Be sure to mark down how far you've gotten on your menus so I know how fast we are progressing. We want to be the best. Thanh, can I see you for a quick second on your way out.

Thanh: You know, Mrs. Doan, this stuff is kind of hard for me.

Mrs. D.: Don't worry, Thanh. I'm going to arrange for Joanne to show you her system for doing all these workbook exercises. It's a lot easier than you think. A few good lessons to get you a system and you'll be up there with the rest of the team. You better run—here's a late pass.

Brief   *Key Facts* – List three key facts verbatim that characterize the main positive and/or negative aspects of the lesson.

Strengths/Weaknesses – Briefly explain how the key facts selected indicate strengths and/or weaknesses in the teacher's performance.

Recommendations – Briefly describe what the teacher could have done to alleviate or avoid the problems that were seen.

♦ ♦ ♦ ♦ ♦ ♦ ♦

CASE STUDY 5.2   Students as Adolescents

Orienting Questions   As you read this case study ask yourself these questions:

Specific
♦ Does this teacher seem to be aware of the adolescent's tendency toward self-consciousness?
♦ How does this teacher's attitude affect the students?

General
♦ What points in this lesson stand out as indicators of this teacher's strengths and/or weaknesses?
♦ What recommendations would you make for addressing the problems this teacher seems to have?

Setting	School – High school in an economically and racially mixed neighborhood
	Subject – Developmental math (forty minutes)
	Teacher – Mr. Powell, regular life science teacher who has been assigned one period of math
	Students – Thirty sophomores, most of whom are in similar developmental skills classes in reading and language arts
	Topic – Probability Ratios
Lesson	Note: This is a fifth-period class coming right after lunch. Most of the boys in the class had been playing basketball during the lunch period.

Time Frame	Dialog	
1 to 3	►	As the class enters the room Mr. Powell is checking the roll. The day's lesson notes are already on the board and handouts have been placed on each student's desk.
	Mr. P.:	Please turn in your homework. (The students let out a groan in unison.)
	►	The students open their notebooks and pass up their assignments. Mr. Powell puts all the assignments in his in-basket and walks to the front of the room to begin the lesson.
	Mr. P.:	Okay class, it's time to begin. Open your lecture notebooks and we'll review what we have covered on probability up to this point.
3 to 8	►	The students shuffle through the pages of their notebooks. Many of the boys are red-faced and sweaty from their lunch-period basketball games.
	Mr. P.:	Omar, I've told you five times to have your shirt tucked in when you enter class. We have a dress code here and I will not get in trouble for your sloppy habits!
	Omar:	I know, Mr. Powell, but I was playing basketball.
	Mr. P.:	I can smell that, Omar. No excuses. This time you're going to the dean's office.
	►	There is a big reaction among the students. Several girls giggle, and a few of the boys begin to make snorting sounds as Omar walks out of the room.
8 to 15	**Mr. P.:**	Okay, enough of that! Let's get to work. Yesterday we explained how probability is a function of all possible outcomes for an event. Look at the handout on your desk. I've prepared the basic formulas used in probability exercises in genetics as well as some history on Mendel and his famous pea experiments. You will need to

Time Frame	Dialog	
		memorize these handouts if you want to pass the test on Friday. Bill, why aren't you looking at your handout?
15 to 20	**Bill:**	I thought we were supposed to have a lab today.
	Mr. P.:	I didn't have time to prepare for the lab so we are having a lecture instead. The information is the same.
	Bill:	Yeah, I guess so, but I was looking forward to the lab. I like labs. You didn't do the last lab we were supposed to have either. I thought we were supposed to have a lab twice a week.
	Mr. P.:	Enough! I told you I didn't have time. I don't have to lecture either. I can just assign readings with written exercises from the text.
	►	The students look sullen and disappointed. Many students are doodling on the handout. All is quiet.
20 to 30	**Mr. P.:**	Today I am going to explain all outcomes that are possible when throwing two six-sided dice. It's all a function of mathematics. Remember, to get outcomes you must multiply. For example, each die has six sides, therefore there are thirty-six possible outcomes.
	Paul:	Mr. Powell, I don't get it. Can't you show us on the board or something?
	Mr. P.:	Just pay attention. You young people have got to learn to listen just like the rest of us. Not everything is "touchy-feely" in this world.
	►	Paul, who was previously trying very hard to pay attention and to understand, tunes out.
30 to 38	**Mr. P.:**	Okay, I'll put the possibilities on the board. Copy them and make sense out of them at home. You can roll the dice to see what you come up with if you want to.
	►	Mr. Powell turns to the board and begins to write pairs of numbers on the board while saying them aloud. Most students either have their heads down or are looking out the window. Only a few are trying to follow what Mr. Powell is doing.
38 to 40	**Mr. P.:**	For homework, do the problems on the board. You'll have a quiz tomorrow on the material in the handout and on what we did in class today.
	►	The bell rings and the students quickly leave the classroom.

Brief   *Key Facts* – List three key facts verbatim that characterize the main positive and/or negative aspects of the lesson.

Strengths/Weaknesses – Briefly explain how the key facts selected indicate strengths and/or weaknesses in the teacher's performance.

Recommendations – Briefly describe what the teacher could have done to alleviate or avoid the problems that were seen.

♦ ♦ ♦ ♦ ♦ ♦ ♦

CASE STUDY 5.3   Students as Products of the Environment

Orienting Questions   As you read this case study ask yourself these questions:

Specific
- ♦ Does this teacher seem to understand or appreciate the students' cultural backgrounds?
- ♦ Has this teacher designed a lesson that furthers the students' understanding of Japanese culture?

General
- ♦ What points in this lesson stand out as indicators of this teacher's strengths and/or weaknesses?
- ♦ What recommendations would you make for addressing the problems this teacher seems to have?

Setting   *School* – Port-of-entry junior high school in poor area of a large urban city

Subject – Social studies (fifty-two minutes)

Teacher – Mrs. Amalfitano, a social studies teacher with thirty years of experience at the school

Students – Thirty-nine seventh-grade students, all of whom have come from various Latin American countries over the past few years

Topic – Japan and Eastern Culture

Lesson

Time Frame	Dialog
1 to 6	► The students hurriedly enter the room and take their seats because they know they have limited time to copy down the homework assignment and then answer the "thought-for-today" question, which is, "We live in a society made up of people from many different cultures. How has this made us a stronger nation?"

Time Frame	Dialog
	Mrs. A.: I have some wonderful things to show you today, so get the thought-for-today question done quickly.
	► Mrs. Amalfitano has placed a variety of pictures, trinkets, and musical instruments common to the Japanese culture around the room.
6 to 17	**Mrs. A.:** Students, today we are going to look at the people of Japan. If you look around the room you'll see many things that give us an idea of Japanese culture. First, let's hear some of your responses to today's question.
	► Ramon eagerly raises his hand to give his response.
	Mrs. A.: I'm so glad to see you want to participate, Ramon. How did you answer the question?
	Ramon: Having many different people here is good because they learn all kinds of different things from each other. My father said the other night at supper that a man from Nigeria who he works with had taught him things he didn't know before about carpentry.
	Mrs. A.: Ramon, that's a very good response. It shows us how all sorts of ideas can be shared by people from different cultures. Dolores, why does our cultural diversity make us a stronger nation?
	Dolores: I don't know.
	Mrs. A.: (Rather indignant) What do you mean you don't know? Surely you can think of something.
	Dolores: I guess it's because we learn from each other.
	Mrs. A.: That's more like it. That's a fine answer.
	Dolores: But maybe I have to be here a little longer so I can meet more people from other countries. Then I think I can answer the question better.
	Mrs. A.: Don't be silly. You see all kinds of people all the time on television. Anyway, your answer was fine.
	► Mrs. Amalfitano pulls down the map of Asia.
	Mrs. A.: (Pointing to the islands that make up Japan) Most people think Japan is just on one piece of land like the United States. But here you see it is really made up of four islands. The capital is Tokyo, the world's most populous city. Has anyone heard about why Japan is such a successful country?
	Irma: They make many, many cars like, you know, Nissan. They make a lot of money selling these cars, especially to people here. That's successful.
	Mrs. A.: You're very right, Irma. Japan is one of the richest nations in the world.

Time Frame	Dialog

Pablo: Back home in El Salvador the priest in our village told us that money is not the most important thing in life. He said I will know I am growing into a fine young man when I care about other people as though they were all part of my family.

Mrs. A.: Wait a second, Pablo. Nobody said you couldn't also make money and still like other people.

Pablo: I guess you're right, Mrs. Amalfitano.

17 to 32 ► Mrs. Amalfitano takes two pairs of chopsticks out of her desk drawer to show the class.

Mr. A.: These are called chopsticks. In Japan they use these the same way we use spoons and forks here.

Olivet: Can I see them, Mrs. Amalfitano?

Mrs. A.: Yes. In fact you and someone else can come up to my desk and I'll show you how to hold the chopsticks properly. Who wants to join Olivet? Okay, Angelica.

► Mrs. Amalfitano shows them how to use the chopsticks as the class looks on. When this activity is done she takes out some large color photos of Japan.

Mrs. A.: Here's a photo of the famous Phoenix Hall near the city of Kyoto. It was originally a villa and is now a temple. Isn't it beautiful?

► Mrs. Amalfitano shows several other photos and then hands out map worksheets.

Mrs. A.: On these worksheets you see that the names of the islands and cities have to be added. Watch up here and write in the names as I show you where they are.

Hillario: Will we also learn about the countries of Africa and Latin America in this unit?

Mrs. A.: Remember, Hillario, the reason I'm spending so much time on Japan is that we have to learn to compete with them if we are to stay the number-one nation in the world. The text tells you a lot about the various countries of Africa and Latin America. You're all from Latin America anyway. Most cultures are alike there so I'd rather use the time to show you things you're not familiar with.

Hillario: I really don't know that much about many countries in Latin America. Besides, I heard the principal, Mr. Howard, talking to the student teacher who helps Mr. Schwartz and he told her that she was going to learn as much from the students as they were going to learn from

Time Frame	Dialog

her because the cultures they come from are so advanced. If these cultures are so advanced why is there so much poverty there?

Mrs. A.: In some ways these countries are still very backward. They don't have the technology that we have or that Japan has. But that's beside the point now. Let's move on.

32 to 45

► Mrs. Amalfitano takes out a chart that has the numbers one to ten written on it in Japanese.

Mrs. A.: Now I want to teach you how to count to ten in Japanese. I'll say each number in Japanese and you repeat after me.

Ana: Gee, Mrs. Amalfitano, it's hard to pronounce these numbers.

Mrs. A.: Do it alone, Ana.

Ana: Oh no! I sound stupid. Please don't make me do it.

Mrs. A.: You have nothing to be afraid of—everyone in this class has language problems.

Ana: I mean I sound stupid trying to speak Japanese.

Pablo: (Speaking aside to Ana) Mrs. Amalfitano doesn't think much of our cultures. She would like us more if she knew how nice our people are.

Ana: Yeah, and I wish we could talk more about what the Japanese believe in and how young people like us are brought up.

45 to 52

Mrs. A.: All right. For the remaining time I'd like you to color in the maps of Japan I handed out today.

Luis: We didn't get to use those musical instruments you brought. Can we do them tomorrow—I love music.

Mrs. A.: If there's time I'll show you the instruments after class, Luis. There's too much we have to cover for me to take any time from tomorrow's class to play instruments.

► A few other students who felt like Luis about the instruments were saddened to hear what Mrs. Amalfitano said to him. The class spends the remaining time coloring in their maps. The students leave the room in an orderly fashion when the bell rings. A few students go over to take a closer look at the instruments on their way out.

Brief *Key Facts* – List three key facts verbatim that characterize the main positive and/or negative aspects of the lesson.

Strengths/Weaknesses – Briefly explain how the key facts selected indicate strengths and/or weaknesses in the teacher's performance.

Recommendations – Briefly describe what the teacher could have done to alleviate or avoid the problems that were seen.

♦ ♦ ♦ ♦ ♦ ♦ ♦

CHAPTER PROJECT   Develop and Use a Student Profile

Goals
1. To develop a student profile that helps understand students in the following areas: mental and emotional development, cultural background, and individual qualities.
2. To use the profile developed as a guide to reaching students.

Planning
1. Determine the various characteristics (e.g., abilities, interests, experiences) to be listed under each area of the profile.
2. Develop the profile using a checklist format, an anecdotal format, or a combination of both formats.
3. Develop a set of interview questions to ask students to gain insights not possible through observations alone.

Partial Implementation
1. Select three students to develop profiles for who have apparently different personalities and backgrounds.
2. Compile information for the profile by observing the three students over several class sessions.
3. Interview the three students individually to gain further insights about them.

Full Implementation
1. Analyze the information obtained from the observations and interviews to fill out the students' profiles.
2. Write a summary of each profile that includes suggestions for dealing with each student considering his or her particular characteristics.

♦ ♦ ♦ ♦ ♦ ♦ ♦

REFERENCES

Ausubel, D. P., Montemayor, R., & Pergrouhi, S. (1977). *Theory and problems of adolescent development* (2nd ed.). New York: Grune & Stratton.

Beard, R. M. (1969). *An outline of Piaget's developmental psychology for students and teachers.* New York: Basic Books.

Bruner, J. S. (1960). *The process of education.* Cambridge, MA: Harvard University Press.

Cross, D. E., Baker, G. C., & Stiles, L. J. (Eds.). (1977). *Teaching in a multicultural society.* New York: Free Press.

Dewey, J. (1928). *Democracy and education: An introduction to the philosophy of education.* New York: Macmillan.

Dewey, J. (1938). *Experience and education.* New York: Macmillan.

Einstein, A. (1950). *Out of my later years.* New York: Philosophical Library.

Elkind, D. (1981). *Children and adolescents: Interpretive essays* (3rd ed.). New York: Oxford University Press.

Gesell, A., Ilg, F. L., & Ames, L. (1956). *Youth: The years from ten to sixteen.* New York: Harper and Brothers.

Heck, S. F., & Williams, C. R. (1984). *The complex roles of the teacher: An ecological perspective.* New York: Teachers College Press.

Markova, A. K., Orlov, A. B., & Fridman, L. M. (1986). Motivating school children to learn. *Soviet Education, 28*(7), 13–64.

McDaniel, T. R. (1985, September). The ten commandments of motivation. *The Clearing House, 59,* 19–23.

Mead, M. (1950). *The school in American culture.* Cambridge, MA: Harvard University Press.

Mickler, M. L. (1985, Fall). Interview with Ralph W. Tyler. *The Educational Forum, 50*(1), 25–32.

Montessori, M. (1948). *From childhood to adolescence.* New York: Schocken Books.

Purkey, W. W. (1978). *Inviting school success: A self-concept approach to teaching and learning.* Belmont, CA: Wadsworth.

Russell, B. (1926). *On education.* London: George Allen & Unwin.

Russell, B. (1927). *Selected papers of Bertrand Russell.* New York: Modern Library.

Shane, H. G. (1977). *Curriculum change toward the twenty-first century.* Washington, DC: National Educational Association.

Smith, B. O., Stanley, W. O., & Shores, J. H. (1957). *Fundamentals of curriculum development* (rev. ed.). New York: World Book Company.

Tyler, R. W. (1975, September). Reconstructing the total educational environment. *Phi Delta Kappan, 57*(1), 12–13.

Waples, D., & Tyler, R. W. (1930). *Research methods and teachers' problems: A manual for systematic studies of classroom procedure.* New York: Macmillan.

◆ ◆ ◆ ◆ ◆ ◆ ◆
ANNOTATED READINGS

Archambault, R. D. (Ed.). (1927). *John Dewey on education: Selected writings.* New York: Random House.

> *A selection of some of Dewey's most poignant thoughts on a variety of topics illustrating his systematic and complete philosophy of education. See Chapter 2 for a discussion of ethics and education, especially the relationship between science and values.*

Bruner, J. S. (1966). *Toward a theory of instruction.* Cambridge, MA: Harvard University Press.

> *A series of related essays on the problems of education in general, and of learning specifically, by one of the foremost experts on cognitive learning processes. See Chapter 1 on patterns of growth through instruction and Chapter 2 on education as social invention for ideas important to understanding and dealing with students.*

Charters, W. W. (1927). *The teaching of ideals.* New York: Macmillan.
>   A systematic examination and analysis of character training in the secondary school, including concrete cases and suggested modes of teaching. See Chapter 16 on the measurement of individual traits and Chapter 17 on the integration of personality.

Crawford, C. C. (1948). *Materials for the study of secondary education: A syllabus for the courses in secondary education.* Los Angeles: C. C. Crawford.
>   A practical guide for the secondary school teacher focusing on everyday situations, needs, and problems found in the classroom. See Chapter 10 on characteristics of the adolescent, Chapter 11 for a discussion on guidance of students, and Chapter 12 on fitting instruction to the individual needs of students.

Elkind, D. (1981). *Children and adolescents: Interpretive essays* (3rd ed.). New York: Oxford University Press.
>   A discussion of Piaget's work and thinking as related to the child, adolescent psychology, and education. See Chapter 7 on cognitive structure and experience in the child and the adolescent.

Feinberg, W., & Soltis, J. F. (1985). *School and society.* New York: Teachers College Press.
>   An examination of the relationship that exists between school and society. See "A Theory of Cultural Reproduction" in Chapter 5 for a discussion of the influence of the school as a dominant culture on various cultural groups.

Fuhrmann, B. S. (1986). *Adolescence, adolescents.* Boston: Little, Brown.
>   A comprehensive text integrating theory and research concerning adolescence as a stage of development, and adolescents as individuals. Numerous ideas and theories are presented, and their practical use in the classroom is emphasized.

Gander, M. J., & Gardiner, H. W. *Child and adolescent development.* (1981). Boston: Little, Brown.
>   A survey and synthesis of major research studies and findings concerning the theories of Piaget, Erikson, Kohlberg, and Havighurst. See Part V for a discussion of development in the adolescent.

Ghose, A. (1966). *Sri Aurobindo and the mother on education.* Pondicherry, India: Sri Aurobindo Ashram.
>   An examination of ways education serves as the basis for bringing humanity, with its varied cultures, together. See Chapter 3 on the moral nature of students and education of the intellect.

Havighurst, R. J., & Taba, H. (1949). *Adolescent character and personality.* New York: John Wiley & Sons.
>   An exhaustive report growing out of studies made on all youths in "Prairie City" who were sixteen years old in 1942, made by the Committee on Human Development of the University of Chicago. Particularly useful are Parts III and IV, respectively, on character and personality development, and methods of studying character and personality.

Judd, C. H. (1927). *Psychology of secondary education.* Boston: Ginn.
>   A view of classroom teaching from a psychological perspective. See Chapters 2, 3, and 4 for a discussion of the social, intellectual, and behavioral maturity of secondary school students.

Marshall, H. H., & Weinstein, R. S. (1984). Classroom factors affecting students' self-evaluation: An interaction model. *Review of Educational Research, 54*(3), 301–325.

> *A paper that presents a model of classroom factors that contribute to the development of students' assessments of their own work and progress.*

Piaget, J. (1970). *Science of education and the psychology of the child* (D. Coltman, Trans.). New York: Orion Press.

> *Discussions of the importance discoveries in genetic psychology have to the field of pedagogy and to the psychological foundations of new methods of teaching.*

Reed, A. J. S. (1985). *Reaching adolescents: The young adult book and the school.* New York: Holt, Rinehart and Winston.

> *A thorough and thoughtful review of adolescent literature containing numerous annotated references. In addition to providing an excellent reference source, the author discusses several techniques for incorporating various types of books into the classroom curriculum.*

Russell, B. (1932). *Education and the social order.* London: George Allen & Unwin.

> *A study of the social pressures that work to prevent children from realizing the ideal of becoming free and productive citizens. While all sixteen chapters provide useful ideas for reaching the students, Chapter 2 on education and hereditary, and Chapter 5 on the home versus the school are particularly relevant.*

Wadsworth, B. J. (1971) *Piaget for the classroom teacher.* New York: David McKay.

> *An examination of Piaget's principle of developmental learning as related to teaching specific subject areas including reading, math, science, and history, as well as to teaching in general. See Part IV for a practical guide to assessing intellectual and cognitive development in the Piagetian mode.*

CHAPTER 6

Carrying Out
Classroom Instruction

INTRODUCTION

Which is more important in classroom teaching—content or method? So goes the perennial debate. The answer is that content and method are inextricably intertwined, and mastery of both is essential to successful teaching. Content is the specific subject matter taught. Its effective use in curriculum planning and development has already been discussed in Chapter 3. A teaching method is the means of transmitting subject content to students. Although content is important, how subjects are taught and the environment in which they are taught are even more important determinants of student growth. It is essential, therefore, to apply maximum thought and attention to selecting and using various methods rather than to teach by proxy through mechanical prescriptive models. Ultimately, success in carrying out classroom instruction depends upon the teacher's creative efforts, sustained by a spirit of inquiry and exploration, to bring into harmony the dynamic and unique relationship between students, teacher, and subject. This chapter examines how "subject matter may be made educative" (Mursell, 1934, p. 493) by various methods.

The ultimate goal of teaching methods is to increase students' subject matter knowledge and learning skills. The measure of any teaching method, therefore, is the students' resulting performance in terms of character formation, that is, good habits and self-discipline; learning skills and mental growth; subject matter knowledge; and communications skills.

Teaching methods fall into the following broad categories: teacher-directed, student-directed, interactive, and problem solving (general method). The characteristics and effectiveness of each are discussed in this chapter.

BASIC THEORIES

♦ Teacher-Directed Methods

Those methods in which the teacher selects, organizes, and presents subject matter to students are called teacher-directed methods. Principal among such methods are lectures, demonstrations, drills, reviews, and questioning.

Lectures

In the days before the written word, knowledge was transmitted orally from a teacher to a student, who would fully commit it to memory and in turn transmit it orally to his or her students. This is how knowledge was passed down through the generations. This ancient mode of imparting knowledge, which is the forerunner of what we know as the lecture, will remain valuable because it is "indispensable in passing on to the rising generation the accumulated wisdom of the society . . ." (Earhart, 1915, p. 28).

There are three basic forms of lecture: formal, informal, and lecture-commentary.

Formal Lectures. This method is characterized by one-way communication from the teacher to the class. The teacher selects and organizes the lecture material ahead of time and then delivers it with few changes in the predetermined format. Students do not participate in a formal lecture, but the teacher may answer student questions after its conclusion. In this way, the teacher may present the subject material in its entirety, imparting it to the students in its accepted and understood form, exposing them to ideas worked out by more mature and experienced minds.

Informal Lectures. Like the formal lecture, this type of lecture is organized by the teacher, who determines the scope and sequence of material. Unlike the formal lecture, it allows the teacher to add spontaneously to the prepared material as the situation demands. Students participate in these lectures by briefly discussing key points; this discussion is closely guided by the teacher.

Lecture-Commentaries. This type of lecture differs from the other two in that its main source of information is not the teacher but a book, article, or other material. At key points, the teacher questions students to monitor their understanding of the topic and source material. Such regular questioning urges students to pay close attention and helps build their mental discipline.

Using Lectures
The lecture can be used to advantage for the following purposes and activities:

1. *To introduce or summarize a unit, lesson, or activity.* An introductory lecture, delivered clearly and succinctly, is an effective way to inaugurate the study of a new topic or set the tone for a class session. The teacher is able to treat the subject broadly. Such a lecture can serve as a transition between topics linking the old and the new, thereby lending continuity to the curriculum.
2. *To explain difficult ideas.* The adolescent student is often unable to figure out the key principles of a subject unit merely by reading assigned material or participating in classroom discussion. From time to time, the teacher may need to serve up those ideas in a predigested, ready-made form that will enable students to progress in the subject. In this way the teacher can interweave ideas more thoroughly than is possible through student discussion alone.
3. *To stimulate student desire to learn.* Presenting students with interesting or even controversial theories or points of view can broaden their understanding. A lecture that expounds a theory of life on other planets, for example, is likely to cause students to search for answers to new questions. If carefully guided, this use of the lecture can teach students to examine ideas carefully and develop a sense of objectivity.
4. *To go over information in a short time.* The secondary school teacher is often in a race against time to cover the required curriculum within a given school year. The lecture method is an efficient way of providing information to students; this information can then be referred to in subsequent learning activities.

The above uses of the three basic types of lecture method enable the teacher to motivate students and capture their interest. A well-organized

lecture planned with sensitivity to students can overcome the short attention span and boredom often experienced by the adolescent student.

The following steps may be taken in order to carry out effective lectures:

1. *Plan the presentation thoroughly.* Determine the focus and purpose
   of the lecture, developing an outline that lists the major and minor
   points to be covered and the main objectives to be reached. Consulting
   a variety of sources, including books, journals, textbooks, and, if time
   permits, other teachers, will help you obtain the best ideas and information to be found on the topic. (*Note:* The basic sources and the
   sequenced preliminary notes gathered for the comprehensive curriculum-development project in Chapter 3 will be very useful in planning
   the lecture presentation.) Such consultation should come only after the
   teacher has explored his or her own mind. By thinking creatively the
   teacher can develop his or her own ideas instead of using secondhand
   ones from others.

2. *Present the lecture so that it is interesting to students.* Open the
   lecture with a challenging question, problem, case study, or demonstration to gain student interest and attention. Make the focus of the
   lecture clear to students from the beginning, and try to relate the subject
   to their concerns and interests and to material that has already been
   covered and that will be covered.

3. *Allow for flexibility.* Allow room for flexibility in the original plan of
   the lecture so you can respond to student interests and needs on any
   given day. Further, if a particular outline for the lecture is followed too
   strictly, students will have little opportunity for original thinking on
   the subject. Although the lecture should be as well planned as possible,
   when it is presented students should be allowed some degree of initiative
   and self-direction even if this means that the order of topics covered
   differs from what you originally planned.

4. *Use the lecture in combination with other methods.* For example,
   material presented in the lecture is better understood and retained by
   students when there is time for questions and discussion of particular
   points.

5. *Provide follow-up activities.* The information and ideas presented to
   the students in the course of a lecture have little chance of being
   understood and retained unless immediately followed by time for reflecting on the material along with opportunities for applying it to a
   variety of problems and situations. Thus, as a method of teaching, the
   lecture should always be planned in conjunction with other modes of
   instruction.

6. *Know the subject as an expert.* Because the lecture is a direct method
   of imparting information and ideas, the teacher must establish himself
   or herself as an authority on the subject. Students quickly perceive the

degree of expertise the teacher has in the subject as well as his or her enthusiasm for teaching the subject. It is important, therefore, that the contents of the lecture be creatively prepared as a product of research, experience, and careful thought instead of inadequately prepared using a "one-step-ahead-of-them" approach, which indicates poor teaching.

7. ***Determine the practical needs for carrying out the lecture.*** In addition to carefully preparing the material to be presented, consider the following needs:
   ♦ Identify and procure instructional resources that will enhance the presentation.
   ♦ Be aware of vocabulary words and terms that need special explanation.
   ♦ Develop a timeline as a guide for the presentation so the various points covered receive the emphasis they deserve.

The lecture is particularly effective in training students to pay attention. Toward this end, students should be required to take careful notes whenever a lecture is presented with the attention that such note-taking demands. To ensure that students will be able to fulfill this requirement, three things should be kept in mind:

1. Make the material and its presentation, that is, tone of voice and inflection, interesting. To do this you have to sincerely care about how the listeners will perceive the presentation. No one is inspired to pay attention to a series of boring words spoken in a monotone.
2. Present the material in a clearly organized fashion so the line of thought can be readily followed. Students find it very difficult to focus their attention when they cannot discern any relationship between the facts and ideas being presented.
3. Show students how to take telegraphic notes in which the essence of thoughts is captured and later used to trigger a more complete remembrance of the presentation.

Figure 6.1 summarizes the advantages of the lecture method and lists the steps in carrying out effective lectures.

Demonstrations

The demonstration is similar to the lecture in its direct communication of information and ideas from teacher to students. Unlike the lecture, which is characterized by an oral approach, it features a visual approach to examining information, ideas, and processes. The demonstration is a unique and particularly effective teaching method in that it allows students to see the teacher actively engaged as a learner and a model rather than as someone merely telling them what they need to know. It allows for the direct observation of real things and how they work, and as such it makes an excellent complement to the lecture, which is more abstract.

FIGURE 6.1 *Effective Lectures*

Use the lecture to advantage for the following purposes and activities:

1. To introduce or summarize a unit, lesson, or activity
2. To explain difficult ideas
3. To stimulate student desire to learn
4. To go over information in a short time

Take the following steps to carry out effective lectures:

1. Plan the presentation thoroughly.
2. Present the lecture so that it is interesting to students.
3. Allow for flexibility in the lecture.
4. Use the lecture in combination with other methods.
5. Provide follow-up activities.
6. Know the subject as an expert.
7. Determine the practical needs for carrying out the lecture.

The demonstration is usually associated with subjects in which a variety of materials are used and actions are performed, such as science, music, art, business education, and physical education. It can, however, be employed equally effectively in other subjects such as English and math. For example, a demonstration of how to construct a complete sentence and a demonstration of how to solve a two-step equation are often more effective than a lecture on either topic.

There are three basic forms of demonstration: pure, with commentary, and participative.

Pure Demonstrations. This is a purely visual method of instruction in which the teacher shows students a particular process in operation, an act of skill performed, or a particular technique applied, while providing no, or a bare minimum of, commentary. This is done so students can focus their complete attention on every aspect of the demonstration.

Demonstrations with Commentary. Although this form of demonstration is still primarily visual, timely and concise explanations are provided where the process, skill, or technique being demonstrated are too complex for students to understand through observation alone. It is a harmonious blend of visual and verbal modes of instruction.

Participative Demonstrations. In this form of demonstration students have the opportunity to attempt either to replicate all or parts of the demonstration given by the teacher or to take part in a group activity, such as discussion or problem solving, that directly relates to the demonstration.

Using Demonstrations

The demonstration method can be used to advantage for the following purposes and activities:

1. *To stimulate interest in a particular topic.* Often the demonstration attracts student attention and generates interest by providing sensory stimulus that the written or spoken word cannot. As Thorndike and Gates say, there are "certain elements of knowledge, certain tendencies to response which can be got only by direct experience with real things, qualities, events, and relations" (1929, p. 263).

2. *To illustrate points efficiently.* The demonstration is useful when time is limited or when an explanation alone is not sufficient. For example, a well-planned demonstration of how to operate a microscope is far more effective than any amount of written or verbal instructions. However, the teacher should not use the demonstration blindly. There are times when only written or oral instructions should be provided so that students exercise their mental faculties and do the thinking needed to understand points that could be easily communicated through a demonstration.

3. *To provide a change of pace.* At times the demonstration method is used for the express purpose of giving students a break from other modes of instruction, especially verbal ones, such as the lecture and drill. This change of pace avoids or alleviates the boredom that tends to set in with prolonged use of one particular mode of instruction. When used in this way the demonstration must be well planned not only in itself but also in relation to prior and subsequent instruction.

4. *To provide a model for teaching specific skills.* The demonstration is effective for providing students a clear idea of how a particular act is to be performed so that the particular skill or skills involved can be correctly practiced for mastery. Examples of areas in which such demonstrations are apt include teaching certain technical skills in music, the fine arts, and athletics, and various pronunciations in a foreign language.

The following steps may be taken in order to carry out effective demonstrations:

1. *Carefully plan the demonstration.* As with all methods of teaching, to be successful you must know exactly what you are doing. This is particularly true of the demonstration, where precision and clarity are crucial to the students' ability to understand what they see. Careful thought and research are needed to make sure that all phases of the demonstration are accurately and logically presented.

2. *Practice the demonstration.* Once a well-thought-out plan has been developed, ample time should be set aside to practice the demonstration.

It is very risky to give a demonstration without having practiced it beforehand, especially when the procedure or topic is relatively complex or unfamiliar.

3. *Develop an outline to guide the demonstration.* To ensure that the demonstration goes smoothly it is a good idea to have an outline that lists the steps to follow, the materials to use, the questions to ask, and the important points to make. Developing such an outline provides the teacher not only with a guide for carrying out the demonstration but also with a well-designed framework into which spontaneous ideas can be incorporated as the situation demands.

4. *Make sure everyone can see the demonstration.* It seems obvious that the teacher would make sure that all students can see the demonstration. Unfortunately teachers sometimes fail to do this, causing a situation that results in student loss of interest and misbehavior.

5. *Introduce the demonstration to focus attention.* Students are more likely to be interested in the demonstration and to understand it if they have at least a general idea of what to look for as it proceeds. A few introductory comments emphasizing the essential features and key terms of the demonstration can serve this purpose as can an outline or diagram on the chalkboard. It is, however, unproductive to use a worksheet as a means of orienting students because it tends to draw their attention away from the demonstration.

6. *Ask and encourage questions.* "Students should be encouraged to ask questions . . . so that their verbal experiences are integrated with their visual ones" (Crawford, 1938, p. 354). Also, students should be asked questions at key points as a way of assessing how well they are understanding the demonstration.

7. *Plan a follow-up to the demonstration.* A demonstration should be followed by activities that help students interpret and further understand the important points that were presented. Such activities could include a lecture with commentary or discussion, or a writing exercise in which students can describe what they have seen.

The demonstration is particularly effective in helping students develop the skill of accurate observation. Such skill is important not only for the immediate purpose of understanding an aspect of a particular subject but also for developing a sense of objectivity. Thus the demonstration has wider implications for students' lives because it helps develop their ability to learn from direct experience. See Figure 6.2 for a summary of the advantages of demonstrations and a list of steps for carrying out effective demonstrations.

Drills
The drill is one of the most direct forms of reinforcing learning. In the drill, essential information on a particular topic is repeated until it is firmly established in the students' minds. "The essence of drill is intelligent repetition and the standard is automatism such that the item worked upon

---

FIGURE 6.2 *Effective Demonstrations*

Use the demonstration method to advantage for the following purposes and activities:

1. To stimulate interest in a particular topic
2. To illustrate points efficiently
3. To provide a change of pace
4. To provide a model for teaching specific skills

Take the following steps to carry out effective demonstrations:

1. Carefully plan the demonstration.
2. Practice the demonstration.
3. Develop an outline to guide the demonstration.
4. Make sure everyone can see the demonstration.
5. Introduce the demonstration to focus attention.
6. Ask and encourage questions.
7. Plan a follow-up to the demonstration.

---

will carry itself through with a minimum of attention" (Charters, 1912, p. 382). Because the aim of the drill is recall and permanent retention of information, the value of learning beyond the needs of the moment should be made clear to students. This can be done if material selected for drill is chosen wisely and always used in subsequent instructional activities. For example, intense drill on the structure and nature of chemical compounds should find its application in a variety of classwork, homework, and lab assignments. Too much reliance upon drill as a mode of learning can be counterproductive, causing "an undue emphasis upon devices which secure automatic skill at the expense of personal perception" (Dewey, 1928, p. 60).

The value of drill is clear: "Most forgetting takes place within the first twenty-four hours after the learning. If something is re-learned [i.e., through drill] after this first fading out period, a larger amount of it remains after the second day's decline" (Crawford, 1938, p. 170). Unfortunately, there is often too much emphasis on giving students a knowledge of where to find certain information rather than on having them commit such information to memory. Such an approach puts students at a loss in many instances where remembering certain information is essential to solving problems. The motto "You can always look it up" is not worthy of the good student. The drill should not be used where other instructional methods, such as discussion, questioning, or problem solving, are more useful.

There are three basic forms of drill: preparatory, review, and remedial.

Preparatory Drills. This form of drill deals with material that is new to students. It is concerned with preparing for future learning needs by anticipating what students will need to know about a particular subject before they begin studying it. As such, it is also an effective diagnostic tool, because it allows the teacher to diagnose where students are likely to have learning difficulties in the course materials ahead. For example, the English teacher drills the class on the structure of a paragraph, knowing that in the long run this will save students much trouble in writing assignments. Or the math teacher drills students on certain geometrical formulas as a preparation for a laboratory exercise in building and measuring geometrical figures. The preparatory drill is "highly productive where a high degree of proficiency — speed, accuracy, facility, definiteness, or precision — in certain reactions, especially those which constitute tool skills, is needed" (Thorndike & Gates, 1929, p. 258).

Review Drills. The review drill is similar to the preparatory drill in all respects except that the material covered has already been introduced. Thus the focus is on reinforcing, clarifying, and consolidating what students have already learned. This form of drill is also very useful for monitoring student progress and the effectiveness of classroom instruction.

Remedial Drills. This form of drill is corrective, focusing on those areas in which students have performed poorly. Because of this, the emphasis in the remedial drill is on accuracy and quality, not on speed. In addition, the teacher must take into account not only students' weaknesses but also their misconceptions and bad habits. Simply drilling students mechanically on information or skills they are weak on, without first clearing up any wrong ideas or misconceptions they may have, can be a waste of time and may even confuse them further.

Using Drills

The drill can be used to advantage for the following purposes and activities:

1. *For permanent retention.* The drill is the most economical method to use where the aim is the retention of specific facts or skills, such as letter combinations for spelling words, multiplication tables and various formulas in math, and rules and procedures in other subjects. This use of the drill is especially useful for memorizing elements of subjects that need to be recalled automatically.
2. *For systematic review and application.* Because information and skills that are learned begin to fade after time has passed, regular drill in connection with a variety of activities allowing for application of the information or skills is needed for continued progress in learning.
3. *For informal quizzes.* This use of the drill highlights its usefulness as a diagnostic tool. When used judiciously it serves to keep students alert as well as to indicate what they do not know.
4. *For forming new habits.* Because the drill is a highly structured and intense learning experience it is very useful as an initial exercise for helping students form new habits where accuracy and speed are important.

The first step in such exercises is a clear idea of the thing to be done. This may be secured through presentation or through the recall of previous ideas. As the [drill] is to be accompanied by attention, by frequent comparison of the thing as it is with the model to be equaled, there is again a constant review of the model or ideal. (Earhart, 1915, p. 185)

5. *For individualized practice.* Students needing extra work in learning particular skills can often benefit from individualized drills that use worksheets, computer programs, flash cards, and original exercises.
6. *For establishing closure.* A quick drill is an efficient way of summarizing a particular learning activity or sequence of activities. Such drill provides a sense of structure and highlights the key points to be remembered and understood. It can also serve as a link with new learning experiences.
7. *For refining skills.* Skills already learned can be refined through well-designed drill that requires performance at a higher level. In this way drill achieves a balance between exact repetition of what has been learned and the introduction of more polished techniques.

The following steps may be taken in order to carry out effective drills:

1. *Use drill discriminatingly.* Material to be practiced should be selected for its utility. Students will accept and thus be in a position to gain more when drill is used for learning they perceive as important.
2. *Determine where to use drill.* Scan every lesson to see if there are any facts, skills, or procedures that need to be made automatic and thus would lend themselves to drill.
3. *Organize material to be drilled.* Students find it easier to retain information when it is grouped or categorized into larger patterns and configurations. For example, drill on all the known chemical symbols is more effective when the symbols are categorized into the two main divisions as they appear on the Periodic Table of Elements.
4. *Make clear the purpose of the drill.* Students retain more and appreciate the need for drill more when they are fully aware of its purpose. Such awareness allows them to focus their attention and provides motivation. Students are quick to tune out or rebel when the drill seems useless.
5. *Present a model.* In addition to knowing the purpose of the drill, students also need to know exactly what they are to do. A model provided by the teacher or a student is necessary to ensure that the correct form or idea is practiced.
6. *Make performance measurable.* Students should know how well they are doing as the drill proceeds. For this, performance needs to be measurable so a comparison between correct and incorrect performance can be made.
7. *Require full attention and accuracy.* Students must feel the need to pay full attention so the desired skill or habit can be employed consis-

tently. Such consistency builds confidence and solidifies correct performance, whereas mere mechanical repetition cannot lead to mastery or understanding.

8. ***Ensure equal participation among students.*** Because drill is an opportunity for reinforcing learning, developing skills, and assessing student progress, it should be used in a way that reaches all students. Thus the teacher must exercise the prerogative of calling on every student over a period of time and allow no calling out of answers.

9. ***Incorporate motor activity into the drill.*** Drill used with corresponding motor activity is an effective way of increasing sensory stimuli to the brain, thus deepening the impression of the material or skill to be learned. For example, acting out a part from a play provides the benefit of motor activity to supplement the ideas and feelings contained in the words.

10. ***Space drill sessions.*** Because drill emphasizes repetition, students are able to attend much better to drill exercises that are relatively brief and spaced at intervals of at least a day apart.

Because the drill requires careful attention and accuracy of performance, it helps students develop a sense of mental discipline. Although the skills and information acquired through drill may be limited in their application, the mental discipline developed applies to many situations. Figure 6.3

FIGURE 6.3 *Effective Drills*

Use the drill to advantage for the following purposes and activities:

1. For permanent retention
2. For systematic review and application
3. For informal quizzes
4. For forming new habits
5. For individualized practice
6. For establishing closure
7. For refining skills

Take the following steps to carry out effective drills:

1. Use drill discriminatingly.
2. Determine where to use drill.
3. Organize material to be drilled.
4. Make clear the purpose of the drill.
5. Present a model.
6. Make performance measurable.
7. Require full attention and accuracy.
8. Ensure equal participation among students.
9. Incorporate motor activity into the drill.
10. Space drill sessions.

summarizes the advantages of drills and lists the steps in carrying out effective drills.

Reviews
"There is a fundamental activity of the mind involved in all review . . . this is the process of correlation, the process of giving meaning to ideas through relating them to other ideas which have more or less meaning established" (Earhart, 1915, p. 180). Thus review differs from drill in that it aims not only to reinforce previously learned material but to give such learning new meaning as the basis for establishing higher levels of understanding, gaining new knowledge, and encouraging the formation of new ideas.

There are basically two forms of review: preparatory and summary.

Preparatory Reviews. The aim of this form of review is to extend learning and associations as the basis for learning new material. Such review integrates past and present learning as previous knowledge is reviewed and applied to develop new habits and understandings.

Summary Reviews. This form of review is used to reinforce learning and, at the same time, widen understanding, attitudes, and appreciation. It looks at what has already been learned from new vantage points, thus encouraging students to higher levels of thinking.

Using Reviews
The review can be used to advantage for the following purposes and activities:

1. ***As an opportunity for student questions.*** The review offers students an excellent opportunity to ask questions to clarify material previously presented or to open up new areas of thought about the same material.
2. ***To foster a sense of accomplishment.*** A well-organized review at the end of a class or topic demonstrates to students how much they have learned and how this information can lead to learning new material.
3. ***As an assessment technique.*** Used in this way the review examines student understanding of information and concepts with the aim of overcoming any apparent weaknesses. Thus tests, quizzes, and drills constitute a form of review.
4. ***To establish new relationships.*** Review serves as the basis for new learning when facts or ideas are selected for application to new problems. For example, "to solve a given problem about triangles, we must review our knowledge of angles and select the relevant facts which apply to our particular problem" (Earhart, 1915, p. 179).
5. ***To organize previous learning.*** Often students only partially remember material previously learned, and even that in a disorganized way. With this problem in mind, review can be carried out with the aim of putting

order to previously learned material so student understanding is made complete and ready for future applications.

The following steps may be taken in order to carry out effective reviews:

1. **Design reviews to put learning to varied uses.** When students have attained an understanding of particular information and ideas, they should be made to apply what they have learned to solving a variety of problems. Such review strengthens their grasp of previously learned material and serves as a functional connection with new learning.

2. **Determine when review is necessary.** Before reviewing certain material it is important to make an accurate assessment of the students' levels of understanding. In this regard, a question to ask is, Do they need further lecture or drill on the material before either enrichment or application is feasible?

3. **Plan the review carefully.** Once specific material has been targeted for review, plans for carrying out the review should be carefully developed, taking into account the nature of the material, the state of the students' minds in terms of interest and understanding, and the relationship with subsequent learning.

4. **Encourage and ask questions.** Interspersing questions throughout the review serves three main purposes:
   ♦ It provides immediate and precise information on how much students understand.
   It allows for a degree of spontaneity and creativity in thought.
   It increases opportunities for students to participate directly in the review.

5. **Design the review to ensure correct understanding.** Because correct understanding of ideas is essential to further and wider learning, it is essential that review carefully moves students toward such understanding. It is sometimes advisable, therefore, to begin a lesson with a review to establish correct understandings and habits before new learning is attempted.

6. **Motivate students to learn through review.** It is possible to design the review so that students are made to feel a need for more information and skill. Their deficiencies of knowledge pointed out by the review can motivate them to further and more intense study.

7. **Make review of material parallel to its initial presentation.** "Material presented through a series of lessons in class should be similarly reviewed and organized to secure intelligent comprehension, and also to aid retention in the mind" (Earhart, 1915, p. 187).

8. **Make review relevant.** Facts and concepts selected for review should be directly related to the problem at hand, thus keeping important information and ideas current. In this way students are provided an organized structure that helps them retain what they have learned.

9. *Individualize instruction through review.* Because students in a given class may be at different levels in their understanding of a subject, review sometimes has to be individualized to address all students' needs and readiness to learn. Such review can come in the form of thought-provoking problems, research questions, and exercises covering material suited to a particular level of understanding.

Review helps students develop their thinking skills. A well-designed review requires students to go beyond mere recall of information to higher levels of thinking by utilizing past experiences and learning to solve varied problems and understand new ideas. Training in this form of review provides students with a model for learning that will be useful to them in all their endeavors, in and out of school. Figure 6.4 summarizes the advantages of reviews and lists the steps in carrying out effective reviews.

Questioning

Questioning is by far the most common teaching method used in the classroom. Teachers would be startled to know how many questions they ask during any given lesson—usually several dozen or more. Questioning is one of the most effective ways of stimulating students to higher levels of thought. To accomplish this, however, questions need to foster the integration of knowledge through convergent thinking, in which information and ideas are applied and analyzed, and divergent thinking, in which information and ideas are synthesized and evaluated. Unfortunately, the use of questioning is frequently not well thought out, and thus the full potential of this method is not utilized. As Crawford notes,

---

FIGURE 6.4 *Effective Reviews*

Use the review to advantage for the following purposes and activities:

1. As an opportunity for student questions
2. To foster a sense of accomplishment
3. As an assessment technique
4. To establish new relationships
5. To organize previous learning

Take the following steps to carry out effective reviews:

1. Design reviews to put learning to varied uses.
2. Determine when review is necessary.
3. Plan the review carefully.
4. Encourage and ask questions.
5. Design the review to ensure correct understanding.
6. Motivate students to learn through review.
7. Make review of material parallel to its initial presentation.
8. Make review relevant.
9. Individualize instruction through review.

> In spite of all our progressive education, the most common purpose that ac-
> tuates questioning in the classroom . . . is that of testing the [students']
> preparation. In other words, it is a recitation [memorization] purpose. Many
> teachers spend most of the time asking questions to find out whether or not
> the students have learned their lessons. This is a blind and futile process, in
> the first place because the teacher cannot get around to any one pupil often
> enough to have an adequate sampling of his knowledge; also because the
> questions that are asked of different pupils are of unequal difficulty, and
> therefore not good for comparison. (1938, p. 263)

Questions that can be answered by recall of information stored in the
memory may be useful in drill and review exercises, but they do not promote
thought.

The questions students address to the teacher and to the class are a
vital part of classroom instruction. "Questioning by the teacher which does
not lead to the asking of questions by [students] is unsatisfactory. If the
[students] are thinking, really trying to solve the problem at issue, they will
have questions of their own" (Strayer, 1914, p. 120). To make optimal use
of the method of questioning it is crucial, therefore, to become aware of
how questioning can be used for a variety of learning purposes.

There are three basic forms of questioning: diagnostic, developmental,
and informational.

Diagnostic Questioning. Diagnostic questioning typically comes in the
form of a drill, quiz, or test to find out what each student does and does
not know about specific course material. Such questions require either recall
of information or thought. Questions emphasizing memory require recall of
what has been previously learned.

> Asking [students] to repeat a definition, a multiplication table, a selection
> of poetry, dates and rules are all of this sort. Tests of thought may be used
> on the same material. The [student], instead of being asked to define a
> grammatical term, may be asked to parse a word whose class is defined in
> the definition; instead of repeating a multiplication table, he may be given
> a problem in multiplication; instead of being given a rule, he may be given
> a question in which the rule is to be applied. (Charters, 1912, p. 300)

Diagnostic questioning provides both the teacher and students with
opportunities to assess the results of their work as a guide for subsequent
efforts.

Developmental Questioning. This form of questioning is used to spur
students to think on their own. For example, when a student asks for help
or appears to have some difficulty understanding a certain point, it is better
to ask him or her a question or series of questions that lead him or her to
discover the answer rather than to simply supply the answer. Because they
provide opportunities for thought and expression, developmental questions

can be particularly effective for gaining and holding students' attention. In addition to eliciting increased student involvement, such thought questions also give the teacher some idea of students' learning needs. "If the teacher can only find where the students are in their thinking, and what their errors and misconceptions are, he has a better basis for a follow-up job" (Crawford, 1938, p. 265).

Informational Questioning. "By informational questions is meant questions that are asked because the questioner is seeking for information that he does not possess. Such questions do arise in school work and are provocative of the greatest interest when asked" (Charters, 1912, p. 297). Unfortunately, students are often unaware of what they do not know. It is not uncommon for a student to say, "Oh, I know that," when in reality he or she has little or no idea of the point in question. It is a sign of successful instruction when students begin to recognize their difficulties in understanding and applying various facts and concepts. Sometimes material should be presented in a way that makes clear to students that their understanding is lacking, thus prompting them to raise questions in an attempt to solve their problem.

Using Questioning

Questioning can be used to advantage for the following purposes and activities:

1. *To hold students accountable for paying attention and participating in classroom instructional activities.* It is the teacher's prerogative to call on any student at any time for an answer to a particular question. Some students, as soon as they observe that they are rarely going to be called on, begin to let their attention slip. "Why bother with this," they may say, "I'll just make sure I study for the tests."
2. *To assess student understanding of course material.* There is no substitute for the direct question to learn where each student is in terms of knowing and wanting to know about particular subject material. As such it represents a primary factor in determining what modifications to make in short- and long-term instructional plans.
3. *To lead students to think.* Questions that require students to apply what they have previously learned to new or modified material prompts them to expand their mental capacities.

   If all the [students] can answer every question asked immediately, the questions have not been very successful from the standpoint of provoking thought. It takes time to think. The question of large scope will be followed, not by a wild waving of hands, but rather by a period of quiet reflection. (Strayer, 1914, p. 115)

4. *To bring students into the instructional process.* Well-designed questions gain students' attention. They also indicate to students that the

teacher is concerned about how they are learning and that he or she values their contribution to the lesson.

5. *To get students to relate and compare experiences and understandings.* Students are often eager to add to other students' answers. It is important, however, that such exchanges be constructive, even if the purpose is correcting what are perceived to be wrong answers. Ideally, students should supplement each others' answers in a spirit of collaboration.

6. *To encourage students to study.* Students who find it necessary to study material in their textbooks and notes or other collateral readings to develop answers to questions posed by the teacher are much more likely to retain that material. "They will forget all except that which has become part of a system or scheme of ideas which have meaning and significance because of their organization" (Strayer, 1914, p. 118).

7. *To create a springboard for discussion or other methods of instruction.* An intriguing question that captures students' imaginations can effectively prepare the class for a discussion to examine the problem or for a demonstration, lecture, or review.

8. *To provide students with opportunities to obtain information from the teacher and each other.* When used properly this use of questioning can enhance the sense of community in the classroom. Students feel free to express to the teacher and fellow students that they do not know something and to share what they have learned.

9. *To allow students to express their opinions about issues or ideas.* Adolescents like their view of the world to be taken seriously. Sometimes the alert teacher can do this by stressing the importance of personal opinion.

10. *To determine the depth of each student's understanding.* For example, "A student's knowledge of grammar should in the last analysis be tested by his ability to use grammatical English, but sometimes it becomes necessary to go behind the correctly used form to find out why the pupil uses the form, and this is done by a question" (Charters, 1912, p. 300).

11. *To increase retention of reading material.* Questions given prior to reading assignments serve to focus student attention on the material and to increase retention of relevant material. In addition to reading assignments, questions can be used in this way for field trips, activities using audiovisual materials, and lab exercises.

The following steps may be taken in order to carry out effective questioning:

1. *Design questions that foster cognitive development.* These questions involve students in the discovery of meaning rather than fragment learning by emphasizing mere factual recall. For example, in a lesson reviewing the parts of the cell, students can be asked why each part is important to the overall health of the cell and what might happen if

certain parts were to malfunction rather than just asked to identify the parts of the cell. Thus, even questions aimed at ascertaining students' knowledge of factual information can stimulate the use of conceptual and ideational skills.

2. *Design questioning so the whole class benefits from both the questions and responses.* It is unwise to think that only the student to whom a question is addressed has something to gain. The value of instruction increases manyfold when students are trained to listen to all questions and all responses.

3. *Design some questions that leave students puzzled.* "A puzzling question may arouse curiosity and open up a whole channel of new investigations. Questions thus become valuable study guides. They may direct and stimulate observation. They may send the student on the quest for new data" (Crawford, 1938, p. 266).

4. *Include in questions at least two facts or concepts that aim at stimulating thought.* Students must be asked to examine and determine the relationship (e.g., comparing, contrasting, integrating) between such facts or concepts to create opportunities for thought. For example, in the following questions notice how two recall-type questions can be combined to form a thought question: Can you list three accomplishments of President Franklin Delano Roosevelt? Can you list three accomplishments of President Herbert Hoover? Which of these two presidents had a greater positive effect on the country?

5. *Give only factual recall questions when conducting a drill.* The main purpose of drill is practice and development of memory and speed in using factual information, such as conjugating verbs in a language class or spelling out chemical elements in a physical science class.

6. *Prepare important questions in advance.* For a given lesson, the teacher should determine what the main divisions of the subject are and then determine questions that require students to provide answers that cover these various sections. In addition, the questions that are chosen should get at the issues from a variety of perspectives and should cover the essential concepts of the lesson. "They should be selective, go to the main points, and yet, taken as a whole, should cover the entire field of the day's work" (Crawford, 1938, p. 268). Preparing questions in this manner helps determine the organization of subject matter in a way that considers student interests and needs.

7. *Avoid building clues into the questions.* The purpose of questioning is to find out what students know and to spur them to thought. Questions that are worded so that the answers are revealed defeat this purpose.

8. *Address questions to the whole class before calling on any one student to answer.* This keeps all the students alert and attentive. When a question is addressed to a single student the rest of the class no longer feels directly involved or obliged to listen to the question or to think about answering it. If it is sometimes necessary to address a question to one particular student, the rest of the class should know that anyone

may be called upon to supply a second opinion or to respond to a closely related follow-up question.

9. *Do not repeat questions or answers unless it is clear that they are not understood by the class.* To do so sends a signal to students that a low level of attention and effort is acceptable. Rather, students should be led to realize that inattention to questions and answers soon leaves them behind the rest of the class and thus requires them to do considerable work in order to catch up.

10. *Frame questions so as to encourage healthy debate among students.* For example, questions that involve choosing between various courses of action can stimulate students to think and express their personal points of view. In addition, such questions often lead to related questions, thus fostering a deeper examination of the topic as well as maximum student participation and interchange.

11. *Plan questions in a logical sequence.* The actual presentation of questions during a lesson may not conform to the planned sequence because of needs and opportunities that may arise. Such planning, however, allows the teacher to address changing situations appropriately and in a controlled manner. Also, a planned sequence of questions creates a sense of integration that makes the lesson as a whole more understandable to students.

12. *Present questions used for drill in a random order.* If students are trained through drill exercises to understand material only in set combinations they will be at a loss when required to deal with such material in a way that differs from the pattern they are familiar with. For example, "Students who learn the multiplication table or French verbs in a fixed rigmarole have difficulty in reacting to specific combinations on their own merits without getting a running start by repeating the rigmarole" (Crawford, 1938, p. 271).

13. *Conduct questioning so the whole class, not just a few students, feels a responsibility to participate.* If day after day the same small group of students are seen answering most of the questions, it is safe to assume that many students are sitting idle—their minds left dormant. Maintaining a daily participation log in which each student's contributions to class discussions and question-and-answer periods are recorded is an excellent way of obtaining broad student involvement—especially when it is explained that the results indicated in the log will influence each student's course grade.

14. *Deal with students' answers respectfully.* If a student has made a sincere attempt to answer a question, the effort should be appreciated and any corrections should be made constructively in collaboration with the student. Ridiculing or abruptly cutting off a student because of an incorrect answer could drive that student into a shell, making the possibility of future participation unlikely if not impossible.

15. *Make necessary corrections to incomplete or incorrect answers to avoid leaving students with wrong or misleading impressions of what*

is right and what is wrong. Rather than supplying the correct answers immediately, however, it is more productive to ask the student who has given an incorrect answer to give reasons to support the answer. This not only shows respect for the student's effort, but also provides some insight into where he or she lacks understanding. After this the teacher can make comments and criticisms, point out what is correct and incorrect, lead students to the right answer, or restate the answer more concisely so that it is more likely to leave a lasting impression in students' minds.

16. *Require students to enunciate their responses to questions clearly so they are audible to everyone in the class.* Answers that can be heard only by the teacher or a few students are of little value and have no place in activities involving the whole class. Students should also be led to realize that how they speak in class, or in any group for that matter, communicates an indirect message of how comfortable they feel as part of the group and thus has social as well as instructional implications.

17. *Develop a system for handling student questions.* In general it is best to be open to spontaneous questions at any point in the lesson, because students eager enough to ask questions are usually well disposed to learning. Sometimes, because of the material being covered and the teaching method being used, it is preferable to have students ask questions in a more disciplined way. One way of doing this is to spend some time near the beginning of class going over questions that grew out of the previous day's lesson. Another way is to have students write down any questions they have as the lesson proceeds and then collect and answer them at a particular point in the lesson. "The environment must make students feel the need to ask questions and feel comfortable in asking them. Supportive responses from teachers and honest acceptance of divergent viewpoints can encourage students to ask more questions and become actively involved in learning" (Heck & Williams, 1984, p. 78).

18. *Learn to recognize questions that are meant to be disruptive.* "If a student's question is irrelevant or insincere, and thrown in to waste time, it should be treated as a disciplinary case . . . and should become the starting point for a little civic education in plain human courtesy" (Crawford, 1938, p. 279). Also watch out for those questions that stem from students' impatience or laziness. Such questions are better left to students to answer through further thought or investigation. There is no harm in explaining how an answer may be found, only in doing work students would be better off doing.

19. *Admit to not having sufficient knowledge rather than feeling compelled to have an answer to every question.* Providing students with incorrect or misleading answers simply to save face will tarnish the very image that is being protected and will be unfair to the students who trust in their teacher's integrity. If you know the subject well, are

actively involved in learning, and have the students' interests at heart, an occasional "I don't know" in response to a student's question will do nothing to harm your standing with students. Indeed, these instances can be used as opportunities to work collaboratively with students to discover the answer to the question. Through such collaborative efforts it is possible to show students firsthand how to solve a problem and, at the same time, to observe firsthand how they approach problem solving.

20. ***Word questions so students are encouraged to answer based on their own experience and understanding, not simply in ways they hope will be most acceptable to the teacher.*** Because adolescents are eager to please their teachers and to be accepted by them, they tend to answer questions in ways they think the teacher prefers rather than in ways that reflect their own thinking. The students' desire to please can be used effectively to help them develop good habits and courteous manners, but it should not be used to inhibit expression or original thought.

21. ***Develop questions that are possible for students to answer.*** Questions should not be too complex or based on information and concepts totally unfamiliar to students. In addition, questions should contain no irrelevant material, because this scatters students' thoughts and leads to confusion. Preparing questions devoid of irrelevant material requires the teacher to know exactly what he or she wants, once again pointing out the value of planning.

22. ***Wait a few seconds after asking a question to allow students time to think before they respond.*** To answer questions adequately, especially questions involving higher-level thinking, students need time to collect and process their thoughts. When the teacher expects immediate responses and moves on to other students when such responses are not forthcoming, either the quickest students alone can keep up or, in general, the students' answers will be based on superficial thought.

23. ***Indicate clearly when questions are to be answered in a specific way.*** For example, when students are to define, compare, evaluate, classify, outline, or support certain information or ideas, they should know which of these functions they are to perform and which material is involved.

24. ***Evaluate the effectiveness of how questioning was used.*** The following questions are a useful guide to such an evaluation:

"Were my questions concise and clear?" "Did they challenge the attention of all the members of the class?" "Did the [students] need to think, to organize their experience with reference to the problem in hand before they answered?" "Did each [student] have a chance to answer?" "Did the [students] ask questions?" (Strayer, 1914, p. 116)

Figure 6.5 summarizes the advantages of questioning and lists the steps in carrying out effective questioning.

FIGURE 6.5 *Effective Questioning*

Use questioning to advantage for the following purposes and activities:

1. To hold students accountable for paying attention and participating in classroom instructional activities
2. To assess student understanding of course material
3. To lead students to think
4. To bring students into the instructional process
5. To get students to relate and compare experiences and understandings
6. To encourage students to study
7. To create a springboard for discussion or other methods of instruction
8. To provide students with opportunities to obtain information from the teacher and each other
9. To allow students to express their opinions about issues or ideas
10. To determine the depth of each student's understanding
11. To increase retention of reading material

Take the following steps to carry out effective questioning:

1. Design questions that foster cognitive development.
2. Design questioning so the whole class benefits from both the questions and responses.
3. Design some questions that leave students puzzled.
4. Include in questions at least two facts or concepts that aim at stimulating thought.
5. Give only factual recall questions when conducting a drill.
6. Prepare important questions in advance.
7. Avoid building clues into the questions.
8. Address questions to the whole class before calling on any one student to answer.
9. Do not repeat questions or answers unless it is clear that they are not understood by the class.
10. Frame questions so as to encourage healthy debate among students.
11. Plan questions in a logical sequence.
12. Present questions used for drill in a random order.
13. Conduct questioning so the whole class, not just a few students, feels a responsibility to participate.
14. Deal with students' answers respectfully.
15. Make necessary corrections to incomplete or incorrect answers to avoid leaving students with wrong or misleading impressions of what is right and what is wrong.
16. Require students to enunciate their responses to questions clearly so they are audible to everyone in the class.
17. Develop a system for handling student questions.
18. Learn to recognize questions that are meant to be disruptive.
19. Admit to not having sufficient knowledge rather than feeling compelled to have an answer to every question.
20. Word questions so students are encouraged to answer based on their own experience and understanding, not simply in ways they hope will be most acceptable to the teacher.
21. Develop questions that are possible for students to answer.
22. Wait a few seconds after asking a question to allow students time to think before they respond.
23. Indicate clearly when questions are to be answered in a specific way.
24. Evaluate the effectiveness of how questioning was used.

♦ Student-Directed Methods

Student-directed methods of instruction, more than any other methods, put the responsibility for learning on students. Because these methods provide students with an opportunity to take a share of the responsibility for planning and carrying them out, they foster the development of self-discipline and thus have implications for student growth extending well beyond the immediate subject matter being studied. Considering how busy the adolescent's life is—studying several different subjects each day, reconciling social and emotional problems, and adjusting to the pressures of entering adulthood in a tumultuous world—it is little wonder that he or she rarely finds time to think. In addition to placing responsibility for learning on students, these modes of instruction also provide students with opportunities to reflect upon what they are doing. Principal among such methods are individualized instruction and study.

Individualized Instruction

Individualizing or personalizing instruction simply focuses the emphasis of the instructional process on each individual student—his skills, abilities, interests, learning styles, motivation, goals, rate of learning, self-discipline, problem-solving ability, degree of retention, participation, strengths, weaknesses and prognosis for moving ahead in various curriculum areas and projects. The teacher becomes more professional and assumes the functions of learning facilitator, guide, consultant, professional diagnostician and prescriber of learning resources, activities, evaluation procedures and total learning packages for each student. (Dunn & Dunn, 1972, p. 31)

Individualized instruction embraces a variety of learning activities from the highly structured drill to the most creative independent research project — all designed to meet each student's specific learning needs.

A child's individuality cannot be found in what he does or in what he consciously likes at a given moment; it can be found only in the connected course of his actions. Consciousness of desire and purpose can be genuinely attained only toward the close of some fairly prolonged sequence of activities. Consequently some organization of subject matter reached through a serial or consecutive course of doings, held together within the unity of progressively growing occupation or project, is the only means which corresponds to real individuality. (Dewey in Thorndike & Gates, 1929, p. 232)

Individualized instruction is not a method to be used sporadically but one to be carefully and consistently integrated into the instructional plan.

Individualized instruction can be used to advantage for the following purposes and activities:

1. *To strengthen writing skills.* Individualized writing assignments such as themes, stories, and essays allow the teacher to both diagnose and address each student's writing problems.

2. *To strengthen reading skills.* Reading is probably the most frequently individualized learning activity. It should be taken as an opportunity to closely monitor each student's difficulties and interests.

3. *To address individual differences.* In most aspects of all subjects, individualized instructional materials and activities can be designed to accommodate students' varying abilities and rates of progress. This takes into account the fact that all students are usually not equally ready for learning at the same level and can often benefit from exercises that are within the range of their abilities. Some students need remedial exercises to address apparent learning deficiencies, whereas others who are more advanced need exercises that offer a challenge. Individualized instruction from this point of view "not only permits the student to proceed at his own pace and level, but on materials and projects that motivate and involve him" (Dunn & Dunn, 1972, p. 45).

4. *To foster self-discipline and confidence.* Individualized learning activities require students to take control of the pace and intensity of learning with a minimum of prompting from the teacher. Thus, such activities not only foster disciplined work habits, but they also provide adolescents with opportunities to fulfill their desire for independence in a constructive way.

5. *To work cooperatively with parents.* Parents often have little idea of the work their children are supposed to be doing at home, and even less of an idea of how to help them. Communication with parents about individualized assignments their children are to do at home presents an excellent opportunity to enlist their understanding and support.

6. *To utilize available technology.* Many of the technological resources available to the classroom, such as the microcomputer, tape recorder, and videocassette recorder, are best utilized for individualized learning activities. These resources, however, should not be overused for individualized instruction because they do not require students to apply the level of mental discipline of more traditional, less automated individualized activities.

7. *To carry out drill and practice exercises.* To be effective, drill and practice exercises that aim at mastery of specific subject matter and basic skills need to allow for the continuous progress of each student. For this reason the individual, not a group, is often the best unit of organization for such exercises.

8. *To carry out independent projects.* Independent projects allow for the integration of learning as it occurs in natural situations and relationships rather than in the logically organized patterns typical of most subject

matter. Independent projects are basically of three types, all aimed at some concrete achievement and related to student interests and needs:

♦ Projects in which students are provided with all the materials and directions they need

♦ Projects in which the general nature of the desired outcome is provided by the teacher but with few or no directions

♦ Projects in which students determine both the goals and the ways to reach them. For independent projects the teacher's role is to observe and assist students. "By indirect yet enthusiastic leadership, the teacher also watches the progress of each student in order to insure that pertinent and valuable facts, principles, and skills are mastered—in correspondence to individual ability" (Colman, 1967, p. 125).

The following steps may be taken in order to carry out effective individualized instruction:

1. *Determine students' learning needs.* "The responses of [students] to any stimulus will not be invariable like the responses of atoms of hydrogen or of filings of iron, but will vary with their individual capacities, interests, and previous experience" (Thorndike, 1906, p. 83). The success a teacher has individualizing instruction is largely determined by how well such activities are related to each student's readiness to learn.

2. *Facilitate students' efforts.* Students frequently waste much time and energy on individualized assignments because they find the directions unclear or the subject matter too difficult. To avoid these problems three things should be kept in mind:

♦ Design individualized assignments so the purpose of the activity is clear and the material is presented in logical sequence.

♦ Whenever possible, provide oral as well as written instructions for individualized assignments.

♦ Circulate around the room as students work on individualized assignments to provide advice and encouragement where needed.

3. *Communicate high expectations.* Because individualized instructional activities depend heavily on self-motivation "there should be a constant attempt to help students establish a standard of workmanship that makes them uncomfortable with inferior work . . . by playing down grades and emphasizing competence, by having available a rich range of resources and activities" (Grambs & Carr, 1979, p. 63).

4. *Let students know what to do if they need help and what to do when they finish.* These activities can serve as the basis for responsible self-direction and can help minimize problems that may come about because of lack of direction or confusion.

5. *Maintain a balance between individualized and group activities.* Keep in mind that the ultimate goal of education is not mere mental facility, but to teach students to think for themselves and learn to cope with the problems and complexities of life. Thus the needs of students will be best served by allowing them to work individually at times and also to actively take part in cooperative learning situations.

6. *Procure and prepare a variety of instructional resources.* Students have different interests, abilities, and strengths. Some benefit from approaching particular topics and ideas in one way and at a certain pace, whereas others need a different approach and pace to cover the same material. Therefore, learning activities must often include instructional resources of varying difficulty and modes of presentation to effectively individualize instruction. For example, some students work more effectively with materials that focus on concrete operations and visual and motor skills; for other students materials focusing on complex or abstract thought processes are more suitable. Whatever the preferred mode of learning, however, instructional resource materials should always be used as part of a learning activity in a way that provides a challenge and an opportunity for the student's creative involvement.

7. *Encourage student involvement in planning individualized activities.* Student involvement in planning individualized activities serves three purposes:
   ◆ It increases the likelihood that individualized instruction will be in tune with student interests, skills, and previous experiences.
   ◆ It provides students with opportunities to take responsibility in planning work for which they will be held accountable.
   ◆ It allows the teacher and students to develop personal relationships through cooperative work.

8. *Plan individualized activities carefully.* Careful planning is the key to effective individualized instruction. The teacher needs to ask three questions when undertaking such planning:
   ◆ Which course material can be best covered through the use of specific individualized activities?
   ◆ When can specific individualized activities be best integrated into the instructional sequence?
   ◆ When can each student benefit most from individualized instruction?

For the most part, individualized instruction places students on their own. They find that the responsibility for sustained effort and eventual success in learning is on their shoulders. Such instructional activities, therefore, represent excellent opportunities for the development of character. Figure 6.6 summarizes the advantages of individualized instruction and lists the steps in carrying out effective individualized instruction.

FIGURE 6.6 *Effective Individualized Instruction*

Use individualized instruction to advantage for the following purposes and activities:

1. To strengthen writing skills
2. To strengthen reading skills
3. To address individual differences
4. To foster self-discipline and confidence
5. To work cooperatively with parents
6. To utilize available technology
7. To carry out drill and practice exercises
8. To carry out independent projects

Take the following steps to carry out effective individualized instruction:

1. Determine students' learning needs.
2. Facilitate students' efforts.
3. Communicate high expectations.
4. Let students know what to do if they need help and what to do when they finish.
5. Maintain a balance between individualized and group activities.
6. Procure and prepare a variety of instructional resources.
7. Encourage student involvement in planning individualized activities.
8. Plan individualized activities carefully.

Study

Effective study methods allow students to transfer what is in their notes, textbooks, and all other collateral material to their heads for the purpose of solving problems and further learning. In training students to use effective methods of study the teacher is, in essence, showing them how they may best help themselves. Thus, study is perhaps the most important student-directed method in terms of laying the foundation for students' continued growth.

There are basically two forms of study: supervised and independent.

Supervised Study. Opportunities for supervised study arise whenever students are working individually on classroom assignments such as warm-up, practice, and review exercises or on independent projects.

Independent Study. All study done outside school, and thus out of the teacher's immediate supervision, can be appropriately called independent study. The homework assignment represents the most important and frequently occurring instance of independent study in the students' school experience. Other study activities in which students are left to their own resources include library research, collateral reading, and independent projects.

Using Study
Study can be used to advantage for the following purposes and activities:

1. *To develop the capacity for autonomous work.* Knowledge of how to focus and organize study prepares the student to successfully engage in autonomous work. "The autonomous approach should lead the [student] to think about his learning processes and take an active and responsible share in them. It will promote the development of his personality by cultivating his critical faculties and sense of responsibility" (Wake, Marbeau, & Peterson, 1979, p. 49).
2. *To develop a sense of objectivity.* Careful study of information, ideas, situations, and their own experiences is crucial if students are to develop a sense of objectivity. They need to have a way of intelligently examining the barrage of messages that come at them relentlessly from all directions. If they never learn to sort out these often-conflicting messages, young people will never develop a sense of objectivity, and they will be left open to manipulation.
3. *To carry out research.* Learning that is self-directed and self-motivated, commonly known as research, is usually the most lasting. Although students depend on the teacher's directions for memorization and drill exercises, they must be able to stand firmly on their own when carrying out research. At the heart of all such efforts to learn in this way is the ability to apply good study habits.
4. *To complete homework assignments.* Because immediate assistance is usually unavailable to students when they do their homework, the learning they derive from such work depends on the study skills they have developed as well as on their sense of purpose and self-discipline.

The following steps may be taken in order to carry out effective study:

1. *Plan activities and assignments that require studying.* All too often students are taught study skills through some form of lecture without follow-up activities that allow them to apply what they have learned. Even worse, students are many times left to figure out for themselves how to organize and focus their efforts to study. Such teaching is contrary to all principles of learning and is bound to fail. To learn effective study methods students need to do work that requires study so essential skills and habits can be developed. For example, "assign term papers to be written if there is to be any instruction on how to write them. Give instruction in making outlines of chapters [important to effective study], and require actual outlines to be made and submitted for careful checking" (Crawford, 1938, p. 102).
2. *Relate study assignments to other subjects.* When secondary school students go home they are faced with the necessity of studying several subjects on any given day. Because of this it is important to communicate with other teachers about the work they are assigning so the

amount of homework students have on any given day is not so much that they cannot do justice to any of it. In addition, such communication can alert teachers to opportunities for planning joint assignments that clearly demonstrate how effective study methods can be applied to various subjects. For example, two or more teachers can get together and plan assignments during a particular week that emphasize library study skills or research techniques, thus reinforcing each other's efforts.

3. *Teach study skills through writing assignments.* Nothing drives home the value of good study habits as well as the writing assignment. Preparing to write a paper on a particular theme or preparing a term paper requires students to apply several skills that promote good study habits, including taking notes, reading for the main idea, outlining, putting questions to oneself, and organizing facts and ideas.

4. *Relate study skills to critical thinking.* During the study of any subject the learner must periodically sit back and sift through all the information that has been taken in. These times of meditation and reflection, of allowing the mind freedom to wonder about what has just been learned and to put disparate facts together in new ways, are at the heart of developing the ability to think creatively. Toward this end students should be assigned study topics that will force them to analyze information and ideas to form new associations.

5. *Conduct classroom instruction in a way that encourages study.* Students feel a strong need to develop their study skills when classroom instruction is carried on in a way that requires them to respond to, present, and evaluate ideas. They want to be able to live up to their teacher's high expectations and they want to do well in front of their peers.

6. *Understand the close relationship between study and learning.*

> Study is the process by which an individual draws on what is [known]. On the other hand, learning means something which the individual does when he studies. It is an active, personally conducted affair. . . . There is, on one side, a body of truth, ready-made, and, on the other, a ready-made mind equipped with a faculty of knowing—if it only wills to exercise it. (Dewey, 1928, p. 390)

The key is to develop in students the interest and capacity to exercise such will.

7. *Teach students the value of a study routine.* The development of a routine is essential to effective study. The prolific author, the accomplished musician, and any other person working to perfect a skill must establish a routine of study and practice to be successful. Sporadic efforts at study are, for the most part, futile. Students should be shown how to develop a study schedule so that a definite time is set aside solely for the purpose of study. Adolescents lead very busy and sometimes confusing lives, so anything short of establishing such a daily routine

is likely to result in either no or very slipshod study. In a limited way an understanding of and a feeling for a routine of study can be fostered through regular, short study sessions during class time. Students who maintain a routine of study, both at home and at school, soon see their efforts begin to generate a self-sustaining momentum.

8. *Avoid providing information better obtained through study.* Sometimes because of overenthusiasm or interest in saving time, teachers provide information that should be obtained by students through study. For example, preparing students in advance for a particular reading assignment by handing out an outline of the material to be covered, a list of key points and their meanings, and a brief summary would leave the student little creative thinking to do. In fact, they are likely to conclude that most of their work has been done for them and all they need to do is remember the information in the outline. Unfortunately, such practices occur often and have a lot to do with many students' inability to think through problems.

9. *Plan for supervised study time.* To help students develop good study habits the teacher should observe them to see how they approach study, thereby determining in what specific areas they need the most assistance. The teacher can walk around the room observing and assisting students with their study assignments, helping each one and sometimes focusing the whole class's attention on a common problem or misunderstanding. What students learn from such supervised study times often helps them transfer study skills to other work outside the classroom.

The development of study skills brings benefits that extend beyond the classroom. Effective study is based on forming the habit of applying the mind to a given problem or task. Students who develop this habit find that they can apply it to all endeavors requiring mental discipline and good work habits. Figure 6.7 summarizes the advantages of study and lists the steps in carrying out effective study.

♦ Interactive Methods

Interactive methods are those in which students or the teacher and the students work cooperatively. They play a major role in the socialization function of the school. Principal among such methods are the discussion and the group project.

Discussions

Discussion takes many forms and serves many purposes in classroom instruction, ranging from the brief exchange to clarify facts during a lecture to a large panel discussion to express a variety of personal viewpoints.

Because of the opportunity it provides the teacher to stimulate interest and to guide the pupils' activities into desirable channels . . . it has become a

---

FIGURE 6.7 *Effective Study*

Use study to advantage for the following purposes and activities:

1. To develop the capacity for autonomous work
2. To develop a sense of objectivity
3. To carry out research
4. To complete homework assignments

Take the following steps to carry out effective study:

1. Plan activities and assignments that require studying.
2. Relate study assignments to other subjects.
3. Teach study skills through writing assignments.
4. Relate study skills to critical thinking.
5. Conduct classroom instruction in a way that encourages study.
6. Understand the close relationship between study and learning.
7. Teach students the value of a study routine.
8. Avoid providing information better obtained through study.
9. Plan for supervised study time.

---

favorite method of teaching [students] how to find, use, express, and apply knowledge and how to work together in a social group. Properly used, the discussional method also provides opportunities for encouraging and testing the results of work with books, lectures, and other materials. It can be directed to securing the expression of information, the debating of issues, the testing of assertions and opinions, and the solution of problems. But a method which may be put to many uses is easily subjected to many abuses. Because of the flexibility and indefiniteness of the discussional procedure, great skill is required to put it to fruitful use. (Thorndike & Gates, 1929, p. 246)

There are three basic forms of discussion: introductory, clarification, and summary.

Introductory Discussions. This form of discussion has a dual purpose: It helps in assessing student readiness for new learning, and it links new learning with previous lessons and experiences. There is no particular time limit for the introductory discussion—it may be brief or it may take most of one class period. Factors that determine when to use the introductory discussion include the nature of the relationship between old and new material, the difficulty of the new material being presented, the questions students raise, and the interest students show in the topic.

Clarification Discussions. Whereas the introductory discussion comes at the beginning of a lesson or segment of instruction, the clarification discussion is generally brief and can be employed at any point in a lesson as the need arises. The aim of this form of discussion is to provide opportunities for students to ask about and discuss material that is unclear to them. When used wisely and consistently the clarification discussion minimizes instances where instruction proceeds without students' full understanding.

Summary Discussions. This form of discussion, characterized by active student participation, is primarily used at the end of a topic or unit to reinforce essential information and ideas. It often serves as an effective link with subsequent topics. A valuable opportunity is wasted when the summary discussion is used as some form of drill in which students more or less recite information from their notes or textbooks. Rather, it should be structured so students are led to consider new and related ideas that require them to organize and express their thoughts about what they have previously learned.

Using Discussions

The discussion may be used to advantage for the following purposes and activities:

1. *To provide an opportunity for students to share ideas and assist each other.* Discussion represents one of the principal means of socialization within the school. The efficacy of group discussions depends largely on the topic or problem the group is given to address. "If it is purely informational, there is much less likelihood of a vital and vigorous discussion" (Crawford, 1938, p. 397). For example, there is little point in holding a group discussion if students are merely asked to contribute facts pulled out of their textbooks. On the other hand, the teacher can make the group discussion a positive learning experience by having students raise or address questions or statements that stimulate thought and interest.

2. *To motivate students to learn by focusing on solving problems they can readily identify with and by providing an opportunity for them to creatively apply information and ideas they have been studying.* "Students are eager to discuss topics that they feel are of vital importance to them" (Callahan, 1971, p. 207). In addition, they are particularly interested in doing well in and contributing to group efforts. The well-planned discussion provides an opportunity for just such cooperative problem solving.

The following steps may be taken in order to carry out effective discussions:

1. *Provide whatever guidance is needed to keep the discussion on track and interesting.* Sometimes a few students begin to dominate the discussion with the result that the rest of the class loses interest. In such cases it is necessary to bring other students into the discussion, for example, by raising a question that immediately captures everyone's attention and to which all can relate.

2. *Familiarize students with the material before it is discussed.* The only way to ensure thoughtful participation is to make sure students know what it is they are discussing. Thus, a discussion may be preceded by a lecture, a demonstration, a laboratory exercise, a reading assignment, or any other activity that gives a basic understanding of and sparks an interest in the particular material that is to be explored further in a class discussion.

3. *Set up a classroom seating arrangement that fosters open communication.* The traditional setup consisting of a series of parallel rows is not conducive to a discussion that involves more than a few people. Usually some form of semicircle where all students can see one another is the best seating arrangement for conducting a discussion.

4. *Include a variety of instructional resource materials to enhance the discussion.* Some topics are more clearly discussed and understood with the aid of visual or written materials. For example, a discussion of the key battles of the Civil War is enhanced by daguerreotypes of the leading generals on both sides as well as by quotations attributed to these generals concerning their strategies for victory.

5. *Plan carefully for the discussion to avoid a long, rambling activity that soon becomes boring and pointless.* An effective plan includes an outline of the topic being covered, lists of major points to address, key questions to ask, and resource materials to utilize, as well as a good idea of how to get everyone to participate in the discussion. The plan that is developed should present a clear picture of the goals to be reached through the discussion.

6. *Create a classroom environment in which all students feel free to express their views and are open to giving or receiving constructive criticism.* Such an environment must be in evidence from the first day of class, when crucial first impressions are being made. If students feel threatened or in any way self-conscious about expressing themselves, their participation in class discussions is likely to be limited. What you will have is a group of the more confident students doing the bulk of the work in discussions while the others recede into the background.

7. *Introduce the discussion at the most advantageous time in the instructional sequence.* "The discussion may be confined chiefly to the final stages of the work in which general ideas, conclusions, and applications are compared, debated, tested, and refined" (Thorndike & Gates, 1929, p. 251). One test of the effectiveness of the discussion is how well it promotes student interest and ability to work independently. After an engaging discussion students should want to explore ideas further on their own, perhaps by locating material to read, experimenting with solutions to problems, or simply formulating questions to address to the teacher or the class.

8. *Foster interest in current events through regular class discussions.* Most adolescents are preoccupied with problems that they feel immediately touch their lives. This, unfortunately, leaves them rather

uninformed and, worse, uninterested in events and problems outside their ken.

At present, our students are not well-informed about current affairs. A gap exists between the school and the real world of everyday affairs. Therefore, more time and attention should be devoted to the critical study of contemporary social and economic issues. (Brar, 1985, p. 57)

The discussion is perhaps the best forum for introducing students to the range of issues and problems facing society and to spark their involvement in examining these issues. In such discussions, objectivity should be the guiding principle. The best way to achieve this is for the teacher to be

the embodiment of the qualities that he wants to promote in his students; otherwise, his words will fall flat on his students. He should develop his own ability to think clearly and rationally. He should be able to see both sides of an issue. (Brar, 1985, p. 57)

9. *Evaluate the discussion for the possibility of making changes in how future discussions are conducted.* Some basic questions should be asked after the discussion to determine its effectiveness, including, Was the purpose of the discussion clear to everyone? Was the discussion organized, focused, and well guided? Did the discussion gain everyone's interest and participation? Was the discussion a valuable learning activity?

Figure 6.8 summarizes the advantages of discussions and lists steps in carrying out effective discussions.

Group Projects
Group projects provide opportunities for students to work cooperatively toward common goals and thus play a primary role in the school's socialization function. Socialization of classroom instruction means creating learning experiences that foster cooperation and interaction among students. This is contrasted with activities that are teacher-centered. When students have the opportunity to work and share with other students, the process of socialization naturally takes place. Through this process each student begins to identify with the group rather than retain only an isolated personal identity.

Socialization involves a give-and-take among members of the class. This give-and-take may involve conflict as well as cooperation, because [students] will not all be of the same mind, and differences of opinion or purpose will have to be ironed out through social action. Considerable teacher skill may be required to weld a group together into a unified body, and to draw into the circle the few who are individualistic; but there is a strong thread of

---

FIGURE 6.8 *Effective Discussions*

Use the discussion to advantage for the following purposes and activities:

1. To provide an opportunity for students to share ideas and assist each other
2. To motivate students to learn by focusing on solving problems they can readily identify with and by providing an opportunity for them to creatively apply information and ideas they have been studying

Take the following steps to carry out effective discussions:

1. Provide whatever guidance is needed to keep the discussion on track and interesting.
2. Familiarize students with the material before it is discussed.
3. Set up a classroom seating arrangement that fosters open communication.
4. Include a variety of instructional resource materials to enhance the discussion.
5. Plan carefully for the discussion to avoid a long, rambling activity that soon becomes boring and pointless.
6. Create a classroom environment in which all students feel free to express their views and are open to giving or receiving constructive criticism.
7. Introduce the discussion at the most advantageous time in the instructional sequence.
8. Foster interest in current events through regular class discussions.
9. Evaluate the discussion for the possibility of making changes in how future discussions are conducted.

---

human nature running through all of us that makes us want to be members of the group and identify ourselves with what the group is trying to do. (Crawford, 1938, p. 379)

The group-project method takes into account that students learn much more than subject matter in school. They learn to work and live with others, developing not only an academic intelligence but a social and ethical intelligence as well. Perhaps more than any other method of instruction, the success of the group project is measured more by the means than by the ends. In addition, group projects offer excellent opportunities for students to cooperatively take part in a variety of school undertakings (e.g., dramatic productions, book fairs) and community events (e.g., international-day festivals, senior citizen center visitations).

There are three basic forms of group projects: panel presentations, symposiums, and task forces.

Panel Presentations. This form of group project involves a group of four to six students who are charged with becoming informed about a particular topic for the purpose of sharing what they learn with the class. The panel meets first to determine just how they want to cover the topic and then to assign each panel member a specific responsibility. Usually one student on the panel assumes a leadership role, coordinating the overall effort. The work of the panel culminates in a presentation to the class in which all panel members make a brief statement highlighting what they have learned. This is followed by a period in which the panel answers questions from the class. Serving on a panel of this type can have a positive and lasting effect on students in that it shows them how to take responsibility for their own learning and the value of working not only for oneself but for others.

Symposiums. The symposium also involves the collaborative efforts of a panel of usually four to six students concerning a particular topic. It is, however, a more formal setting, with students representing different points of view making their presentations and then opening up the activity to take questions from the audience. Whereas most of the important information and ideas in the panel discussion come out during the open questioning period, the main points in the symposium are made during each student's prepared speech. The burden of preparing a speech for presentation to the class puts the students participating in the symposium under more pressure than those in a panel presentation. Therefore, the teacher should keep track of how students are getting along and provide encouragement and advice as needed.

Task Forces. This form of group project is like the panel presentation and the symposium in that it involves a group of four to six students in work covering a particular topic and culminating in a group presentation to the class. It differs from these other two forms of group work in the way it covers the topic. The task force selects or is assigned an actual problem to learn about through a combination of firsthand observations and interviews in addition to study. The aim is to look at a real problem the way those in a particular field look at it and then to make recommendations for solving the problem. For example, the task force could choose to examine the problem of air pollution, determining what areas should be covered and assigning each student a particular area to cover. Next, they can contact the person or persons in a local government agency who deal with such problems. The task force members can then synthesize their class notes, readings, and other research on air pollution with what they learn from people in the field. As a final step the task force can formulate their understanding of the problem as the basis for making a set of recommendations. Typically, such recommendations are presented in a panel presentation that may include one of the experts with whom they have been in contact. The result is an interesting and informative classroom activity and a memorable learning experience.

Using Group Projects
The group project can be used to advantage for the following purposes and activities:

1. *To encourage students to work cooperatively and take responsibility.* By working toward a common goal students have the opportunity to develop respect and tolerance for each other in a way not readily available through other methods of instruction.

2. *To allow for a degree of informality and freedom in the classroom.* Because the group project has a clear focus and mode of operation, it is an excellent way to provide a change of pace from the rigidity of the formal daily routine while maintaining a controlled atmosphere.

3. *To make use of resources extending beyond the classroom.* Group projects often require students to augment the information and ideas found in their notes and textbooks with that obtained from a variety of outside sources such as library research and experts in the field.

4. *To motivate students to learn.* Students are grateful for an opportunity to plan some of their school work and find it a natural source of motivation because of the sense of ownership such work provides.

5. *To provide students with opportunities for taking a leadership role.* In most group projects there is usually a need for one student to assume a leadership role so the group's efforts can be kept on the right track. It is important to plan such opportunities for leadership carefully. "The welfare of the total group has to be placed above the experience derived by the one who leads the [group]. It is much more important to have strong leadership than a frequent rotation" (Crawford, 1938, p. 386).

6. *To allow students to role-play.* An engaging use of the group project is a simulation in which students can assume the roles of persons they are studying. For example, to enrich study of a unit on democratic forms of government in a tenth-grade history class, a group of students can carry on a debate assuming the roles of members of the British Parliament in the late eighteenth century. Role-playing is a way of bringing alive information and ideas they have read and heard about.

7. *To permit students of similar interests and abilities to work at their own speed and to their full capacity.* A slow student who tends to be a few steps behind the class may benefit greatly from participating in a small group project with students also needing more time to grasp the course material. On the other hand, a bright student who usually monopolizes class discussions may have difficulty maintaining the pace set by a small group of teacher-selected students who have intelligence equal to or greater than his or hers.

8. *To provide a manageable learning environment for shy and overly self-conscious students.* A shy student lacking the courage to participate in full class group activities may open up verbally and socially in a small group of his or her peers.

The following steps may be taken in order to carry out effective group projects:

1. *Provide leadership and guidance to groups so that they work together with a sense of self-discipline and purpose.* It is important to help students define the topic to be investigated and determine procedures for deploying their time and skills most effectively.

2. *Make group projects more than merely looking up and reciting information.* The project should focus on challenging problems that require students to use their imaginations, both individually and collectively.

3. *Determine whether the group's plans are within their capabilities.* If students chart an overambitious plan the result is likely to be, at best, an aborted effort and, at worst, a sense of frustration and loss of confidence.

4. *Be available to students as they proceed with their project.* Students need to know that help is available if personality differences arise or if they get bogged down on a particular point.

5. *Organize group projects so that over the course of time students have opportunities to work with a number of different partners in the class.* Getting used to dealing with a variety of different personalities is good practice for honing social skills.

6. *Plan in advance for those things that facilitate small-group work in the classroom.* Even if groups have been well formed and have worthwhile topics to study, their efforts could fail if basic requirements such as special seating arrangements, materials, and instructions are not planned for adequately in advance.

7. *Establish rules.* Each student should be aware of his or her responsibility to participate in the total group effort. And each group should know it is responsible for maintaining decorum in the classroom so the work of other groups is not disturbed.

8. *Monitor and encourage self-monitoring of each group's work.* This will determine whether the plan that has been developed is being followed and whether any modifications in the plan would help students better reach their objectives.

Figure 6.9 summarizes the advantages of group projects and lists the steps for carrying out effective group projects.

♦ Problem Solving as a General Method

"A problem is a functional unit rather than a structural one; psychological rather than logical; and hard to fit into a formal outline" (Crawford, 1938, p. 202). The problem-solving approach cannot be described by a set order of procedures or a sequence of steps to follow. It takes many forms as it is incorporated into various methods of instruction. Regardless of the method of teaching with which the problem-solving approach is used, the following

---

FIGURE 6.9 *Effective Group Projects*

Use the group project to advantage for the following purposes and activities:

1. To encourage students to work cooperatively and take responsibility
2. To allow for a degree of informality and freedom in the classroom
3. To make use of resources extending beyond the classroom
4. To motivate students to learn
5. To provide students with opportunities for taking a leadership role
6. To allow students to role-play
7. To permit students of similar interests and abilities to work at their own speed and to their full capacity
8. To provide a manageable learning environment for shy and overly self-conscious students

Take the following steps to carry out effective group projects:

1. Provide leadership and guidance to groups so that they work together with a sense of self-discipline and purpose.
2. Make group projects more than merely looking up and reciting information.
3. Determine whether the group's plans are within their capabilities.
4. Be available to students as they proceed with their project.
5. Organize group projects so that over the course of time students have opportunities to work with a number of different partners in the class.
6. Plan in advance for those things that facilitate small-group work in the classroom.
7. Establish rules.
8. Monitor and encourage self-monitoring of each group's work.

---

are some basic principles to follow to assure that it results in an increase in students' ability to think through problems in and out of school.

1. ***Present problems to be solved in ways that encourage each student to approach them in his or her own characteristic way rather than with mechanical uniformity.***

    The specific elements of an individual's method or way of attack upon a problem are found ultimately in his native tendencies and his acquired habits and interests. The method of one will vary from that of another as his original instinctive capacities vary, as his past experiences and his preferences vary. (Crawford, 1938, p. 203)

    It is a great mistake to reduce problem solving to mere routine involving a set of prescribed steps to be mechanically applied.

2. ***Judge the success of students' attempts at problem solving by the ability they have developed to apply their minds and to approach other problems.*** Measuring success this way, not by the correctness of specific information or answers students have acquired in a particular instance, emphasizes the importance of understanding the problem-solving process.

3. *Avoid using the problem-solving method to the exclusion of other methods of instruction.* "It should be used along with habit formation, information and experience getting, development of emotional attitudes or convictions, and the arousing of appreciations. It should not be allowed or forced to swallow up these other types of learning" (Crawford, 1938, p. 203). It is artificial, and ultimately counterproductive, to view problem solving separate from other learning activities or to use it where other methods are more suitable.

4. *Provide students with the relevant information they need to deal with the major elements involved in a problem.* Such information could include essential facts or a brief list of resources needed to carry out the investigation. Sometimes, however, finding essential facts or resources is part of the problem to be solved; this information should not be provided in these instances.

5. *Determine whether the problem to be solved is inductive or deductive.* Induction involves students in using specific facts to discover general principles or laws to which they apply. Deduction involves students in using general principles to solve specific problems. Such a determination makes for a clear presentation of the task to be completed — the presentation of the problem being the critical first step in the problem-solving process. In addition, it makes monitoring of student progress more accurate.

6. *Take an active part in developing materials to use in problem solving.* Just as the dedicated, enthusiastic teacher takes responsibility for curriculum development and instructional planning rather than relying solely on the textbook or commercial materials, he or she also selects and adapts such materials for use in problem-solving activities, creatively integrating them into the methods of instruction to be used.

7. *Structure some activities to encourage cooperative thinking.* For example, the whole class can be asked to list what they feel are the most important things to consider when doing homework. Then for each important thing they can list some of the problems that can occur. Finally they can list possible solutions for each problem. Once students have thought about doing homework and listed their ideas in this way, the ideas can be discussed for everyone's benefit. Such "think-tank technology" is one of the most effective ways for groups of people to share ideas and cooperatively solve problems. In addition, problems posed by the students are likely to be seen by them as more immediate and interesting, and the solutions more likely to be acted upon.

8. *Show students that thinking is a guide to action.* For this, problems they are given to solve should require them to make choices in a quest to accomplish what are recognized to be worthwhile goals. The students' ability to see the value of thinking in this way opens up possibilities for it to be applied to many other areas of their lives, including educational and career planning, interpersonal relationships, and social issues.

9. *Open new areas for problem solving by presenting tasks that make students aware of difficulties and relationships they may not have expected.* Often adolescents do not know what they do not know and thus discovering that certain problems exist remains beyond them unless some concrete information or task is provided.

10. *Teach students good research techniques to broaden their perspectives and to provide opportunities for independent thinking.* To most students, research ends with their textbooks or, at most, with a brief review of a limited selection of sources in the library. Impress on students the concept that research includes elements characteristic of genuine investigation, such as selecting and defining a problem to be solved, collecting objective information from relevant sources, analyzing and interpreting the data collected, formulating conclusions, and testing possible solutions. The students' potential for and interest in research is often greatly underestimated and thus left untapped as a way of developing their thinking skills. Attempts to help students obtain the maximum benefits from research will prove futile, however, if the teacher is not actively involved in and familiar with the use of such procedures.

11. *Explain to students that emotional reactions have to be controlled and seen in perspective for thinking to be objective and accurate.* Discussion on this point is best done when students are in a calm mood and thus more open to accepting the advice and to considering the merit such advice may have. When you are either unusually elated or depressed your view of things is often out of focus with reality, and it is unwise to make decisions until a sense of balance returns. With this bit of wisdom in mind students can often avoid jumping to wrong conclusions not only in academic problems but in most of the personal and social problems that confront them as well.

12. *Design problem-solving activities so that the solutions students discover are translated into action.* Such learning is commonly known as discovery learning. As Grambs and Carr point out, "A good working definition of discovery learning is intentional learning through problem solving and under teacher supervision" (1979, p. 232). Problem-solving activities that result in nothing more than a collection of facts are unlikely to make a permanent impression on students. Because the most enduring record of thinking lies in the action such thinking generates, it is much more likely that students will assimilate the material covered and the processes used in problem solving if the solutions they arrive at require them to take some course of action. In addition, they will acquire the "capability to deal with future similar problems with greater facility" (McNeil, 1985, p. 154).

13. *Create a classroom environment that encourages creative, independent thinking.*

Such a classroom setting might be thought of as a learning resource center or a laboratory, and the teacher might be seen as a resource person. The role of resource person implies that the teacher provides a variety of ideas and materials from which the learner can examine a range of choices. (Heck & Williams, 1984, p. 73)

In addition, the creation of such a classroom environment is greatly enhanced when the teacher demonstrates respect for students' feelings and opinions. Such sensitivity builds a sense of trust and confidence that is essential to student ventures into new territory and is frequently called for in problem solving.

Figure 6.10 lists some basic principles to follow that will ensure that problem solving results in increased student ability to think through problems both in and out of school.

◆ The Daily Lesson

All curriculum development and instructional planning culminate in the daily lesson. Indeed, the daily lesson is the touchstone upon which all the teacher's efforts are measured. A teacher may develop great skill in a particular subject area and may construct a sophisticated set of materials and teaching strategies, yet if these skills, materials, and strategies are not

---

FIGURE 6.10 *Effective Use of the Problem-Solving Approach*

The following are some basic principles to follow to assure that problem solving results in an increase in the students' ability to think through problems in and out of school.

1. Present problems to be solved in ways that encourage each student to approach them in his or her own characteristic way rather than with mechanical uniformity.
2. Judge the success of students' attempts at problem solving by the ability they have developed to apply their minds and to approach other problems.
3. Avoid using the problem-solving method to the exclusion of other methods of instruction.
4. Provide students with the relevant information they need to deal with the major elements involved in a problem.
5. Determine whether the problem to be solved is inductive or deductive.
6. Take an active part in developing materials to use in problem solving.
7. Structure some activities to encourage cooperative thinking.
8. Show students that thinking is a guide to action.
9. Open new areas for problem solving by presenting tasks that make students aware of difficulties and relationships they may not have expected.
10. Teach students good research techniques to broaden their perspectives and to provide opportunities for independent thinking.
11. Explain to students that emotional reactions have to be controlled and seen in perspective for thinking to be objective and accurate.
12. Design problem-solving activities so that the solutions students discover are translated into action.
13. Create a classroom environment that encourages creative, independent thinking.

---

translated into the development of daily lessons that interest students and increase their ability to learn, they are essentially worthless.

Up to this point the focus has been on selecting and developing instructional objectives, resources, and methods—all vital elements in the creation of the daily lesson. In this section, the focus is on how to effectively implement the major parts of the daily lesson—beginning the lesson, reviewing work from the previous lesson, introducing objectives, presenting new material, assigning homework, and summarizing the day's work. A problem analysis for each of the six parts of the lesson that combines troubles and remedies to form a series of "how to" statements is presented. In this conception of the daily lesson, the lesson plan is seen as a device for integrating the vital elements and facilitating implementation of the major constituent parts of the lesson. This section concludes with a recommended lesson plan format that has proven successful in a variety of settings.

Beginning the Lesson

The first few minutes of the lesson often determine whether the day's work is going to be useful or useless. It is crucial, therefore, for this part of the lesson to be well thought out, with nothing left to chance. So many unpredictable and potentially disruptive events occur at the beginning of the lesson that anything short of a clear and firm opening routine is likely to spell disaster.

Consider the following potential problems and suggested solutions when beginning the lesson.

1. How to avoid confusion and chaos at the beginning of class
   ♦ Be on time to class. Nothing gets a lesson off to a bad start like the teacher coming late to class. Besides setting a poor example, the time students are left unsupervised while waiting for the teacher to show up dissipates whatever attention and feeling for orderly learning they might have had.
   ♦ Know the daily and weekly school schedule well, including all changes that occur on any given day for assemblies, half days, and the like. It is wise to routinely brief yourself for a few minutes each morning just for this purpose and to regularly post updated schedules in the classroom.

2. How to deal with tardy students
   ♦ Establish a policy from the first day of class that anyone not in his or her seat by the tardy bell is automatically marked tardy.
   ♦ Treat repeated tardiness with definite punitive actions including letters to and conferences with parents, lowered behavior grades, detention, and exclusion from special events.
   ♦ Give unannounced pop quizzes from time to time immediately after the late bell rings. Those who make a habit of coming late to class will know that they run the risk of missing quizzes that will play a part in determining their grade.
   ♦ Never take tardiness lightly. Being on time to fulfill one's respon-

sibilities is at the heart of good character. Any weakness shown by the teacher in this area can only harm students and lead to a poor learning environment.

♦ Develop a set, organized procedure for dealing with and recording tardies. Remember, the idea is to open the lesson with an air of organization and purpose. Therefore, anything that might waste time, such as having to stop several times to record tardies, should be eliminated. This is possible where procedures are well organized and consistently applied.

♦ Confer with students who are chronically tardy. A demonstration of personal concern often prompts them to share their reasons for coming late to class and makes them receptive to constructive advice.

3. How to take attendance

♦ Do not hold up the beginning of class to take attendance. Always plan an opening activity for students to do while you take attendance.

♦ Make multiple copies of the class seating chart and use this for taking attendance. If a certain student is absent write the date in pencil under his or her name on the seating chart. Should that student come in late the absence can be changed to a tardy. If the student is absent then the date listed on the seating chart will make it that much easier to process the student's admit slip when he or she returns. In any event, the information on the seating chart can be transcribed into the official roll book at a later time when there will be no interference with classroom instruction.

♦ If possible, have a trustworthy student monitor take roll at the beginning of class, listing the names of those who are not there. Then at some point during the lesson the names of those listed as absent can quickly be checked against the seating chart.

4. How to avoid excessive talking and noise at the beginning of class

♦ Establish from the first day of class that there is always going to be some work to do from the moment the late bell rings. Such work could include a thought for the day to which the students are to write a brief response, a set of questions to be answered, or notes relating to material that will be discussed later in the lesson. The latter two activities are particularly effective when put on overhead transparencies because they can easily be used again later in the lesson and with several other sections of the same course.

♦ Give detention to any student who fails to stop talking after the late bell. Rather than make a big scene with students who are noisy at the beginning of the lesson, give one warning and then calmly write out detention slips for them. The class will soon realize that anyone who disrupts the beginning of class will get detention.

5. How to handle student problems and questions

♦ Develop a routine for dealing with the various problems and questions that come up at the beginning of class. For example, make it clear that only emergencies will be dealt with during the first ten minutes of class and that anything else will be handled at an appointed time.

♦ Make announcements at a specific time during the lesson and create a bulletin board of daily announcements for students to refer to on their own time.

♦ Create five folders, one for each day of the week, on which the assignments given on that day are listed and into which students can put work that is due. In this way the collection of assignments and work being turned in late can be handled with the least possible disruption to the lesson. The assignments placed in the folders can be recorded toward the end of the day.

♦ Have students write down any questions they have about the subject material. These questions can then be addressed during the lesson so the whole class can participate in and benefit from the responses.

♦ Admit to class only those recent absentees who have their readmit slips. Again, consistency is paramount. Once students realize that these rules and procedures are going to be strictly enforced they will follow them carefully.

♦ Hand out corrected work or official school announcements and forms toward the end of the lesson. If corrected work is going to be reviewed during the lesson, hand it out just prior to the review. Assigning monitors to perform this function is one way to save valuable class time.

6. How to deal with students who do not have materials needed for the lesson. It is very hard for students to get to work when they have nothing to work with.

♦ Have students keep an organized notebook that is graded periodically. Let students (and their parents) know exactly how the notebook is to be organized and maintained and how it will be graded.

♦ Where appropriate, use peer pressure to get students to bring all their materials, such as notebooks, pens and pencils, and textbooks, to class. One way of doing this is to point out that certain groups are at a disadvantage when a member or members of the group do not have the materials needed to contribute fully to the group effort.

7. How to gain students' attention from the beginning of class

♦ Make the opening activity interesting and useful to students. Pose questions and present problems that challenge students to think and that provide them with the practice and reinforcement they need to go on to further learning.

♦ Spend the first few minutes of class walking around the room helping students as they work on the opening activity. If you do not do this, students may think of this time as nothing more than "dead time" during which the teacher takes care of official business such as marking the roll book or signing readmit slips.

♦ Be enthusiastic about the material to be learned. The teacher has absolutely no right to expect students to be interested in the material covered in the lesson if he or she is not. They will, however, naturally feel attracted to material that obviously excites the teacher.

♦ Hold students responsible for the work they do in the opening activity. This could be accomplished by periodically collecting and grading the work, by questioning students at random, or by discussing the material.

Reviewing Work from the Previous Lesson

Secondary school students usually have five subjects every day and thus five different sets of ideas to keep in their heads from one day to the next. It is no wonder that the review part of each lesson is so important to their being able to pick up the thread of thought from the previous day so learning can proceed.

The following potential problems and suggested solutions should be considered when reviewing the previous day's work.

1. How to develop a set of review questions
   ♦ Ask questions that make students recall the most important information and ideas presented the previous day.
   ♦ Ask questions that require students to think about what they learned the previous day in relation to new problems and material to arouse their interest in the possibilities of and need for further learning.

2. How to use the opening minutes of class to recall the previous day's material
   ♦ Put several problems that relate directly to the previous day's work on the board or on an overhead transparency to be done as soon as students take their seats.
   ♦ Have three or four students at a time come to the board to do the opening problems and explain how they arrived at their answers.
   ♦ Assess how well students handle the opening problems both at the board and as you walk around the room to determine what ideas are not fully understood and which students are having particular difficulty.

3. How to use review to give a new and clearer view of material that has already been covered
   ♦ Relate the previously learned material logically to other material students already know.
   ♦ Present previously learned material in a more sophisticated way, thus taking into account the cyclical nature of the learning process. For example, in review, material originally acquired only as factual information may be reinforced at a higher level of learning as the basis for a series of problem-solving exercises.
   ♦ Whenever possible, hold open discussions in which students relate previously learned material to their own life experiences. With a little imagination most material in all subject areas can be treated in this way.

4. How to avoid boring review sessions
   ♦ Vary the teaching methods used for reviewing material. The review, rather than being a dull formality, should be an exciting activity that opens up new vistas for learning. In addition to having students look at previously learned material from different perspectives, as suggested above, the review should sometimes be carried out through discussion, demonstration, questioning, individualized instruction, and other methods of instruction.
   ♦ Set up a buddy system of tutoring in which students who have not fully grasped previously learned material can be brought up to the level of the rest of the class and are thus ready to get the most out of review sessions. In addition to this, individual meetings with students at free times before, during, and after school can serve a similar purpose. Students who are not prepared for review sessions quickly become bored and tune out what is going on.
   ♦ Include student ideas and comments throughout the review session. Students have limited interest in activities in which they are involved solely as listeners no matter how creative the teacher's presentation is. This is especially true where material they think they have already learned is gone over again, even in modified form.

Introducing Objectives for the Lesson

A statement of the objectives for the lesson lets students know where the day's work is headed and why. Without this they are left to meander through the various activities of the lesson purposelessly, thus exacerbating any existing problems of motivation and attention.

Consider the following potential problems and suggested solutions when introducing the objectives for the lesson.

1. How to select and present objectives effectively
   ♦ Prepare well before developing objectives. The quality of the objectives that are developed directly depends on the quality of curriculum research and planning that has been carried out. If the teacher has not immersed himself or herself in the subject and given careful thought to organizing it for classroom instruction, students will sense that the objectives developed are mechanical, not substantive.
   ♦ Emphasize quality, not quantity, when selecting objectives. The hallmark of the inexperienced teacher is the lesson plan containing enough objectives for several lessons. Repeatedly telling students they are going to learn something and then not following through or, worse, covering the material hastily and superficially, makes for uninterested and confused students.
   ♦ State objectives clearly. The purpose of stating the objectives of the lesson to students is to motivate them and to give direction to their work. All the time and effort spent on trying to develop high-quality objectives could be wasted if they are general and vague or com-

municated in a way students cannot understand. Rather, objectives should be definite, specific, and practical. Students generally do not relate well to objectives that are merely theoretical. A simple rule to follow is, if objectives are worth reaching they are worth explaining clearly.

♦ Involve students in formulating objectives. When students are made part of this process, not only do they understand the objectives better, but they also feel they have a stake in reaching the objectives.

♦ Select objectives that reinforce rather than conflict with each other. Rarely are classroom activities, each motivated by specific objectives, isolated events. Students learn better when they can see how their work to achieve one thing relates to or makes possible the achievement of other things.

Presenting New Material

The main part of the lesson is the presentation of new material. The first problem for the teacher concerning this part of the lesson is to determine the function and structure of the material to be presented, which is a problem of subject matter. The second problem is to determine how the material will be taught, which is a problem of method. Only after considering these two problems carefully can the teacher proceed to develop specific lesson plans for presenting the new material.

The following potential problems and suggested solutions should be considered when presenting new material for the lesson.

1. How to make sure all students pay attention when new material is presented

   ♦ Do not present too many ideas and objectives at one time. It is far more productive to cover one point thoroughly than many points superficially.

   ♦ Select a particularly interesting activity for introducing new material. Students are used to fast-moving media such as television and music videos and thus are going to make up their minds about how much effort to exert during the first few moments that new material is presented.

   ♦ Immediately involve students in thinking about and discussing the new material. It is wise to come prepared with a set of questions designed expressly for this purpose. The main point is to get them talking about or doing something with the new material rather than listening passively. Here, too, their involvement should not be seen as drudgery, such as filling in uninteresting worksheets or taking copious notes, but as stimulating work that relates to their own experiences.

   ♦ Notice when students need further review to grasp the new material. In such cases go back one step to solidify their understanding of previous material and then draw parallels to the new material.

2. How to avoid having students miss new material
   - Establish a policy that no students are allowed out of the room for at least the first half of the lesson except for emergencies.
   - Create a buddy system among the students so each student knows he or she can get any notes and materials missed because of an absence.
   - Set aside some time for students to work in pairs or small groups to pool ideas and thus help each other gain a fuller understanding of new material. Such cooperative study groups are most effective when the teacher is available to answer questions that may arise.

3. How to make sure the best conditions are created for learning new material
   - Use several teaching methods to reach one learning objective. For example, introduce new material with a brief lecture, followed by a discussion of what was just presented, reinforced by an individualized or small-group activity, and summarized by a joint student-teacher demonstration. By following this pattern of instruction students have several opportunities in a variety of learning modes to grasp the new material. At the same time the teacher has several opportunities to observe each student deal with the new material, which will help him or her provide assistance and modify instructional plans.
   - Organize the material well so students can see the connections between various facts and ideas. The ability to organize material in this way is directly related to the effort and thought that has gone into developing the course curriculum. Without having immersed oneself in the subject for the purpose of instructional planning, attempts to present new material effectively are not much more than guesswork. A good textbook may help solve the problem of how to organize material, but if this alone is used as a guide, instruction takes on an impersonal, disinterested tone.
   - Prepare instructional resources carefully. This includes gathering resources that make the new material clearer, more interesting, and understandable to students who have a variety of learning styles. In addition, all selected resources should be previewed to determine their exact contents and readiness for classroom use.
   - Pace instruction so that it is possible for students to remain interested and alert. Effective pacing of instruction begins with lesson planning, in which the nature and importance of each activity is considered and allotted a prescribed amount of time. Although in reality the planned time allotments may have to be modified as the lesson is taught, they do provide a guide for monitoring the progress of instruction. Avoid lingering on one point with a single student. The teacher's main responsibility is to all students in the class and this should be made quite clear to students. If there is a compelling reason to remain on one activity much longer than planned, do so,

but if such a practice becomes routine any sense of order and chance of covering all the required course material will disintegrate.

♦ Establish a network among teachers in the same subject area as a way of exchanging ideas and resources to enrich instruction. Such a network could eventually be extended across school and even district bounds.

Homework Assignments

The homework assignment is the students' opportunity to carry on learning at home that was begun in the classroom. As such, it is the true measure of how well they have learned how to learn. Thus, it should not be treated as mechanical or uninteresting work. On the contrary, it should be made as motivating as possible to encourage students' consistent and full efforts.

The following potential problems and suggested solutions should be considered when giving and reviewing homework assignments.

1. How to make homework assignments relevant
   ♦ Select what is to be done for homework thoughtfully, not mechanically. For example, using a thoughtful approach the teacher would ask, What material do the students need work on? How much work can they handle in one assignment? Have they had adequate preparation for doing the assignment? Is the work to be done interesting? Does the assignment call for learning at different levels (e.g., drill, problem solving)? The teacher who considers none of these questions and uses materials he or she has neither developed nor taken the time to carefully review is using a mechanical approach to giving homework assignments. If homework is as important as we tell students it is, then the planning, preparation, and presentation of such assignments have to be treated accordingly. Otherwise we have no right to expect students to take the assignments or us seriously.
   ♦ Design homework assignments so they are an extension not only of what has been covered in the classroom but also of the process of learning that has been used. This reinforces students' learning skills.

2. How to make homework assignments clear
   ♦ Establish a routine way of letting students know what their homework assignment is, when it is due, and what is expected of them. This could include posting the assignment in a specified place on the board or in designated folders and then briefly explaining what is to be done. In addition, some time should be provided for student questions concerning the work.
   ♦ Provide any instructions or lists of resources that students might need to successfully complete the assignment. These are especially important for assignments that are relatively complex.

♦ Explain the purpose of the assignment and its relation to work just presented. Leaving such explanations to simple verbal instructions is most often not enough to avoid the situation in which students get home and have completely forgotten how to begin the assignment. Therefore, it is helpful to work through a sample problem or two from the assignment in class to increase the likelihood that when the students reach home they will know how to proceed.

3. How to make sure students do their homework
   ♦ Tell students from the first day of class that homework is a major part of their grades and then follow through with this.
   ♦ Make no exceptions to the rule that students who do slipshod work on their homework will not get decent grades.
   ♦ Collect homework assignments regularly, not in bunches or sporadically.
   ♦ Make sure the assignments are reviewed one way or another (i.e., with teacher comments written on them or as a class review activity).
   ♦ Design homework assignments so they are interesting, yet challenging, and within student capabilities. Students are more inclined to do their homework when they see that it helps them understand the subject—they are interested in finding something that promotes personal success. All too often homework assignments are given mechanically, quite oblivious to any help the students might need.
   ♦ Communicate to the parents or guardians what is expected of students concerning homework assignments. They are in a position to assist their children and see that a proper, stable environment for study is maintained.

4. How to review homework assignments
   ♦ Use a variety of methods for reviewing homework assignments. For example, sometimes a review can be the opening activity, and a few students can put their work on some of the homework problems on the board for a general discussion concerning ideas and procedures or for a drill where specific information needs to be repeated and memorized.
   ♦ Coordinate the review of homework with the presentation of material during the lesson. In this way the review can serve either as an introduction or a follow-up to learning related material.
   ♦ Have students keep a section of their notebooks just for homework so they and the teacher can have easy access to the assignments.
   ♦ Avoid checking homework in a way that communicates to students that it is not very important. Sometimes because of the sheer amount of homework to correct, along with numerous other tasks, the teacher merely glances at each student's assignment only long enough to see that something is written on the page. Rather than feeling homework assignments are opportunities for independent learning and disciplined work, students in such a class come to see homework as

something to get out of the way as quickly and mechanically as possible. In situations where the volume of work and scarcity of time do not allow all homework to be carefully checked, it should be made clear that on any given day a thorough check of the homework can be made and that failure to have the assignment or to have done a decent job will negatively affect grades. In addition, reviewing homework in conjunction with other classroom activities, as mentioned above, can also relieve some of the pressure of having too much work to correct at any one time.

Lesson Summaries

The summary of the lesson is a sensitive period in which much may be gained or lost. If it is planned for and carried out effectively students can leave class with a clear idea of what they just learned and an interest in continuing where they left off. On the other hand, an ineffective summary can leave students confused and consequently unprepared and uninterested in further learning.

Consider the following potential problems and suggested solutions when summarizing the lesson.

1. How to provide for summaries in the lesson
   - As with the pacing of instruction, the key to an effective summary begins with planning. Rather than planning for a single summary at the end of the lesson, it may become evident during planning that because of the diversity of activities and complexity of subject matter a brief summary should be provided after each main point in the lesson is covered.
   - Establish a routine for wrapping up the day's work. For example, students can be required to stop all work several minutes before the bell to collect their thoughts on what has been learned each day. In addition, establishing such a routine will decrease the likelihood that the summary will receive inadequate time or attention, as frequently happens. Having such a well planned and purposeful activity near the very end of the lesson will also make for much more controlled class dismissals.

2. How to use summaries effectively
   - Avoid summaries that merely reiterate in condensed form what was covered during in the lesson. Such an approach is boring and is not much help in solidifying student understanding of the material.
   - Use the questioning method to enhance the summary. A few well-designed questions can be a stimulating way of making students collect their thoughts and connect various ideas presented during the lesson. Students appreciate the challenge such questions represent and the opportunity they provide to get a new and wider view of ground already covered.

♦ Use the summary as a way of diagnosing student strengths and weaknesses and of assessing the effectiveness of the teaching methods and materials that have been used. Used this way, the summary also provides the teacher with a valuable opportunity to collect his or her thoughts and observations as a preparation for subsequent planning and instruction.

Table 6.1 summarizes the elements to consider for effectively carrying out the daily lesson.

Preparing the Daily Lesson Plan

When observing successful veteran teachers it is often noticed that they do not work from detailed lesson plans. Rather, they seem to be relying on a few sentences written in the daily plan book or on sheer recall of the material. What is not observed, however, is the huge amount of work these teachers have put into lesson planning earlier in their teaching careers and the time and effort they continue to spend outside the classroom. Indeed, it is this significant effort that gives veteran teachers the ability to function without detailed daily plans if they choose to.

For the new teacher to attempt to function without developing carefully thought out lesson plans, though, is to court disaster. More than anything else the success of new teachers depends on their knowing what they are doing, including understanding the subject, determining the scope and sequence of topics to be covered, selecting various teaching strategies, and relating instruction to the particular students to be taught. The development of daily lesson plans represents the most effective and creative way for teachers to bring into focus their understanding of all four of these critical elements to meet the daily practical needs of the classroom.

The lesson plan format presented in Figure 6.11 takes into account all the important factors that need to be considered for teaching a lesson:

♦ Listing of the course element (unit) and specific topic to which the material in the lesson is related
♦ Statement of the overall objective for the lesson (e.g., To increase skills in doing two-step equations)
♦ Statement of objectives for each activity in the lesson. When these activity objectives are reached the overall objective for the lesson will have been accomplished
♦ Listing of the criteria by which progress toward each activity objective is to be measured
♦ Listing of the activities to be carried out during the lesson, culminating with a summary activity
♦ An approximate time allotment for each activity
♦ A summary evaluation section for indicating how much progress students made toward reaching each activity objective
♦ Listing of the materials and resources needed for teaching the lesson
♦ Listing of vocabulary words to be presented and defined

TABLE 6.1 *Considerations for Effectively Carrying Out the Daily Lesson*

LESSON PART	CONSIDERATIONS
Beginning the lesson	1. How to avoid confusion and chaos at the beginning of class 2. How to deal with tardy students 3. How to take attendance 4. How to avoid excessive talking and noise at the beginning of class 5. How to handle student problems and questions 6. How to deal with students who do not have materials needed for the lesson 7. How to gain students' attention from the beginning of class
Reviewing work from the previous lesson	1. How to develop a set of review questions 2. How to use the opening minutes of class to recall the previous day's material 3. How to use review to give a new and clearer view of material that has already been covered 4. How to avoid boring review sessions
Introducing objectives for the lesson	1. How to select and present objectives effectively
Presenting new material	1. How to make sure all students pay attention when new material is presented 2. How to avoid having students miss new material 3. How to make sure the best conditions are created for learning new material
Homework assignments	1. How to make homework assignments relevant 2. How to make homework assignments clear 3. How to make sure students do their homework 4. How to review homework assignments
Lesson summaries	1. How to provide for summaries in the lesson 2. How to use summaries effectively

- Indication of important notes to be put on the board during the lesson
- Listing of the homework assignment

SUMMARY

In this chapter several main points about carrying out classroom instruction were presented:

1. The methods of transmitting subject content and the subject content itself are inextricably intertwined, and mastery of both is essential to successful teaching.

FIGURE 6.11 *Recommended Lesson Plan Format*

LESSON PLAN

Element _____   Topic _____   Class _____   Date _____

Overall Lesson Objective _____

Objectives	Criteria for Measuring Progress	Summary Evaluation
1.	1.	1.
2.	2.	2.
3.	3.	3.
4.	4.	4.

Time Allotment	Activities	Materials/Resources	
_____	1.		
_____	2.		
_____	3.		
_____	4.		
	*Summary activity		

Vocabulary   Board Notes   Assignment

2. The lecture, perhaps the most ancient method of teaching, can be used to introduce or summarize a unit, explain difficult ideas, stimulate student desire to learn, and cover information in a short time. It is particularly effective in training students to pay attention.

3. The demonstration, a combined visual and oral approach to conveying information and ideas, can be used to stimulate interest in a particular topic, illustrate points efficiently, provide a change of pace, and provide a model for teaching specific skills. It is particularly effective in helping students develop the skill of accurate observation.

4. The drill, one of the most direct forms of reinforcing learning, can be used for permanent retention of information, systematic review and application, informal quizzes, forming new habits, individualized practice, and refining skills. It is particularly effective in helping students develop a sense of mental discipline.

5. The review, a method of teaching that aims not only at reinforcing previously learned material but also at giving such learning new meaning, can be used to provide opportunities for student questions, foster a sense of accomplishment, assess student understanding, establish new relations, and organize previous learning. It is particularly effective in helping students develop thinking skills.

6. Questioning, by far the most common teaching method used in the classroom, can be used to hold students accountable for paying attention and participating in classroom activities, assess student understanding of course material, lead students to think, get students to relate and compare experiences and understandings, encourage students to study, create a springboard to discussion or other methods of instruction, and provide students with opportunities to obtain information from the teacher and each other. It is particularly effective for allowing students to form and express opinions about issues and ideas, thus fostering cognitive development, especially at the conceptual and ideational levels.

7. Individualized instruction, a method that focuses the emphasis of the instructional process on each individual student, can be used to strengthen reading and writing skills, address individual differences, foster self-discipline and confidence, work cooperatively with parents, utilize available technology, and carry out drill and practice exercises and independent projects. It is particularly effective in helping students take responsibility for learning.

8. Study, a method that allows students to transfer what is in their notes, textbooks, and all other collateral material to their heads for the purpose of solving problems and further learning, can be used to develop the capacity for autonomous work, develop a sense of objectivity, carry out research, and complete homework assignments. It is particularly effective in helping students form the habit of applying their minds to problems and tasks, and thus for extending learning beyond the classroom.

9. Discussion, the primary interactive method of teaching, can be used to

provide an excellent opportunity for students to share ideas and assist each other and to motivate students to learn. It is particularly effective for creating a classroom environment in which all students feel free to express themselves.

10. The group project, a way of providing opportunities for students to work cooperatively toward common goals, can be used to allow for a degree of informality and freedom in the classroom, make use of resources extending beyond the classroom, provide students with opportunities for taking a leadership role, and permit students of similar interests and abilities to work at their own speed and to their full capacity. It is particularly effective in furthering the school's socialization function.

11. Problem solving, a general method that takes many forms as it is incorporated into various methods of instruction, can be used effectively to increase students' ability to think through problems in and out of school.

12. The daily lesson, the touchstone upon which all the teacher's efforts are measured, represents the culmination of all curriculum development and instructional planning.

13. The development of the daily lesson plan represents the most effective and creative way for the teacher to bring into focus his or her understanding of subject matter, of methods of instruction, and of the particular students to be taught, to meet the daily practical needs of the classroom.

♦ ♦ ♦ ♦ ♦ ♦ ♦
PRACTICAL MODEL 6.1   Teaching Resource Units

Introduction   This practical model describes how to design teaching resource units as a way of using a conceptual approach to provide students with effective independent learning activities. The emphasis in this model is on student creativity and thought, with the teacher serving as a guide and facilitator.

Submitted by   Teresa Coda, high school science teacher, Santa Monica, California

Purpose   To show teachers how they can use teaching resource units as independent learning exercises to enrich classroom instruction and foster students' sense of responsibility and confidence

♦ Teaching Resource Unit

Effective teaching resource units consist of the eight sequential sections described below.

Section 1. Daily Calendar of Activities
Construct a daily plan of the activities to be used for the entire teaching resource unit. This calendar of activities serves as guide for carrying out

the teaching resource unit and also allows for additional comments to be noted as the unit is carried out so that constructive modifications can be made for subsequent uses of the unit.

Section 2. Introduction to the Concept
Provide a written and oral statement explaining the conceptual approach to be taken in carrying out the teaching resource unit. In addition, briefly discuss with students the importance of the topic to be studied and its relevance to the world around us.

Section 3. Orienting Questions
Present students with an anticipatory set of "how" and "why" questions to orient them to the objectives of the unit. These questions should stir up the students' minds by showing them what they do not know and fostering a keen interest in obtaining the knowledge they seem to be lacking.

Section 4. Motivational Activities
Develop a series of lead-in activities to motivate the learners and at the same time introduce them to the unit. Effective lead-in activities spur a healthy curiosity in the students about the material to be covered. For each activity describe how it is to be carried out, what is to be told to the students, and how the students are to perform their tasks. Students should be given a list of questions to prepare them for subsequent hands-on activities (see Section 5) and to further pique their interest in the ideas and information being covered.

Section 5. Planning Hands-On Activities for Each Concept
This section may extend for many pages as it describes the various hands-on activities to be used in the classroom to carry out the teaching resource unit. No more than one significant concept should be covered per lesson. In addition, the activities used should stress the learning of specific process skills where appropriate while providing ample opportunities for students to use their imaginations to explore each concept to the fullest extent possible.

Section 6. Student-Developed Lists of Concepts Learned
The students should identify and express concepts they have discovered within the unit through the hands-on activities. They should also list any other ideas and unresolved questions that may have come to mind in the course of the various learning experiences. To carry out this section effectively the students should do the following four tasks:

1. State the concepts they have discovered in their own words as clearly as possible.
2. List the discovered concepts sequentially so that they build upon each other and thus lead to a wider understanding of the unit.

3. List any subordinate concepts under the main concepts where such detail seems possible and useful.
4. Prepare lists of examples describing various applications where the concepts appear to be operative in everyday life.

Some of these student-developed concepts and applications can serve as the basis for individual or group projects (see Section 7).

Section 7. Individual and Group Writing Assignments and Projects
It is useful to have individual or group writing assignments and projects as a follow-up to the hands-on activities as a form of reinforcement, an evaluative tool, and an opportunity for self-expression and cooperation. Students should be encouraged to pose relevant questions regarding the hands-on activities as the basis for beginning these assignments and projects. Effective writing assignments should include three phases:

1. Prewriting activities in which an outline and approach to the assignments are developed
2. Writing activities in which ideas and feelings about what has been learned are expressed
3. Rewriting activities in which the written work is modified based on constructive teacher, peer, and self-criticism

In addition, it is useful for these assignments and projects to provide students with a list of resource materials they may wish to refer to as they complete their work.

Section 8. Methods for Evaluating Learning
It is important to evaluate how well students are progressing, in as nonthreatening an environment as possible. The following four forms of evaluation are helpful in creating such an environment:

♦ *Monitoring by observation.* Many forms of learning, especially learning of process and laboratory skills, are best monitored by observing students as they are engaged in particular activities.
♦ *Monitoring by verbal examination.* Prepare a list of conceptual "how" and "why" questions to test students for understanding and application of the main ideas covered in the units.
♦ *Monitoring by problem solving.* Design a variety of exercises that require students to deal with problems by applying the concepts they have learned. This form of assessment allows for originality while providing for the development of essential thinking skills.
♦ *Monitoring by student evaluations.* Students should be given numerous opportunities to cooperatively review and discuss each other's writing assignments and projects.

◆ ◆ ◆ ◆ ◆ ◆ ◆

CASE STUDY 6.1   Student-Directed Methods

Orienting Questions

As you read this case study ask yourself these questions:

Specific
- ◆ How carefully has this teacher prepared the students for this group project activity?
- ◆ Is this lesson being carried out in a way that fosters student cooperation and interaction?

General
- ◆ What points in this lesson stand out as indicators of this teacher's strengths and/or weaknesses?
- ◆ What recommendations would you make for addressing the problems this teacher seems to have?

Setting

School – High school in a large metropolitan area

Subject – History (fifty-two minutes)

Teacher – Ms. Olmos

Students – Thirty-five tenth graders with below-average reading skills

Topic – The British Parliament

Lesson

Note: Under Time Frame the numbers represent the minutes that elapse as the period progresses. Under Dialog the names of the students and the teacher appear as they speak. The symbol ► represents a brief description of a particularly noteworthy action or observation.

Time Frame	Dialog	
0 to 3	►	The students enter the room and quickly begin answering the day's warm-up question: " 'The greatest happiness for the greatest number.' What does it mean?"
	Ms. O.:	When you have finished the warm-up, copy down the vocabulary words listed on the side board. I hope you are looking up these words every day. They are important to know. On the next test you'll be asked to define some of them.
	Pablo:	Ms. Olmos, I missed the words from last Friday because of the band concert we gave at Pierce Elementary School.
	Ms. O.:	Ask someone. Everyone should have the words and their definitions in their notebooks.
	Pablo:	Okay.
3 to 6	Ms. O.:	Let's discuss your answers to the warm-up. What does "the greatest happiness for the greatest number" mean?

Time Frame	Dialog	
	►	A dozen voices are heard simultaneously with answers. One student, Enrique, is the loudest.
	Enrique:	It means when a lot of people in a country are doing okay.
	Ms. O.:	Something like that. Anyone else?
	►	Again, numerous voices call out.
	Ms. O.:	What do you think, Wanda?
	Wanda:	Hmmn. I don't know.
	Ms. O.:	It means that a majority of the people, that's 51 percent, in a country are happy. When the majority are happy that means the greatest number are happy. Let me give you an example you can relate to. How many of you want homework tonight? (One student raises his hand.) How many don't want homework? (All the other students raise their hands.) So you see, the majority don't want homework, so that is what you feel is the greatest good.
	Mark:	Yeah, it would be real good not to have homework.
6 to 10	Ms. O.:	Oh, that was just an example. You are going to have homework. (Changing the topic) I'd like us to get into discussion groups in a moment. As you will see when you read this sheet I'm handing out, each group is going to prepare a speech to present to the class.
	Lily:	What do you mean write a speech?
	Ms. O.:	Here, read this sheet; it tells you what to do.
	►	The instructions on the sheet are brief: "Your group must make a speech before the British Parliament. First you have to make a decision concerning whether or not to favor social reform. Once you have decided which side to take you should work together to write a speech arguing your position before the British Parliament. You may use your worksheet from yesterday's lesson on reform to prepare your speech." In addition, there are several questions listed on the sheet, some under the heading "Favoring Reform" and some under the heading "Against Reform."
10 to 15	Ms. O.:	We are now going to form seven discussion groups.
	►	As soon as this is said most of the students begin talking and quickly moving to be in a group with their friends.
	Ms. O.:	Wait a second. (The students do not respond.) I said hold it! (Everyone quiets down.) This time I have made up groups for you.

Time Frame	Dialog	
	Frank:	You never did that before. I want to be with Louis and Chick.
	Ms. O.:	I think it would be good for you to learn to work with other people for a change.
	►	Ms. Olmos reads out the group assignments and the students take their places. (Each group has at least one student who has demonstrated good leadership qualities.) She then finishes handing out the instruction sheets.
15 to 39	**Susie:**	Ms. Olmos, how do we begin?
	Ms. O.:	(Coming over to Susie's group and at the same time addressing the whole class) First, decide who your group recorder is going to be.
	►	Several of the students in Susie's group enthusiastically volunteer Susie, who is considered the brightest one in the group and who always does her assignments. Susie accepts, taking it in stride.
	Ms. O.:	Next, decide among yourselves which side you want to take on this issue. Third, answer the questions listed on the instruction sheet because these will help you write your speech. Although we may not actually have time to write our speeches this period, we at least will be ready to write them first thing tomorrow and then present them to the class. Which reminds me, one person has to be selected to give the speech. (Again, several students volunteer Susie).
	►	Ms. Olmos spends the next twenty minutes going around to each group to make sure they are proceeding well.
	Ms. O.:	(Speaking to the class) I notice that in each group some people are doing all the work and some are taking a free ride. Every group member must answer at least one of the questions on the instruction sheet. I'll be checking to see that this is being done.
	Mia:	(A student who was one of those taking a free ride, speaking to her neighbor) Look, she lists the page numbers in the text where we can find the answers. This is easy. (She then turns to page 507 in her textbook, locates the information she needs, and copies it down verbatim.)
39 to 52	**Ms. O.:**	I'm glad to see that everyone is now working. (Going over to a particular group) Who is the leader here?
	Ramon:	I am, Ms. Olmos. We have most of our answers already done.

Time Frame	Dialog

Ms. O.: What position has your group taken?

Ramon: We are definitely for reform, of course.

Ms. O.: Why are you for reform? Wait, Ramon. Bill?

Bill: Because reform is good. The people against reform want to cheat people.

Ms. O.: Have you discussed this among yourselves?

Ramon: No, not really. We know we all agree, so we spent our time finding the answers in our books.

► Ms. Olmos realizes that all seven groups have chosen to be for reform and that there has been little or no discussion except in one group where she asked them to imagine who would be the reformers and who the Tories today.

Ms. O.: You know, the whole idea of this activity was to get you to discuss the issues involved. I haven't seen much discussion. Therefore, before you all write your speeches tomorrow, spend the first ten minutes discussing how the situation in England in those days relates to problems in the world today.

Susie: Oh no, Ms. Olmos. I've already started to write our speech.

Ms. O.: Don't worry, just wait to finish it until after you have your little discussion. You'll be fine.

► The bell rings to end class. Several students approach Ms. Olmos, wanting to ask her opinion of their ideas for relating the question of reform to today's world.

Brief   *Key Facts* – List three facts verbatim that characterize the main positive and/or negative aspects of the lesson.

Strengths/Weaknesses – Briefly explain how the key facts selected indicate strengths and/or weaknesses in the teacher's performance.

Recommendations – Briefly describe what the teacher could have done to alleviate or avoid the problems that were seen.

◆ ◆ ◆ ◆ ◆ ◆ ◆

CASE STUDY 6.2   Questioning

Orienting
Questions   As you read this case study ask yourself these questions:

Specific
◆ Does this teacher include questions that encourage the development of thinking skills?
◆ Are the questions posed relevant and useful in helping students understand the topic of the lesson?

General
◆ What points in this lesson stand out as indicators of this teacher's strengths and/or weaknesses?
◆ What recommendations would you make for addressing the problems this teacher seems to have?

Setting   *School* – Private high school in an upper-middle-income and racially mixed neighborhood

Subject – Art I (sixty minutes)

Teacher – Mrs. Pane, the school's vice principal, who still teaches one class a day

Students – Twenty-five eleventh and twelfth graders

Topic – Greek and Roman Sculpture

Lesson

Time Frame	Dialog
0 to 3	► The first bell has rung. Students enter the classroom and sit five to a table. The teacher is taking roll as they enter. The overhead projector is projecting a transparency of Greek and Roman sculpture on a screen. The homework assignment is written on the board.
3 to 7	**Mrs. P.:** Good morning. Today we are going to start a unit on Greek and Roman art. Before I start, copy your homework assignment from the board. (She then proceeds to read aloud the assignment.) Read pages 160 through 170 and answer only the questions marked "history." Has everybody got that? It's due Monday.
	► Moans and groans are heard as the students write the assignment down.
7 to 10	**Mrs. P.:** Okay, I'd like everyone to move to a spot where you can see the screen. Can everyone see?
	► The students shift their chairs to get better viewing positions.

Time Frame	Dialog	
10 to 13	**Mrs. P.:**	All right then, on the left you see a Greek sculpture and on the right you see a Roman one. The Greek one is bronze and was done by an artist named Paroclytis. The Roman one is marble and we don't know who made it. Compare the sculptures. How are they different?
13 to 17	►	Several hands go up.
	Mrs. P.:	John?
	John:	The Greek one isn't wearing any clothes, and the Roman one is.
	Mrs. P.:	Okay, good. What else is different about them? Dave?
	Dave:	The Greek one is much stronger looking, but the Roman one looks more realistic.
	Mrs. P.:	Right. The Greek figure is very fit and muscular. What does he look like he might be?
	►	Many students call out answers such as "athlete," "soldier," and "warrior."
17 to 23	**Mrs. P.:**	I heard someone say athlete; that's very good. In fact he is an athlete. He is called *The Victorious Athlete.* How do we know he is victorious? Can anybody guess?
	►	The class does not respond.
	Mrs. P.:	What's he pointing to with his hand, Joan?
	Joan:	Something on his head.
	Mrs. P.:	Right. What did athletes who won first place in Olympic competition receive?
	Joan:	Oh, that's right, a wreath. But why doesn't he have clothes on?
23 to 28	**Mrs. P.:**	It would be hard to run a race in a toga and sandals, wouldn't it? But does he look like a real person? Compare him to the Roman. Erich?
	Erich:	The Roman guy looks more real. His face is wrinkled and he's wearing clothes and he's kind of bald. But the Greek guy is too perfect.
	Mrs. P.:	Think back to your Western Civ class when you were freshmen. What do you remember about Greek society? What did the Greeks want to achieve? Anybody remember? Paul?
	Paul:	Well, they were great thinkers and they also invented the Olympic games.
	Mrs. P.:	Right. So this perfection of mind and body, or its idealized image, is reflected in their art. Does everybody see that?
	►	Most heads nod affirmatively.

Time Frame	Dialog	
	Mrs. P.:	What about the Romans? What did they stand for? Barb?
	Barb:	They were conquerors.
	Mrs. P.:	Yes, and engineers. Very practical people. The sculpture here is called the *Roman Patrician*. It was made as a death mask when this man died. That's why it's so realistic. It's the face of a man who actually lived in ancient Rome. Why would anyone want a mask of someone who had just died? Adam?
	Adam:	I don't know for sure, but I guess to remember him.
28 to 39	**Mrs. P.:**	Exactly, and to honor him on special occasions like the anniversary of his death. Now, before I forget, I want to remind you to bring in your permission slips for the field trip next Wednesday. We're going to the Getty Museum in Malibu. *The Victorious Athlete* is there and you'll get a chance to see him up close.
	John:	You mean we're gonna see that same statue?
	Mrs. P.:	Yes, and some Roman ones too. Now, I have some short questions for you to discuss and answer. First I'll go over the questions with you in case you don't understand them. Question 1. Which sculpture do you find more interesting and why? Question 2. Does American culture compare more to the Greeks or to the Romans? Question 3. Which sculpture reflects a truer image of man? Are there any questions?
	Russell:	Yes. What do you mean by "image of man"?
	Mrs. P.:	I mean types of sculpture that present a truer depiction of an ideal. In other words, a realistic representation.
	Russell:	Now I see.
39 to 47	►	The class begins discussing and writing answers. Mrs. Pane walks around the room answering questions and observing the students at work.
47 to 60	**Mrs. P.:**	Okay, I'd like you to stop and we'll quickly go around the room to get your reactions.
	►	Several students share their answers with the class.
	Mrs. P.:	Great. Most of you had some really good answers. Please put your names on the sheet with your answers to the three questions and leave them at my desk. The bell is about to ring.
	►	The bell rings and the students leave in an orderly fashion.
Brief		*Key Facts* – List three key facts verbatim that characterize the main positive and/or negative aspects of the lesson.

Strengths/Weaknesses – Briefly explain how the key facts selected indicate strengths and/or weaknesses in the teacher's performance.

Recommendations – Briefly describe what the teacher could have done to alleviate or avoid the problems that were seen.

♦ ♦ ♦ ♦ ♦ ♦ ♦

CASE STUDY 6.3   Interactive Methods

Orienting Questions   As you read this case study ask yourself these questions:

Specific
- ♦ How effective is this teacher in communicating information and ideas to the students?
- ♦ Does this teacher blend verbal and visual modes of instruction effectively?

General
- ♦ What points in this lesson stand out as indicators of this teacher's strengths and/or weaknesses?
- ♦ What recommendations would you make for addressing the problems this teacher seems to have?

Setting   *School* – High school in an inner-city area

Subject – General biology (forty-five minutes)

Teacher – Mr. Stevens, a former research biologist who is in his first year of a career change

Students – Thirty-eight sophomores with a variety of ethnic and academic backgrounds

Topic – Plant Classification

Lesson   *Note:* Mr. Stevens had given a brief outline of plant classification the previous day. The majority of the students showed no real interest. He had asked each student to bring in one leaf and one seed to use for today's lesson.

Time Frame	Dialog
0 to 5	► The students enter the classroom slowly and take their assigned seats. The following is written on the front board: "Have your notebooks, leaves, and seeds out and ready for today's lesson." While Mr. Stevens is taking

Time Frame	Dialog

attendance some of the students are asking friends for leaves and seeds because they did not bring them as directed.

5 to 9 — **Mr. S.:** I'm glad to see that most of you are prepared for today's class. As we said yesterday, seed plants can be divided into two main groups, monocots and dicots. Sue, can you recall the characteristics of a monocot plant?

Sue: Sure. The veins run in the same direction and they have one part to their seed.

Mr. S.: Good. Tom, describe a dicot.

Tom: A what?

Mr. S.: A dicot. Don't you remember anything from yesterday or were you asleep again?

Tom: Not really.

► A few hands go up trying to respond to the question that Tom could not answer. Mr. Stevens calls on one of these students, who then gives the right answer.

Mr. S.: Now, by looking at the leaves and seeds you brought in, let's determine which group they belong to. In other words, we want to classify them.

9 to 24 ► Mr. Stevens walks around the room trying to improve the attention of the class. He picks up different samples and the students discuss the classifications. There is quite a variety of specimens and many of the students react positively to the investigation. Others are looking at the clock anxiously. Mr. Stevens points out the students who failed to bring in samples.

Mr. S.: (As he notes the names of the students who failed to bring in samples) Why didn't you bring anything in?

Rosa: I forgot to.

Mark: I live in an apartment and we ain't got no bushes or trees.

Jeanne: I wasn't sure what you wanted us to bring in.

Mr. S.: Who finds it easier now to understand monocots and dicots after seeing these samples?

► Many hands go up.

Mr. S.: And what about the rest of you? Leroy?

Leroy: Oh, I don't really care that much about plants.

► The same students who were not interested in the class before mumble agreement with Leroy's statement.

Mr. S.: But plants are such an important part of our world.

Tom: Yeah, but who can make any money knowing about plants?

Time Frame	Dialog	
24 to 29	►	The students begin to laugh and talk among themselves. Mr. Stevens tries to get their attention, making a lot of effort to do so.
	Mr. S.:	Now let's get back to work.
	Rosa:	(Trying to be funny) Yeah, plants are sure a lot of work.
	►	Again the class becomes disruptive.
	Mr. S.:	(Loudly) I mean it now. No more of this. You people don't realize why plants are so important.
	►	Mr. Stevens thinks briefly to himself and then asks a question.
	Mr. S.:	Rosa, what did you eat for dinner yesterday?
	Rosa:	What?
	Mr. S.:	What did you eat for dinner last night?
29 to 39	**Rosa:**	Pizza with the works.
	Mr. S.:	What plants did it have on it?
	Rosa:	Plants?
	Mr. S.:	Yes, did it have mushrooms, peppers, onions, tomatoes, or things like that?
	Rosa:	Sure it did.
	Mr. S.:	Then you ate plants.
	►	Mr. Stevens asks more of the uninterested students about their dinners and they begin discussing edible plants. More and more of them want to add their opinions. The classroom gets noisy with excitement and Mr. Stevens has to settle them down after a few minutes.
39 to 45	**Mr. S.:**	Okay, okay. Now for the last few minutes of class I want you to write down in your notebooks as many plants as you can that we eat. Whoever can list the most will not have to do tonight's homework.
	►	The students frantically start writing down ideas while Mr. Stevens writes the assignment. This is the first time he has written on the board during the period. He checks the lists at the bell and tells one student that he does not have to do the homework because he has the longest list.
Brief		*Key Facts* – List three key facts verbatim that characterize the main positive and/or negative aspects of the lesson.

Strengths/Weaknesses – Briefly explain how the key facts selected indicate strengths and/or weaknesses in the teacher's performance.

Recommendations – Briefly describe what the teacher could have done to alleviate or avoid the problems that were seen.

◆ ◆ ◆ ◆ ◆ ◆ ◆

CHAPTER PROJECT   Develop a Detailed Methods Plan for Covering a Particular Course Topic

Goals
1. To plan for the use of various teaching methods to reach the same and different instructional objectives.
2. To address individual, small-group, and whole-class needs in the plan that is developed.
3. To present a modeling demonstration of a segment of the developed plans.

Phases
One, two, or three phases of the chapter project can be completed as is deemed appropriate to student needs and the design of the course.

Planning
1. Select and outline the course material to be covered for the project.
2. List the objectives to be reached for this particular segment of the course.

Partial Implementation
1. Develop a lesson plan for reaching one particular objective through the coordinated use of three different teaching methods.
2. Develop a lesson plan for reaching two or more objectives using one teaching method.

Full Implementation
1. Present a modeling demonstration of the beginning and any other part of either lesson plan that is developed.
2. Discuss with those who observe the modeling demonstration any suggestions for improving the plan and the performance.

◆ ◆ ◆ ◆ ◆ ◆ ◆

REFERENCES

Brar, P. S. (1985, March). Training in clear thinking. *The Educational Review, 91,* 57–58.

Callahan, S. G. (1971). *Successful teaching in secondary schools* (rev. ed.). Glenview, IL: Scott, Foresman.

Charters, W. W. (1912). *Methods of teaching.* Chicago: Row, Peterson & Company.

Colman, J. E. (1967). *The master teachers and the art of teaching.* New York: Pitman.

Crawford, C. C. (1938). *How to teach.* Los Angeles: Claude C. Crawford.

Dewey, J. (1928). *Democracy and education: An introduction to the philosophy of education.* New York: Macmillan.

Dunn, R., & Dunn, K. (1972). *Practical approaches to individualizing instruction.* West Nyack, NY: Parker.

Earhart, L. B. (1915). *Types of teaching.* Boston: Houghton Mifflin.

Good, T. L., & Brophy, J. E. (1984). *Looking in classrooms* (3rd ed.). New York: Harper & Row.

Grambs, J. D., & Carr, J. C. (1979). *Modern methods in secondary education* (4th ed.). New York: Holt, Rinehart and Winston.

Heck, S. F., & Williams, C. R. (1984). *The complex roles of the teacher: An ecological perspective.* New York: Teachers College Press.

McNeil, J. D. (1985). *Curriculum: A comprehensive introduction* (3rd ed.). Boston: Little, Brown.

Mursell, J. L. (1934). *Principles of education.* New York: W. W. Norton.

Strayer, G. D. (1914). *A brief course in the teaching process.* New York: Macmillan.

Thorndike, E. L. (1906). *The principles of teaching: Based on psychology.* New York: A. G. Seller.

Thorndike, E. L., & Gates, A. I. (1929). *Elementary principles of education.* New York: Macmillan.

Wake, P. A., Marbeau, V., & Peterson, A. D. C. (1979). Innovations in secondary education in Europe. Strasbourg: Council for Cultural Cooperation, Council of Europe.

◆ ◆ ◆ ◆ ◆ ◆ ◆

ANNOTATED READINGS

Alcorn, M. D., Kinder, J. S., & Schunert, J. R. (1970). *Better teaching in secondary schools* (3rd ed.). New York: Holt, Rinehart and Winston.
  A comprehensive text designed to give beginning teachers help in solving the complex problems of teaching. See Chapters 7 and 8 for a discussion of teaching methods and basic instructional procedures.

Callahan, J. F., & Clark, L. H. (1982). *Teaching in the middle and secondary schools* (2nd ed.). New York: Macmillan.
  A basic self-instructional text on teaching methods featuring a series of learning modules offering practical explanations of teaching procedures. See Chapters 7, 8, 9, and 11 for modules on various methods of instruction.

Cooper, J. M. (Ed.). (1977). *Classroom teaching skills: A workbook.* Lexington, MA: D. C. Heath.
  A workbook providing practice in major teaching skill areas through analytical exercises as well as guidelines and suggestions on how these skills may be practiced in microteaching. See Chapter 4 on lesson presentation skills and Chapter 5 on questioning skills.

Gilstrap, R. L., & Martin, W. R. (1975). *Current strategies for teachers: A resource for personalizing instruction.* Pacific Palisades, CA: Goodyear.
  A book designed to help make teachers increasingly aware of what they are doing and what they might do in terms of their instructional methods. For each of the dozen teaching strategies presented there is a background section offering information on the origins of the strategy and a competency worksheet consisting of a list of checkpoints of the observable behaviors that usually comprise the strategy.

Henson, K. T. (1981). *Secondary teaching methods.* Lexington, MA: D. C. Heath.
  A basic text in secondary school teaching emphasizing practical applications of the principles of teaching. See Chapter 11 for an examination of various teaching strategies and recommendations for their use in the classroom.

Hoover, K. H. (1977). *Secondary/middle school teaching: A handbook for beginning teachers and teacher self-renewal.* Boston: Allyn and Bacon.
  A text consisting of six learning modules featuring classroom simulations. Each module can be used for small-group activities or for self-instruction. See Module 3 on discussion-focused methods and techniques and Module 4 on personal-social instructional techniques.

Hunkins, F. P. (1976). *Involving students in questioning.* Boston: Allyn and Bacon.
  This book provides numerous theories, techniques, and examples to assist the teacher in using questioning as a method for increasing student involvement and interest in learning.

Hunter, M. (1982). *Mastery teaching.* El Segundo, CA: TIP Publications.
  A book designed to help the beginning teacher develop effective classroom techniques. See Chapter 10 on designing effective practice sessions in the classroom.

Hyman, R. T. (1979). *Strategic questioning.* Englewood Cliffs, NJ: Prentice-Hall.
  This book presents various questioning strategies appropriate for different situations in teaching to help teachers become effective, strategic questioners. The questioning strategies are presented in a way that allows the teacher to develop a framework to guide all efforts at questioning in the classroom.

Kilpatrick, W. H. (1925). *Foundations of method: Informal talks on teaching.* New York: Macmillan.
  A book based on a course taught by the author, one of the foremost educators of this century, to discuss the principles on which method in general are founded. The various topics, problems, and recommendations are presented in conversational style, making them particularly easy to relate to and understand.

Kim, E. C., & Kellough, R. D. (1974). *A resource guide for secondary school teaching: Planning for competence* (4th ed.). New York: Macmillan.
  An excellent workbook featuring an organization of basic resource materials designed to improve secondary school teaching. See Chapter 11 for recommended guidelines and exercises concerning the use of specific teaching strategies.

Martin, B. L., & Driscoll, M. P. (1984, August). Instructional theories: Maximizing their strengths for application. *Performance and Instruction Journal, 23*(6), 1–4.
  The purpose of this article is to explore the philosophical basis and points of view for several instructional theories as a means of maximizing the strengths found in these theories for classroom application.

Orlich, D. C., Harder, R. J., Callahan, R. C., Kravas, C. H., Kauchak, D. P., Pendergrass, R. A., & Keogh, A. J. (1985). *Teaching strategies: A guide to better instruction* (2nd ed.). Lexington, MA: D. C. Heath.
  Presentation of a broad spectrum of instructional methodologies, techniques, and approaches tailored to the secondary school classroom. See Chapter 7 on decisions to make for conducting classroom discussions and Chapter 8 on decisions to make for using the inquiry approach to learning.

Waples, D., & Tyler, R. W. (1930). *Research methods and teachers' problems: A manual for systematic studies of classroom procedure.* New York: Macmillan.

> *A book intended to facilitate systematic studies of teachers' classroom problems by focusing on studies conducted by in-service teachers to solve urgent problems of particular classroom situations. See Chapter 4 on problems involving methods of teaching.*

Weil, M., & Joyce, B. (1978). *Social models of teaching: Expanding your repertoire.* Englewood Cliffs, NJ: Prentice-Hall.

> *An informative and practical guide to using teaching models that emphasize group processes. The models presented are the "Role Playing Model," the "Jurisprudential Model," and the "Simulation Model." The discussion for each model includes a classroom scenario and an outline of classroom activities as the basis for a balanced and better understanding of related theories.*

Wong, B. Y. L. (1985, Summer). Self-questioning instructional research. *Review of Educational Research, 55*(2), 227–268.

> *This article reviews studies on student self-questioning as it is designed and used to improve their processing of prose. It is pointed out that self-questioning training provided to students is successful in improving their prose processing.*

CHAPTER 7
◆ ◆ ◆ ◆ ◆ ◆ ◆

Managing the Classroom Environment

INTRODUCTION

In Chapter 5 we saw that students' backgrounds and individual natures influence how they respond to various classroom activities and situations. This chapter examines the ways in which the teacher's management of the classroom environment can positively influence student growth and, to some extent, counteract or redirect negative influences, such as a poor home or community environment, that are beyond his or her control. Classroom management in this sense considers not only the organization of routines and procedures but also how these affect students' abilities to learn and work with each other. Thus, successful classroom management depends on establishing and maintaining conditions that facilitate effective teaching. "Management provides the stage, the settings, and the properties necessary for the satisfactory performance of learning and teaching activities" (Waples & Tyler, 1930, p. 394).

The term *management* denotes the act of considering, organizing, and directing those elements or factors essential for the accomplishment of specific goals. Successful classroom management, therefore, involves all the factors that contribute to effective teaching, including:

1. Developing curriculum plans
2. Procuring and using instructional resources
3. Understanding the nature of students
4. Carrying out daily lessons
5. Organizing classroom routines and procedures and maintaining classroom control
6. Assessing the effectiveness of instruction and student progress

Factors 1, 2, 3, and 4 have been discussed in Chapters 3, 4, 5, and 6, respectively, and factor 6 will be discussed in Chapter 8. This chapter focuses on factor 5.

Teachers should take a positive approach to classroom management. "Management should be approached with an eye toward maximizing the time students spend in productive work, rather than from a negative viewpoint stressing control of misbehavior" (Good & Brophy, 1984, p. 183). Further, because each classroom situation differs depending on the particular students and the subject being taught as well as the teacher's personal style, all decisions concerning classroom management must be based on the educational objectives developed so they address the particular needs of each classroom situation.

BASIC THEORIES

♦ Establishing Classroom Routines and Procedures

Daily classroom routines and procedures are the framework from which all instructional activities proceed. Although routines and procedures can make classroom instruction more efficient, they can also dampen student initiative when applied too rigidly to activities requiring individual and group creativity and thought. The key to effective classroom management is to achieve a balance in its use as a means and as an end:

At times there has been considerable controversy concerning the kind of management which was most to be desired in the schoolroom. Those who have thought of management as a means only have been apt to overemphasize routine; while those who have thought only of the opportunity afforded for growth in self-control have neglected to realize the importance of habit in situations which are invariable. The adherents of the one type of control want everything done at the tap of the bell, in accordance with the rules which have been made by the teacher. Their opponents would do away with "mechanized routine," and would expect children to exercise their judgment as each question arises. This difference in point of view is easily reconciled when we look at management now as a means and again as an end. (Strayer, 1914, p. 157)

The teacher who wastes several minutes during a lesson taking roll, several minutes handing back the previous day's papers, and several minutes at the end of class with an unorganized and ineffective closing activity as order seems to fall apart is doing a less-than-adequate job. Wasting ten out of fifty minutes, even assuming everything runs smoothly in the remaining forty minutes, renders this teacher an 80 percent teacher. Unfortunately, many do fit the 80 percent profile, either because they are unaware of the value of routines and procedures or because of their inability to establish them.

The most important routines and procedures to consider for effective classroom management include planning for the first day, having students enter, move about, and leave the classroom in an orderly manner, making seating arrangements, establishing procedures for collecting and distributing materials, providing a clean and attractive room, and preparing records and reports. Table 7.1 summarizes the tasks involved in these routines and procedures.

Planning for the First Day

As soon as students enter a teacher's classroom for the first time they begin trying to figure out how strict the teacher is, how much work is going to be required, and how organized all activities are. An excellent way of demonstrating your attitudes concerning discipline and organization is to establish routines and procedures for carrying out essential classroom functions and activities from the very first class session. The following practices are recommended when planning for the first day.

1. Make classroom routines and procedures clear to students from the first day.
   ♦ Well before the first day of class determine what routines and procedures need to be established for a well-managed classroom and what form these routines and procedures should take. To do this it is useful to consult other teachers for ideas and recommendations about what works in a variety of classroom situations. Information of this nature is among the most valuable the veteran teacher has to share with the new teacher.
   ♦ Avoid leaving anything to chance on the first day—everything should be planned. The teacher should not appear unprepared or disorganized. And students should not be allowed to treat this day merely as a social occasion. The first day should exemplify how the classroom will be run throughout the year.

TABLE 7.1 *Establishing Classroom Routines and Procedures*

ROUTINE OR PROCEDURE	TASKS INVOLVED
Planning for the first day	1. Make classroom routines and procedures clear to students from the first day. 2. Develop routines and procedures jointly with students. 3. Ensure success on the first day.
Having students enter, move about, and leave the classroom in an orderly manner	1. Determine how students are to enter the room. 2. Determine how students are to move about the room. 3. Determine how students are to leave the room. 4. Plan for emergencies.
Making seating arrangements	1. Determine the different types of seating arrangements that will be used. 2. Assign students to permanent seats. 3. Develop a seating chart that facilitates recordkeeping.
Establishing procedures for collecting and distributing materials	1. Determine which materials need to be collected and distributed daily. 2. Develop plans for collecting and distributing materials. 3. Store materials in a neat and organized fashion. 4. Assess the effectiveness of the procedures used for distributing and collecting materials by asking several pertinent questions.
Providing a clean and attractive room	1. Establish rules for keeping the room clean. 2. Provide ample cleanup and waste disposal facilities and materials. 3. Add a few artistic touches in the room to make it attractive and pleasing to the eye. 4. Designate some areas in the room for exhibiting student work.
Preparing records and reports	1. Communicate with school administrators concerning requirements for recordkeeping. 2. Set up an organized and neat class record book. 3. Use recordkeeping to help assess student progress and to communicate with parents.

♦ Communicate details of the routines and procedures through concise oral and written instructions, providing immediate opportunities for students to follow these guidelines and recognize that they are going to be an essential part of how business is conducted in the classroom.

2. Develop routines and procedures jointly with students.

♦ Actively involve students right from the first day in managing their own classroom by holding a group discussion and planning session that focuses on developing essential classroom routines and procedures.

♦ Let students know that as the term progresses they will have a role in monitoring the effectiveness of the routines and procedures established and, when necessary, modifying them to address new or changing situations.

3. Ensure success on the first day.
   ♦ Concentrate on successfully establishing those routines and procedures that are essential for conducting daily classroom business (e.g., taking roll).
   ♦ Make it obvious to students that following the established routines and procedures makes for a more interesting and less stressful learning environment. For example, point out how following the procedure for taking roll during the first five minutes of class provides them time to copy the key notes for the day from the chalkboard or an overhead projection.
   ♦ Avoid getting bogged down with administrative details. Although the first day is the best time to establish essential classroom routines and procedures, the main objective is to kindle student interest in the course. Because students come to class on the first day without any special preparation, the teacher must make sure to plan interesting activities that do not require any student preparation. For example, in a math class students might be presented a few particularly interesting problems to solve, individually and then together, giving them an idea of how the subject matter will be covered and at the same time introducing them to the first topic of the course. The routines and procedures established on the first day should be seen as the organizational structure that makes interesting instructional activities possible.

Having Students Enter, Move About, and Leave the Classroom in an Orderly Manner

How students behave and respond in class from day to day is closely related to how they enter, move about, and leave the classroom. If they are allowed to dash in noisily, get out of their seats without permission, and rush out in a frenzy as soon as the bell rings, then you can be sure attempts to conduct orderly instructional activities will be extremely difficult. The following practices are recommended for having students enter, move about, and leave the room in an orderly manner.

1. Determine how students are to enter the room.
   ♦ Structure the beginning activity of every period so that it seems necessary and natural to students to enter the room in an orderly way and get right to work.
   ♦ Avoid having students line up in the hall and enter the room in pairs. Although this might have merit with very young children, adolescents find it offensive and either rebel directly against the

practice or harbor resentment that manifests itself in various ways in the classroom. It is much wiser to obtain students' cooperation and give them the opportunity to take responsibility for their actions.

♦ Follow the procedure that is set up without fail. A procedure or routine is of little use if students perceive that it must be followed only sometimes.

♦ Make is absolutely clear at what point students entering the room will be marked tardy and how those coming late, for whatever reason, are to enter the room. Failure to clearly communicate these points or to consistently apply them will eventually lead to a virtual free-for-all at the beginning of the period.

2. Determine how students are to move about the room.

♦ Discuss with students the various activities and situations that could require them to get out of their seats and how this is to be done when it is necessary. Again, the aim of this discussion is to get students to understand how they will benefit by functioning in an orderly way. For example, make it clear when and how students are to go to the chalkboard or to the individual learning carrels.

♦ Establish and strictly adhere to the policy that no one gets out of his or her seat without asking for and receiving permission. This policy should be established on the first day of class and then closely monitored, because any erosion of this practice will soon lead to chaos.

♦ Design the physical layout of the room so that moving about can be done easily and safely. To do this it is helpful to visit other classrooms to see how other teachers of the same subject arrange their floor plans to facilitate necessary movement about the room.

♦ Clearly designate any workplaces in the room other than students' regular seats, such as study carrels, laboratory stations, or library areas. In addition, make it clear when such areas are to be used and how students are to go to and return from these areas. Students will respect the value of these areas more if they know that a standard of decorum exists and must be followed. Of course, they must also find the work they are assigned to do in these areas is purposeful and helps them learn the subject.

♦ Foster a sense of community. In developing procedures for moving about the room, point out that the welfare of the whole group is each person's responsibility. If any student fails to do his or her part, delay and loss of time in the work can result, which affects the progress of the entire class. By following the definite procedures that have been established, students can help create and maintain an environment that increases their opportunities for learning.

3. Determine how students are to leave the room.

♦ Develop a routine for concluding the lesson. There should be no doubt in students' minds how the last several minutes of every class period will be conducted. Any doubts about how the lesson is going to end each day invariably lead to confusion and the taking of liberties, rendering the final minutes of the period useless.

♦ Make the closing activity of the period meaningful and make sure enough time is left to finish it. Students should come to realize that the day's closing activity provides an opportunity to better understand the day's work and prepare for the next lesson. When the closing part of the lesson is planned and conducted in this way, students naturally feel calm and absorbed in their work, making dismissal a simple and orderly part of the daily routine.

♦ Establish a policy for discussions at the end of the period. As a general rule students should quickly leave the room when the final bell rings. Students who want to have a brief meeting to discuss an exam grade, an idea presented during the lesson, or any other concern should be asked to indicate this at some point during the lesson. This avoids an impossible situation at the end of the period, in which several students' concerns have to be dealt with in a few minutes. Short notes or direct requests made during the lesson give the teacher time to determine whose concerns require attention at the end of the period, whose concerns require a more lengthy meeting at some later time to be arranged, and, when possible, whose concerns can be addressed during the lesson. Failure to establish such a policy creates several problems, including cutting short the crucial few minutes between periods needed to prepare for the next class, allowing students to have an excuse for arriving late at their next class, and making it difficult to help students who have legitimate concerns requiring attention.

4. Plan for emergencies.

♦ Determine the various kinds of emergencies for which students should be prepared. Reviewing school administrative manuals and memoranda will provide details on required procedures for dealing with most emergencies that can occur in the school. These procedures are developed in accordance with state education statutes and codes. The specific emergency plans developed for each school also take into account the structural design and layout of the school plant and the size of the school population so that all movement necessitated by emergencies can proceed quickly and smoothly.

♦ Establish and communicate procedures concerning what to do in the event of an emergency. It is important to periodically practice these procedures, because the safety of all demands that each situation always be followed by a specific response. For example, "If a fire drill is to be effective, everyone must drop the work in hand when the signal is given and march out of the building in an order and by a route which has been determined previously and from which there is no variation" (Strayer, 1914, p. 158).

Making Seating Arrangements

Careful thought should be given to how students are to be seated in the room.

> Some organized procedure for the assignment of students to definite seats or stations is necessary to expedite attendance check, to facilitate the learning of students' names, to take care of special needs (for example, students with defective vision or hearing), and to ensure a more orderly working atmosphere for the class as a whole. (Alcorn, Kinder, & Schunert, 1970, p. 337)

In addition, the way students are seated in the classroom can serve either to encourage or discourage an open and cooperative working environment. For example, using the same arrangement, with all seats in straight rows regardless of the learning activity being conducted, tends to isolate students from one another and ignores the flexibility that is possible by moving chairs and desks. The following practices are recommended for making seating arrangements.

1. Determine the different types of seating arrangements that will be used.
   ♦ Review the instructional plans to determine the various kinds of learning activities to be conducted during the semester as a guide to deciding what kinds of seating arrangements will be most appropriate for the different activities. For example, "for watching a movie, or listening to a lecture, some variations of the ordinary row setup may be desirable; for committee work, small circles of chairs may be best; for a discussion, a circle or some segment of a circle may be suitable" (Clark & Starr, 1986, p. 98). Figure 7.1 shows some examples of possible seating arrangements.
   ♦ To determine the degree of flexibility possible in making seating arrangements, take into account the facilities and equipment available. For example, in a room where the desks are very heavy and therefore difficult to move it is more effective to alter the seating arrangements for various learning activities by moving students rather than desks. By strategically placing the desks (i.e., so students can easily move from their regular seats to work in groups of various combinations) and instructional resource materials you can increase the options possible even when the classroom furniture is relatively immobile.
   ♦ Take into account the nature of the students to determine how flexible to be in making seating arrangements. The degree of flexibility in making seating arrangements also depends on what students can responsibly handle. For a relatively large and immature group of students a stable seating structure is likely to prove more successful than a looser one that provides numerous opportunities for students to move about the room to change seats. In class situations with

FIGURE 7.1 *Possible Classroom Seating Arrangements (Strengths of each seating arrangement noted in parentheses)*

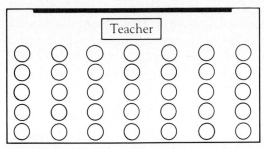

(a) Parallel rows
   (Lecture and individual assignments)

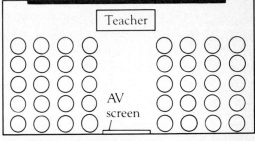

(d) Facing parallel rows
   (Lecture, questioning, discussion, demonstration, and individual assignments)

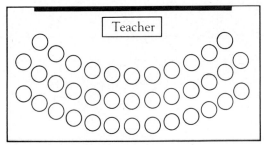

(b) Semicircular rows
   (Lecture and demonstration)

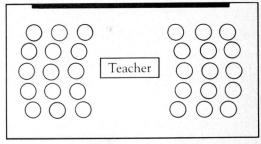

(e) Facing semicircular rows
   (Discussion, demonstration, and questioning)

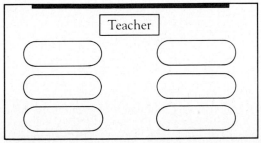

(c) Parallel desks
   (Group projects and independent study)

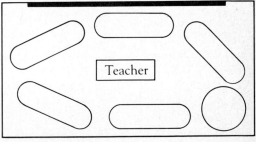

(f) Facing desks
   (Group projects and demonstration)

potential problems, changing seats can be limited to times when students must work individually or in pairs at study carrels set up at a few places in the room. Sometimes, however, creatively using seating arrangements can help interest immature or problem students in the class work while presenting them with opportunities to develop responsibility for how they conduct themselves. The teacher's confidence in his or her ability to control the class, the type of facilities available, and the nature of the students are the important factors in determining how to arrange seating.

2. Assign students to permanent seats.
    ♦ Establish one set seating arrangement during the first, or at least by the second, class session regardless of the degree of flexibility allowed for seating students for various instructional activities. Any attempts at creative seating arrangements can work only when students know they have a regularly assigned seat to move from and return to. Failure to establish a permanent seating arrangement soon results in a daily free-for-all, leaving students with the impression that anything goes in the classroom. In addition, assigning regular seats prevents races each period for favorite spots, facilitates taking roll, and simplifies numerous other routine problems.
    ♦ Observe students carefully to determine early on which students tend to stimulate conversation, fooling around, or showing off. This should serve as the basis for reseating students as necessary. Relying on changing students' seats as a principal means of controlling problem behavior, however, puts the teacher in a weakened position. "Reseating may eventually result in new alliances, and create the same problem again. If seating were the teacher's only disciplinary device, it could never keep ahead of the game" (Crawford, 1938, p. 33).
    ♦ As soon as possible learn which students need special seating arrangements. Students with defective hearing or vision greatly benefit from sitting closer to the front of the room, as do students with particularly short attention spans.
    ♦ Determine how seats are to be assigned. There are essentially three methods for assigning permanent seats: by alphabetical order, by random order, and by student choice. It should be no surprise to learn that students who sit toward the front of the room tend to be more involved and attentive and consequently to gain more from instructional activities than those who sit in the back rows. Therefore, whatever method is used it is highly recommended that seating assignments be changed at midsemester to give those who sat toward the back of the room a chance at the front rows of seats.

3. Develop a seating chart that facilitates recordkeeping.
    ♦ Use a simple, easy-to-hold seating chart for making a preliminary check of attendance and tardies. The chart should consist of a series of boxes, one for each student, arranged according to the floor plan

of the chairs and desks in the room. In this way the teacher can quickly glance at the chart, notice who is absent or tardy, and make the appropriate notation in pencil for later transcription to the official roll book.

♦ As an alternative method, combine the seating chart with official recordkeeping. This can be done effectively by using what is known as a "Delaney Book" with "Delaney Cards," named after the New York City school teacher who developed the system. The Delaney Book consists of several thin cardboard sheets (enough for two per class) with rows of slots. The Delaney Cards are each approximately two inches wide by three inches long and contain designated spaces for all relevant information that needs to be recorded for students, including name, address, telephone number, homeroom section and teacher, exam, quiz, and report card grades, and on the reverse side a continuous calendar for noting absences and tardies. The advantages of this system are that it speeds up attendance checks, facilitates recordkeeping, and allows for considerable flexibility when seating arrangements are changed, because cards merely have to be shifted from one slot to another.

Establishing Procedures for Collecting and Distributing Materials

The hallmark of effective classroom management is the efficient execution of all routine tasks that can potentially take time away from learning activities. The collection and distribution of materials is among the routine tasks that can be most disruptive to instruction if not well planned, simply because it occurs at many points during every lesson. Although genuine learning activities should be the most important part of the daily lesson, the problem of teaching students to follow essential routine classroom procedures such as collecting and distributing materials needs to receive the same care that is normally given to teaching subject matter if the classroom is to function smoothly. Students must learn to follow such routines efficiently "as a means of attaining desired outcomes of greater importance" (Waples & Tyler, 1930, p. 435). The following recommended practices should be followed for establishing procedures for collecting and distributing materials.

1. Determine which materials need to be collected and distributed daily.
   ♦ Make a list of the various supplies, handouts, equipment, classwork and homework, and related instructional resources that are usually collected and distributed at different points during each lesson.
   ♦ Use the above list to develop a matrix for categorizing materials according to type, purpose, and frequency and timing of collection and distribution. Once a materials matrix is developed, space can be created on it to list materials that are used occasionally or for special purposes.

2. Develop plans for collecting and distributing materials.

   ◆ Review the materials matrix to determine the most efficient ways for collecting and distributing each type of material. For example, for classwork assignments that are routinely collected, graded, and then returned, it is useful to use a scheme that maintains all the papers in an order corresponding to the seating arrangement. This helps in checking for cheating or copying and also makes it easier to record grades. It also makes handing back assignments much easier.

   ◆ To avoid unnecessary movement of students and delays or confusion, assign monitors to collect and distribute materials. Such monitorial assignments should be regularly rotated so that all students eventually have an opportunity to share in the responsibility of efficiently collecting and distributing materials to the class. For some activities, such as a laboratory exercise, the best way to distribute and collect materials is to unobtrusively circulate around the room to avoid interrupting students' work.

   ◆ Prepare materials for distribution by counting them out in bunches for the different rows before the period begins. A materials matrix like the one recommended above provides an excellent reference guide for making such advance preparations. When the time comes to use the materials in the lesson they can be quickly distributed by the assigned monitors and then collected in a similar fashion.

   ◆ Inform students in advance of the equipment and materials they will need and be expected to pass in. To minimize confusion, list on the board or in a handout any equipment or materials they will need or any assignments that should be handed in.

   ◆ Collect papers from all students at the same time rather than allowing work to drift in haphazardly over the course of a few days. The key is to routinize such procedures so students learn them more easily, just as they learn subject matter more readily when it is organized rather than taught haphazardly.

3. Store materials in a neat and organized fashion.

   ◆ Draft a floor plan for storing materials in the classroom, taking into consideration how frequently they are used, how much space they take up, and the facilities available. Store the various materials according to the floor plan to assess its practicality and make any necessary modifications so that a workable and neat system is in place from the first day of class.

   ◆ Use labels and stickers on the edges of shelves so the various materials stored around the room are easy to locate when they have to be given out or put back where they belong. Poor housekeeping in the classroom sets a poor example for students, whom we expect to be doing their part at home to maintain an orderly and clean environment.

Good housekeeping is to be recommended not only because of its aid to efficiency and the saving of time and energy, but also because of its close relationship to character. Untidiness, confusion, and disorder in the classroom are closely related to a corresponding lack of moral and personal organization, or just plain laziness. (Crawford, 1938, p. 33)

4. Assess the effectiveness of the procedures used for distributing and collecting materials by asking several pertinent questions.
   ♦ Have the materials that need to be distributed and collected throughout the course been clearly identified for advanced planning?
   ♦ Have procedures been established for distributing and collecting different types of materials at various points during the lesson?
   ♦ Have students been given opportunities to learn and follow the procedures that have been established?
   ♦ Have students been kept regularly informed in advance of what materials they need to bring to class or turn in?
   ♦ Are the materials stored neatly and labeled for easy identification?
   ♦ Are the procedures that have been established strictly followed?

Providing a Clean and Attractive Room
Whenever students enter the room they are affected, positively or negatively, by the existing environment. A clean, attractive room provides a sense of security and discipline, and communicates to students that the teacher cares how they feel when they are there. In addition, an orderly and attractive classroom fosters good work habits and attitudes. On the other hand, a dirty, disorganized room quickly lets students know the teacher is not in full control and perhaps is not concerned that they have a nice place in which to work. The following are recommendations for providing a clean and attractive room.

1. Establish rules for keeping the room clean.
   ♦ Let each student know he or she is responsible for the area around his or her seat. Because students appreciate being in a clean room, peer pressure is usually sufficient for getting them to follow through on this responsibility.
   ♦ Assign students on a weekly rotating basis to general cleanup duty. This three- or four-student team is charged with keeping common areas of the room clean and straightening out the stored materials and equipment.
   ♦ Develop a policy jointly with students for dealing with those who fail to do their part in keeping the room clean. In this way peer pressure will again come into play, increasing the likelihood that rules will be followed.
2. Provide ample cleanup and waste disposal facilities and materials.
   ♦ A good rubber doormat does wonders toward keeping the floor free from excessive grit and grime, especially on rainy days.

♦ Wastepaper baskets at handy places around the room invite students to dispose of paper scraps and other trash in an orderly fashion.
♦ Having a good broom and dustpan in the room for the weekly cleanup crew to use makes their job easier and, consequently, the room neater.
♦ Providing adequate shelf and cupboard space for valuable materials will not only keep the room looking neater and protect those materials, but will also reveal any junk lying around that should be thrown away.

3. Add a few artistic touches in the room to make it attractive and pleasing to the eye.
♦ At strategic places in the room select and post interesting and colorful materials that are relevant to the subject being taught. There is no excuse for a classroom that has nothing but bare walls and bulletin boards, save for the obligatory fire drill and time schedule. Students sense how much effort the teacher is making on their behalf, and the appearance of the room is one of the first indicators they notice.
♦ In addition to posting subject-related materials around the room, "a few beautiful pictures, vases, or potted plants make it seem nearly sacrilegious to throw trash on the floor; thus they render a double-service [attractive appearance and cleanliness]" (Crawford, 1938, p. 37).

4. Designate some areas in the room for exhibiting student work.
♦ One area should be for displaying exemplary work, thus providing students with an incentive to do well.
♦ One area should be for original ideas, materials, and designs contributed by students so that they realize everyone will have an opportunity at some point to have their work put up for display.
♦ One area should be for work resulting from group projects, thus allowing students to feel not only a sense of personal pride but a sense of collective achievement as well. Creating these opportunities is important to help adolescents achieve a balance between individual and cooperative recognition and well-being. Identification with others' needs and accomplishments is a sure sign of character development and maturity.
♦ In addition to displaying students' work, involve them in designing, decorating, and maintaining bulletin boards and instructional displays. Make them feel that it is their room and thus their responsibility to share in creating and maintaining an attractive environment.

Preparing Records and Reports

All teachers are required to maintain numerous official and unofficial records and to complete a variety of reports as part of their regular classroom duties. The ability to maintain a record book containing accurate and complete information on student grades, behavior, and attendance is a good measure of the teacher's organizational skills considering the sheer volume of data involved and the pressure of performing many other duties.

Because the secondary school teacher deals with from 150 to 200 different students each day, good recordkeeping is absolutely necessary for monitoring each student's progress over the course of a semester. In addition, recordkeeping is a source of considerable concern to school administrators primarily because such records are legal documents but also because data about grades and attendance need to be regularly reported to and evaluated by central office personnel. The following practices are recommended for preparing records and reports.

1. Communicate with school administrators concerning requirements for recordkeeping.
   ♦ Ascertain as soon as possible, preferably before the first day of school, what information needs to be recorded, how it should be recorded (e.g., symbols to use, documents to use), and when it is needed for periodic and final review.
   ♦ Develop a calendar that indicates when various information and reports need to be submitted to the school's administrative offices. Using a records calendar as a guide and reminder relieves some of the pressure and uncertainty that usually weighs on the teacher's mind. Classroom recordkeeping in itself is a manageable task, but when considered in addition to all the other tasks and responsibilities of the secondary school teacher it often becomes a source of pressure and frustration.
   ♦ Consult periodically with the appropriate school administrator (e.g., grade counselor, assistant principal) to make sure your recordkeeping is on track and your records calendar is accurate. Failure to do this can become a source of much misery if the end of the semester approaches and it becomes apparent that information was not recorded as required.
2. Set up an organized and neat class record book.
   ♦ Based on communication with school administrators and other experienced teachers, determine specifically what information to keep in the class record book. Typically such information concerns student grades, attendance, punctuality, and behavior. A sloppy record book is likely not only to bring a reprimand from the school administration but also to be a contributing factor to poor classroom control. For example, once some students realize that tardies are only sporadically recorded, or that readmit notes after absences are only occasionally checked, they will soon take advantage of the situation by coming late or being absent more often. Any situation, such as keeping poor records of punctuality and attendance, that tempts students to do their worst represents a failure of responsibility on the part of the teacher.

♦ Take sufficient time to become thoroughly familiar with the class record book used at your school and to carefully plan how and where various kinds of information are to be recorded.

♦ Fill in any information as soon as possible in the record book, such as dates, holidays, and class rosters if available. This will provide a needed sense of organization and readiness for handling the constant flow of information that has to be recorded.

♦ Add labels and tabs to the class record book to expedite the location of different class and information sections. This is in keeping with the aim of making recordkeeping an organized and relatively automatic process rather than a distracting burden.

3. Use recordkeeping to help assess student progress and to communicate with parents.

♦ Develop a uniform method of recording grades by converting all marks on quizzes, tests, reports, and other projects into letter grades, percents, or points so that there is a common denominator for comparing all marks given in a particular course. Students and parents who are dissatisfied with report card grades are much easier to deal with when they can be shown grade records that are readily understandable and consistently maintained.

♦ Designate a section in the class record book for citizenship.

In reporting [and recording] citizenship, the teacher is advised to keep anecdotal records of significant student behavior rather than base his report on vague remembrances or impressions derived from a recent, perhaps atypical, example of student behavior. (Alcorn et al., 1970, p. 338)

♦ Although anecdotal behavior records usually focus on misconduct, they should also contain any information that can provide insights into students' strengths and weaknesses. This information could include descriptions of how they approach their school work, how they work and deal with others, how they respond to constructive criticism, and how they are affected by different situations. Obviously, there is neither time nor space to keep voluminous anecdotal records on every student. Therefore, anecdotal records should be concise and particularly helpful in developing an accurate personal profile of each student.

♦ **Maintaining Classroom Control**

One of the primary aims of education is to prepare students for a productive life in a democratic society based on a spirit of cooperation and freedom. It would be unrealistic, however, to think that all necessary cooperation among students can result from spontaneous impulse. Consideration for others does not, with most students, arise spontaneously but has to be taught, and it can hardly be taught except by the exercise of authority.

Maintaining classroom control is not possible without establishing authority. Authority, however, can be of two kinds—caring and uncaring. If the aim of using authority to control the class is simply to "make my life with these brats easier," the students will sense this uncaring attitude and view the teacher as something of a tyrant. The result is likely to be controlled rebellion at best, or open hostility at worst. "We do not consider an individual disciplined only when he has been rendered as artificially silent as a mute and as immovable as a paralytic. He is an individual annihilated not disciplined" (Montessori, 1912, p. 86). If, on the other hand, authority is used to provide an environment in which all students, whatever their level of social, emotional, and intellectual development, are given an opportunity to grow and realize their higher instincts and capabilities, students will sense the teacher's personal concern for their lives and thus respect his or her authority.

The principal areas to consider for maintaining classroom control include establishing classroom behavior standards, preventing misbehavior, fostering self-discipline, and handling behavior problems (Table 7.2).

TABLE 7.2 *Maintaining Classroom Control*

AREA	RECOMMENDED PRACTICES
Establishing classroom behavior standards	1. Develop and clearly communicate behavior standards. 2. Assess how well the behavior standards have been communicated. 3. Assess the effectiveness of the behavior standards.
Preventing misbehavior	1. Establish rapport with students. 2. Develop class morale and loyalty. 3. Deal with students and situations consistently. 4. Deal with misbehavior in an impersonal manner. 5. Communicate effectively with students. 6. Locate sources of misbehavior.
Fostering self-discipline	1. Provide opportunities for students to take responsibility and deal with problems. 2. Emphasize courtesy and consideration in the classroom. 3. Allow students to monitor and take responsibility for their own learning and behavior.
Handling behavior problems	1. Use rewards and punishments wisely. 2. Monitor the effects various rewards and punishments have on students. 3. Communicate and work with parents. 4. Communicate and work with fellow teachers. 5. Communicate and work with administrators.

Establishing Classroom Behavior Standards

The basis for running an effective classroom, or any enterprise involving a group of people, is that all have a clear understanding of what is expected of them as they work individually and together. In particular, the need of adolescents

> to experience a sense of independence from adults and the confusion and anxiety associated with their rapidly changing bodies and increased analytical skills make them increasingly vulnerable to peer group influences. Therefore, [they] need the safety and security that can be found in clear expectations and well-defined norms. (Jones & Jones, 1981, p. 68)

A classroom in which students are neither aware of nor perceive standards for how they are to conduct themselves is bound to lack the focus and discipline needed for successful teaching and learning. The following recommended practices should be followed for establishing classroom behavior standards.

1. Develop and clearly communicate behavior standards.
    - Involve students in developing classroom behavior standards. This can be done effectively by setting aside a period at the beginning of the year that focuses on the question, What behavior rules and standards do we need to create and maintain a positive learning environment? During this period students can be asked to list the areas in which they think behavior problems can occur along with proposed rules and standards relating to those areas. It is particularly helpful at this point to assist students in stating behavior standards in a positive way. For example, explain to students that rather than coming up with a rule that says, "Don't call out to answer the teacher's questions," a better feeling and response will result if the rule is changed to, "Raise your hand and wait to be called on to answer the teacher's questions." The teacher can then review student ideas and list the results on the board under two categories: "Areas of Possible Behavior Problems" and "Behavior Rules and Standards to Follow." Once student ideas have been placed on the board the teacher can lead a general class discussion from which a final set of behavior standards can be agreed upon. "A procedure of this type tends to take the onus of rule making and enforcement off the teacher. Arbitrary imposition of rules on students is an invitation to rebellion; however, students tend to abide by their own rules quite willingly" (Clark & Starr, 1986, p. 101). Ultimately, however, it is the teacher's responsibility to see that appropriate behavior standards are established, communicated, and followed.
    - Let students know through explanations, distributed and posted materials, and especially your actions, exactly what behavior is acceptable and what is not from the time they enter the classroom until the time they are dismissed. It is helpful to consider the various

degrees of misbehavior as the "lines of defense" at which efforts to maintain control of the classroom take place, with the goal being to stop misbehavior at the first line of defense (i.e., minor behavior infractions) if possible. The first evidence of even minor disruptive behaviors (e.g., unnecessary talking) has to be quickly detected and corrected to avoid a struggle at a line of defense that is closer to jeopardizing the maintenance of an orderly classroom (e.g., getting out of the seat without permission). If the case of students getting out of their seats without permission is not handled at the first occurrence, you can be sure the line of defense will advance to some more serious misbehavior.

♦ Communicate the behavior standards to the parents. Early contact with parents concerning classroom behavior standards is important for obtaining their support and for developing a trusting and open relationship with them.

> They are more likely to feel positive about and support issues they clearly understand and have had an opportunity to discuss. By discussing norms and responsibilities early in the year, the teacher is also able to work with the parents before any concerns regarding their child's misbehavior make contacts less positive. (Jones & Jones, 1981, p. 81)

2. Assess how well the behavior standards have been communicated.
   ♦ If students understand the behavior standards they should be able to answer the following questions: What should be done upon entering the room? What action or gesture by the teacher signals that instruction is beginning? What is the policy for tardies? What are the rules for talking during discussions and group activities? What are the rules for moving about and leaving the room? How are questions to be asked and answered during the lesson? What are the procedures for using instructional resources? What are the procedures for distributing and collecting materials? What responsibility does each student have for keeping the room neat and clean? How are citizenship grades determined? By establishing and communicating behavior standards so that the students can answer these questions, expectations are made clear. Thus the students

> need not approach the class with anxieties arising from unclear understandings about what behaviors are and are not acceptable. When a problem arises involving a clear breach of a listed [standard], the teacher is free to act without fear that he is responding in an arbitrary fashion. (Armstrong, Denton, & Savage, 1978, p. 151)

   ♦ When students misbehave ask them if they are aware of the behavior standards they are not following. It may be difficult to get a straight answer, but you will at least get some idea of how students perceive the behavior standards and interpret them in a variety of situations.

3. Assess the effectiveness of the behavior standards.
   ◆ Develop a behavior standards matrix for keeping a daily log of observations and information indicating how well students are following the various standards that have been established.

   The log should contain narrative descriptions of behavior along with interpretations about its possible meanings. . . . Probably the easiest way to do this is to use only the left half of the page for keeping the log of behavior. Interpretations can be written on the right half of the page later, when you review your notes and think about what you have observed. (Good & Brophy, 1984, p. 55)

   ◆ A periodic review of this matrix can point out patterns and areas of misbehavior by individual students or by the whole class.
   ◆ Determine whether the behavior standards are accomplishing their primary purpose of providing a classroom environment conducive to effective instruction. To do this it is important to assess not only the standards themselves, but also the way they are communicated and the consistency with which they are carried out. It is misleading to think it is the behavior standards that are inadequate if they have not been clearly communicated or consistently applied.
   ◆ Involve students in assessing the effectiveness of the behavior standards. During the first few weeks of school, hold periodic discussions centering around the following questions: Do we all understand the behavior standards we have established? Are we doing our best to follow the behavior standards? Do we need to make any changes in the behavior standards or in the way they are carried out? Are we behaving in a way that enhances or detracts from our ability to learn? As the semester progresses similar discussions can be held periodically, especially when there seems to be some deterioration in the students' classroom behavior. Students should also be asked to consider how much work and learning they accomplish during lessons in which they abide by the behavior standards as compared with lessons during which they are disorderly. If such comparisons are made at times when neither the teacher nor the students are reacting, the students will acknowledge that it is in their best interest to learn as much as they can and that abiding by the behavior standards helps them do this. Involving students in assessing their behavior in this way conveys the teacher's respect for them. Students are much more likely to respect the teacher and one another if they feel genuine respect from the teacher.

Preventing Misbehavior

Teachers rarely lose control of the classroom all at once because of a particular incident. Rather, control tends to slip away, slowly at first, and then deteriorate rapidly until the situation becomes unmanageable. "Being lenient at first and 'tightening up' later seldom succeeds. The cumulative effect of a period of leniency makes return to strict standards later almost impossible" (Crawford, 1938, p. 68). The key to preventing a loss of classroom control is to work with students to establish classroom behavior standards from the beginning of the semester. When students clearly understand what is expected of them and feel responsible for living up to those expectations, the likelihood of misbehavior is considerably lessened. They have to perceive, however, that the teacher means business. The behavior standards that have been mutually agreed upon must be applied with firmness and consistency. Any wavering or equivocation on the teacher's part in the area of classroom management is quickly interpreted by students as weakness and leads to misbehavior as well as a search for other possible weaknesses (e.g., Is homework checked regularly? Are tardies always recorded? Is participation in class required?). The following recommended practices should be followed for preventing misbehavior.

1. Establish rapport with students.
   - Simply learning students' names conveys a message of interest and care. Students feel a sense of closeness with the teacher when they are addressed by their names rather then merely being called "you" or being pointed to. Because the secondary school teacher has so many students each day, remembering everyone's name by the end of the first or second week of the semester is difficult. As an aid to learning students' names it is helpful to use the seating chart when checking roll and during the lesson when calling on students, because this provides opportunities to associate names with faces. Learning students' names as soon as possible at the beginning of the semester is so important that taking a few minutes after class to review the seating chart while trying to remember the faces that go with the names is a worthwhile use of time.
   - Demonstrate to students that all your efforts are for their sake. To students the clearest sign of a caring attitude is a classroom in which instructional plans, routines and procedures, and behavior standards and policies are carefully thought out and implemented. Students know when the teacher has taken time to create the best learning environment possible for them, and they know when only minimal effort has been exerted on their behalf. Even if they do not register this consciously, they certainly sense it somewhere. No amount of superficial friendliness or familiarity can substitute for thoughtfully creating a positive learning environment. In fact, students will take advantage of such superficiality to manipulate the teacher into being less demanding and strict in the areas of homework, grades, and behavior standards.
   - Take interest in each student's personal problems and concerns. Set aside some time in your daily schedule to chat a few minutes with students. They appreciate an adult who is willing to listen to their

thoughts sympathetically. This also allows the teacher to get to know students in a way not possible through reviewing cumulative records or even observations in the classroom.

♦ "Being helpful to students is always advantageous, but receiving help from them is still more so. A youngster who has done a service for the teacher is the teacher's friend for a long time because of it" (Crawford, 1938, p. 53). Insightful teachers are able to win over problem students, or those they see as potential problems, by involving them in activities of service, such as helping straighten out desks and files or setting up audiovisual equipment. Students who are given opportunities to help in this way feel the teacher's personal interest, attention, and trust, and this leads to the formation of a bond that can substantially diminish the likelihood of antagonism and misbehavior.

♦ Treat all students equally. When some students get privileges that are denied others, resentment toward the teacher and those students who seem to be favored is the natural outcome. When students have these negative feelings a sense of instability is created, making effective classroom control a more difficult task than it would otherwise be.

♦ Treat students as individuals worthy of respect. Belittling students in front of their peers causes great bitterness and often compels them to talk back in an attempt to save face. Thus students are actually led to behave worse than they ordinarily would have—hardly a situation conducive to effective classroom control. Some problems are better handled individually. "A private session enables the teacher or the pupil to admit his error more gracefully, and promotes mutual understanding and cooperation" (Crawford, 1938, p. 71). Also, it is very important after disciplining a student to show him or her you hold no hard feelings. The teacher's message to the student who has been disciplined should be, "What is done is done and hopefully the lesson has been learned so we can move on to better things."

When a [student] has been corrected, he should be completely "restored to grace" and accepted on a level of equal favor with the others . . . this holds out hope for the future and transfers the [student's] attention from an unhappy past to what may become a happy future. (Crawford, 1938, pp. 72–73)

2. Develop class morale and loyalty.
   ♦ Develop group tasks that the whole class can take part in, such as "a class excursion, a class party, winning a class banner for 100 percent punctuality, a class motto, class flower, class song, class officers, a contest with another class, a program given for another class to witness as guests . . ." (Crawford, 1938, p. 54). All of these

tasks represent opportunities for students to work with and assist each other as they strive toward a common goal.

♦ Provide opportunities for group decision making and responsibility. For example, students who have had a large part in developing the behavior standards for their classroom will readily identify with and take pride in the results of their cooperative effort. Whenever possible, it is preferable to ask the class how they think a particular thing should be done instead of simply telling them how to do it. If the teacher is going to open up decision making to the whole class, some protocol has to be followed to avoid chaos and to ensure a truly collaborative effort. Too often, common responsibilities are regarded as no one's responsibility. Therefore every effort must be made to help students work out a system whereby duties are equitably shared and, if possible, cheerfully carried out.

♦ Have positive expectations of students. By expecting the best from students and communicating this expectation by the way you behave and teach, many potential behavior problems can be avoided. This does not mean, however, that the teacher should not look for or ignore indications of potential problems. Careful observation of students with the aim of determining how best to help them and the overall learning environment is always appropriate—indeed, required.

3. Deal with students and situations consistently.

♦ Once standards of behavior are established in the classroom they must be applied consistently. Reprimanding a student at one time for a particular act of misbehavior and ignoring the same act by the student at another time negates the very purpose for establishing a set of behavior standards. Instead of having the atmosphere of calmness and discipline that is created when everyone knows what to do and what to expect, confusion and poor behavior will result.

♦ Do not be coaxed into changing a decision. Unfailingly, students will test the teacher to see how much they can make him or her reconsider decisions that have already been made. Of course, there should be some opportunity for students to express their grievances. But, if a pattern develops where the teacher is seen frequently yielding to pressure, manipulation, anger, or threats (e.g., "I'm going to tell the principal on you") the students will never take the teacher's word on anything seriously. Although students would seem to want such a situation, a close examination will show that, for most, there is a sincere desire to have a classroom that is orderly and directed by a teacher whose words and actions they can trust and respect.

♦ Make apparent the reasonableness of rulings dealing with misbehavior before those rulings come into question. In this way students will be much more understanding and accepting when those rulings are actually applied. Waiting to explain why certain rulings are made until after incidents occur sets the stage for confrontation and puts the teacher in the weakened position of having to defend his or her actions.

4. Deal with misbehavior in an impersonal manner.

   ♦ When students misbehave it should be made absolutely clear that it is not them you dislike, but their behavior. Students who regard the teacher's disciplinary actions as personal attacks become alienated and either close off completely to the teacher or resort to increasingly disruptive behavior, as if to say "I could care less." When firm words and actions are necessary it should be "done on behalf of the interest of the group, not as an exhibition of personal power. This makes the difference between action which is arbitrary and that which is just and fair" (Dewey, 1938, p. 59).

   ♦ Understand that opposition should not be confused with hate. You can oppose students' misbehavior or laziness without hating the students. In fact, the most effective disciplinary actions are those where the teacher outwardly displays a degree of indignation appropriate to suit the offense but inwardly feels a deep sense of responsibility and affection for the students. A show of force can have a positive effect only when students firmly believe you are on their side. Otherwise, appearances of anger, contempt, and impatience indicate to students that the teacher is unable to control the class, or himself or herself for that matter. Teachers

     must simultaneously assert both their right to be treated with respect and their responsibility to ensure that students treat each other with kindness. Teacher warmth and concern can exist side by side with firmness. Indeed, effective teaching involves blending these key ingredients. (Jones & Jones, 1981, p. 101)

5. Communicate effectively with students.

   ♦ When there is a problem with a student or several students, deal with it directly rather than through a third party. Students resent and worry considerably more about what they hear was said about them than criticisms that are directly communicated. "By talking directly to [students], teachers show respect for them while ensuring that they receive accurate (rather than secondhand) information about adults' feelings and concerns" (Jones & Jones, 1981, p. 102).

   ♦ Provide opportunities for students to express themselves. Observation of a typical lesson in a secondary school will reveal that almost all the talking is done by the teacher. This is pedagogically unsound and also stifles the students' need to share their concerns and ideas. Merely providing opportunities, however, is not enough. The context in which those opportunities are provided, that is, the classroom environment, has to be nonthreatening so the characteristically self-conscious adolescent feels encouraged to participate freely in class.

♦ Speak effectively. The tone of your voice has a lot to do with getting and keeping the class's attention.

A low, well-modulated voice has a calming effect on an unstable, restless group. If the noise level of a class begins to rise to a point where it interferes with learning, the teacher should first gain the complete attention of his students and then address them in a quiet, positive manner. (Alcorn et al., 1970, p. 344)

6. Locate sources of misbehavior.
   ♦ Determine whether students are kept occupied throughout the lesson by asking some basic questions: "Have a set of instructional activities been carefully planned for each day's lesson? Are the instructional activities interesting and do they allow for various styles of learning? Is the pace of instruction too slow or too fast, and is the work too easy or too difficult? (In both cases the students will become bored, frustrated, and restless.) Do the students know what they should be doing? Do the students have the materials they need to do their work (e.g., an organized notebook, pens and pencils, textbooks)? Are lesson and overall curriculum plans sequenced in a way that is readily understandable to the students? Is instruction carried on in a dull, unenthusiastic manner?
   ♦ Determine whether students are kept informed of how they are doing. It is a mistake to take for granted that students know exactly how they are behaving or progressing academically. Without feedback from the teacher, students usually feel a sense of uneasiness that eventually turns into indifference and misbehavior.
   ♦ Assess the quality of your teaching by asking the following questions: Is the material presented logically and clearly? Are various methods of instruction used knowledgeably and skillfully? Has the subject been, and does it continue to be, studied to increase depth of understanding (i.e., by the teacher)? Are the effects of instruction on the students regularly monitored?
   ♦ Determine whether any aspect of the physical environment is contributing to misbehavior. A cluttered, unattractive room makes students feel uncomfortable and invites disorder. In addition, basic physical needs, including proper room temperature and adequate ventilation and lighting are essential for good discipline and good health.
   ♦ Determine whether students' personal problems play a role in their misbehavior. Careful observation of students combined with individual conferences can usually reveal underlying causes of misbehavior, such as a poor home environment, poor peer relationships, or emotional and mental instability. Discussions with parents, other teachers, and counselors are also important for determining underlying causes of misbehavior.

Fostering Self-Discipline

Discipline is most effective and lasting when it comes from students themselves. External controls make the teacher's job manageable and provide an atmosphere in which students can recognize the benefits of orderly behavior. Ultimately, however, internal control in the form of self-discipline is what students need to develop if they are to function as productive members of society and succeed in whatever endeavors they embark upon. Self-discipline is based on the students' cooperation and desire to do what is right, not merely on imposed authority.

Before it is possible to begin to foster self-discipline in students, three conditions must exist in the classroom:

1. The teacher has developed a reasonably high degree of personal self-discipline as demonstrated by his or her work, speech, and behavior toward others.
2. The teacher has a sincere interest in furthering students' personal growth in a way that will extend beyond the relatively short span of time they are in his or her class.
3. The teacher has given careful thought to developing instructional plans, routines and procedures, and classroom behavior standards.

It is difficult to say which of the three conditions is most important, because the absence of any one of them makes fostering self-discipline in students almost impossible. It would appear, though, that if conditions 1 and 2 exist, there is every likelihood that condition 3 will be developed in time, with experience. The following recommended practices should be followed to foster self-discipline in students.

1. Provide opportunities for students to take responsibility and deal with problems.
   ♦ Assign duties that allow them to make judgments, take responsibility, and work out problems on their own. When they know they are in charge of certain duties they will tend to exercise the self-control needed to do a good job.
   ♦ Help students measure their progress in developing self-discipline. Because attitude and effort are the two main ingredients for developing self-discipline, it is important to remind students that the spirit in which these duties are carried out, not simply the results obtained, is most important. They should be told that outward success in any endeavor despite poor attitude and effort is really no success in terms of their personal growth. For example, getting good grades by cheating or without developing good study habits shows weakness of character, and thus failure in terms of personal growth.
   ♦ Avoid imposing authority on students. As with anything else, self-discipline is developed through practice. If students are merely ordered about they may follow the directions given, but when the

orders have to come from within, that is, through self-discipline, they will find themselves at a loss.

2. Emphasize courtesy and consideration in the classroom.
    ◆ Be courteous and considerate. Students learn a valuable lesson in self-discipline when they see the teacher handle a wide variety of situations with dignity and control. Adolescents yearn for role models to follow to give some meaning and direction to their lives. The teacher who respects everyone as an individual presents a caring and healthy presence, which illustrates to students an effective way of dealing with others.
    ◆ Help students understand the value and need for courtesy and consideration. When necessary, by example and instruction, teach students the worth of good manners and courtesy. The student who can practice saying "I am sorry" in a nonthreatening atmosphere will often continue to use this behavior outside the classroom.

3. Allow students to monitor and take responsibility for their own learning and behavior.
    ◆ Regularly integrate independent learning activities into the daily lessons. When these activities are designed well they promote the development of self-discipline by making students focus their attention and efforts to complete the tasks at hand.
    ◆ Develop a system that allows students to monitor their own progress. A self-monitored system should provide students with a way to keep track of the daily progress in their academic and behavior grades throughout each grading period. The students can be issued a form each grading period on which they are to record a predetermined number of points as they complete various instructional tasks, including tests, homework, quizzes, and class participation. A similar form can be issued for students to record points for following appropriate standards of behavior in various areas, including attendance, punctuality, entry and dismissal behavior, bringing materials, work habits, and cleanup.
    ◆ Avoid misusing rewards and positive reinforcement. If students are given rewards that are out of proportion with what they accomplish or as a sort of bribe to do better, they soon gravitate to a mediocre level of performance. Indulging students concerning their academic work and classroom behavior counteracts all other attempts at fostering self-discipline in them. Students develop self-discipline and respect the teacher and themselves much more when they know their rewards are deserved.

Handling Behavior Problems

Behavior problems of varying degrees of seriousness inevitably have to be faced by every teacher at one time or another. The guiding principle to follow in handling behavior problems is to be objective, consistent, impersonal, yet firm. Objectivity is not possible, however, when "teachers fall into the unconscious trap of expecting a student to behave a certain way and then systematically coloring their interpretations of the student's behavior, so that he or she appears to fulfill the teacher's expectation" (Good & Brophy, 1984, p. 48). One indication that behavior problems are being dealt with effectively is when students begin to accept being disciplined, viewing the teacher's actions as necessary and fair. "If the action is just, and is taken calmly, and is lacking in any touch of personal feeling on the part of the teacher—except perhaps one of regret that it is necessary—the [student] is likely to take it in the same spirit and profit by it" (Crawford, 1938, p. 71). The following recommended practices should be followed for handling behavior problems.

1. Use rewards and punishments wisely.
   - Students should be led to understand that readiness to accept what they have earned, whether it be rewards or punishments, is a sign of maturity. This can only be done if classroom behavior standards are clearly established and if students perceive the teacher to be fair and caring.
   - The personality of each student and the nature of each situation should be the factors that guide the determination of rewards and punishments and classroom policies. The key is not to confuse consistency with rigidity. At different times and in different situations rewards or punishments that are blindly applied according to fixed prescriptions will hurt rather than help students. "The punishment that would not even reach a [student] with a 'thick rust on his soul' might utterly crush the spirit of another whose temperament was different" (Crawford, 1938, p. 69).
   - Any reward or punishment that fails to bring a better attitude toward work and behavior is at best inappropriate and might very well be harmful. This can be avoided by following the simple principle that a reward or punishment should clearly be a natural consequence of the thing done.
   - Avoid using rewards and punishments to compare one student with another. A student should never be told that he or she has done better than so-and-so, or that he or she never manages to do as well as so-and-so. The first can produce disdain and contempt, and the other frustration and jealousy.

2. Monitor the effects various rewards and punishments have on students.
   - Ask, Are the rewards and punishments working? It is important when answering this question to keep in mind that the ultimate goal is the development of self-discipline in students. Therefore, immediate positive responses by students can be deceiving. What needs to be ascertained is how students work and behave over a period of time, especially when they think the teacher is not watching. If superficial changes in behavior are taken too seriously

it may lead to justification of a particular technique (sometimes a very poor one) as a solution to almost every problem. Thus the variables in situation, student (maturity, background), or ultimate goals are completely overlooked. (Alcorn et al., 1970, p. 362)

♦ Determine whether the rewards and punishments are being applied in a timely manner. They should not be given on impulse, nor should they be delayed to such an extent that students lose the valuable effect of associating their work and behavior with the rewards or punishments that result.

♦ Try to get an accurate perception of how students view the use of rewards and punishments. Do they think they are applied fairly and consistently? Do they resent the punishments and take the rewards for granted? Do they understand the reasons why rewards and punishments are used?

3. Communicate and work with parents.

♦ As a natural follow-up to contacts with parents at the beginning of the year concerning classroom behavior standards and policies, the parents should periodically be kept informed of how their children are behaving in the classroom. Such communication should reflect a balanced approach by focusing not only on poor behavior but on good behavior as well. This builds credibility with both parents and students—a crucial factor in handling behavior problems.

♦ Maintain an accurate, up-to-date file containing each student's home telephone number and address and their parents' work telephone numbers to facilitate communication with parents as soon as it is necessary. Many a phone call that could have helped in a difficult situation was not made because the teacher either did not have time to get to the office after school or had the wrong phone number. An up-to-date home information file that is kept close at hand is absolutely necessary for maintaining timely contact with parents.

♦ Let parents know that you want and need to join forces with them to help their children obtain the maximum benefit from their education. When parents are consulted only after problems are far advanced, they justifiably ask, "Why did you wait so long to tell me about this? I could have done something." The parents are then left to think that either the teacher does not know what is going on in the classroom or, worse, does not care about helping their children. A much more effective approach is to consult parents when problems are just beginning and relatively easy to handle. A cooperative relationship can be established with parents by describing their child's problems as objectively as possible and by encouraging them to ask questions and make suggestions. The key is to make them feel their assistance is wanted and needed.

♦ Send notes home to maintain open communication with parents. Most notes are sent home to inform parents of misbehavior or academic failure. Although these are justifiable reasons for sending notes, they should not be the only reasons, as is usually the case. Personal notes can help establish a good relationship with the home if they are also used "to request assistance, suggest a conference, inform parents about progress, offer suggestions, or discuss future plans" (Lemlech, 1979, p. 100). Also, parents appreciate receiving letters explaining the subjects their children are studying, the classroom learning goals, and upcoming field trips and other special activities.

4. Communicate and work with fellow teachers.

♦ Discuss those students that are particularly difficult to handle, reach, or understand with other teachers who have had some experience with them. First, this allows the teacher to view problems from the perspective of colleagues who are working in the same environment. Second, this helps the teacher differentiate between problems with particular students that are common to those other teachers are experiencing and those that appear to be unique to his or her classroom. Third, and perhaps most important, the teacher can benefit from the greatest resource available to the field of teaching—the accumulated wisdom of experienced teachers.

♦ Ask other teachers at your school and other schools how they handle various behavior problems. Many opportunities to talk to other teachers are readily available in the lunchroom, office, or during preparation periods. Further opportunities, however, have to be sought out, including visitations to other schools, attendance at professional conferences, and correspondence. Although the knowledge gained from doing this may not apply specifically to your students, it can suggest many excellent ideas that may be adapted and effectively applied to your classroom setting.

5. Communicate and work with administrators.

♦ Find out what the school's policies are concerning the handling of various behavior problems. This includes determining what procedures to follow for a range of problems that cannot be dealt with sufficiently in the classroom so that those at the appropriate levels in the administrative chain of command can be properly involved.

♦ Avoid turning to school administrators to solve your classroom discipline problems, except in severe cases. Those charged with running the school simply do not have the time to handle problems that should rightfully remain within the teacher's jurisdiction. Further, they are not in a position to understand or deal with many classroom behavior problems because they do not know exactly what has happened or the classroom dynamics that contributed to the problem.

♦ Send students to the office only after several steps that have been established for handling various behavior problems at the beginning of the semester have been taken. For example, when a student is sent to the dean's office it should be either for a major offense such as fighting or for incorrigible behavior that fails to respond to any of the teacher's efforts. Administrators and students perceive the teacher's inability or unwillingness to deal with behavior problems as a sure sign of weakness. In the first case, the teacher's professional future is clouded, and in the second, the teacher's command in the classroom is undermined. This does not mean that administrators should not be consulted about behavior problems. As experienced educators and relatively dispassionate observers, they definitely should be consulted just as long as problems are not routinely dumped in their laps.

♦ Determine when behavior problems need to be referred to school counselors rather than the dean, assistant principal, or principal. Although most behavior problems must be solved in the classroom, some require the assistance of guidance counselors. Students often benefit from discussions held in the privacy of the counselor's office, especially if personality conflicts with the teacher or underlying emotional disturbances are involved. Students usually regard the counselor as a sympathetic adult who is in a neutral position with respect to problems they have with teachers and fellow students. Consequently students often find it possible to confide in the counselor feelings that might otherwise never be made known to their teachers or even to their parents. Discussions with counselors, therefore, can frequently provide the teacher with valuable insights and information about their students that is essential to better classroom control.

SUMMARY

In this chapter several points about managing the classroom environment were presented:

1. The teacher's management of the classroom environment can positively influence student growth and, to some extent, counteract negative influences that are beyond his or her control (e.g., poor home or community environments).
2. Successful classroom management involves all the factors contributing to effective teaching, including developing curriculum plans, procuring and using instructional resources, understanding the nature of students, carrying out daily lessons, organizing classroom routines and procedures and maintaining classroom control, and assessing the effectiveness of instruction and student progress.
3. The teacher who is aware of the value of classroom routines and procedures and can effectively establish them is better able to maximize the amount of time available for genuine instructional activities.
4. An excellent way of demonstrating a sense of discipline and organization

is to establish, in the very first class session, the routines and procedures for essential classroom functions and activities.

5. How students behave and respond in class from day to day is closely related to how they enter, move about, and leave the classroom.

6. Careful thought should be given to how students are seated in the room to expedite checking attendance and learning students' names and to encourage an open and cooperative working environment.

7. The hallmark of effective classroom management is the efficient execution of all routine tasks that can potentially take time away from learning activities. Because it occurs at many points during the lesson, the collection and distribution of material is among the routine tasks that can be most disruptive.

8. Whenever students enter the room they are affected, positively or negatively, by the condition of the room. A clean, attractive room provides a sense of security and discipline and communicates the teacher's regard for how students feel when they are there.

9. All teachers are required to maintain numerous official and unofficial records and to complete a variety of records as part of their regular classroom duties. In addition, good recordkeeping is necessary for monitoring each student's daily progress over the course of a semester.

10. Maintaining classroom control is not possible without establishing authority. To be effective and gain students' respect, however, authority must be used to provide an environment in which all students, whatever their level of social, emotional, and intellectual development, are given opportunities to grow and realize their higher instincts and capabilities.

11. The basis for running an effective classroom, or any enterprise involving a group of people, is that all have a clear understanding of what is expected of them as they work individually and together. Therefore, a key factor in preventing classroom control from slipping is to work with students to establish behavior standards from the beginning of the semester. When students clearly understand what is expected of them and feel responsible for living up to those expectations, the likelihood of misbehavior is considerably lessened.

12. Three conditions must exist in the classroom to foster self-discipline in students: (1) the teacher has developed a reasonably high degree of personal self-discipline as demonstrated by his or her work, speech, and behavior toward others; (2) the teacher has a sincere interest in furthering students' personal growth in a way that will extend beyond the relatively short span of time they are in his or her class; and (3) the teacher has given careful thought to developing instructional plans, routines and procedures, and classroom behavior standards.

13. The guiding principle to follow in handling behavior problems is to be objective, consistent, impersonal, yet firm. Rewards and punishments must be used wisely and their effects on the students monitored carefully; communication with parents, fellow teachers, and administrators must be maintained.

◆ ◆ ◆ ◆ ◆ ◆ ◆

PRACTICAL MODEL 7.1   A Student-Monitored Classroom Management System

Introduction   This practical model outlines a successful classroom management system that provides students with a clear sense of their responsibilities for maintaining a classroom environment conducive to learning.

Adapted from   Nels C. Sorenson and William L. Roueche. Their article "Classroom Management System for the Physical Science Classroom" appeared in the March 1986 issue of *The Clearing House*.

Purpose   To create and cooperatively implement a classroom management system that improves student attitudes toward the teacher and the subject taught

Setting   Any secondary school classroom

◆ Procedures for Setting Up the Classroom Management System

Step 1. Identifying Required Classroom Behaviors
To begin, the teacher must identify the student behaviors necessary for classroom control and successful academic performance. Some behaviors that could be selected include promptness, classroom entry, bringing appropriate supplies and materials, initiative, completion of activities and assignments, and nondisruptive classroom behavior.

Step 2. Selecting Student Self-Management Procedures
Next, the classroom management plan should list procedures that are to be used to train students to record, monitor, and evaluate required classroom behaviors, thus helping them become responsible for their own classroom behavior. Provide students with a printed form, entitled "Participation Point Rules" (Figure 7.2), that describes each required classroom behavior and the corresponding assigned point value, to be recorded by each student on a weekly "Participation Report Card" (Figure 7.3).

Step 3. Communicating the System to Students
On the first day of class the teacher should pass out the participation point rules form and the participation report card. The teacher should then carefully explain and demonstrate the importance of each required classroom behavior. These points should be emphasized during the first few weeks of the semester so students understand and become accustomed to the behavior expected of them.

Step 4. Rewards in the Classroom
In this classroom management system participation points earned and accumulated by students can be exchanged for an "Activity Center License" (Figure 7.4) and an "Academic Enrichment License" (Figure 7.5). For an activity center license a student needs to accumulate 1000 points. This

FIGURE 7.2 *Participation Point Rules*

HOW TO GET POINTS	HOW TO LOSE POINTS
1. Attendance (plus 25 points)	1. Embezzling points (minus 100 points)
2. Entry behavior (plus 5 points)	2. Failure to keep daily records (minus 20 points)
3. Bringing materials (plus 10 points)	3. Using license illegally (minus 50 points)
4. Punctuality (plus 10 points)	4. Disruptive behavior (minus 75 points)
5. Behaving well (plus 10 points)	
6. Doing all classwork (plus 10 points)	
7. Keeping classroom clean (plus 10 points)	

license can then be used for one class period to play a game, listen to the radio or a tape with earphones, do homework, study for another class, write a letter, or to quietly converse with another "licensed" student. For an academic enrichment license a student needs to accumulate 750 points. This license can be used to go to the library, research an assigned report, research an essay or oral presentation, or do independent reading of approved or class-based magazines and books.

♦ Conclusion

The advantages of using this student-monitored classroom management system are that on-task time is increased, disruptive classroom behavior is reduced, and students show a more favorable attitude toward the subject. In addition, because this system gives the teacher more time to devote to teaching and designing learning activities and minimizes the number of classroom discipline problems, it increases his or her enthusiasm for teaching the subject.

♦ ♦ ♦ ♦ ♦ ♦ ♦

CASE STUDY 7.1   Planning for the First Day

Orienting Questions   As you read this case study ask yourself these questions:

Specific
♦ What are some things this teacher should do differently right from the next day to avoid losing control of this class?

FIGURE 7.3 *Participation Report Card*

Balance Forward _____

Week _____

Maximum Points Possible (7 Categories)

1. (25) 2. (5) 3. (5) 4. (10) 5. (10) 6. (10) 7. (10)

Daily Record								DT	DED	TOT
Monday	1. ___	2. ___	3. ___	4. ___	5. ___	6. ___	7. ___	___	___	___
Tuesday	1. ___	2. ___	3. ___	4. ___	5. ___	6. ___	7. ___	___	___	___
Wednesday	1. ___	2. ___	3. ___	4. ___	5. ___	6. ___	7. ___	___	___	___
Thursday	1. ___	2. ___	3. ___	4. ___	5. ___	6. ___	7. ___	___	___	___
Friday	1. ___	2. ___	3. ___	4. ___	5. ___	6. ___	7. ___	___	___	___

DT = Daily total
DED = Deducted points
TOT = Grand total

339

FIGURE 7.4 *Activity Center License*

Name _____ Date _____ Period _____

Rules

1. Student must be passing course (i.e., 70 percent average) to date.
2. License must be acquired twenty-four hours in advance.
3. License is good for one class period.
4. Specific procedures for using the license must be followed or privileges will be lost for one semester.
5. Points required to earn this license = 1000.

Activities Allowed with This License

1. Converse with another licensed student at the classroom learning center.
2. Play chess, cards, Scrabble®, or other approved game with licensed student at the learning center.
3. Listen to tape or radio at the learning center (using earphones only).
4. Do homework or study for a test for this or another class.
5. Other. Specify: _____

_____

_____

_____

_____

♦ Has this teacher demonstrated a sense of discipline and organization or provided for student involvement in establishing routines and procedures?

General

♦ What points in this lesson stand out as indicators of this teacher's strengths and/or weaknesses?
♦ What recommendations would you make for addressing the problems this teacher seems to have?

Setting   *School* – Central city magnet school, grades 4–12

Subject – Computer skills (fifty-five minutes)

Teacher – Mr. Warren, an emergency-credentialed teacher whose training consists of three weeks in a school district intensive program for new emergency-credentialed teachers

Students – Thirty-five students from seventh grade through twelfth grade

Topic – Introduction to the Course

Lesson   *Note:* Under Time Frame the numbers represent the minutes that elapse as the period progresses. Under Dialog the names of the students and the teacher appear as they speak. The symbol ► represents a brief description of a particularly noteworthy action or observation.

_____
FIGURE 7.5 *Academic Enrichment License*

Name _____ Date _____ Period _____

Rules

1. Student must be passing course (i.e., 70 percent average) to date.
2. License must be acquired twenty-four hours in advance.
3. License is good for one class period.
4. Specific procedures for using the license must be followed or privileges will be lost for one semester.
5. Points required to earn this license = 750.

Activities Allowed with This License

1. Library pass to research the following topic (please list): _____
   _____

2. Classroom permit to research the following seminar or special interest topic (please list): _____
   _____

3. Reading permit to do class-based reading of magazines or books pertinent to the following current issue related to the subject (please list): _____
   _____

4. Interview permit to interview the following faculty or staff member (please name): _____
   _____

5. Other. Specify: _____
   _____
   _____
   _____

Time Frame	Dialog	
	►	Mr. Warren, using one of the techniques he learned during the district's intensive, three-week training course, has arranged the desks and chairs in the room into a series of seven clusters.
1 to 5	**Mr. W.:**	(As the students begin entering the classroom) Hi. I'm Mr. Warren.
	►	A small group of students come up to Mr. Warren to introduce themselves and ask him about the class and himself.
	John:	(To Mr. Warren at his desk) You new here?
	Mr. W.:	Yep. This is my first day. I think I'm going to like it.
	Stella:	You don't give a lot of homework, do you?
	Mr. W.:	Enough to help you learn the subject. But don't worry, it won't be too much.
	Stella:	Good.
	Burton:	Can we sit where we want? Most teachers let us.

Time Frame	Dialog	
	Mr. W.:	Well, sit anywhere for now, but in the future I might want to arrange things in a particular way.
	▶	After Mr. Warren says this, several students who had taken the first seat they came to scramble to sit with their friends.
5 to 9	**Mr. W.:**	I'm sending around a sheet of paper and I'd like everyone to write their names on it. Write so I can read it because I'll be using this sheet to enter your names in the roll book.
	▶	This sheet is sent around and the students put their names on it.
	Viva:	Mr. Warren, in the other classes we've had today I think the teachers used some kind of list from the office to call roll.
	▶	A few of the students agree that this is what they remember seeing.
	Mr. W.:	Hmmn. Well I guess they could have put the class list inside my orientation packet. But I thought I looked through it. For now, let's sign the sheet.
	▶	The sheet continues circulating around the room.
9 to 21	**Mr. W.:**	While the sheet is going around I'd like to say a few words about what we'll be doing this semester.
	▶	Mr. Warren speaks for about seven minutes, telling the students the different topics they will be covering and the computer skills they will be trying to develop.
	Mr. W.:	Where is the sheet now?
	▶	No one seems to know.
	Mr. W.:	It must be somewhere!
	Corey:	Here, it fell under this desk. The wind must have blown it.
	Mr. W.:	Thanks. Who hasn't signed it yet?
	▶	One cluster of students all say "me." They all sign the sheet and hand it to Mr. Warren.
	Mr. W.:	Okay, when I call your name please say "here" and then, if necessary, correct my pronunciation of your name.
21 to 30	▶	Mr. Warren calls the names, marking the attendance and checking for spellings and pronunciations as he goes.
	Mr. W.:	Good. I'll enter your names into my roll book later. Tomorrow roll should go a lot quicker.

Time Frame	Dialog	
30 to 45	**Irene:**	Mr. Warren, you haven't told us about how we are going to get to use all these computers. They look so complicated. I don't think I can ever figure out what to do.
	Mr. W.:	Don't worry, we'll start slowly and move ahead at a pace everyone will be able to keep up with. I guess this is a good time to tell you about what we've got in this place. Actually, I haven't really looked over all the equipment and software that's here, but I can give you a general idea for now.
	►	Mr. Warren then proceeds to say a few words about the kinds of computers they will be using and where the software and related manuals are kept.
	Irene:	Who gets to use the best computer? I don't want to be on an old one.
	Mr. W.:	Oh, we'll work out some fair way of assigning people to the computers. Probably on a rotating basis or something like that.
	►	A few boys who happen to be seated near one of the newer-looking computers get out of their seats and begin looking over and touching the computer.
	Kevin:	(One of the boys out of his seat) Hey man, this will be great for video games. (He then wildly fingers the keyboard, making believe he's playing an exciting video game.)
	Mr. W.:	(To the boys out of their seats) You guys, don't be too rough on the computer. That keyboard can break if it is mishandled. In fact, you better get back to your seats. I don't want to dampen your enthusiasm, but you shouldn't move around on your own before we've organized things yet.
	►	The boys go back to their seats.
45 to 49	**Mr. W.:**	Tomorrow we are going to have our first lesson to help us prepare to use the computers.
	Laura:	Do we need to set up a section in our notebooks to copy anything down?
	Mr. W.:	Most of the notes you need I'll be giving you on dittoed sheets, but it would be a good idea to have some paper handy to take down any notes that might seem useful.
	►	By this time most students have grown restless and are talking with their neighbors.

Time Frame	Dialog
49 to 55	**Mr. W.:** That's about it for day one. (He begins transferring the names on the sheet that was sent around into his roll book.)

► When the bell rings the students rush out, leaving most desks and chairs askew. |

Brief   *Key Facts* – List three key facts verbatim that characterize the main positive and/or negative aspects of the lesson.

Strengths/Weaknesses – Briefly explain how the key facts selected indicate strengths and/or weaknesses in the teacher's performance.

Recommendations – Briefly describe what the teacher could have done to alleviate or avoid the problems that were seen.

♦ ♦ ♦ ♦ ♦ ♦ ♦

CASE STUDY 7.2   Handling Behavior Problems

Orienting Questions   As you read this case study ask yourself these questions:

Specific
♦ Does this teacher's use of punishment as a way of handling a behavior problem seem likely to bring about a better student attitude toward classwork?
♦ Why do you think this teacher has reacted so strongly to the behavior problem that has occurred during this lesson? What has her reaction caused the students to feel?

General
♦ What points in this lesson stand out as indicators of this teacher's strengths and/or weaknesses?
♦ What recommendations would you make for addressing the problems this teacher seems to have?

Setting   *School* – Junior high school (all girls)

Subject – General science (forty-five minutes)

Teacher – Ms. Turnbull, a first-year teacher

Students – Thirty-two girls of average ability

Topic – Mendeleyev's Periodic Table of Elements

Lesson

Time Frame	Dialog	
	►	As the girls enter the classroom and take their seats they are talking loudly, and some are shouting to friends across the room. The following assignment is projected from an overhead transparency: "Define the following terms and write them in your lecture notebook: chemical families, inert, and chemically active."
0 to 2	**Ms. T.:**	All right, girls, class has begun and your assignment is on the overhead. Follow the directions. You have five minutes to complete the assignment. If you don't finish, it is to be done for homework.
	►	The students are quiet while Ms. Turnbull is speaking and start right in on the assignment. Soon, however, the talking starts up again and gets progressively louder.
	Mr. T.:	Girls, I expect you to be silent as you complete the work.
	►	Ms. Turnbull glares at the three students who are doing the majority of the talking. They stop when they realize they have been spotted. When they stop talking, the room is quiet.
2 to 5	**Ms. T.:**	(Turning off the overhead projector as many students grumble that they have not had time to copy the assignment) I like it when you follow directions and concentrate on your work. I know you learn better when you cooperate because everyone did so well on the surprise quiz Tuesday. Remember how quiet you were on Monday? Let's see if we can repeat that performance. Today's topic is about how the periodic table is arranged.
	►	Ms. Turnbull turns on the overhead projector and changes the transparency to one that displays a series of questions:
		1. Who thought of the arrangement of the periodic table?
		2. How did he/she come up with the process of determining the sequence of how the elements should be arranged?
		3. What information can we learn from studying the periodic table?
5 to 10	**Ms. T.:**	Please copy these questions into your notebooks. We'll soon read the section of the text that will help you answer these questions, but first let's see if we can think of how someone would arrange the elements into a table. Angela, how would you arrange the elements?

Time Frame	Dialog	
	Angela:	I would arrange them by color.
	►	The class laughs loudly. The talking begins again. The same three girls are particularly laughing and talking loudly.
	Ms. T.:	Angela, that remark just earned you detention. Meet me after school to work out a time that is convenient. Does anyone want to try to think of how you would arrange the elements?
	►	No one responds. The talking has ceased. Two students are passing notes to each other.
10 to 15	**Ms. T.:**	Then open your books and turn to page 273 to 282. (Ms. Turnbull writes the page numbers on the chalkboard as she is speaking.) You will have fifteen minutes to read this section. Remember to record the new vocabulary terms. You may begin.
	►	Ms. Turnbull is sitting at her desk. Immediately, the three girls begin to talk to each other and the people next to them. Soon everyone is talking and the volume of sound becomes louder.
15 to 17	**Ms. T.:**	Girls! I expect silence as you read. If you cannot remain quiet we will read this section out loud. I have an assignment for you to complete in class, but if we spend time reading the section out loud I'm afraid you'll have to do this assignment at home. I wanted to give you a night without homework. You need to decide if you would rather have homework and talk, or be quiet and finish the assignment in class. It's up to you.
	►	Everyone stops talking. When Ms. Turnbull has finished, however, the same three girls begin talking again. A few students tell them to be quiet, but they keep right on talking.
17 to 35	**Ms. T.:**	All right. You obviously want to read aloud and have homework. So, Nancy, will you please begin reading on page 273.
	►	Ms. Turnbull calls on different students to read. She calls on the three "talkers" who find it necessary to ask where the place is and use silly voices or pronounce words in a strange way. This wastes time as it makes the rest of the class laugh.
35 to 40	**Ms. T.:**	I'm very tired of all the talking. Patty, Yvette, and Noelle (the three misbehaving girls), I want each of you

Time Frame	*Dialog*	

		to copy the entire section we read in class today on separate sheets of paper. I want this work on my desk tomorrow before school starts. You will learn to be quiet! I am also going to speak to your parents if this talking continues in the future. The rest of the class has the last five minutes to copy the questions I have prepared. I expect these questions to be answered and on my desk tomorrow. I will not tolerate this misbehavior. If you choose to talk during class time, then we will meet after school. You need to decide if you want to learn or play games.
	►	Ms. Turnbull changes the transparency on the overhead to display the questions that are to be written out and answered for homework.
40 to 45	**Ms. T.:**	You have the last five minutes to copy these questions.
	►	Ms. Turnbull returns to her desk and sits down. She takes out some papers and begins to grade them. The class silently copies the questions.
	Ms. T.:	Class is over (turning off the overhead projector). I expect the assignment on my desk tomorrow. Class is dismissed.
	►	Several students come up after class and say that they did not finish copying the questions. Ms. Turnbull tells them that is too bad and they should get them from someone who has finished. She also informs them that any questions not completed will be marked wrong. The students leave feeling angry, and Ms. Turnbull leaves feeling the same way.

Brief   *Key Facts* – List three key facts verbatim that characterize the main positive and/or negative aspects of the lesson.

Strengths/Weaknesses – Briefly explain how the key facts selected indicate strengths and/or weaknesses in the teacher's performance.

Recommendations – Briefly describe what the teacher could have done to alleviate or avoid the problems that were seen.

♦ ♦ ♦ ♦ ♦ ♦ ♦

CASE STUDY 7.3   Establishing Classroom Behavior Standards

Orienting
Questions   As you read this case study ask yourself these questions:

Specific
♦ Does this teacher let the students know through her words and actions what behavior is acceptable and what is not in the classroom?
♦ What makes you think the students were not involved in developing behavior standards for this class?

General
♦ What points in this lesson stand out as indicators of this teacher's strengths and/or weaknesses?
♦ What recommendations would you make for addressing the problems this teacher seems to have?

Setting   *School* – High school with students from three widely different communities

Subject – World history (fifty minutes)

Teacher – Mrs. Rivas, in her last year before retirement

Students – Thirty-five sophomores

Topic – Medievel Europe: The Feudal Contract (second week of the new semester)

Lesson

Time Frame	Dialog	
−5 to 0	►	The bell to move to second block rings and the students begin pouring into the classroom. On the board is written: "Review the feudal contract. Quiz tomorrow."
0 to 5	►	The announcements for the day come over the loud speaker. The principal begins speaking. The students are talking so loudly that the announcements can barely be heard. Mrs. Rivas is busily preparing the overhead projector and makes no effort to quiet the class.
	Mary:	(Speaking as she raises her hand) Mrs. Rivas, what time has cheer practice been changed to? I couldn't hear what they said.
	Mrs. R.:	I wasn't listening, Mary. Go check in the office. Don't worry about a pass for this. Just tell them I sent you and come right back. (To the class in general) You know I have told you that you will be given infractions for talking during the announcements. Please take this rule

Time Frame	Dialog	
		about not making noise during the announcements seriously.
	►	Mrs. Rivas has not given any infractions all week.
5 to 15	►	Mrs. Rivas puts a transparency on the overhead projector that shows the feudal contract. The students continue to talk among themselves as roll is taken.
	Mrs. R.:	Now class, the feudal contract grew out of certain customs and traditions. Obie, was it a written or oral contract?
	Obie:	What was the question?
	Mrs. R.:	Weren't you listening?
	Obie:	Yes, I was, but I couldn't hear you.
	Mrs. R.:	(Impatiently) Was the contract written or oral?
	►	Obie flips through the textbook looking for the answer.
	Obie:	It was an oral contract.
	Mrs. R.:	That's right.
15 to 35	►	Mrs. Rivas explain the concept of fief and the feudal contract obligations. The students seated toward the front of the class are taking notes. Those seated toward the back of the room are chattering among themselves.
	Mrs. R.:	(To several students who are talking) Jennie, Eric, Tommie, Lisa, and Nikki, if you persist in talking I will give you each an infraction. Nikki, can you state the obligations that the lord had to the vassal?
	►	Nikki hears her name called, realizing that Mrs. Rivas has noticed that she was talking to the student behind her.
	Nikki:	What?
	►	Mrs. Rivas repeats the question.
	Nikki:	Some days of military service, that was their obligation.
	Mrs. R.:	No, Nikki. That is one of the vassal's obligations to the lord. Were you taking notes?
	Nikki:	Yes, Mrs. Rivas.
	Mrs. R.:	I don't believe that, otherwise you would know the answer.
35 to 45	Mrs. R.:	Tommie, can you help Nikki with the answer as she's apparently having some difficulty.
	Tommie:	With what?
	Mrs. R.:	Explain the obligations of the feudal contract. This is what I've been talking about for the last forty minutes.
	Tommie:	I don't understand this contract.

Time Frame	Dialog
	Mrs. R.: If you and others near you would bother listening to the explanations instead of talking you might understand. Tommie, all you were doing was talking to Nikki.
	Tommie: Nikki was explaining the feudal contract to me.
	Mrs. R.: How could she? She didn't know the answer herself.
45 to 50	**Mrs. R.:** Class, take the last few minutes to review the questions at the end of Chapter 6 in your textbooks. This will help get you ready for tomorrow's quiz on the feudal contract.
	▶ Several students do the review questions. Most of the students simply put their books away and start talking.
	Mrs. R.: (As the bell rings the class is almost halfway out the door) Class dismissed. Don't forget to study your notes for the quiz.

Brief   *Key Facts* – List three key facts verbatim that characterize the main positive and/or negative aspects of the lesson.

Strengths/Weaknesses – Briefly explain how the key facts selected indicate strengths and/or weaknesses in the teacher's performance.

Recommendations – Briefly describe what the teacher could have done to alleviate or avoid the problems that were seen.

♦ ♦ ♦ ♦ ♦ ♦ ♦

CHAPTER PROJECT   Develop and Implement a Classroom Management System

Goals
1. To develop a system for organizing and managing classroom activities and routines.
2. To increase the effectiveness of classroom operations and the time available for instructional purposes.

Phases   One, two, or three phases (i.e., planning, partial implementation, full implementation) of the chapter project can be completed as deemed appropriate to students' needs and the design of the course.

Planning
1. Determine the major areas that constitute a classroom management system (e.g., discipline, routines, and procedures).
2. Define each of the major areas, listing the factors in each area that need to be considered for effective classroom management.

Partial Implementation

1. Develop policies, standards, procedures, and routines that are applicable to the major areas of classroom management that have been delineated.
2. Determine the best ways to communicate and establish the policies, standards, procedures, and routines that have been developed.

Full Implementation

1. Create a daily classroom management log in the form of a matrix, listing the policies, standards, procedures, and routines vertically down the lefthand column, and comments and dates horizontally across the top as a way of monitoring the day-to-day effectiveness of the system that has been developed.
2. After using the system for approximately two weeks, analyze the information that has been recorded on the daily classroom management log to identify areas of difficulty.
3. Propose solutions for overcoming the difficulties identified by modifying the classroom management system.

◆ ◆ ◆ ◆ ◆ ◆ ◆
REFERENCES

Alcorn, M. D., Kinder, J. S., & Schunert, J. R. (1970). *Better teaching in secondary schools* (3rd ed.). New York: Holt, Rinehart and Winston.

Armstrong, D. G., Denton, J. J., & Savage, T. V., Jr. (1978). *Instructional skills handbook.* Englewood Cliffs, NJ: Educational Technology Publications.

Clark, L. H., & Starr, I. S. (1986). *Secondary and middle school teaching methods* (5th ed.). New York: Macmillan.

Crawford C. C. (1938). *How to teach.* Los Angeles: Claude C. Crawford.

Dewey, J. (1938). *Experience and education.* New York: Macmillan.

Good, T. L., & Brophy, J. E. (1984). *Looking in classrooms* (3rd ed.). New York: Harper & Row.

Jones, V. F., & Jones, L. S. (1981). *Responsible classroom discipline: Creating positive learning environments and solving problems.* Boston: Allyn and Bacon.

Lemlech, J. K. (1979). *Classroom management.* New York: Harper & Row.

Montessori, M. (1912). *The Montessori method.* New York: Schocken Books.

Strayer, G. D. (1914). *A brief course in the teaching process.* New York: Macmillan.

Waples, D., & Tyler, R. W. (1930). *Research methods and teachers' problems: A manual for systematic studies of classroom procedure.* New York: Macmillan.

◆ ◆ ◆ ◆ ◆ ◆ ◆
ANNOTATED READINGS

Callahan, J. F., & Clark, L. H. (1982). *Teaching in the middle and secondary schools* (2nd ed.). New York: Macmillan.
   A basic self-instructional text on teaching methods. See Chapter 9 on motivation, discipline, and control.

Cooper, J. M. (Ed.). (1977). *Classroom teaching skills: A workbook.* Lexington, MA: D. C. Heath.

A workbook providing practice in major teaching skill areas through analytical exercises as well as guidelines and suggestions on how these skills may be practiced in microteaching. See Chapter 8 on classroom management.

Good, T. L., & Brophy, J. E. (1984). *Looking in classrooms* (3rd ed.). New York: Harper & Row.

This book offers a method for observing, describing, and understanding classroom behavior as the basis for improving student attitudes and for developing an effective teaching style. See Chapters 6 and 7 on effectively preventing and coping with classroom problems, respectively.

Heck, S. F., & Williams, C. R. (1984). *The complex roles of the teacher: An ecological perspective.* New York: Teachers College Press.

A book focusing on the dynamic interactive contexts within which teaching and learning take place. See "Understanding Students: A Basis for Effective Discipline" in Chapter 4.

Henson, K. T. (1981). *Secondary teaching methods.* Lexington, MA: D. C. Heath.

A basic text in secondary school teaching emphasizing practical applications of the principles of teaching. See Chapter 3 on discipline and self-discipline and Chapter 4 on classroom management.

Kim, E. C., & Kellough, R. D. (1987). *A resource guide for secondary school teaching: Planning for competence* (4th ed.). New York: Macmillan.

An excellent workbook featuring ideas and exercises focusing on the developmental elements necessary to becoming a competent professional. See Part IV on classroom management, discipline, and legal guidelines.

Orlich, D. C., Harder, R. J., Callahan, R. C., Kravas, C. H., Kauchak, D. P., Pendergrass, R. A., & Keogh, A. J. (1985). *Teaching strategies: A guide to better instruction* (2nd ed.). Lexington, MA: D. C. Heath.

A book presenting a broad spectrum of instructional methodologies, techniques, and approaches tailored to the secondary school classroom. See Chapter 10 on how to manage a class.

Redl, H. B. (Ed. and Trans.). (1964). *Soviet educators on soviet education.* London: Free Press of Glencoe, Collier-Macmillan.

See pages 28–41 for excellent ideas on fostering self-discipline in adolescents by A. S. Makarenko, one of the foremost Soviet educators.

Strother, D. B. (1985). Classroom management. *Phi Delta Kappan, 66*(10), 725–728.

An article discussing recent studies on effective teaching that focuses on the creation of positive environments for learning through using management and organizational skills.

CHAPTER 8
♦ ♦ ♦ ♦ ♦ ♦ ♦

Evaluation

INTRODUCTION

Evaluation is the process of attributing value to something. In the classroom, this process allows the teacher to determine the worth of his or her efforts and all aspects of the instructional program. Evaluation is used throughout the school year as the basis for determining which aspects of the instructional program need adjustment and which students need individual help. Because "central to all learning is the ability to reflect on and learn from experience" (Donoghue, Snow, & Spencer, 1986, p. 75), classroom evaluation is also an integral part of the teacher's continuing process of learning for professional growth.

Evaluation has three main purposes: to determine each student's readiness for learning, to determine how well each student is progressing, and to determine what each student has achieved. These three purposes are commonly associated with initial, formative, and summative evaluation, respectively.

Initial evaluation is essential at the beginning of the semester and major course units so that instructional plans and activities can be tailored to meet student needs and interests. It is pedagogically unsound to start a semester or unit and continue for weeks without knowing the students' fitness for the intended level of instruction. Initial evaluation need not always be elaborate or formal, but sufficient opportunities to determine student readiness for learning, both individually and collectively, should be afforded. An effective initial evaluation must address two main questions:

1. What are the students' current levels of understanding in the subject area? (What learning have they already accomplished? What skills and competencies have they acquired?)
2. What are the student's learning needs? (What are their strengths and weaknesses? What are their individual learning styles?)

The results of initial evaluation provide the teacher with a guide to planning effective daily lessons in terms of types of activities to use and the level and pace of instruction to follow. In addition, initial evaluation provides the basis for determining the goals and overall instructional plan for the semester.

Formative evaluation is carried out continuously. The teacher as classroom researcher regularly conducts formative evaluation. Despite the many modes formative evaluation may take, it has one main goal—to provide the teacher with information for improving the classroom instructional program by letting him or her know as accurately as possible how instruction and management of the classroom environment are affecting the students. Effective formative evaluation must address four main questions:

1. Are the students interested and involved in the instructional activities?
2. Do the students demonstrate an understanding of the basic concepts presented?
3. Are the students ready for each succeeding topic as it is covered?
4. Are instructional activities, methods, and resources employed effectively and according to plan?

Although initial evaluation alone is usually considered diagnostic, formative evaluation is also diagnostic in that it provides information about the strengths and weaknesses of the students and of the classroom instructional program. In addition, initial and formative evaluation are the keys to attaining a balance in which classroom instruction challenges but does not frustrate students. Thus, the results of formative evaluation help the teacher determine what to change to increase the effectiveness of daily instruction. The results are valuable, however, only if they are obtained using appropriate techniques and instruments in a timely manner. For example, any exam used as part of formative evaluation should be criterion-referenced rather than norm-referenced because the former is based on what has actually been taught and the latter on general knowledge of the subject. An effective method for developing small- or large-scale criterion-referenced classroom tests will be presented in a later section.

Summative evaluation is typically conducted at the conclusion of a unit, grading period, or semester. Its purpose is to determine what the students have achieved, both in terms of learning the subject and developing self-discipline. In this sense it is used "to grade the students and judge our own teaching success" (Clark & Starr, 1986, p. 348). Although an air of finality usually surrounds summative evaluation, it also has a diagnostic function. In fact, it should be seen as only one point in a process that continues throughout each student's school career. For instance, the final report card, when used properly, is as much a diagnosis of the student's strengths and weaknesses as any informal classroom quiz or weekly test. The difference is in scope. Initial and formative evaluations focus on students' work over relatively brief periods of time, while summative evaluation looks at their work over a much longer time span. For example, the teacher using summative evaluation effectively would view end-of-unit exam scores as the basis for modifying subsequent instructional plans and activities, and would see final semester grades as key indicators for communicating to the students' new teachers where and how instruction might begin.

BASIC THEORIES

◆ Measurement

There are two aspects of evaluation. Measurement (or assessment) is the quantitative aspect, and interpretation the qualitative. This section focuses on classroom observations and testing as means of accurately measuring student performance in class. The measurement function is the necessary first step in the evaluation process that makes interpretation and subsequent corrective action possible. Failure to obtain sufficient accurate information about what is happening in the classroom makes all attempts at initial, formative, and summative evaluations fruitless or, worse, misleading. Such failures have serious implications for students, considering that decisions based on these various evaluations determine what, how, and with whom they will learn. Many a student's life has been deeply affected by the results of school evaluations.

Using the evaluation process to measure academic progress alone is shortsighted. An effective measurement program must provide diagnostic information about student behavior and personal growth as well. "Thus the results of the testing program will show what the [student] has learned to do to protect his health, to be punctual, to live harmoniously with others, to meet his obligations, to control his emotions, and to earn his living rendering valuable social service" (Crawford, 1938, pp. 451–452).

Classroom observations and testing are the principal methods for obtaining information essential to initial, formative, and summative evaluations. This section focuses on how to effectively observe and record students' classroom behaviors. Table 8.1 summarizes these essential methods of measurement.

Making Classroom Observations

The classroom is the teacher's living educational laboratory. The wealth of information and insights that can be derived from carefully observing what happens in the classroom from day to day can benefit the teacher and, consequently, the students far more than any educational theories or prescriptions ever could. To make optimal use of classroom observations, however, it is necessary to know what areas are most important to observe and how to maintain a concise, up-to-date record of what is observed.

Classroom observations should center around student classwork, participation in instructional activities, and behaviors. Observing performance in these areas provides information about work habits, personality, and social adjustment that cannot be obtained through pencil-and-paper tests. The following recommended practices should be followed for observing student classwork, participation, and behaviors.

1. Observe and review student classwork.
   ◆ Review the instructional plan to determine the different types of classwork expected of students. For example, in a science class, in addition to the usual review and workbook exercises, students will probably be involved in some form of lab work. Make a list of the different types of classwork that indicates how frequently (e.g., daily, weekly, irregularly) students can be expected to engage in each type of work. This list can then guide the teacher in observing and

TABLE 8.1 *Essential Methods of Measurement*

METHODS	TASKS INVOLVED
Making classroom observations	1. Observe and review student classwork. 2. Observe student participation in instructional activities. 3. Observe student behavior.
Recording observations	1. Maintain anecdotal records.
Testing	1. Develop classroom tests. 2. Administer tests. 3. Score tests and report results. 4. Understand the role of standardized testing within the framework of the classroom instructional program.

recording useful information about each student and the class as a whole. It can also help minimize the effects of the observations on students' work.

Observers are notoriously unreliable; students behave differently when they know they are being observed. However, to a degree, these limitations can be reduced by careful observation. A helpful technique is to determine in advance what to look for and how to look for it. (Clark & Starr, 1986, p. 350)

◆ Develop daily lesson activities so that ten to fifteen minutes of every period are set aside for firsthand observation. During this time, walk around the room to work with individual students. These few minutes of individual work with students on a regular basis provide insights about their understanding and approach to solving problems that cannot be obtained with such accuracy any other way. In addition, this individual attention contributes to a feeling of closeness in the teacher-student relationship, which helps create a positive classroom environment.

◆ Allow for a degree of flexibility when setting standards for how different types of classwork are to be done. This flexibility is necessary if observations of students' classwork are to yield an objective picture of how they respond to various problems and situations. Preconceived notions of how classwork should be done blind the teacher to the unique problems, learning styles, and attributes of each student. The degree of flexibility allowed, however, must be kept within limits, always considering the specific skills to be developed, procedures followed, and instructional objectives attained.

◆ Collect and carefully review samples of students' classwork periodically to determine their strengths and weaknesses. The secondary school teacher does not have the time to review all the written work of every student. It is possible, however, to assess students' writing skills by examining representative samples of the written work commonly required of them. This sampling technique results in increased attention to and interest in classwork, because the students know their work may be checked and evaluated at any time.

Sampling is not only involved in appraising the individual's behavior, but it may also be involved in appraising the effectiveness of curriculum experiences in use with a group of students. It is not always necessary to find out the reaction of every individual in order to see the effect that the curriculum is producing. (Tyler, 1950, p. 71)

◆ Regularly review students' notebooks. Maintaining a good notebook requires perseverance and the ability to record ideas and information logically and concisely. Much insight into students' work habits and problems can be gained by seeing how they organize and record the material presented in class. In addition, where clear instructions have been given for how the notebook is to be maintained, such reviews provide information about each student's ability and willingness to meet those requirements. Students who have difficulty keeping up with the class can often benefit considerably from suggestions for improving the organization and completeness of their notebooks.

2. Observe student participation in instructional activities.

   ◆ Review the instructional plan and make a list of the various activities and ways in which students are expected to participate in class, including responding to questions, posing questions, involvement in discussions and group work, and presentations to the class.

   ◆ Use the list that is developed to employ a participation-point system to be used as one factor in determining students' grades. This system encourages student participation if it is used consistently in conjunction with a nonthreatening cooperative classroom environment.

   ◆ Plan instructional activities to encompass the variety of personalities and learning styles of the students in the class. Some students are incorrectly assessed to be slow or uninterested when, in fact, they are simply not given the chance to show what they can do. Unfortunately these students often do not realize their predicament and also believe they are lacking in some way. For example, students who are reticent about speaking in front of the class might feel more comfortable participating in demonstrations or group presentations. On the other hand, students who have difficulty with written work might thrive on opportunities to ask questions and present their ideas to the class.

   ◆ Avoid allowing a handful of students to dominate classroom participation. Too often, teachers allow a pattern to develop in which a small group of students answer and ask most of the questions raised in class. The constant flow of responses creates the illusion that instruction is proceeding well, when in reality most of the students are sitting passively.

3. Observe student behavior.

   ◆ Classroom observations are extremely useful for helping the teacher effectively carry out the school's socialization function. Frequently students reveal more about themselves when they interact with one another rather than with the teacher, whom they are often trying to please or create an image for. It is particularly important, therefore, to see the level of concern and respect they show for each other to obtain valuable information about their social adjustment and emotional growth. Students' reactions to criticism, praise, authority, offers of assistance, and requests for assistance can also provide useful information about their personal growth.

   ◆ Observe how students handle individualized assignments, noticing in particular their levels of concentration, confidence, and interest.

The way in which a student works by himself or herself may or may not indicate that student's ability to work alone. A student who is able to remain on task when working alone may be revealing several things. He or she may be exhibiting confidence in the ability to solve problems or to grasp the concepts that are being studied. (Heck & Williams, 1984, p. 98)

♦ A student who seems to be avoiding classwork may actually be silently calling for help. It takes careful and regular observation to understand what is behind a student's overt behavior.

♦ Observe how students approach various types of tasks to obtain an understanding of their work habits. Again, these observations should be as objective as possible, allowing for each student's ability level and style of learning. Students should not be expected to fit any one mold in their approaches to doing classwork. In addition to ascertaining students' personal styles and needs, however, the information obtained over a period of time from numerous observations should provide important general information about students' work habits, including their use of time, use of materials (e.g., textbooks, notebooks, study guides, dictionaries), perseverance, and ability to organize and plan. In addition to watching individual students as they work, the teacher should sometimes ask them to describe orally what goes through their minds as they work on different problems. The combination of specific and general information can later serve as the basis for developing individualized learning plans and remedial activities.

♦ Observe students' communication skills, including their ability to speak clearly, write legibly and coherently, listen attentively, and read with comprehension. These observations can also provide information that is helpful in identifying any physical defects they may have, such as speech, coordination, hearing, or vision problems.

♦ Observe students' behaviors that relate directly to the instructional objectives for the course and the daily lessons. This not only provides information about students' progress but also about the quantity and quality of the opportunities provided to the students to express the behavior implied by the objectives. This is in keeping with the basic principle of evaluation that "any evaluation situation is the kind of situation that gives an opportunity for the students to express the type of behavior we are trying to appraise" (Tyler, 1950, p. 73).

Recording Observations

The wealth of information obtained through classroom observations needs to be recorded and organized in a way that ensures accuracy and ready access so insights can be gained about the learning and development of the students. Such records are particularly important because they provide information that not only supplements test data but, in many cases, is the only information available about certain aspects of the students' development (e.g., work habits, perseverance, regard for others). Without regularly recorded written accounts to refer to, the teacher is left with only general impressions of classroom observations. Over time these impressions begin to fade, blend into one another, or become distorted—resulting in an inaccurate and biased picture of what is going on. The anecdotal record is one of the most effective ways of maintaining records of classroom observations for gaining a better understanding of each student's unique pattern of behavior and needs.

1. Maintain anecdotal records.
   ♦ Determine the format to use for keeping anecdotal records. A simple method is to have a large index card (four inches by six inches) for each student on which entries are made describing significant positive or negative incidents that occur. For example, on the card for Student X, it might be recorded that on September 29 he requested supplementary enrichment exercises to do at home, and that on November 4 he was observed making fun of two learning disabled students who had received poor midterm exam scores. (The first note reveals an interest in the subject and the second one a degree of immaturity.) A more complete method is to keep an anecdotal records notebook containing several types of information, including a *significant incidents* sheet for each student and each class, and a *significant behaviors* sheet for each student that lists specific behaviors related to habits, interests, personal and social adjustments, and learning needs that cannot be evaluated by any other means.
   ♦ Record observations in a timely fashion so recollections remain vivid and thus accurate. To do this requires limiting and controlling both the observations made and the information recorded in a way that is manageable within the busy daily classroom routine. It is recommended, therefore, that just a few types of behavior be observed at any one time. For example, as students are engaged in completing an assigned workbook exercise, the teacher can circulate through the room assisting students and making written or mental notes about their approaches to solving problems. This information can then be concisely recorded on the significant behaviors sheets for individual students. Although a few behaviors may be targeted for observation at a particular time, the teacher must remain flexible and alert enough to note any unusual student behavior that may prove necessary to record. The aim is not to have volumes of notes to read but concise accounts of observations that provide a representative sample of student behavior in the various areas in which information is desired. Observation notes that are too lengthy and disorganized become an amorphous mass of words and discourage further efforts in this area.
   ♦ On each anecdotal record sheet, allow space for a factual account of the observation, an analysis of the observation, and, where ap-

propriate, a recommendation for action. The factual accounts should be as objective as possible, expressed in nonjudgmental terms. Although each observation may be analyzed for meaning, any final decision should be reserved until after several anecdotes have been collected for each student. "It is only after observing a [student] a number of times in a variety of settings that his basic pattern of behavior begins to emerge" (Gronlund, 1971, p. 417). For example, a review of Student X's significant behaviors sheet may reveal that for the week preceding unit exams he tends to become particularly introverted and irritable.

♦ Develop student profiles as a means of integrating information obtained through classroom observations with other evaluation information (e.g., testing). Maintaining student profiles allows for a simultaneous examination and comparison of student behaviors and academic work and thus places the teacher in a better position to understand the relationship between the two as the basis for determining and addressing student needs.

Testing

There are many types of testing carried out in the classroom, including quizzes, weekly pretests and posttests, unit exams, midterms, final exams, and various standardized tests. The type of testing used depends upon its purpose. On the large scale, standardized tests compare the performance of students in a school or district with those in other parts of the state or in the rest of the nation. On the small scale, daily quizzes diagnose each student's progress and learning needs in a specific segment of a course topic.

The value of the results obtained from testing is determined by the quality of the test used and by the interpretive skills of the teacher. Test scores in themselves have no meaning. Using them simply to record obligatory weekly entries in the roll book loses sight of the real purpose of measurement and is a mockery of the evaluation process. The results of testing should be regarded as a measure of students' work that can, after thoughtful analysis and interpretation, serve as the basis for providing individual guidance, planning remedial activities, and adjusting the instructional program.

For the teacher to use classroom testing to accurately measure students' work and progress requires a knowledge of how to develop and administer various forms of tests, as well as an understanding of the role of standardized testing within the framework of the classroom instructional program. The following recommended practices should be followed in developing and administering tests and in gaining an understanding of the role standardized tests should play.

1. Develop classroom tests.
   ♦ Become familiar with the various types of classroom tests (i.e., quizzes, weekly pretests and posttests, unit exams, midterm and final exams),

the nature of the information they yield, and when they are best employed. (See Table 8.2 for a list of characteristics for the various types of classroom tests along with recommendations for their use.)

◆ Become familiar with the various forms tests can take (i.e., objective, essay, performance), the reasons for using each form, and the principles for creating test items or activities characteristic of each form. (See Table 8.3 for a description of each form of test.)

◆ Review the instructional plan to develop a preliminary classroom testing schedule that indicates what type of test (e.g., quiz, unit exam) to use at particular points throughout the semester as different topics are covered. This schedule can serve as a framework for organizing initial, formative, and summative evaluations. The preliminary testing schedule will naturally be modified as the semester proceeds and evaluation information obtained through observations and testing indicates the need for changes in the level, pace, and scope of instruction as well as the need for obtaining additional evaluation data at different points in the semester.

◆ Begin preparation of classroom tests by determining the type and form of test to be used and then relating the learning objectives involved to the subject-matter content to be tested. The most effective way of doing this is by using a table of specifications. (See Table 8.4 for a sample table of specifications, including the steps to

TABLE 8.2 *Characteristics of Various Types of Classroom Tests*

RECOMMENDED USES	TYPES OF TESTS					
	Quiz	Pretest	Posttest	Unit Exam	Midterm	Final
Initial evaluation	F	A	N	N	N	N
Formative evaluation	S	S	F	S	S	R
Summative evaluation	N	N	S	F	A	A
Few items	F	R	R	N	N	N
Many items	R	F	F	A	A	A
Short-answer	S	S	S	F	A	A
Essay	N	S	S	F	A	A
Time limit	F	S	S	F	F	F
Untimed	N	F	F	S	S	R
Teacher-made	A	F	F	A	F	F
Oral response	S	R	R	N	N	N
Written response	F	F	F	A	A	A
Single topic	A	F	F	N	N	N
Many topics	N	S	S	A	A	A

Key: A = Always, F = Frequently, S = Sometimes, R = Rarely, N = Never

TABLE 8.3 *Three Forms of Classroom Tests*

TEST FORMS	DESCRIPTION
Objective	Aims at objectivity in scoring; two or more persons should reach similar scores when grading the same tests.
	Requires a relatively large number of items to obtain desired results.
	Used to sample relatively large segments of course content.
	Scoring is mechanical and relatively fast.
	Typical test items include multiple choice, true/false, matching, and completion.
	Effective for measuring recall and recognition of factual information.
	Frequent use encourages memorization of information rather than higher levels of thinking.
Essay	Scoring is subjective; responses allow for originality, creativity, and varying writing styles.
	Requires only a few well-designed questions to obtain the evaluation information desired.
	Used to sample a specific segment of course material because of depth of response called for.
	Encourages understanding of concepts, organization of ideas and information, and development of writing skills.
	Stresses creativity and imagination and thus effectively measures higher levels of thinking and understanding.
Performance	Provides opportunities to see what students do in real-life situations.
	Emphasizes ability to interpret information, apply learning, think carefully, and reason logically.
	Emphasizes demonstration of skill rather than memorization or manipulation of information.

follow for constructing the table.) This allows the teacher to construct tests that address the learning objectives and course topics according to their relative importance and to the emphasis they are given in class. In this sense, all tests developed from a table of specifications are criterion-referenced. To ensure that this is accomplished, it is useful as a preliminary step when creating a table of specifications to develop a rating index for organizing the skills and activities corresponding to the subject content being tested. (See Table 8.5 for an example of one such rating index.) "This planning enables the teacher to design the test to fit the situation, rather than a haphazard test that does not correspond to the objectives either in content or behavior emphasis" (Callahan & Clark, 1982, p. 309). Even if a particular topic or learning objective is considered very important, it is unwise and unfair to include many tests items on

TABLE 8.4 *Table of Specifications for Test on Punctuation Skills*

STEPS TO FOLLOW

1. Determine course topic(s) to be tested.
2. Review the instructional plan and daily lesson plans pertaining to the topic(s) to be tested.
3. Determine the importance that has been given to various objectives and concepts relating to this topic(s), noting emphasis on the test in terms of percentages.
4. Determine the levels of thinking (e.g., recall, application) to be tested, noting emphasis on the test in terms of percentages.
5. Use the table of specifications to write specific test items according to the emphasis indicated for both the course content and levels of thinking involved.

SUBJECT MATTER	RECALL RULES OF USAGE	FIND IN A SENTENCE	USE IN A SENTENCE	CORRECT ERRORS IN A SENTENCE	PERCENT OF TEST
Periods	10	10	9	6	35
Commas	5	8	4	3	20
Question marks	5	7	5	3	20
Exclamation points	3	5	5	2	15
Apostrophes	2	5	2	1	10
PERCENT OF TEST	25	35	25	15	100

TABLE 8.5 *Rating Index for Organizing Skills and Activities*

The skills activities listed below cover a two-week period on the topic of punctuation. The activities have been divided into five degrees that reflect the increasing difficulty of the activities at each succeeding level. Activities cover all four skill areas at each degree of difficulty. Thus, the skills activities under Degree 1 must be successfully completed before those under Degree 2 are begun. The number of skills activities listed reflects the relative importance and emphasis given to the different skill areas at each level of difficulty. Information on the rating index can be used in developing a table of specifications to determine the importance of specific skills areas and the degree of difficulty involved in the various activities.

SKILL AREAS*	DEGREE 1	DEGREE 2	DEGREE 3	DEGREE 4	DEGREE 5
Recall rules of usage	7	7	7	7	7
Find in a sentence	2	4	5	4	4
Use in a sentence	2	3	5	5	4
Correct errors in a sentence	3	3	4	4	3

*Subject matter involved in all four skill areas: periods, commas, question marks, exclamation points, and apostrophes.

that topic or learning objective if it has not been given corresponding emphasis in classroom instruction. Further, because using a table of specifications to develop classroom tests requires reflecting on what has been taught and how, it gives the teacher an opportunity to evaluate whether various course topics and objectives are being covered with the attention and time they deserve. As a basic principle, all tests except those used strictly for initial diagnosis should reflect the emphasis in our teaching. This principle points out the problem of relying too much on commercially developed, district-made, or even department-made tests in place of teacher-made tests. In too many instances the teacher is minimally involved in developing course curriculum and in developing instruments to evaluate student progress and the worth of the instructional plan. Rather, the textbook, workbook, and related assessment instruments are his or her mainstay. This is hardly characteristic of true professionals, who immerse themselves in all aspects of their field and take the major share of responsibility for the development and quality of the material they use.

♦ Determine the number and type of items to be on the test. The length of the test should depend on the type of test used (e.g., quiz, final exam). The number of items on the test should be sufficient to obtain an accurate sampling of students' work in terms of their understanding of the material being tested. Using a table of specifications to construct tests helps increase the accuracy of the resulting test information by ensuring that enough items cover specific information and ideas so that students have the chance to demonstrate what they really know. For example, if a unit exam on the American Revolution includes only one multiple-choice question on the concept of sovereign rights, some students may get the correct answer simply by guessing, when in reality they do not have the slightest idea what the concept means. In contrast, some students who answer incorrectly may actually understand the concept but have a hard time discriminating between two of the possible choices that are given. An analysis of the test results for this particular item, therefore, would still leave the teacher in the dark about students' understanding of the concept tested. A few more items that address the concept from different perspectives, or a fill-in, short-answer, or essay question requiring careful, informed thought about the concept, would give much more valid information. It is also important to have only a few different types of items on a single test to avoid confusing the students and causing them to allot time and effort unproductively.

♦ Determine whether the test is to be a speed test, where a time limit is set for completing the exam, a power test, where students are allowed whatever time they need to answer all the questions they can to the best of their ability, or some combination of the two.

The advantage of power tests is that the responses to the various questions clearly indicate the students' levels of understanding. On speed tests the teacher cannot be sure whether poor or incomplete answers are due to lack of understanding or lack of time. Speed tests have their use, but more often in the form of quizzes and drills to provide students with practice for increasing their capacities to think quickly and decisively—skills very much needed to function in today's world. In addition, speed tests are useful in testing students' abilities to demonstrate specific skills such as typing, shooting baskets, or using a soldering iron. A speed test should be designed so that no one is likely to finish all the test items. If several students are able to complete the test with much time to spare, it becomes impossible to determine how much more they would have been capable of doing. It also creates the potential behavior problem of students sitting around with nothing to do. A power test does not mean the students have unlimited time to complete the test. Some time frame has to be set up in accordance with the length of the class period. Within that time frame, however, the teacher should try to determine the maximum amount of time anyone would need to complete the test or sections of the test if they have any understanding at all of the material. Such considerations help determine not only the time frame for a power test but its length as well.

♦ Prepare test items by reviewing the table of specifications that has been developed and then systematically typing or writing each item on an index card. This allows you to easily rearrange the test items in various permutations until the most satisfactory order is achieved. The individual items should then be placed in a test-item file for future reference and for adding comments or modifications as they are used in the classroom. The specific course topic and the level of thinking involved should be indicated on the test-item index card. For example, for three questions relating to a particular theorem on a geometry exam, the item that requires recognizing the correct wording of the theorem should have an index card labeled "Theorem A/Recall"; the item that involves determining whether the theorem has been applied correctly to solve a problem should be labeled "Theorem A/Application"; and the item that involves using the theorem in conjunction with another theorem to solve a complex problem should be labeled "Theorem A/Synthesis."

♦ Determine the order of the items on the test by following three basic principles: (1) avoid placing questions so that the answer to one serves as a clue to answering the next one, or the answer to a question is supplied in the statement of the next question; (2) keep questions of the same type (e.g., true/false, essay) together so students can remain in the same mental gear as they progress through the various segments of the test; and (3) put some questions that most students can handle toward the beginning of the test to help build their confidence. When items are arranged so that the easiest ones come first and then progressively get more difficult, some students may simply give up after reaching a certain point. Interspersing items of varying levels of difficulty throughout the test is more likely to maintain students' confidence and efforts.

♦ Give clear oral or written directions explaining how students are to complete the test to minimize confusion and create positive and calm testing conditions. The directions should state the time available for completing the test or different parts of the test; how the test is to be graded, including the point value of each item and section; the procedure to use for answering different types of questions (e.g., "Fill in the blank with the word that best completes the sentence" or "Select the one choice that you think is best"); how to ask questions if something on the test is not clear (e.g., "Raise your hand and quietly wait until I come to you"); what to do upon completion of the test (e.g., "When you are done, please place your test sheet face down and wait quietly for it to be collected"). In addition, it is important to let students know whether they will be penalized for making a wrong guess, or if they should try to answer all the questions as best they can.

♦ Make sure that a sufficient number of readable copies of the test are available. Leaving the typing and duplication of the test until the last minute often leads to mistakes, including numerous typographical errors, missing information, poor spacing or alignment of words, blank test sheets, smudged lettering, and off-center printing, all of which are disconcerting to students. Testing situations produce enough anxiety in students. They do not need the added pressure of struggling to decipher what is written on the test sheet. Therefore, design the test sheet so all the material on it is easy to read. Also, it is hard to impress upon students the importance of a test when it is evident that the test has been carelessly prepared. The students are wiser and more sensitive than you think—you cannot set standards for them and not follow any yourself.

♦ Maintain a topical/chronological testing file that includes a complete file of tests developed and administered, all tables of specifications used for developing the tests (as an aid to subsequent modifications of the tests), all the individual test-item index cards, and reports of the results of the tests that especially indicate student progress, the effectiveness of specific test items, and the value of the information obtained.

2. Administer tests.
   ♦ Establish arrangements and procedures to be followed in testing situations, including materials permitted on the desk, seats to take, requesting assistance, requesting permission to leave the room, handing in completed papers, and use of time after completing the test.

◆ Determine whether the test is to be administered orally or in written form. For practical reasons most tests are given in written form. There are times, however, when tests, especially the completion and true/false types, are better given orally. For orally administered tests, students should be asked to write down a series of numbers in a column corresponding to the number of test items. Then each questions or statement should be read twice, and only twice, as the students supply either the needed word or "true" or "false." There are three main advantages to periodically administering tests this way. First, the teacher's vocal inflection makes the meaning of the questions or statements clear and unambiguous, thus eliminating students' reading comprehension skills as a determining factor. Second, it provides an opportunity to compare students' work when all students are given exactly the same amount of time to hear, reflect upon, and answer questions. Third, because students are compelled to listen carefully, it provides them with sorely needed practice in focusing their attention. Care should be taken in reading the test items to speak clearly and at a pace that is comfortable to all.

◆ Count out the number of tests needed, including several extra copies to allow for the occasional blank sheet or printing mistake. While doing this, it is just as easy to put the tests in bunches corresponding to the seating arrangement for quick distribution.

◆ Before handing out the tests, make sure the proper seating arrangement is being used, see that everyone has the materials they need (e.g., including pens, pencils, scratch paper, reference sources), insist upon silence and attention, and read aloud the directions for completing the test, allowing a few minutes for any questions the students may have.

◆ Administer two or three versions of the test in which the order of the items varies to discourage cheating. Students also feel inhibited about cheating if the teacher stays noticeably alert and circulates through the room once in a while to monitor everyone's progress. Ideally, cheating should be avoided by creating a test situation that is devoid of any sense of competition and is instead perceived by students as an opportunity to demonstrate what they know and to find out what they do not know so they can receive help accordingly. A patient who is undergoing various tests in a doctor's office would not think of cheating to make certain readings look better. The teacher's aim should be to get students to perceive themselves in a position similar to that of the patient, with the teacher as the "doctor" in charge of their diagnosis and treatment.

◆ Maintain physical conditions conducive to test taking by keeping the room quiet and providing students with ample work space. Also take into account the psychological conditions that may influence students' test performances. For example, students are unlikely to do their best on tests given as punishment or on tests where they are threatened with severe consequences if they do poorly.

♦ Prepare an answer key by taking the test yourself. At the same time, note any suggestions or clarifications that need to be announced when the test is administered. In addition, written notes should be made about any test items that may be difficult for students to understand.

3. Score tests and report results.
   ♦ Develop scoring keys as an efficient method for grading objective tests (i.e., completion, true/false, multiple choice, matching). Scoring keys can take several forms, including transparent sheets that contain the correct answers just above, below, or to either side of where student responses to each item will appear, to be placed over each test paper; sheets that similarly contain the correct answers but instead have a cutout ("window") through which student responses will appear, to be placed over each test paper; or a teacher-completed version of the test against which each test paper is matched. The use and accuracy of scoring keys are greatly facilitated by physically designing test papers so that the spacing of questions and answers is relatively uniform and kept in alignment.
   ♦ Avoid fast and unreliable methods of scoring, such as having students exchange and grade each others' tests or having a monitor or aide grade tests of any consequence. Student work deserves and requires the personal scrutiny and judgment of the teacher for purposes of fairness and determining necessary remediation. These fast methods are useful, however, for saving class time when correcting and reviewing workbook exercises, drills, classwork problems and examples, and certain quizzes.
   ♦ Prepare model responses to essay questions to facilitate objective, timely scoring. "Sometimes you will not want to use the item after you try to answer it!" (Clark & Starr, 1986, p. 368). You might also think of some ways to improve the question. Rather than scoring each student's set of essay questions on a test, it is better to score the first essay question for each student, then the second, and so on. This encourages better concentration on the specifics of each question in relation to the prepared model response and allows you to compare how students are responding to each question. Because it is difficult to score essay questions objectively a few steps should be taken to minimize subjective grading, including scoring student responses anonymously and determining the criteria by which each response is to be judged (e.g., creativity, organization of ideas, accuracy of information, usage, neatness).
   ♦ Record test scores in a way that facilitates analysis of the results so that needs that are common to the class as a whole or to large groups within the class are readily identifiable. These needs are then used as a guide to making any necessary changes in the instructional program and teaching practices. Any method of recording test scores should also facilitate the diagnosis of each student's strengths and

weaknesses so plans that address individual needs can be designed. To accomplish this, results from every test should be maintained in the form of tables, charts, or sheets for the class as a whole and for each student. In addition to recording test score information in terms of number or percentage of right and wrong, a way of comparing this information from test to test needs to be devised because scores on tests of varying lengths and levels of difficulty may have different meanings. This requires reducing test scores on all tests to some form of common denominator such as a frequency distribution where, for example, it becomes apparent how students have fared in comparison to each other and to the course material covered.

> If the teacher tabulates the frequency of error, analyzes strong and weak points in the class performance, and then does something about them, he has a chance to serve the students much more abundantly than when he merely uses testing as a form of scorekeeping. (Crawford, 1938, p. 468)

♦ Report test results in a timely manner to maximize the benefit this information holds for the students. Students are naturally interested in knowing how well they did on a test and what was wrong with the items they missed. This initially keen interest wanes, however, in proportion to the amount of time the teacher takes to correct and hand back the test papers. When a test is not handed back within a reasonable amount of time, students lose track of what was on the test and tend to think that the teacher really does not take the test or its results seriously. Thus, what should be a meaningful learning experience turns into a waste of time. An effective way to report testing scores to students is to return the corrected papers within a few days and to provide ample time for class review and discussion of the test. Individual conferences should be set up for students who have questions. This timely approach demonstrates to students that their work is receiving careful attention for the purpose of determining their capabilities, progress, and learning needs.

4. Understand the role of standardized testing within the framework of the classroom instructional program.
   ♦ Become familiar with the basic principles of standardized testing, including the main characteristics of achievement and aptitude tests (the two types of standardized tests most relevant to the classroom teacher) and the possible uses of the information obtained from each of these tests. (See Table 8.6 for a description of standardized achievement and aptitude tests.) Although the classroom teacher has little or no role in constructing standardized tests, the importance of these tests in determining the students' continued promotion through school and eventual entrance into college demands an understanding of the principles pertinent to their construction and use.

TABLE 8.6 *Standardized Achievement and Aptitude Tests*

TEST TYPE	DESCRIPTION
Achievement	Used to obtain information in a designated area such as general knowledge, basic skills, or subject knowledge.
	Focuses on what has been learned in the designated area being tested.
	Designed to be used for the largest number of students and schools possible.
	Items are of the objective type.
	Content is tested and procedures for administering and scoring are standardized to make it possible to give in different places at different times.
	Results are norm-referenced to allow for comparison with others at the local, state, or national levels.
	Results are used to determine grade placements, promotion, graduation, attainment of minimum competency, and teacher effectiveness.
Aptitude	Designed to obtain information for predicting future performance in a specific area, activity, or skill.
	Results used to direct students to areas in which they are most likely to achieve their potential.
	Measures types of learning common to most students and therefore can be administered to students from many different backgrounds.
	Frequently given in the form of a multiple-aptitude test battery as a guide to career planning.
	Requires students to draw upon their out-of-school as well as in-school experiences.

♦ Understand the limitations of standardized tests and the statistical information they provide, and avoid being unduly influenced by them. When a teacher attributes too much importance to standardized tests and focuses the instructional plan on doing well on them, competition becomes the predominant goal, teacher creativity wanes, and the life goes out of classroom instruction and learning.

The test-makers themselves admit that their multiple choice tests of aptitude and achievement do not measure creativity and motivation. . . . If [the student] is subtle in his choice of answers it will go against him; and yet there is no other way for him to show any individuality. (Hoffman, 1962, p. 91)

♦ Always remember that no matter how detailed and sophisticated the statistical reports of the results from standardized testing may be, they have little to do with student needs. The teacher's firsthand, informed judgment based on classroom observations and testing should never be replaced by some formalized statistical substitute. "In seeking high ability, let us shun overdependence on tests that are blind to dedication and creativity, and biased against depth and subtlety" (Hoffman, 1962, p. 217).

♦ Understand the value of standardized tests. They are useful in measuring educational development over a period of several years, placing students in certain types of instructional programs such as honors and advanced placement courses, and comparing students against national, regional, or state norms.

♦ Prepare students to take standardized tests. Beyond stressing the importance of these tests to their success in school, it is necessary to plan activities that expressly familiarize students with the types of questions that appear on the test and teach them strategies for selecting answers and making optimal use of the allotted time. These activities can become opportunities for developing decision-making and study skills.

♦ Interpretation

Measurement is not an end in itself. If the teacher becomes a slave to statistics, the evaluation process loses sight of its original purpose of fostering personal growth and thus of higher human sensibilities such as character development. The measurement aspect of evaluation is valuable only to the extent that it culminates in careful, informed interpretation that leads to effective action.

The degree of success achieved in determining student progress and achievement and the effectiveness of classroom instruction depends first upon the accuracy and completeness of the information obtained from classroom observations and testing and second upon the teacher's ability to analyze the selected information carefully. To be most useful, analysis of the results of evaluation "will not be a single score or a single descriptive term but an analyzed profile or a comprehensive set of descriptive terms . . ." (Tyler, 1950, p. 78).

To say that a student is at the seventy-seventh percentile or is a B+ student is virtually meaningless in terms of being able to help that student. Infinitely more effective is the collection and interpretation of a variety of information bearing on the student's physical, intellectual, emotional, and spiritual growth in a way that permits the teacher to sit down with the student, his or her parents, and his or her other teachers to discuss strengths and weaknesses discovered, goals to move toward and actions to take. Therefore, in effective classroom evaluation the teacher must focus on selecting relevant information, analyzing it, and addressing the problems and needs the information reveals. A classroom grading system based on the areas important to student growth is essential for successful interpretation and evaluation. Figure 8.1 summarizes the steps involved in developing a classroom grading system.

FIGURE 8.1 *Interpretation*

Developing a Classroom Grading System
1. Determine the areas to look at for grading.
2. Assign relative values to the various areas designated for determining grades.
3. Communicate grading information.
4. Determine the relationship between achievement and citizenship grades.
5. Adjust grades according to inherent abilities and effort.

Developing a Classroom Grading System

A classroom grading system is used for several purposes: it informs students, parents, and other school personnel about educational and social progress; it motivates students to build on their strengths and improve their weaknesses; it helps predict the possibilities of students' continued success in conjunction with decisions concerning promotion and class placement; and it guides the development of instructional plans and learning activities for both the class and individual students.

Distinction should be made between the marks given to students on tests and classroom activities and the grades issued for report cards. Marks represent a quantitative body of information, while grades represent a qualitative judgment arrived at after review and analysis of marks and consideration of other factors such as effort, improvement, and the relative value of the various marks. The following recommended practices should be followed for developing a classroom grading system.

1. Determine the areas to look at for grading.
   - All areas of student work in the classroom should enter into the determination of their grades, including tests, homework assignments, quizzes, classroom participation, special projects or activities, and classroom assignments.
   - Make it clear to students at the beginning of the year what different types of work determine their grades. (See Practical Model for an effective way of involving students in the grading process.) There is a better chance that students will view their grades as fair if they understand the methods used to judge their work and the standards on which their grades are based. Student morale suffers more than in any other classroom situation when students think their grades are the result of totally subjective, snap decisions.
   - Devise an efficient system of recording information about students' work in the areas designated for grading. A natural place for this information is the class roll book. The roll book does not always have ample space for all the information that needs to be recorded, in which case a separate book can be kept solely for recording grading information. Space should still be set aside in a designated section

of the roll book to record at least a summary of the information in the grade book. Maintaining accurate and complete grading records is necessary not only for determining student progress but also as the documented basis for communicating with parents, school personnel, and the students themselves.

♦ Collect complete information in each of the designated areas to obtain a reliable picture of each student's work for both diagnostic and grading purposes. The volume of information collected should not render the grading system impractical or unwieldy, or the teacher might be tempted to fall back on combining a few test scores with some general impressions to determine grades.

2. Assign relative values to the various areas designated for determining grades.

♦ Use the amount of class time spent on work in each area as an indicator of the emphasis and importance of the work to the instructional program. For example, homework assignments requiring approximately twenty-five hours of work over a six-week period should make up a larger percentage of the grades for that period than a single mark for a term paper that took approximately five hours of work. Whatever method is developed for assigning values to the various types of work, the main goal is to make sure it accurately reflects student efforts and progress.

♦ Review the instructional plan to compare the values assigned for grading with the objectives set for the course to see if there is any need for adjustments in the values assigned, time allotted to various types of work, or emphasis placed upon certain objectives. While the objectives listed in the instructional plan will affect the grading system, conversely, a classroom grading system can also help monitor and constructively modify the instructional plan.

3. Communicate grading information.

♦ The primary purpose of a classroom grading system is to communicate information that will meaningfully contribute to student growth. In those unfortunate instances where a grading system is used merely to record marks and summarily judge students, the goal of students becomes getting high marks, and learning is seen as secondary.

♦ Design a grading system that is easy for students, parents, and other school personnel to understand. A system that is overly complex, although accurate and fair, may lead to confusion and unnecessary mistrust. If students and parents lose confidence in a teacher's grading system, any possible value of those grades in understanding and addressing student needs is also lost.

♦ Once the grading system is developed, based on a careful review of the instructional plan, the school's grading policies, and other teacher's ideas, it should be explained to students with examples of exactly how it works. A thorough explanation should convey to students that the primary purpose of the grading system is to help them discover and work on their strengths and weaknesses. They should also understand that the grading system establishes the teacher's standards and expectations and defines the work they are responsible for. Within the first few days of a semester, the main features of the grading system should also be communicated to the parents by letter. The grading system should be explained in person at the first open house. The letter should be written in simple, succinct language that describes the areas of work to be looked at for determining grades, the relative importance of work in each area, and how the grades can be interpreted and used to help students continue to progress in school. In addition, parents should be invited to ask any questions or voice any concerns they may have about the grading system. Such time spent communicating with students and parents should significantly minimize potential misunderstandings and arguments over grades.

♦ After report cards are issued, set aside time to speak to the class as a whole. Meet students individually to explain the grades and make plans for building on strengths and correcting weaknesses.

Knowledge of results is useful or not depending upon when and where the learner receives the corrective information, under what conditions such corrective information can be used, even assuming appropriateness of time and place of receipt, and the form in which the corrective information is received. (Bruner, 1966, p. 50)

♦ Comply with any school policies on advance parent notification of the possibility that their child will receive a failing grade (i.e., a danger of failure notice). Regardless of whether such a policy exists, it is wise to inform parents when it seems apparent their children are headed toward a failing grade. When information on report cards surprises either students or parents, a breakdown in communication is clearly indicated.

♦ Prepare for any conferences with parents or students. Before any scheduled conference, review the pertinent records relating to the student's background, ability, and school work, and carefully select samples of test papers, homework assignments, and projects that tangibly portray the student's strengths and weaknesses. In conducting conferences, listen carefully to the other person's point of view and concerns. Keep in mind that the purpose of these conferences is to share ideas and mutually agree upon a course of action to take. Therefore, the tone of the conference should be constructive and not seek to blame anyone.

4. Determine the relationship between achievement and citizenship grades.

♦ Because almost all report cards call for citizenship grades in addition to grades for academic achievement, it is necessary to find out how school policy defines citizenship. Usually, no single grade is issued for citizenship; rather, separate grades for cooperation, effort, attendance, and punctuality are given. In any event, the importance of these grades as indicators of personal growth must be recognized by teachers, students, and parents alike, and taken seriously when making decisions concerning placement, promotion, and individual assistance. Measuring academic achievement and citizenship, assigning grades for both, and then, for all intents and purposes, disregarding the citizenship grades in making various administrative and instructional decisions, is a travesty of the evaluation process.

♦ Before the school year begins, decide the relationship between achievement grades and classroom behavior. The outcome of this decision should then be communicated to students and parents at the beginning of the school year so all know what to expect. When such guidelines are not established, confusion and bitterness at report card time often result. For example, students who receive lower academic grades than they expected feel the teacher has lowered their grades because of poor behavior. Many complaints from parents also stem from the perception that their children's achievement grades have been lowered because of poor conduct. One school of thought maintains that behavior should influence achievement grades because "one of the purposes of a course is to develop right attitudes" and "a teacher teaches the whole child; not just his mind. Good citizenship is a part of the whole child. A child who knows the facts but is uncooperative has not learned cooperation; therefore he has not achieved one of the important objectives of the course" (Crawford, 1938, p. 478). There is a compelling argument for this line of thinking when only one grade that combines achievement and citizenship is issued. In most schools, however, the grade-reporting policies require the teacher to issue separate grades for citizenship and achievement and to allow for clarifying comments in which it is possible, and indeed advisable, to point out the relationship between the grades given in these two areas. For example, on the report card of Student X, who receives an achievement grade of A and a cooperation grade of D (or U), it would be useful to explain that Student X clearly demonstrates superior intellectual capacity but seems to have problems with his or her social and emotional growth, and that these problems need to be addressed if he or she is to realize his or her full potential and become a functioning member of society. A guiding principle in determining what grades to give and comments to make is that grades should accurately reflect students' work and behavior and serve to further the possibilities for their social, emotional, and intellectual growth.

5. Adjust grades according to inherent abilities and effort.
   ♦ Determine students' *accomplishment quotients* by finding the ratio between what they actually do compared to what they can do based

on their abilities. Careful day-to-day classroom observations in conjunction with measurements of student progress as the semester proceeds are the most effective methods for accurately finding this quotient. As discussed above, these two methods are at the heart of the classroom evaluation process, with information from one being useful in explaining and verifying information from the other.

♦ Decide the degree to which grades will be determined by the factors involved in the accomplishment quotient, that is, inherent ability, progress, and achievement. The need to do this invariably arises because some students are able to achieve high test scores with a minimum of effort, while others, even while doing their best, are barely able to achieve passing scores. When making this decision it should be kept in mind that the accomplishment quotient reveals vital information about each student's character. "Character education is an important outcome, and should certainly be taken into account. Cooperation, interest, industry, dependability, and sincerity are much more important than dates, facts, or formulas" (Crawford, 1938, p. 478). As with the question of achievement and citizenship grades, the decision to use an accomplishment quotient in determining grades should be made before the school year begins in consultation with other teachers and the professional literature and cognizant of prevailing school policies and the nature of the course curriculum. Once the semester begins, this method should be carefully communicated to students and parents.

♦ Determine whether grading according to effort and progress rather than achievement will serve the students' best interests in terms of motivation and subsequent course and grade placements. Ideally the best grades should be given to those who do everything in their power to perform their best. In reality, however, many administrative decisions, such as course and grade placements, are made according to the level of achievement attained. For example, a student who makes excellent effort and progress in an elementary algebra class but is able to achieve only a C average will be ill-served by placement in an accelerated intermediate algebra class the next semester. On the other hand, this student will be equally ill-served in terms of continued motivation by receiving a grade of C. The solution to this dilemma lies in a sincere effort to do what is in the student's best interest. In this case, the student might be given a B with comments recognizing the value of his or her superior effort. Placement in subsequent math classes should be decided carefully and in consultation with other math teachers. In addition, special attention should be given to finding out whether the student is working as effectively as possible. The student who works hard without corresponding results often may have poor study skills or may not understand some fundamental concept. Poor performance does not always represent an inability to learn.

SUMMARY

In this chapter several main points about evaluation were presented:

1. Evaluation is the process of attributing value to student work, the teacher's efforts, and all aspects of the instructional program.
2. Classroom evaluation has three main purposes: to determine each student's readiness for learning, to determine how well each student is progressing, and to determine what each student has achieved. These three purposes are commonly associated with initial, formative, and summative evaluation, respectively.
3. The three basic forms of evaluation all have a diagnostic function. The difference is in scope. Initial and formative evaluation focus on students' work over relatively brief periods of time, while summative evaluation looks at their work over a much longer time span.
4. There are two aspects of evaluation. Measurement (or assessment) is the quantitative aspect, and interpretation the qualitative. Measurement is the first step in the evaluation process, making interpretation and subsequent corrective action possible.
5. Classroom observations and testing are the principal methods for obtaining information essential to initial, formative, and summative evaluations.
6. Classroom observations should center around student classwork (e.g., individualized assignments), participation in instructional activities (e.g., asking or answering questions), and behaviors (e.g., interaction with other students).
7. The wealth of information obtained through classroom observations needs to be recorded and organized in a way that ensures accuracy and ready access so insights can be gained about the learning and development of students.
8. There are many types of testing carried out in the classroom, including quizzes, weekly pretests and posttests, unit exams, midterms, final exams, and various standardized tests. The type of testing used depends upon its purpose.
9. Test scores in themselves have no meaning. Rather, the results of testing should be regarded as a measure of student work that can, after thoughtful analysis and interpretation, serve as the basis for individual guidance, planning, remedial activities, and adjusting the instructional program.
10. In developing classroom tests the following guidelines should be considered: become familiar with the various types of classroom tests and the forms these tests may take; review the instructional plan to develop a preliminary classroom testing schedule that indicates what types of tests to use at particular points throughout the semester as different topics are covered; determine the type and form of test to be used and then develop a table of specifications to address the learning objectives and course topics according to their relative importance and to the emphasis they are given in class.

11. The measurement aspect of evaluation is valuable only to the extent that it culminates in careful, informed interpretation that leads to effective action.

12. A classroom grading system informs students, parents, and school personnel about educational and social progress, motivates students to build on their strengths and improve their weaknesses, helps predict the possibilities of students' continued success in conjunction with promotion and class placement, and guides the development of instructional plans and learning activities for both the class and individual students.

13. A distinction should be made between marks students achieve on tests and classroom activities and grades issued for report cards. Marks represent a quantitative body of information, while grades represent a qualitative judgment arrived at after reviewing and analyzing marks and considering other factors such as effort, improvement, and the relative value of the various marks.

14. The main points to consider in developing a classroom grading system include determining the areas to look at for grading (e.g., classwork, test scores), assigning relative values to the various areas designated for determining grades, communicating grades, determining the relationship between achievement and citizenship, and adjusting grades according to inherent abilities and effort.

♦ ♦ ♦ ♦ ♦ ♦ ♦

PRACTICAL MODEL 8.1   Student-Maintained Grade Averaging Sheet

Introduction   This practical model presents a way of involving students and parents in the grading process in a format that makes clear the areas of work on which grades are based and that encourages consistent, purposeful effort in these areas.

Submitted by   Tom Harvey, high school history teacher, Sante Fe Springs, California

Purpose   To provide students with a way of monitoring their own progress throughout each marking period as the basis for jointly planning corrective action with the teacher throughout the semester as it is needed

♦ Grade Averaging Sheet

The grade averaging sheet (Figure 8.2) is collected every two or three weeks, checked by the teacher, and then sent home for a parent's signature. The six steps listed below should be followed when completing the grade averaging sheet.

1. To avoid inaccurate and incomplete records, enter information (scores and percents) under each of the six areas as soon as it is available.

FIGURE 8.2 *Grade Averaging Sheet*

Name ————————————— Date ——————— Class ———

AREAS	SCORE	POINTS POSSIBLE	AVERAGE

Area 1: Tests
1. (e.g., Unit on World War II) —————————————
2. ——————————————————————
3. ——————————————————————
4. ——————————————————————
Totals ————————————

Area 2: Homework
1. (e.g., Workbook questions for Unit 5) ————————
2. ——————————————————————
3. ——————————————————————
4. ——————————————————————
5. ——————————————————————
6. ——————————————————————
7. ——————————————————————
8. ——————————————————————
9. ——————————————————————
10. ——————————————————————
Totals ————————————

Area 3: Quizzes
1. (e.g., Causes of World War II) —————————————
2. ——————————————————————
3. ——————————————————————
4. ——————————————————————
Totals ————————————

Area 4: Class Participation
1. (e.g., Participation in group discussion) ——————————
2. ——————————————————————
3. ——————————————————————
4. ——————————————————————
5. ——————————————————————
6. ——————————————————————
7. ——————————————————————
8. ——————————————————————

FIGURE 8.2 *Continued*

AREAS	SCORE	POINTS POSSIBLE	AVERAGE
9.			
10.			
Totals			

Area 5: Special Projects
1. (e.g., Library research project on Truman)
2.
3.
Totals

Area 6: Class Assignments
1. (e.g., Complete problems for Unit 5)
2.
3.
4.
5.
6.
7.
Totals

Composite Total

Parent's Signature _____ Date _____

2. For each entry get an average score by figuring what percent of the total points possible the actual score is.
3. Under each area find the overall average as indicated.
4. Multiply all six overall average scores as follows to reflect the relative importance attributed to each area: Area 1 × 25; Area 2 × 35; Area 3 × 10; Area 4 × 15; Area 5 × 5; Area 6 × 10.
5. Add the products obtained in step 4 and divide the sum by 100. The resulting score indicates the overall quality of your work in the course.
6. Maintain a corrective action log that contains ideas developed from the joint planning meetings held with the teacher to constructively address weaknesses and problems indicated in one or more of the six areas of work.

♦ ♦ ♦ ♦ ♦ ♦ ♦

CASE STUDY 8.1   Observing Students' Classwork

Orienting
Questions   As you read this case study ask yourself these questions:

Specific
♦ Has this teacher been able to accurately evaluate the students' note-taking abilities?
♦ Do you think this teacher allows for a reasonable degree of flexibility in how classwork is to be done?

General
♦ What points in this lesson stand out as indicators of this teacher's strengths and/or weaknesses?
♦ What recommendations would you make for addressing the problems this teacher seems to have?

Setting   School – Public high school in upper-middle-class neighborhood

Subject – Tenth-grade English honors course (fifty-six minutes)

Teacher – Ms. Depesto, emergency-credentialed teacher whose degree is in life science

Students – Thirty-five average to above-average students

Topic – Notetaking skills

Lesson   Note: Under Time Frame the numbers represent the minutes that elapse as the period progresses. Under Dialog the names of the students and the teacher appear as they speak. The symbol ► represents a brief description of a particularly noteworthy action or observation.

Time Frame	Dialog	
1 to 5	►	The late bell rings and all the students are sitting in their seats. Ms. Depesto takes roll from the seating chart.
5 to 11	**Ms. D.:**	Class, today I will be evaluating your notetaking ability. Therefore, for the next twenty minutes I will lecture and you will be required to take notes. Then for the last twenty minutes of the period you will be asked to write a summary of the lecture using the notes you have taken. Before you leave, turn in the summary you have written so it can be graded.
	David:	Excuse me, Ms. Depesto, what will the lecture be on?
	Ms. D.:	The lecture is on the human brain, but that is irrelevant since you are being graded on your ability to take notes from whatever material is being presented. The material is strictly for today's use and you will not be asked to refer to it again in this class.
	David:	All right! I love science.

Time Frame	Dialog	
	Maddie:	(The best student in class) Excuse me, Ms. Depesto, but I'm not very good in science. Shouldn't you present a different lecture, one pertaining to English?
	Ms. D.:	No! Besides, I already told you that the material being presented is irrelevant to our main purpose for today.
11 to 38	►	Ms. Depesto proceeds to lecture for twenty-six minutes. David enthusiastically takes notes, but Maddie gets bogged down with some of the unfamiliar terminology.
	Maddie:	Excuse me, Ms. Depesto, but how do you spell that last word?
	Ms. D.:	Maddie, if I have to stop and spell every difficult word in this lecture I will never finish. The whole point of this evaluation is to see how well you can take notes that capture the essence of the lecture.
	►	Ms. Depesto notices that time is running out so she speeds up the lecture. Most of the students are lost and unable to grasp the complex concepts being presented.
38 to 56	**Ms. D.:**	(As she reads the last sentence of the prepared lecture) There, now you have until the bell rings to hand in a summary.
	►	The students frantically look over their notes and begin to write. Most of the students write about three brief sentences based on the first five minutes or so of the lecture. The bell rings and the students turn in their papers. Maddie is the last one to turn hers in.
	Ms. D.:	(Talking to herself as she looks over Maddie's paper, a two-paragraph summary) Well, it is obvious that Maddie is not a very good notetaker. She didn't understand what I was saying at all. This summary is poor. (She puts an F on the paper.)

Brief   *Key Facts* – List three key facts verbatim that characterize the main positive and/or negative aspects of the lesson.

Strengths/Weaknesses – Briefly explain how the key facts selected indicate strengths and/or weaknesses in the teacher's performance.

Recommendations – Briefly describe what the teacher could have done to alleviate or avoid the problems that were seen.

◆ ◆ ◆ ◆ ◆ ◆ ◆
CASE STUDY 8.2   Communicating Grades to Students

Orienting
Questions   As you read this case study ask yourself these questions:

Specific
◆ Does it seem likely that this teacher's way of communicating grades contributes to student growth?
◆ Does the way grades are used and communicated by this teacher foster cooperation or competition among the students?

General
◆ What points in this lesson stand out as indicators of this teacher's strengths and/or weaknesses?
◆ What recommendations would you make for addressing the problems this teacher seems to have?

Setting   *School* – Urban high school in middle-class, multiethnic community
Subject – Twelfth-grade U.S. Government class (sixty minutes)
Teacher – Mr. Sellers, first-year history teacher
Students – Forty students, all considered high achievers
Topic – Reviewing Tenth-Week Grades

Lesson

Time Frame	Dialog	
1 to 4	►	Mr. Sellers stands in front of the class taking roll and signing tardy and absence slips.
	Mr. S.:	Read Chapter 6 and let me finish taking attendance.
	►	The class is still noisy.
4 to 8	**Mr. S.:**	Please, ladies and gentlemen, I need a semblance of order.
	►	The class quiets down, but several students complain about the sun in their eyes. There is a vote, and although a majority want the shades down, Mr. Sellers wants them up so they stay up.
8 to 11	**Mr. S.:**	Okay, do you want to know your point total or the letter grade they translate into first?
	►	The students discuss this for a few minutes. The general feeling is that they want to know their point totals first.
11 to 18	**Mr. S.:**	Your grade is based on your scores on the three tests as well as on your classroom contributions.
	►	Mr. Sellers goes through the class roster alphabetically and gives the students their point totals.

18 to 27	**Mr. S.:**	I want to commend these students for having perfect attendance. (He reads ten names.) I would next like to congratulate those who had only one absence. (He reads an additional six names.)
	▶	Mr. Sellers then writes on the blackboard the students' point totals in descending order from the highest to the lowest (i.e., 163 to 102).
27 to 34	**Mr. S.:**	The maximum number of points you could have gotten was 170.
	▶	He then turns and writes what the breakdown looks like if he uses the 90, 80, 70, 60 distribution for A through F where A = 163, B = 136, C = 119, D = 102, and F = 101 or below. He then tells the students the grade distribution for some of the other classes he teaches.
34 to 40	**Mr. S.:**	Where do you think A goes and why?
	▶	Several students offer solutions. Mr. Sellers tells them that 155 and up is definitely an A. He says, however, that he might give A's to the three students with grades between 151 and 148. Mr. Sellers then asks the same question for B.
40 to 44	**Mr. S.:** **Andrea:**	The natural break is at 135. Well, I think you should have the same spread for all grades. If you have a twenty-point spread for A, you should have one for B—therefore it should be 128.
	▶	Mr. Sellers explains that he doesn't think that is a good distribution because not enough students would be in each level. In addition, he thinks that it doesn't make sense qualitatively. He then writes down the grade distribution for C = 127–135, D = 106–126, and F = 106 and below.
44 to 51	**Kevin:** **Mr. S.:**	What happens if you miss a test? You get a zero. Okay, now I want you to read Chapter 6. We are going to start on that tomorrow. Now let me enter your grades in the book.
	▶	There is a lot of talking. Several students come up to Mr. Sellers to try to "talk up" their grades. After he finishes entering the grades, he writes the classroom distribution on the blackboard. (A = 5, B = 18, C = 10, D = 4, F = 3)
51 to 55	**Mr. S.:**	Did anyone think the grading system was wrong?
	▶	No one protests.
55 to 60	**Mr. S.:**	I'm going to move quickly on Chapter 6. I hope you all come prepared tomorrow.

► The bell rings and the class is dismissed. One girl (Betsy) comes up to question her grade, saying she really needs a B. Mr. Sellers ask if she's afraid her parents are going to beat her.

Mr. S.: (To Betsy) Your grades have gone down. That's the wrong direction! Your absences and tardies have also pulled your grade down.

Betsy: You can't give me a C!

Mr. S.: I'm not giving you anything. It's what you've earned in this class. In the future, study and don't miss class!

► With that, the conversation ends and Betsy leaves the room.

Brief   *Key Facts* – List three key facts verbatim that characterize the main positive and/or negative aspects of the lesson.

Strengths/Weaknesses – Briefly explain how the key facts selected indicate strengths and/or weaknesses in the teacher's performance.

Recommendations – Briefly describe what the teacher could have done to alleviate or avoid the problems that were seen.

♦ ♦ ♦ ♦ ♦ ♦ ♦
_____

CASE STUDY 8.3   Observations of Students

Orientation   The following are two summaries of classroom observations made to determine the particular learning needs of individual students. After reading each summary, comment on each student's learning style and needs and then outline a plan of action for helping each student.

Students   Julie B. and Vaughn R.

♦ **Observation #1:   Notes on Julie B. (eighth-grade general science class)**

Julie looks very tired, possibly due to her allergies. She talks during roll even though she has been asked to stop and to get out her homework. She fidgets all period. When questions are asked, she waves her hand furiously trying to attract attention so she will be called on to put one of the homework problems on the board. When she is called on, however, she says she doesn't know if her answer is right. She is told to put the problem on the board anyway, and she does. Once all the problems have been put on the board, each student is asked, in turn, to present his or her work to the class. Julie hesitates going to the board to explain her work. When she finally does go to the board it turns out that she has correctly solved the problem, so she is praised and appears very happy with herself.

When new material is introduced, Julie becomes frustrated, saying that she just can't seem to understand it. She raises her hand at every step to ask for clarification of the material. During guided practice she also asks many questions and appears to catch on eventually. She always wants to know the right answer so she can write it down to refer to. Near the end of the period when a test is handed back, Julie sees that she received 93 percent and she jumps in the air for joy and looks much better as she leaves the room than when she entered it.

◆ **Observation #2:   Notes on Vaughn R. (twelfth-grade English class)**

Vaughn has expressed an interest in going to college to study English, and he has started off his senior year very enthusiastic about English class. His verbal and written skills are not well developed, however, and at times he does not understand the discussions on literature. He is interested in literature and reading but has become a little uncooperative about writing.

Vaughn does not work well in a group, particularly when it comes to a group writing activity. On a recent literature test (essay test) he did very poorly because he could not express himself well in writing. It appears that he has lost confidence in his ability to improve his writing skills and thus is very anxious about his grade for English. Vaughn has a very strong need for affirmation and attention in order to keep him working.

◆ ◆ ◆ ◆ ◆ ◆ ◆

CHAPTER PROJECT   Develop a Classroom Grading System

Goals
1. To develop a system that accounts for and integrates all facets of student work as the basis for determining grades
2. To develop the capability to accurately determine student progress and achievement

Phases
One, two, or three phases (i.e., planning, partial implementation, full implementation) of the chapter project can be completed as deemed appropriate to student needs and the design of the course.

Planning
1. Determine the areas to be looked at to evaluate student performance (e.g., classwork, homework, test scores).
2. Develop an evaluation profile to record grading information for each student. use a matrix design for the profile, listing the behaviors to be looked at under each performance area down the lefthand column, with dates listed across the top. Allow space on the profile for making brief comments that may be useful.

Partial Implementation

1. Determine how the different facets of student work are to be graded (i.e., point system, numerical grades, letter grades, or some other form) and weighted (e.g., test scores equal 40 percent of the grade; classroom participation equals 15 percent).
2. Develop a preliminary observation/testing schedule that indicates when specific types of behavior are to be observed and tests given.
3. Record information on the evaluation profile covering a three-week period for five students.

Full Implementation

1. Review the five evaluation profiles and write a two- or three-paragraph analysis of the information on each profile.
2. Based on the analysis of the evaluation profiles:
   a. Determine an interim (unofficial) composite grade for each student, explaining how the grades were arrived at.
   b. Recommend specific instructional activities for each student to address areas of work in which they appear to be weakest (e.g., develop an activity to successfully involve a student in class discussions where there are indications that his or her class participation is poor).

◆ ◆ ◆ ◆ ◆ ◆ ◆
REFERENCES

Bruner, J. S. (1966). *Toward a theory of instruction.* Cambridge, MA: Harvard University Press.

Callahan, J. F., & Clark, L. H. (1982). *Teaching in middle and secondary schools* (2nd ed.). New York: Macmillan.

Clark, L. H., & Starr, I. S. (1986). *Secondary and middle school teaching methods* (5th ed.). New York: Macmillan.

Crawford, C. C. (1938). *How to teach.* Los Angeles: C. C. Crawford.

Donoghue, R., Snow, R., & Spencer, K. (1986, Summer). Personal reviewing and recording—Principles in practice. *Forum, 28* (3), 75–77.

Gronlund, N. E. (1971). *Measurement and evaluation in teaching* (2nd ed.). New York: Macmillan.

Heck, S., & Williams, C. R. (1984). *The complex roles of the teacher: An ecological perspective.* New York: Teachers College Press.

Hoffman, B. (1962). *The tyranny of testing.* New York: Crowell-Collier.

Tyler, R. (1950). *Basic principles of curriculum and instruction.* Chicago: University of Chicago Press.

◆ ◆ ◆ ◆ ◆ ◆ ◆
ANNOTATED READINGS

Armstrong, D. G., Denton, J. J., & Savage, T. V. (1978). *Instructional skills handbook.* Englewood Cliffs, NJ: Educational Technology Publications. *A book providing a systematic model of instruction composed of a series of interrelated subsystems. Throughout, the book emphasizes using evaluation data to assess specific areas of the instructional program. See Chapter 4 on diagnosing learning and Chapter 7 on evaluating the effectiveness of instruction.*

Broadfoot, P., & Fenner, R. (1985). Pupil profiles: The promise and the peril. *The New ERA, 66*(2), 35–38.

> *An excellent article outlining the main advantages of profiling in the classroom. It discusses how the profile can be used as a method for making various kinds of student assessments.*

Crawford, C. C. (1949). *Functional education.* Los Angeles: C. C. Crawford.

> *A comprehensive text in which the emphasis is on action rather than mere knowledge, behavior rather than mere thoughts, and socially significant results rather than mere wishes or attitudes. See Chapter 25 for a thorough discussion of measurement in the classroom.*

Eisner, E. W. (1985). *The educational imagination: On the design and evaluation of school programs.* New York: Macmillan.

> *A book stressing the importance of context in making educational decisions, especially in the area of curriculum development. See Chapter 10 for a discussion of the functional forms of evaluation.*

Henson, K. T. (1981). *Secondary teaching methods.* Lexington, MA: D. C. Heath.

> *A basic text in secondary school teaching emphasizing practical applications of the principles of teaching. See Chapter 14 on test construction, administration, and scoring and Chapter 15 on evaluation.*

McNeil, J. D. (1985). *Curriculum: A comprehensive introduction* (3rd ed.). Boston: Little, Brown.

> *A text that provides examples of curriculum drawn from a variety of educational programs and settings to allow the reader to connect generalizations with reality. See Chapter 10 for a description of recommended evaluation models, an examination of controversial technical issues in curriculum evaluation, and a discussion of norm-referenced versus criterion-referenced tests.*

Smith, F. M., & Adams, S. (1966). *Educational measurement for the classroom teacher.* New York: Harper & Row.

> *A comprehensive text focusing on the use of teacher-made and standardized tests as tools of instruction. Part I presents an introduction and perspective on the nature, importance, and role of measurement in education. Part II presents numerous recommendations for developing and using teacher-made tests. Part III examines the various aspects of standardized testing as they relate to classroom teaching.*

Tyler, R. W. (Ed.). (1969). *Educational evaluation: New roles, new means.* Chicago: University of Chicago Press.

> *A collection of writings by some of the foremost experts on educational evaluation, focusing on the aims and purposes of evaluation. A number of evaluation methods and uses are examined and their implications for the classroom teacher are critically discussed.*

Waples, D., & Tyler, R. W. (1930). *Research methods and teachers' problems: A manual for systematic studies of classroom procedure.* New York: Macmillan.

> *A book intended to facilitate systematic studies of teachers' classroom problems by focusing on studies conducted by in-service teachers to solve urgent problems of particular classroom situations. See Chapter 4, Part V, on investigating and solving problems in testing and diagnosis.*

Index